AUGUST HOME'S

VOLUME 2

AUGUST
HOME
SPECIAL
PUBLICATIONS

2200 Grand Avenue
Des Moines IA 50312
www.augusthome.com

WELCOME OLD FRIENDS AND NEW

Here's one of my favorite stories that really applies to *Cuisine*. There was a young couple that had just recently married and were celebrating their first Thanksgiving together.

The new bride prepared the entire dinner including a turkey that was exceptionally moist. Her husband noticed that the front end of the turkey had been removed prior to roasting and assumed that its tenderness had something to do with this unusual technique.

When he asked his wife why she had removed the front end of the turkey, she replied that she didn't know—it was how her mother had cooked turkey for years.

So, they called her mother to ask why she had always cut off the front end of the turkey before roasting. And she gave the same response, "because your grandmother always prepared it this way." Frustrated, they called grandma, and asked her the same question. Her response was the same, "because this is how your great grandmother taught me how to roast a turkey."

Finally, they called great grandma at the nursing home and asked her the secret of cutting off the front end of the turkey. She finally gave them their answer—"My roasting pan wasn't big enough to hold a large turkey so I had to cut off the front end to make it fit in the pan!"

This is what *Cuisine* is all about— knowing the "whys" and "how comes" of cooking. There is obviously so much more to cooking than just recipes.

John Meyer

VOLUME 2

Cuisine

THE YEAR AT A GLANCE

Please contact us to find out about other *Cuisine* products and services:
By Phone: 1-800-311-3995
By Mail: 2200 Grand Avenue, Des Moines IA 50312
By Email: Cuisine@CuisineMagazine.com
Or Visit Our Web-Site: www.CuisineMagazine.com

ISSUE No 7
JAN/FEB 1998

AUGUST HOME'S

Cuisine

AN ILLUSTRATED GUIDE TO CREATIVE HOME COOKING

™

CHOCOLATE ESPRESSO TORTE
WITH CHOCOLATE GLAZE

Also in this Issue:
OSSOBUCO
FOCACCIA
FISH EN PAPILLOTE

Cuisine

Editor
John F. Meyer

Art Director
Cinda Shambaugh

Associate Editor
Charles Smothermon

Senior Graphic Designer
Holly Wiederin

Graphic Designer
Martin Davis

Photo Director
Lark Gilmer

Senior Photographer
Crayola England

Test Kitchen Director
Ellen Boeke

Food Stylist
Lori Powell Gordon

Editorial Assistant
Jennifer L. Welter

Electronic Publishing Coordinator
Douglas M. Lidster

Pre-press Image Specialist
Troy Clark

Publisher
Donald B. Peschke

Corporate
V.P. Planning & Finance: Jon Macarthy
Subscriber Services Director: Sandy Baum
New Business Director: Glenda K. Battles
New Business Manager: Todd Bierle
Renewal Manager: Paige Rogers
Billing Manager: Rebecca Cunningham
Asst. Subscription Manager: Joy Krause
Promotion Assistant: Rick Junkins
Production Director: George Chmielarz
Production Assistant: Susan Dickman
Production Artist: Jon Snyder
Creative Director: Ted Kralicek
August Home Books: Douglas L. Hicks
New Media Manager: Gordon C. Gaippe
Assoc. Graphic Design Director: Susie Rider
Senior Graphic Designer: Cheryl Simpson
Controller: Robin K. Hutchinson
Senior Accountant: Laura J. Thomas
Accounts Payable Clerk: Mary Schultz
Human Resource Assistant: Kirsten Koele
Customer Service Manager: Jennie Enos
Administrative Assistant: Julia Fish
Receptionist: Jeanne Johnson
Librarian: Sherri Ribbey
Photo Intern: Elizabeth Meyer

From the Editor:

I can honestly say that *Cuisine* gets a little better each issue. Oh sure, the look and content of the magazine is improving and subscribers are increasing—that's great. But what I'm really talking about is the excitement and fun the staff shares around here.

For an editor, it's exciting to see your staff step back, after completing an issue, and say "this is the best one yet!" It's pretty cool to watch them research future articles before I even pass out assignments. And it's amusing to hear their chatter rise and fall with each "hi-test" caffè latte they consume, thinking they need to review the espresso article—again.

And enthusiasm is contagious. Don is our publisher (a publisher is the stoic guy who worries about money all the time). Twenty years ago, Don started a great woodworking magazine called *Woodsmith*. He had fun designing, building, and then writing about it.

To make a long story short, his passion grew into a big company with five magazines, and all his time was taken up with worrying about corporate stuff—until recently.

Now, Don frequents the test kitchen eagerly sharing his *Cuisine* cooking experiences. Don's a better publisher than a cook. But like us, he's excited and having fun—again.

John Meyer

This focaccia is perfect for beginners. It's like making bread with training wheels. The starter is simple, and the dough's easy to work. You end up with authentic focaccia without any disasters.

August Home's Cuisine

AN ILLUSTRATED GUIDE TO CREATIVE HOME COOKING

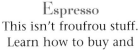

Tips

SHINY FROSTING

Frosting gets dull-looking when the surface dries. To make it shiny again, blow-dry the icing right before serving. Use the low setting (for both fan and heat) so you don't melt the frosting off the cake.

R. McAllister
Farley, IA

FROZEN COOKIE SHEET

If you don't have a marble slab for making candy or rolling pastry dough, use the back of a frozen cookie sheet. Just place it in the freezer about 20 minutes before you need it.

R.B. Himes
Vienna, OH

MARINADE IN BAG

Some recipes call for meat to be marinated for a few hours in a dish—"turning occasionally" to penetrate all sides. I used to marinate in a large casserole dish. The

meat didn't always fit, and I often spilled the marinade when I went to turn it.

Now, I just put the meat and marinade in a Ziploc® bag. Using a Ziploc bag isn't as messy, and there's one less dish to wash. If you get most of the air out of the bag, it should hold the marinade all around the meat. To make sure the marinade gets to all sides, just flip the bag occasionally.

R. Coy
Dayton, OH

DRYING TOMATOES

Dry your own by slicing ripe tomatoes $1/2$" thick or Romas in half, lengthwise. Place on a cooling rack, cut-side-up. Lightly salt them. Place rack on cookie sheet. Dry in a 190° oven for 6–10 hours. Freeze them on the rack and then store in plastic bags in freezer.

T. Hanson
Monticello, MN
Editor's Note: You can pack dried tomatoes in a jar filled with olive oil and fresh herbs. Refrigerate up to 2 weeks.

CLEAN BUNDT PAN

Cleaning inside the tube of a Bundt pan is a pain. So I place a small paper cup over the cone to keep batter from falling down the hole.

P. Van Scoten
Castroville, CA

FREEZING CABBAGE

If you want to make stuffed cabbage leaves, don't cook the leaves to make them pliable. It's a lot easier just to freeze the cabbage. An added benefit is it doesn't stink up your house.

The night before I want to use it, I cut out the core (so the leaves will peel off easily). Then I put the cabbage in the freezer. The next day, I let the cabbage thaw out a few hours before I start stuffing the leaves.

Freezing breaks down the structure of the leaves. They're pliable and don't crack or break when I pull them from the head or roll them for stuffing.

J. Kroop
Passaic, NJ

FROZEN BLUE CHEESE

You can store blue cheeses in the freezer. Freezing doesn't damage the cheese. And it will still crumble perfectly and taste great. Use it as you would fresh.

A. Colombini
Galveston, TX

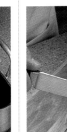

VEGETABLE RACK

Instead of using a metal roasting rack, make a grid of carrots, celery sticks, and onions. This acts like a "mirepoix" to flavor the pan drippings and elevates the meat for even roasting.

D. Lane
Anchorage, AK

THIN MEAT SLICES

For stir-fry or carpaccio, it's easier to slice meat or fish thinly if it's partially frozen. Put it in the freezer for 15–20 minutes. Check on it every five minutes until it turns firm but not stiff.

C. Singletary
Virginia Beach, VA

BROWN LETTUCE?

If lettuce starts turning a little brown (but not slimy) it may not be suitable for salads—but it is for sauteing.

Sauteed salad greens like lettuce, radicchio, and endive make an unusual but tasty side dish.

Saute lettuces just as you would spinach. Cook them quickly in a little olive oil, minced garlic, and salt. They taste great, and you can't tell that the greens were once a little brown.

A. Palazzo
Las Vegas, NV

SEND US YOUR TIPS

We'd like to hear from you. Just write down your cooking tip and mail it to Cuisine, Tips Editor, 2200 Grand Ave., Des Moines, IA 50312, or contact us through our E-mail address shown below. Please include your name, address, and daytime phone number in case we have questions. We'll pay you $25 if we publish your tip.

E-mail address: Cuisine@cuisinemag.com

Tips

FROM THE TEST KITCHEN

PARCHMENT CONE

For a quick pastry bag that you won't have to wash, pull out your parchment paper. Cut a 12" square of paper (it doesn't have to be perfect). Fold it in half twice, so you end up with a smaller square.

Cut an arc along the open sides of the square. When you unfold it, you'll have a circle. Then cut out one quarter of the circle.

Roll up the remaining three quarters around the center point—it becomes the tip of your bag. Keep the hole in the tip as small as possible. You can always cut more off later if you want a bigger hole.

Fold the lip of the cone over a little so the bag won't unroll. The mouth of a jar works great to hold the bag steady during folding and filling.

 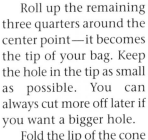

NO ZESTER?

In a lot of dishes, I call for citrus zest for flavor and garnishes. If you don't have a zester, use a peeler. With a "Y" peeler (it works best), remove the outermost colored layer of skin from the citrus using a sawing motion. This peel contains all the aromatic oils—not the bitter white pith. Then thinly slice or mince the strips.

OSSOBUCO

Finding ossobuco on a restaurant menu here in the states is as elusive as a six-figure income. Because of the cut of meat used, this traditional Italian dish needs

a long, slow, moist cooking process called braising. Seems that many of the Italian restaurants consider this long process too costly to prepare.

So if you can't find ossobuco out, definitely try this classic at home. (Besides, ours will probably be better.)

Ossobuco [AW-soh BOO-koh; OH-soh BOO-koh] is a popular northern Italian classic. Made from sliced veal shanks (*see next page*), the center contains the bone which exposes its rich marrow. That's how ossobuco got its name—"osso" meaning bone and "buco" meaning hole. Bone with a hole! The marrow is considered a delicacy by ossobuco connoisseurs.

Look at the photo above and you'll see a small spoon sticking out of the bone. This spoon is known as the "tax collector" because it's used to get *every last bit* of the flavorful marrow.

But ossobuco is much more than just the tasty marrow. It's a combination of white wine, fresh vegetables, and rich stock that forms a liquid around the shanks. By braising the shanks in the oven, the liquid slowly tenderizes the once sinewy shanks.

The combination of these liquids, gelatinous bones, and marrow develop into a rich, thick sauce that covers the tender veal shanks. Ossobuco is simple and satisfying.

Milan Cuisine: Located in Italy's north region of Lombardy, Milan is a mecca of industry and food. Its simple but elegant diversified cuisine is influenced by France and the expansive farm lands made rich by the great Italian lakes. Lombardy borders the Po Valley where the rice for risotto is grown. It raises more cattle (mainly dairy) than any other region in Italy.

What's interesting is that veal is a natural by-product of dairy farming. So it's easy to understand how Milan gave birth to two very classic Italian dishes—risotto alla milanese and ossobuco. In Milan, they're often paired together. To me, the risotto is too rich with ossobuco. I serve it with a little lighter baked semolina gnocchi found on page 14.

When you make ossobuco, you'll see what I mean by Milan's elegant simplistic approach to food.

Veal — A Quick Overview

Veal farming was a controversial subject a few years back, and there still seems to be a reluctance to eating it. But new industry practices and careful monitoring have changed the dark side of raising veal. In fact, I gave up eating veal until I was sure that these poor conditions had been rectified.

Most veal production is a natural cycle in dairy farming. Dairy cows have to give birth once a year to produce milk. In general, female calves are kept to replace the older cows. The male calves are then sold to farmers who specialize in veal production.

Most veal farms are family owned where the calves are individually cared for. They're fed twice daily on nutritionally balanced milk, enjoy plenty of light and fresh air. They also have their own *spacious* stall.

Identification of Veal: Veal is the meat from calves approximately 18 to 20 weeks old (over 21, it's beef). There are three types of veal based on the way the calves are raised and fed.

Special-Fed Veal: Also known as Nature-Fed, Milk-Fed, or Formula-Fed. These calves are fed a nutritional liquid diet which produces a creamy pink, fine-textured meat. About 85% of the veal sold today is Special-Fed.

Grain-Fed Veal: Grain-Fed calves given grains, hay and formulas. Their meat varies in color from dark pink to light red and contains some fat and even marbling. Grains and grazing cause the meat to darken. It's usually marketed at 5 to 6 months old.

Bob Veal: Calves, less than 30 days old, used to suckle a dairy cow's initial milk containing antibodies.

Selection of Veal: Veal quality is based on color and texture. Creamy color and fine texture indicate good quality. Any fat that is attached, should be very white. And while little of the veal is graded (prime, choice, good, etc.), all of it is inspected.

But don't look for marbling. Most veal is too young and *lean* to develop any significant marbling that would contribute to flavor. The enjoyment of veal comes from its tenderness and the delicate flavors it easily absorbs.

Veal Shanks: Ossobuco is made from veal shanks—usually from the hindshank because it has the most meat. The shanks are cut into 1½ to 2–inch thick parallel slices. This exposes the center bone and its rich, flavorful marrow. Veal shanks are a tough cut so they have to be braised.

Key Cooking Process: Braising

At the right, you can see the tough connective tissues in and around this veal shank. What you can't see are the smaller muscle fibers that infiltrate the meat.

The trick to cooking tough meats is to eliminate sinewy connective tissues without breaking down the muscle fibers (shredding). A long, slow, moist-cooking process called braising is the ticket.

Cooking is a form of water extraction. Muscle fibers are primarily water. As fibers are exposed to heat, they constrict and squeeze out water. The more exposure to heat, the more water loss (meat shrinks and drys out). Think about grilling a steak well done.

The connective tissues, which are mainly collagen, also constrict during cooking, further squeezing water from the muscles (drying).

But braising causes this tough meat to go through an interesting and flavorful cycle. Although the shanks are surrounded by liquids and steam during cooking, they literally get drier and tougher for a time. But once the collagen reaches a certain temperature, it melts away into a rich gelatin.

Now, the dry muscle fibers, depleted of moisture and free from constricted tissues, relax and begin to absorb the surrounding flavorful liquids. Braising is complete.

Ossobuco (Serves 6)

Work Time: 45 minutes
Cook Time: 1½ – 2 hours
Make Bouquet Garni with:
    Peel of 1 lemon
¼ cup parsley sprigs
2 sprigs fresh thyme
1 bay leaf
Tie:
6 veal shanks, 2" thick (about 5 lbs.)
Sprinkle with:
1 t. salt
½ t. pepper
Dredge in:
½ cup all-purpose flour
Brown in:
¼ cup unsalted butter
1 T. olive oil
Remove Shanks and Saute:
1½ cups chopped yellow onion
½ cup chopped carrot
½ cup sliced celery
Add and Saute Briefly:
2 t. chopped garlic
3 anchovy fillets
Deglaze Pan with:
1 cup dry white wine
Add with Veal Shanks and Sachet:
1½–2 cups chicken stock, *see page 8*
2 cups fresh tomato pulp
Garnish with Gremolada on page 11

Nutritional Information per Serving:
Calories 691; Total fat 24(g); Calories from fat 32%; Sodium 684(mg)

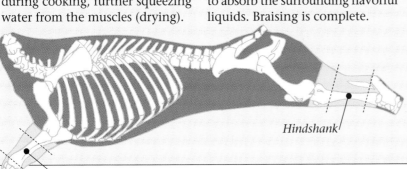

Hindshank

Foreshank

THE STOCK

For ossobuco, you would ideally make a veal stock using the same procedure as in brown stock (*Page 18 in Issue 5*). You would just substitute veal bones for beef bones. But don't use beef here. It's stronger flavor and fat would simply overpower the veal.

The bones and marrow from veal produce a very rich, delicate-flavored stock (like adding butter). Many people add them to soups for richness. But they're hard to come by—especially in smaller cities.

If you can't find veal bones for stock, make a chicken stock. Its mild flavor is much more compatible with veal than a beef stock.

I'm showing you how to make a white (clear) chicken stock so you can use it for other recipes. If you want to, you can brown the bones and vegetables to make a darker stock.

Preparation: In cold water, soak chicken bones two hours to clean and help develop flavor, *see Step 1*.

While the bones are soaking, cut the aromatic vegetables, and saute them slowly until they caramelize (develop a little color), *see Step 2*. This adds color and richness to the stock.

Next, add the drained bones, fresh herbs, and *cold* water, *see Step 3*. Hot water chemically disrupts the rich gelatin from blending with the stock.

Simmering: To prevent clouding, simmer (never boil) the ingredients. As scum appears, remove it, *see Step 4*.

Simmer two hours and then strain the stock. Don't press the ingredients into the sieve, *see Step 5*. This too, can cause the stock to cloud.

Chill the stock and remove the solidified fat, *see Step 6*. It's no longer needed to flavor the stock.

CHICKEN STOCK
(MAKES 8 CUPS)
WORK TIME: 20 MINUTES
COOK TIME: 2 HOURS
SOAK IN COLD WATER:
2   chicken carcasses, cut up
SAUTE:
2   T. olive oil
2   stalks celery, coarsely chopped
2   carrots, coarsely chopped
2   onions, coarsely chopped
1/2 leek (green part only)
ADD AND SAUTE:
2   cloves garlic
ADD DRAINED CHICKEN WITH:
    Water to cover
1/4 cup parsley sprigs
2   bay leaves
2   sprigs thyme
1   t. peppercorns
SIMMER, STRAIN, AND CHILL STOCK.
SKIM SOLIDIFIED FAT FROM SURFACE.

MAKING THE STOCK

1 Cut chicken into pieces and place in large bowl. Fill with cold water and soak 2 hours to remove impurities. I use wings if I don't have bones.

2 Over a medium heat, saute the celery, carrots, onions, leek until the onions turn golden. Then add the garlic and cook about 1 minute more.

3 Drain the bones and add to pot. Add *cold* water to cover 2" above ingredients in pot. Add parsley, bay leaves, thyme, and peppercorns.

4 Bring to a boil, then reduce heat to just below a boil. Simmer for 2 hours, occasionally skimming foam from surface of stock.

5 Strain stock through a sieve. Let this happen naturally by not pressing. Pressing can cloud the stock. Discard scraps.

6 Chill stock for several hours to solidify fat. The cold fat surfaces to make skimming easier. Especially important if you use chicken wings.

INGREDIENT PREPARATION

I've told you before about *mise en place* [MEEZ ahn plahs]. This is a French term referring to having all your ingredients prepared and ready before cooking. Well, this is it—get your mise en place in order and ready to go.

Tomatoes: Even if you're fixing ossobuco in the dead of winter, use fresh tomatoes! Remember, the flavor of veal is very delicate, and canned tomatoes could be too strong.

Through the center, cut the tomato in half. This exposes all the seed chambers. The photo below illustrates the correct cut and incorrect cut. Now, squeeze out the seeds, *see Step 7*.

Next, slide the cut side of the tomato up and down on a grater until only the skin is left, *see Step 8*.

Lemon: Veal and lemon naturally go together. Remove the zest from one lemon by using a peeler, *see Step 9*. The large pieces of zest are easy to handle. Avoid the bitter white pith.

Bouquet Garni: A bouquet garni [boo-KAY gahr-NEE] is a bunch of herbs either tied together, or placed into cheesecloth, *see Step 10*, and then tied, *see Step 11*. This allows you to remove the herbs easily when you're finished cooking.

Tying the Shanks: Because the shank's connective tissues dissolve during cooking, I like to tie each piece to keep the meat attached to the bone.

Use a surgeon's knot by first making several loops and tightening, *see Step 12*. Then complete the surgeon's knot with a simple knot. Tie all shanks this way, *see Step 13*.

With the shanks secure, salt and pepper them liberally, *see Step 14*. You are now ready to start cooking.

▼ *The right tomato is cut correctly to expose **all** its seed chambers. The left one only exposes two.*

7 Before making pulp, you have to seed the tomatoes. Cut through their equators. Then, gently squeeze each half to release the seeds.

8 To make the tomato pulp, rub the cut side of tomatoes against a coarse grater. Grate them until only the skin is left—throw that away.

9 Make a long lemon zest with a "Y" peeler. Using a sawing action, cut the outer peel (not the white pith). Large zest handles easily.

10 For a bouquet garni, place parsley, thyme, lemon zest, and bay leaf in a piece of cheesecloth. Gather corners around herbs.

11 Form a bundle and tie the neck with kitchen twine. Always leave a long piece of twine to tie to pan handle for easy removal.

12 Tie shanks to secure meat while cooking. Use a surgeon's knot. This is formed by making several loops before tightening.

13 After tightening the first loop, tie a simple knot to secure. The surgeon's knot minimizes indentations and remains secure.

14 Sprinkle both sides of shanks with salt and pepper. This not only permeates the meat, but it also enhances the flavor of the sauce.

BRAISING

Braising is a classic cooking technique that's made for ossobuco. Tougher cuts of meats are first browned in a fat, then tightly covered and left to cook in a little liquid for a long period, either on the stove or in the oven.

But we're going to use the oven for ossobuco. I prefer the oven's gentle ambient heat to extract the bone's gelatin. It seems to make a more mellow, smoother sauce.

Browning: After flouring the tops and bottoms of the shanks, brown them. You'll notice that I'm doing this in butter. This is a result of Milan's fondness for French culture and Lombardy's bountiful dairy industry.

Browning the meat cooks the flour to make it blend well with the fats for thickening. It also darkens the sauce and enhances its flavor.

Caramelizing: Remove the shanks after browning and then saute your vegetables using the same pan. You want to cook them gently until they start to caramelize (turn golden). This adds color and flavor by extracting the natural sugars in the vegetables.

Now add the garlic and anchovies, and saute them just until you begin to smell the garlic. Sauteing garlic too long or too hot can turn it bitter.

Deglazing: After smelling the garlic, add the wine and scrape the pan. This is "deglazing"—loosening up all the browned, flavorful particles from the bottom of the pan.

Reduce the wine until it almost disappears. Now, add the liquid ingredients, bouquet garni, and browned shanks. Heat just until boiling. You're ready to put this baby in the oven.

ANCHOVIES
Small species of herring with delicious white flesh that turns dark when preserved in salt and olive oil. Anchovies are frequently used as a seasoning in Mediterranean cooking (the best are from this area). When cooked, the subtle flavor comes primarily from preservatives. Don't worry, the fillets dissolve.

PUTTING IT ALL TOGETHER

15 Dredge shanks in flour. Don't coat the sides, since they won't brown. Place on cooling rack to keep flour from getting gummy.

16 Heat butter and oil over medium-high heat in large pan. Brown shanks. You get better browning if you don't move them around.

17 Turn shanks and brown on second side. Browning takes about 5 minutes a side. After browning, remove and set shanks aside.

18 Turn the heat down to medium, and in the same pan, add onion, carrot, and celery. Saute until the onion caramelizes (golden).

19 Add garlic and anchovy. Saute until you smell garlic cooking. Never put your head over a pan (it could splatter). Fan aroma to you.

20 Add wine and deglaze pan. As wine is boiling, scrape the pan to loosen flavorful particles. Reduce until wine is almost gone.

21 Add chicken stock, tomato pulp, and bouquet garni to the pan. Tie bag to handle of pan with long end of kitchen twine.

22 Now add the shanks to pan. Bring liquids to a boil and spoon some mixture over shanks to moisten. It's now ready for the oven.

FINISHING OSSOBUCO

While braising, you want to do three things to the shanks: baste, turn, and control the temperature.

Basting: Every 30 minutes, baste the shanks with their own sauce. This keeps them moist and continually adds the flavor so important to veal.

Turning: Halfway through the braise, turn the shanks over to equalize the heat on all sides.

Temperature: Controlling the temperature just so the sauce barely bubbles is critical. This allows the flavorful gelatin to blend into the sauce.

Finishing the Sauce: Once the veal shanks are tender, remove them to a platter. Now finish the sauce.

Remove the bouquet garni—it has served its purpose and you can throw it away.

Using the grate with medium or large holes, run the sauce through a food mill. This will make it smoother, yet maintain some character.

Adjust the sauce with salt and pepper, and then pour it over the shanks. Top with gremolada. Your braised veal shanks are now classic ossobuco! **AH**

BAKING AND PRESENTATION

23 Cover pan with a tight-fitting lid. Roast at about 325°. Adjust oven temperature to keep the shanks just below a slow boil.

24 Every 30 minutes, baste the shanks with the sauce forming in the pan. Remember to check your temperature every time you baste.

25 After cooking the shanks for about an hour (halfway), turn each piece over to equalize the heat. Make sure sauce is just below a boil.

26 When the shanks have finished cooking (total 2 hours), place on hot serving platter. *Remove the kitchen twine.* Keep shanks warm.

27 Use a food mill with medium or large holes to process sauce into a bowl. Adjust taste with salt and pepper. Keep warm.

28 Prepare gremolada while the shanks are cooking. Toss together the minced lemon, parsley, and garlic. Chill until ready to use.

29 When you're ready to present the ossobuco, cover warm shanks with hot sauce. Reserve some for a side. Then sprinkle with gremolada— use as much as you wish. The gremolada adds a refreshing taste and color.

GNOCCHI

The origins of gnocchi's name should be left in the closet. The fact is, "gnocco" means "stupid person" or "blockhead" referring to the people who made

uninspired dishes of dumplings without any flavor or sauce. This was the unfortunate beginning of gnocchi.

In the Italian food arena, gnocchi [NYOH-kee] has come to mean dumpling. Dumplings are pieces of dough *usually* made from flour (a starch) and water and then poached, baked, or fried. Good dumplings are made by adding flavorful ingredients or by being served in a soup or sauce. Are you familiar with Jewish matzo balls or spätzle from Germany? These are well-known dumplings.

Well, gnocchi is from Italy and there's different kinds from different regions. But the very basic recipe refers to gnocchi di patate—potato gnocchi.

Light Gnocchi: I don't know about you, but I've eaten some gnocchi that have made me feel like I've swallowed whole baked potatoes.

Just like any dumpling, gnocchi has to be light. The perfect gnocchi has just enough flour to hold it together without breaking apart when poached. The more flour that's added, the heavier they'll be.

Think about it. The more liquid in the dough, the more flour you have to add to make the gnocchi hold together. That's why I don't add eggs. Is this hard? Not really.

Potatoes: If you read the mashed potato article in Issue 2, you'll remember that using the right potato was critical—it is here, too.

Use a floury potato (russet, also called Idaho). Russets have a low-water, high-starch content.

Baking: The only way to cook russets for gnocchi is to bake them. Boiling causes the potatoes to retain too much water. *Remember*, the more liquid, the more flour needed to make the gnocchi hold together.

And don't wrap the potatoes with aluminum foil. This traps moisture.

Shaping: You're going to shape the gnocchi into little pillows. Besides being light, good potato gnocchi has the ability to hold sauces.

A dimple is made on one side. This provides a spot for sauce to gather, as well as making the gnocchi a uniform thickness for even cooking. The other side has ribs formed with a fork for sauce to cling to.

Give this a shot. Many Italian cooks are judged by their gnocchi prowess. Just don't be a "gnocco."

I'll say it again. There has to be just the right ratio between flour and liquid to keep the gnocchi light. So, while kneading in extra flour in Step 3, do several float tests.

POTATO GNOCCHI *(100 PIECES)*

WORK TIME: 1 HOUR 20 MINUTES
COOK TIME: 2 MINUTES

BAKE, PEEL, AND RICE:
2   lbs. russet potatoes

COMBINE WITH:
1¹/₂ cups all-purpose flour
¹/₂ t. kosher salt

KNEAD IN:
¹/₄ cup all-purpose flour

GARNISH WITH:
     Parmesan cheese, shredded

FRESH TOMATO SAUCE

(MAKES 5 CUPS)

WORK TIME: 30 MINUTES
COOK TIME: 25 MINUTES

SAUTE:
¹/₄ cup extra virgin olive oil
1   cup chopped yellow onion

ADD AND SAUTE:
1   T. minced garlic

ADD AND COOK OVER MEDIUM HEAT:
6   cups Roma tomatoes, roughly chopped
¹/₄ cup fresh basil chiffonade
1   t. salt

NUTRITIONAL INFORMATION PER 10 PIECES WITH ¹/₄ CUP SAUCE: CALORIES 192; TOTAL FAT 4(G); CALORIES FROM FAT 17%; SODIUM 280(MG)

FLOAT TEST

To see if gnocchi has just the right amount of flour, try the float test. Before shaping, pinch a bit of gnocchi dough and flatten it slightly. Drop it in water that's just under a boil. If it starts to feather, it needs more flour. If it doesn't float after 2 minutes, it has too much flour.

1 Bake potatoes at 400° for 50 minutes, or until fork-tender. Peel potatoes, then press them through a ricer.

2 Combine hot potatoes, 1¹/₂ cups flour, and salt in a mixing bowl. Stir with wooden spoon until ingredients are well mixed.

3 Turn mixture onto lightly floured surface. Knead in just enough remaining ¹/₄ cup flour to make a smooth dough that isn't very sticky.

4 Test dough to make sure it has enough flour. (See tip box, left.) Roll pieces of dough into ³/₄"-thick ropes. Cut ropes into ³/₄" pieces.

5 Place piece of cut dough on fork. Press with thumb to indent one side and create ridges on other. Roll ends up until they *almost* touch.

6 Cook gnocchi in batches—don't overcrowd. Use a large pot with salted water just under a boil. Cook until they float—about 2 minutes.

Authentic Fresh Tomato Sauce: *Saute onions in olive oil for 5 minutes. Add garlic and tomatoes.*

Simmer 30 minutes. Run through food mill. Add basil and salt. Serve over gnocchi and top with cheese.

BAKED SEMOLINA GNOCCHI

(SERVES 6)
WORK TIME: 2 HOURS
COOK TIME: 25 MINUTES

BRING TO SIMMER:
4 cups 2% milk

ADD:
3 T. unsalted butter
1/2 t. salt
 Dash white pepper
 Dash ground nutmeg

WHISK IN:
1 cup ground semolina

COOL, THEN ADD:
3 egg yolks, beaten
2 T. 2% milk
3/4 cup Parmesan cheese, grated

SPREAD, CHILL AND CUT OUT. PLACE IN BAKING DISH. DRIZZLE WITH:
1/4 cup unsalted butter, melted

SPRINKLE WITH:
2 T. fresh sage chiffonade

COMBINE AND TOP SEMOLINA WITH:
1/4 cup dry bread crumbs
2 T. Parmesan cheese, grated
1 T. unsalted butter, melted

BAKED SEMOLINA GNOCCHI WITH BUTTER AND SAGE

1 In 3-quart saucepan, heat milk until steaming. Add butter, salt, and pepper. Scrape whole nutmeg with a paring knife to add fresh bits. Stir until butter is melted.

2 Add semolina in a slow, steady stream, whisking constantly. Rapidly bring to a boil, then reduce heat to low. Cook 15 minutes, stirring constantly with wooden spoon.

3 Remove from heat and cool for 10 minutes, stirring once or twice. Combine egg yolks and milk. Add 3/4 cup Parmesan and egg mixture to semolina. Stir until smooth.

4 Spread mixture 1/2" thick in a baking sheet that's been sprayed with cooking spray. Spray the rubber scraper with cooking spray to keep it from sticking. Chill for 1–2 hours.

5 Use a 2" round cookie cutter to cut semolina sheet. Arrange rounds in a buttered 2-quart casserole dish so they angle and slightly overlap. Drizzle with 1/4 cup butter.

6 Sprinkle sage over gnocchi. Make topping and sprinkle over the entire casserole. Bake at 400° for 25 minutes or until golden. The bottom stays moist and the top gets crusty.

SPINACH GNOCCHI

(MAKES ABOUT 60 GNOCCHI)

WORK TIME: 30 MINUTES

COOK TIME: 2 MINUTES

COOK AND DRAIN:

1   10-oz. package frozen chopped spinach, thawed

SAUTE:

2   T. unsalted butter

$^1/_4$ cup finely chopped onion

COMBINE WITH SPINACH AND ONION:

$^2/_3$ cup ricotta cheese

$^1/_2$ cup Parmesan cheese, grated

1   egg, large

$^1/_4$ t. kosher salt

Dash ground nutmeg

STIR IN:

$^2/_3$ cup all-purpose flour

TOMATO CREAM SAUCE

ADD TO FRESH TOMATO SAUCE ON PAGE 13:

1$^1/_4$ cups heavy cream

NUTRITIONAL INFORMATION PER 6 PIECES WITH $^1/_4$ CUP SAUCE: CALORIES 258; TOTAL FAT 16(G); CALORIES FROM FAT 56%; SODIUM 426(MG)

SPINACH GNOCCHI WITH TOMATO CREAM SAUCE

1 Frozen spinach works great. Follow package directions for cooking. Drain well. Try to get out as much liquid as possible by pressing spinach with the back of a spoon.

2 Over medium heat, saute onion in butter until translucent. In a mixing bowl, combine onion, spinach, cheeses, egg, salt, and nutmeg. Mix well. Stir in flour.

3 Lightly flour countertop (to prevent a big mess, put wax paper down first). Using 2 spoons, place a heaping teaspoon of spinach mixture per gnocchi onto floured surface.

4 Lightly flour your hands and roll pieces of spinach mixture into balls. They'll be slightly sticky. On the first ball, do float test on page 13 to make sure they have enough flour.

5 Indent each piece with finger. This makes gnocchi a uniform thickness and provides a hiding place for sauce. Cook gnocchi in salted, barely boiling water until they float.

6 For tomato cream sauce, heat the tomato sauce until it's hot. Whisk in cream, and heat—don't bring to boil. Serve over spinach gnocchi or any of the other gnocchi.

MAPLE SYRUP

Nobody knows for sure how maple syrup making began, but there's plenty of legends. Here's my favorite: The wife of Indian Chief Woksis got up late one morning—

the chief had already left. She started searching for a bucket to gather water so she could boil meat for the chief.

She found a bucket under a maple tree—filled with "water." "I won't be going down to the creek today!" she thought. She boiled venison all day.

Suppertime rolled around and the chief was ravenous after a hunt. An inviting aroma filled the air. This was unusual—not that his wife was a rotten cook, but Woksis wasn't exactly living on truffles and foie gras, either.

He now experienced something he had never known before—a delicacy. The maple sap had boiled into a delicious, thick, sweet syrup that made this venison taste like none other. It was the meal of a lifetime.

When the chief asked his wife why this meal was so special, all she could think of was that bucket of water. The truth hit her like a lightning bolt: That

bucket laid right under the gash in the tree where Woksis had thrown his tomahawk last night. The "water" was sap from the maple tree—maple syrup making was born.

When I decided to go to Vermont and learn how the very best maple syrup is made, Woksis' wife wasn't available, so I visited Jacques "Jake" Couture and his wife, Pauline. They've been "sugaring" (making maple syrup) their whole lives. It's still much the same process Woksis' wife used—boiling. It's just a larger scale (and most people omit venison).

The Sugarbush: Syrup comes from sugar maples—a grove of them is a "sugarbush." To be mature enough for one tap, a tree needs to be at least a foot thick. Huge trees can take more taps, but over four is bad for any tree.

A good sugarmaker takes care of those trees. And apparently, tapping

doesn't hurt them. Some trees have been tapped every year since 1892!

Tapping: Tapping's done by early March. A $7/16$-inch-diameter hole is drilled $2\frac{1}{2}$ inches into the tree, and a spout is tapped in for the sap to flow through. Jake's got more than 4,000!

▲ *You still see a lot of buckets for collecting sap. But most people now use tubing.*

▲ *Jake's evaporator is going full-bore! He'll make 15 gallons of syrup an hour.*

▲ *Old timers used a dipper to know when to "draw off." The syrup would be thick enough to form an "apron" when poured.*

▲ *The sap works its way through baffles in the evaporator as it boils down.*

Collecting: Some people still collect sap the old-fashioned way—in buckets, *see Photo at left*. Sometimes the sap is even taken to the sugarhouse in horse-drawn sleighs!

But most sugarmakers, like Jake, run a network of tubing between all their trees. The tubes run into a main line that delivers the sap right into a big tank inside the sugarhouse.

The Run: Sap won't start running until the weather's just right—warm days into the 40's, and cold nights in the 20's. And "running" probably isn't the right word. Sap comes out just a few drops at a time.

It takes 40 gallons of sap to make just 1 gallon of syrup. That's because sap is only 2–4% sugar when it comes out of the tree—it looks and tastes like water. We need to do a *lot* of boiling to concentrate that sap into syrup.

Boiling: As soon as the sap starts running, you need to start boiling. The sooner it's boiled, the better qual-

▲ *Now a hydrometer is used to gauge the thickness of the syrup. The sugarmaker can "draw off" when it's just right.*

ity the syrup will be. Usually the sap is boiled the same day it's collected.

Evaporator: The evaporator is what boils the sap down into syrup. The sap runs through a maze of channels called "baffles" over a roaring wood fire. It's kind of like reducing a sauce—as the liquid evaporates, it gets thicker and the flavor intensifies.

Drawing Off: When the syrup is just the right thickness, it's "drawn off"—drained into buckets. If it's too thin it won't be high enough quality and can wind up spoiling. If too thick,

it can crystallize. Sugarmakers go by temperature, density readings from a hydrometer, and "aproning"—whether the syrup's thick enough to pour from a ladle in big, sticky sheets.

Filtering and Bottling: It's filtered and bottled while still hot. Filtering removes any impurities. And bottling while hot makes sure it won't spoil.

Grading: The lighter the color (not thickness!), the better the grade. But as the season goes on, each batch of syrup gets darker. The trees are changing—getting ready for spring.

There's nothing like Vermont light amber, or "Fancy." The delicate flavor is indescribable. Medium amber has a stronger maple taste, and is also great "eating" syrup. Then there's the dark amber. It's the strongest of the three grades—perfect for cooking.

Vermont Quality: Vermont has the highest quality standards of any state or Canadian province. That's why it's the best. It *must* be thicker, and it's graded not only by *color*, but also by *taste*. I think both Jake and the chief would agree—Vermont maple syrup has no equal. **A**ᴴ

▲ *A lot of other products, like these maple candies, can be made from maple syrup.*

▲ *The quality of maple syrup is strictly controlled in Vermont. Not only does it have to be thick—color and flavor are checked, too. The lightest-colored syrup is the best.*

BUTTERMILK PANCAKES

I'm ashamed to admit this. Up until recently, my concept of homemade pancakes was using box mix with real eggs and milk instead of water. Then I was shown the error of my ways. I had *real* homemade pancakes! With *real* maple syrup! (*See Pages 16 & 39.*) What a difference in taste—their fluffy texture is perfect for soaking up all that great syrup and butter! Oh my.

There's three keys to making these perfect pancakes: buttermilk, a little cake flour, and beaten egg whites.

Cake flour: Using some cake flour, instead of only all-purpose flour, keeps the pancakes light. No worries about gut-bombs with these!

Beaten egg whites: The beaten egg whites hold tiny air pockets in the batter to make the pancakes fluffier.

Buttermilk: Using buttermilk gives the pancakes richness, body, and flavor.

MAKING THE BATTER

BASIC BUTTERMILK PANCAKES
(*MAKES 12 PANCAKES*)
WORK TIME: 15 MINUTES
COOK TIME: 5 MINUTES
COMBINE:
1 1/2 cups all-purpose
    flour
1/2 cup cake flour
2 T. sugar
4 t. baking powder
1 t. salt
SEPARATE AND BEAT:
2 eggs, large
COMBINE EGG YOLKS WITH:
2 1/2 cups buttermilk
1/4 cup vegetable oil
STIR INTO DRY INGREDIENTS;
FOLD IN EGG WHITES

NUTRITIONAL INFORMATION PER 3 PANCAKES: CALORIES 461; TOTAL FAT 18(G); CALORIES FROM FAT 35%; SODIUM 900(MG)

1 Preheat your griddle, *see step 7*. Measure and whisk together flours, sugar, baking powder, and salt.

2 Separate egg yolks and whites. Beat the whites until stiff peaks form, but don't get them too dry.

3 Beat the egg yolks. Then add the buttermilk and vegetable oil. Whisk to combine wet ingredients.

4 Pour wet ingredients into dry. Whisk to combine, but don't overmix—a few small lumps are okay.

5 Gently fold in your whites by cutting down into the mixture and turning it over in a rolling motion.

6 Your finished batter should look like this, with a thick and fluffy marshmallow texture.

BUCKWHEAT PANCAKES

REPLACE BASIC RECIPE FLOURS AND SUGAR WITH:

1 cup all-purpose flour
1/2 cup cake flour
1/2 cup buckwheat flour
2 T. brown sugar

NOW FOLLOW BASIC BUTTERMILK RECIPE.

The buckwheat pancakes cook fast, so watch out. Electric griddle: 350°.

CORNMEAL PANCAKES

REPLACE BASIC RECIPE FLOURS WITH:

1 cup all-purpose flour
1/2 cup cake flour
1/2 cup cornmeal

FOLLOW BASIC RECIPE; ADD:
1 1/2 cups berries (raspberries or blueberries)

Don't mix berries into the batter—place them in the cakes on the griddle.

WHOLE WHEAT BANANA PANCAKES

REPLACE BASIC RECIPE FLOURS AND SUGAR WITH:

1 cup all-purpose flour
1/2 cup cake flour
1/2 cup whole wheat flour
2 T. brown sugar

FOLLOW BASIC RECIPE;
ADD TO EGG YOLK MIXTURE:
2 bananas, mashed
1 cup chopped pecans

Use a fork to mash ripe bananas—a mixer makes them soupy. Add to yolks, buttermilk, and oil. Whole wheat cakes cook quickly! Electric griddle: 350°.

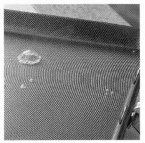

7 I use my stove-top griddle for pancakes. Bring it to medium-high heat and then oil it lightly. For electric griddle: 375°.

8 You can tell when the griddle's hot enough by sprinkling water drops over it. If it's hot enough, the drops will dance.

9 Always do a test pancake because the first one usually fails. Use a 1/3 cup to pour batter onto the griddle.

10 When the cake looks dry on the edges, and bubbles break to form holes that don't close, it's time to flip.

11 Incorrect heat can cause the cakes to burn, remain raw inside, or turn anemic. Adjust the heat for above result.

12 When you get a good test cake, fill the griddle and cook as in Steps 9 and 10. Of course serve immediately.

ORANGE BUTTER

For Orange Butter, mix one stick softened butter, zest from one orange, and 2 t. orange juice.

Roll butter in plastic wrap. Twist ends to form log and freeze. Cut medallions and use for taste twist.

Pancake presentation isn't rocket science. Make any size or shape you want. Sensationalism works for me. Truth is, I couldn't eat half this huge stack, but I sure like it sitting in front of me.

FOCACCIA

Focaccia fever has hit epidemic proportions around here.

I've got a brother who's sending me Portuguese sea salt

from Newark, I've got a staff that's fighting to help make

it (just to eat it), and I've got a boss (our publisher, Don, *see Editor's Letter*) who's so into focaccia, he came to the test kitchen every time it was made.

I suppose since focaccia is sort of new to American cuisine, it's viewed with a certain reverence. I've made a hundred focaccia over the last month, and found that there *is* something mysteriously unique about each one —an unknown ambiguity. A little ugly yet peasantly beautiful. Simple but elegant—hallmarks of Italian cooking.

What is It? Focaccia's an Italian bread that's been around for centuries. It's chewy, full of flavor, and anything but fancy. This is simple food. But it blows you away just because it *is* so simple—and still so good.

Here's something else simplicity does for you: it gives you a perfect place to showcase quality ingredients like fresh herbs, great olive oil, and the best and freshest vegetables. All these fantastic flavors will be able to "pop out" on a focaccia.

Now, people who like a lot of rules might get a little uncomfortable — because there aren't any (or at least not strict ones). Focaccia is extremely forgiving. Make different shapes and sizes, and put anything on it you want — just don't call it pizza!

Making Focaccia: Just the mere mention of breadmaking scares people away. But this is one bread that's hard to screw up. Why? We're pulling out a little breadmaking mystique by using a "biga" ("starter" in Italian).

This starter is the key to everything. It's only a mixture of flour, water, and yeast that you set out on your counter overnight. The simple starter will give you rising action to spare, beautiful texture (lots of big holes!), and outrageous taste. I'll get even *more* into this in a minute.

I'll warn you—making focaccia is addictive. It got Don out of the office! Might as well mix up a starter...

BASIC FOCACCIA DOUGH

MAKES 2 (14-INCH) LOAVES,
16 SLICES PER LOAF
WORK TIME: 40 MINUTES
COOK TIME: 15 MINUTES
FOR THE STARTER:
BEAT TOGETHER:

2 cups bread flour
1 cup water (60°)
2 t. active dry yeast

FOR THE DOUGH:
MIX INTO STARTER:

2 cups warm water (80°–90°)
4 t. fine sea salt
6 cups bread flour *(start with 5 1/2 cups and add if necessary)*

BRUSH WITH:

2 T. extra virgin olive oil

NUTRITIONAL INFORMATION PER SLICE:
CALORIES 110; TOTAL FAT 1(G); CALORIES
FROM FAT 10%; SODIUM 296(MG)

MEDITERRANEAN FOCACCIA

TOPPINGS FOR ONE FOCACCIA:
DRIZZLE 2 T. EXTRA VIRGIN OLIVE
OIL OVER AND TOP FOCACCIA WITH:

1/2 cup red and yellow pepper strips
1/3 cup canned artichoke hearts, quartered
1/4 cup kalamata olives, pitted
1 T. chopped garlic

SPRINKLE FOCACCIA WITH:

2 t. coarse sea salt

BAKE AND TOP WITH:

2 T. flat leaf parsley leaves

With the starter in your bowl, begin.

Mixing: Keep stirring as you add flour, *see Step 3*. Add *only* as much of the total 6 cups as it takes to get the dough to pull away from the sides of the bowl as you stir. Now turn it onto your floured surface.

Kneading: Add in the rest of the flour as you knead, *see Step 4*. Keep in mind, any dough may need slightly more or less flour than called for. Stop adding it when the dough's still just a little bit sticky. As you knead, you're developing gluten in the dough, *see Step 5*. This will let the focaccia rise and develop structure — holes.

Last, cover and let proof about 2–3 hours, *see Step 6*.

STARTER — "BIGA"

Italian bakers use weaker flour than us. To compensate, they use starters.

Starters develop a powerful rising action that gives bread better texture (holes), even if your flour's sub-par, or you add a little too much. It's forgiving. Flavor is outstanding due to a long, slow fermentation overnight. Like I've said before, that's *always* best for taste.

Making the Starter: One key to the starter is to measure properly. Pour the flour from one cup into your measuring cup until it overflows. Then level off the top with a straightedge.

Combine everything in a bowl and start stirring, *see Steps 1–2*. This starter will be stiff. Keep stirring until it strings or forms ropes.

1 Combine 2 cups bread flour, 1 cup room-temperature (tap) water and 2 teaspoons of yeast in a mixing bowl.

2 Beat 100–125 strokes — it'll be smooth, but ropey when pulled. Cover loosely with plastic wrap. Let sit overnight at room temperature.

MIXING AND KNEADING

3 Stir starter to deflate. Add the warm water, fine sea salt, and *only enough* of the flour so that dough pulls away from bowl when you stir.

4 Turn dough onto floured surface. Start kneading by folding half of dough toward you. You'll be gradually adding rest of flour as you knead.

5 Using heels of your hands, push dough vigorously away from you. Repeat steps 4 and 5 until dough is smooth, stretchy.

6 Place dough in lightly floured bowl. Then dust dough with flour. Cover with plastic wrap. Let rise at room temperature for 2–3 hours.

SHAPE, PROOF AND TOP

Now you have a nice soft dough. Quick and light handling are the keys to forming good focaccia.

Initial Shaping: This simple initial shaping procedure makes dough easy to work with.

Cut the risen dough in half. Gently shape it into two balls, *see Step 7*. (The recipe gives you enough for two, but I'm showing you one for clarity.)

Handle the dough as gently as possible. There are two reasons for this: too much handling releases air (air makes the desired big holes in the finished bread), and the final proofing will take less time.

Proofing: If you were careful with the dough, it'll proof quickly this time—the aggressive starter helps, too.

Now take a good long look at step 8. You want the dough to be seriously poofy before you move on. This is what makes good focaccia—the dough has *got* to be airy.

Final Shaping: I'm sorry, but I'm saying this again because it's so important: *Be gentle with the dough*. The little pockets of air bake into big holes.

Turn the dough onto a floured surface. Using all your fingers, play the dough like a piano, poking and prodding it gently, *see Step 9*. This starts shaping it. Then, drape the dough over your knuckles to stretch it, *see Step 10*. Let gravity do the work.

If the dough is tough, rubbery and won't hold a shape, you've overworked it. The gluten strengthened from all the work. No problem. Cover the dough with plastic and leave it alone a few minutes. The gluten will relax and you can finish shaping.

Topping: Brush olive oil on the dough so you can fold it in half for moving. It also gives the crust a great shine, *see Steps 11–12*. Could it be that it tastes good, too? Hmmm.

Coat topping with olive oil to prevent burning, *see Step 13*. And, don't forget the coarse sea salt, *see Step 14*.

7 Cut risen dough into two pieces. Gently shape pieces into balls. Dust with flour. Cover with plastic. Let rest (on surface) 30 minutes.

8 I know I said 30 minutes, but if it's not *real* soft (like this) give it more time. It's ready when the dough doesn't spring back when you poke it.

SHAPE AND TOP

9 Heat oven to 475°. Place a ball of dough on floured surface. Poke gently with fingers to begin shaping—flatten and stretch it *just a bit.*

10 Drape the dough over your knuckles and let it stretch itself into shape. Don't work it too much—you'll lose air, and it'll *look* stretched.

11 Lay dough circle on floured surface. Poke gently to make some more dimples. Brush plenty of olive oil all over the surface.

12 Fold dough in half, oiled surfaces together, and transfer to floured peel—unfold. The oil will keep the dough from sticking to itself.

13 Drizzle some olive oil over all the toppings and toss to coat. A coating of oil will keep the toppings from burning in the hot 475° oven.

14 Arrange toppings on focaccia. Poke the dough and the toppings gently. Sprinkle the focaccia with coarse sea salt. You're ready to bake.

BAKING FOCACCIA

At this point, all you have to do is sit back and wait for your reward. These things take no time to bake, and baking couldn't be easier!

Baking: I've said it before—you've got to have a peel! A peel is the biggest skin-saver this side of asbestos. It's *the* tool for moving focaccia (that's baked on a stone) in and out of the oven.

Oh yeah—the baking stone. It's a must. The dough hits a hot surface immediately and there's no fluctuations in heat. It also absorbs moisture making a chewy, crispy crust.

Slide focaccia into the oven, *see Step 15.* Peek at it in 5 minutes—sometimes there are massive bubbles that form—pop them.

Now, finish cooking it until it turns a rich golden brown. It's done!

Cooling: Cool on a rack, *see Step 16.* Fresh herbs can only be added after cooling or they'll turn black. **AH**

BAKING

15 Slide focaccia from peel to baking stone in a 475° oven. Pop any huge bubbles that form. Bake for 15–20 minutes—until it looks done to you!

16 Cool focaccia on rack *slightly.* Then add the fresh Italian parsley leaves (fresh herbs turn black if too hot). Brush leaves and edge of crust with olive oil.

FOCACCIA VARIATIONS

Just about anything goes on focaccia. But if you start slapping *heavy* meat, *heavy* cheese and sauce on one, you might decide to call it something else.

Make these variations just like the main recipe. But notice that not all ingredients go on before baking.

POTATO, ONION, ROSEMARY

This one opened some eyes—it's fantastic! Dredge thinly sliced yellow onions and potatoes (Yukon Golds or reds) in olive oil. Brush the dough with olive oil and top it with the onions and potatoes. Sprinkle on 1 T. chopped fresh rosemary (won't turn black) and plenty of coarse sea salt.

TOMATO, PARMIGIANO-REGGIANO

This is my favorite—there's nothing in the way of these great flavors. So buy the very best ingredients you can find. Seed 2–3 nice Roma tomatoes and slice them about $1/4$" thick. Brush dough with olive oil, top with tomatoes and coarse sea salt. Now brush tomatoes with olive oil, and bake. Just before it comes out, layer on thin slices of the best Parmigiano-Reggiano cheese. Bake another 2–3 minutes.

PANCETTA, BASIL, TOMATOES

The pancetta is the star here—this Italian rolled bacon is dynamite. And my combination accents its great flavor. Cut it into 1" pieces, then saute until just slightly crisp. It'll cook the rest of the way on the focaccia. Brush the top of the dough with olive oil, then top with the pancetta, thinly sliced (and seeded) Roma tomatoes, and coarse sea salt. Bake, let cool 15 minutes, *then* top with fresh basil leaves.

FISH*en*PAPILLOTE

Cooking fish "en papillote" is the best way to make it indoors. It's simple. It keeps fish moist and tender, and best of all, the house doesn't end up stinking like fish.

You've been there. Cooking "en papillote" eliminates potential problems.

En papillote [ahn pah-pee-YOHT] is a French technique that refers to food baked in a parchment-paper packet. It bakes at a very high 450°. At this temperature, when moisture is released from food, it creates steam. It's this encased steam that creates a hot, moist cooking environment—causing the packet to puff up.

This little handmade pressure cooker cooks the fish just until tender, and keeps fish smells in check.

Why en papillote: Besides odor control, there are other great reasons you should try cooking en papillote.

Speed: Because of the hot steam, fish (or any lean meat) is done in a quick 10–15 minutes. The packets even assemble quickly, too.

Healthy: The very nature of parchment cooking is healthy. You only use lean cuts of meat to cook en papillote. And thanks to the steam, no extra fats are needed to enhance flavor or moisture in the food. I'm not a fan of steaming, but I like this.

Forgiving: Lean fish is fragile. It can easily dry out when overcooked. With en papillote, you can cook these packets a couple of minutes too long and still get a good result.

Versatile: So you don't like fish? No problem. I tested both recipes with chicken breast and they worked great. Just add 5 minutes of cooking time. Fattier types of fish and meat don't work well. Their fats tend to be accentuated in the closed environment.

Clean-up: What can I say? This stuff is cooked in paper. Except for a few bowls, there's not much to wash.

But best of all, it's *fun, different, and elegant.* Everyone has their own packet that they tear open, releasing a burst of aromas and a vision of food. Not bad for a piece of paper.

COOKING IN PARCHMENT

There's really no big trick to how cooking en papillote works. But it does help to know some basics.

Steam Heat: How do you steam without water? Well, food contains natural moisture which is released into the packet as it heats. At this high temperature (450°), steam is generated, creating pressure in the packet. Perfect for hot, fast, moist cooking.

But parchment packets don't create so much pressure that the trapped steam breaks down delicate foods. Parchment is naturally permeable. As the steam builds and puffs up the pack, it can ease the pressure by releasing through the paper (like a relief valve on a pressure cooker).

Steaming in parchment beats steaming over water, too. It's more concentrated, keeping flavors intense because little escapes. Steaming over water doesn't add flavor—it tends to dilute flavors of the food above it.

Have you ever noticed how the water used in steaming becomes colored? That's from flavor and nutrients in your food getting leached away. Parchment packets keep all those good things with the food.

Parchment Paper: What is cooking parchment paper? It's a special, light, grease- and moisture-resistant paper. It's usually called kitchen parchment.

I had a hard time finding parchment paper at the supermarket. If you can't find it there, it *is* available at kitchen stores, cake-decorating stores, and through mail-order catalogs.

What type: Parchment paper comes white and unbleached. Both worked equally well. The only difference is an environmental preference.

Making the Packet: The key to parchment cooking is a tight seal.

First, make the paper big. You want enough of a border around the food to make a double seal. This allows the packet to puff without blowing out the sides. Also, don't stack ingredients too high or you'll have the same problem.

Brush paper with butter or oil to make a tight seal. You could just brush the edges, but I brush the whole thing so the fat can add flavor to the dish.

Finally, match the paper edges carefully and crease the folds tightly. I always double-fold all my edges.

Shapes: Traditionally, the paper is cut into a heart shape, but squares or rectangles work equally well.

SEA BASS EN PAPILLOTE
(SERVES 4)
WORK TIME: 45 MINUTES
COOK TIME: 10 MINUTES

BRUSH CUT PARCHMENT WITH:
1/4 cup butter, melted

DIVIDE AND PLACE AMONG PACKETS:
3 cups sliced leek

TOP WITH:
4 sprigs fresh thyme
4 sea bass fillets (6 oz. each), 1" thick

DIJON MIXTURE: BLEND AND BRUSH FISH:
1/4 cup Dijon mustard
2 T. dry white wine
1/8 t. white pepper

DIVIDE AMONG PACKETS:
1/2 cup sliced shallots
1 cup finely chopped Roma tomatoes, peeled
12 whole shiitake mushroom caps
4 lemon slices

NUTRITIONAL INFORMATION PER SERVING:
CALORIES 287; TOTAL FAT 10(G); CALORIES FROM FAT 32%; SODIUM 551(MG)

SELECTING FISH FILLETS

In order to have good results with these recipes, your fish has to be *absolutely* fresh. I buy my fish from a fish market that I know has its seafood flown in daily from the coast. Some supermarkets can't always do this—ask about the freshness before you buy.

When selecting fillets, your eyes and your nose are your best tools.

Fillets should be slightly translucent and evenly colored. Dark spots indicate bruising, bleeding, or some other contamination. The flesh should be tight and firm, too.

How the fish is stored is also big. Fillets should not be in direct contact with ice. They should be on trays that are set on ice. Melting ice deteriorates the fillets.

And here's the bottom line on "fishy" smelling fish. *There should be no bad odor.* Do you think I'd have my nose that close if it did? Don't let anyone tell you any different.

FISH RECOMMENDATIONS
Lean white fish is perfect for parchment cooking. The fillets stay moist and easily absorb flavors. Oily fish contain some fats that could produce a bad taste in the steamy packets. They're better suited for baking or grilling.

SOME GOOD VARIETIES ARE:
• Black Sea Bass • Cod
• Flounder • Grouper • Halibut
• Ocean Perch • Orange Roughy
• Red Snapper • Rockfish • Sole

▲ *Gently press fish with your finger. If fresh, it will feel firm and spring back.*

▲ *Take a sniff. Fresh fish smells clean. If it isn't, you'll know it right away.*

INGREDIENT PREPARATION

For parchment cooking, most of the work is in the ingredient preparation.

Leeks: Leeks hide a lot of dirt and sand in all those layers. Wash sliced leeks in a bowl of ice water, *see Step 1*.

Mushrooms: To me, shiitake mushrooms have more flavor than any other mushroom. That's why I use them here. Pick shiitakes with small caps, or you'll end up over-stuffing your packets.

The stems of shiitakes are tough and woody, so remove them, *see Step 2*. Toss them or save to make a stock.

Tomatoes: You'll want to peel and seed the tomatoes. Romas can be tough to peel, but worth their flavor.

To loosen their skin, cut a shallow "X" on base and then drop them in boiling water, *see Step 3*. After one minute, remove and place Romas in ice water to stop the cooking. The peel will pull right off, *see Step 4*.

Lemons: The lemon slices add flavor. They're also a garnish when you make a lot of decorative channels with a canelle, *see Step 5*. Then slice rounds.

Packets: These packets are heart shaped. If you're like me, you'll need to sketch the outline on the parchment paper before cutting it out, *see Steps 6-7*. (My valentines are bad, too.)

Finally, brush one side of parchment with butter, *see Step 8*. Put a little under the paper edges to "glue" it down so the edges don't curl up.

ASPARAGUS BUNDLES
For a fancy side dish to go with this fancy meal, bundle fresh asparagus spears and julienned carrots. Tie with chives that've been dipped in hot water until limp. Steam bundles 5 minutes.

1 Slice leeks and shallots to form circles. Separate them into rings. Rinse leeks in a bowl of ice water to remove any dirt. Repeat if necessary.

2 Use shiitake mushrooms with small caps. The flavorful stems are woody and inedible. Cut them off and save (freeze) them for stocks.

3 Blanch tomatoes to make them easy to peel. Cut an "X" on the bases of tomatoes, then place them in boiling water for 1–2 minutes.

4 Remove tomatoes from boiling water, and place in ice water to stop any cooking. The peels come right off. Seed and chop tomatoes.

5 Lemon slices look neater if you cut a lot of shallow, equidistant grooves with a canelle. Cut from stem to base. Then slice into rounds.

6 Cut a 12" x 16" piece of paper, and fold it in half like a book. Mark the largest half of heart you can, starting from the folded edge.

7 Cut out the heart half. Use it as a template to cut out three more hearts from equal-sized pieces of parchment paper.

8 Brush a little dab of butter under paper to keep it flat. Then brush unfolded hearts entirely. This helps seal in steam and adds a little flavor.

ASSEMBLING THE PACKETS

Here's the critical part to successful parchment cooking—building the food and securely sealing the pack.

The Base: Spread the leeks to within two inches of the paper edges. This determines your base so no food goes past this. Then place a full sprig of thyme on the base, *see Step 9*. Putting fresh herbs under the fish adds flavor and keeps the herbs green.

Mustard Mixture: Next, place the fish on the base and brush with the mustard-wine mixture, see Step 10. The Dijon and wine give the fillet a much needed taste "jump-start."

Top the Fillet: Sea bass is very white and mild. Top the fillet with shallots and tomatoes to add color and flavor. Then, place mushroom caps along the sides. If you put them on top, the pile gets too high. Finally, set a lemon slice on top, *see Step 11*.

Folding: Begin folding by bringing the two halves together. Start sealing at the top of the heart, pleating it as you go for a tight seal, see *Steps 12–13*. Twist the end to complete the seal, *see Step 14*. To ensure a tight crease, run your fingernail along each pleat.

Baking: Two packets fit on a baking sheet. Use one with edges for errant juices, *see Step 15*. Allow "puff" room in the oven. When done, *immediately* serve unopened packets. **Aн**

MAKING THE PARCHMENT PACKETS

9 Construct packets one at a time. Arrange a bed of ½ cup sliced leeks on right side of paper. Then put a sprig of fresh thyme on top of leeks.

10 Lightly salt the fish fillet and then put it on the bed of leeks. Now brush the fillet lightly with the Dijon-wine mixture.

11 Arrange 2 T. shallots and ¼ cup tomatoes on top of fillet. Place 3 mushroom caps along the side of fillet. Set a lemon slice on top.

12 Fold left side of paper over fish and *match* edges. Begin folding at the top of the heart. Fold over ½" of edges and pleat about every inch.

13 Continue folding and pleating until you reach the point of the heart. Make sure all edges continually match and folds are tight.

14 Now, *repeat* the folding and pleating to make a double fold. Twist the point tightly to seal. Use your fingernail to crease the edges.

TIMING FISH FOR DONENESS

Since your fish is all wrapped up, it's hard to tell when it's done. You'll have to go on faith, here. I consistently had good luck with 10 minutes at 450° for a 1"-thick fillet. So for fish, allow 10 minutes per inch. But I wouldn't go much thicker than 1½" because your packet will be too full and not fold and seal well.

15 Place packets on large baking sheets. Bake packets at 450° (*see box to the left*). If you sealed them well, the packets will puff up.

16 Serve packets *immediately* or they'll deflate. Let each person tear open their packet. Part of the experience is that first burst of aroma.

The traditional fish en papillote is a great dish. I really liked the concept so I kept experimenting. I found that a square packet worked just as well as a heart. (Actually, it was a little easier!)

I landed on a spicy Asian combination using shrimp and scallops. The shellfish worked great, and the recipe gave a fun twist to a classic technique.

SHRIMP AND SCALLOPS EN PAPILLOTE *(SERVES 4)*

WORK TIME: 60 MINUTES
COOK TIME: 10 MINUTES
FOR MARINADE, COMBINE:

²/₃	cup hoisin sauce
3	T. dry sherry
2	T. sesame oil
1	T. cornstarch
1	T. sugar
2	t. red pepper flakes
10	cloves garlic, chopped
10	slices ginger, cut into strips

ADD:

12	sea scallops
8	jumbo shrimp, cleaned

DIVIDE AMONG 4 PACKETS:

12	iceberg lettuce leaves

ADD SEAFOOD; DIVIDE AMONG EACH PACKET:

³/₄	cup diced red bell pepper

BAKE; GARNISH WITH SLICED SCALLIONS AND TOASTED SESAME SEEDS.

MARINATING SEAFOOD

1 In a mixing bowl, combine hoisin sauce, sherry, sesame oil, cornstarch, sugar, and red pepper flakes. Chop garlic and add to marinade.

2 Peel a piece of gingerroot, then cut 10 *thin* slices. Now, stack a few slices together and cut into thin strips (julienne). Add to marinade.

3 Peel the uncooked shrimp. Using your thumbs, pull the shells apart. Gently pull the shrimp from the shell, leaving the tail "feathers" attached.

4 Remove the dark "vein" (that's a joke—it's the intestinal tract). Cut down the back to reveal the vein. Rinse it out. This is called deveining.

5 Add scallops and cleaned shrimp to marinade, stirring to coat. Chill mixture (20 minutes) or until you're ready to assemble the packets.

PUTTING IT ALL TOGETHER

One of the differences of this recipe from the Sea Bass en Papillote is that it has a marinade. This creates a spicy sauce with big flavor.

Scallions: There's little difference in taste between the green and white part of a scallion. In Asian cooking, the green part of the scallions is used for color. Use the cut green pieces for sprinkling in the packs after baking.

But the white ends don't go to waste. They are made into "brushes" that will garnish the rice.

To make brushes, cut whites into two-inch pieces. Cut thin strips halfway down each piece, leaving the end intact. Put the pieces in ice water and the strips will curl, making brushes.

Sesame Oil: I use sesame oil instead of butter to brush the parchment in this recipe. The sesame oil fits in better with this recipe, and its aroma really pops out with that first blast after opening the packets.

Packets: These square packets are the easiest thing going in en papillote cooking. There's hardly any trimming of the paper and sealing the straight edges is easier than the curves.

Stack all the ingredients on one side of the parchment, fold over the open side (like a book), and start sealing. As with the heart, double-fold the edges and crease the edges with your fingernail for a tight seal. **АН**

RICE DIAMONDS
Shaped rice is more interesting than a big scoop on your plate. Cook sticky rice as directed, then pack it hot into oiled cookie cutters. Push shapes out. Garnish with scallion brushes and pickled ginger.

6 Dice red pepper. Diagonally slice green parts of scallions. Cut strips at green end of white parts. Put in ice water to fan brushes.

7 Cut four 12" x 24" pieces of parchment. Fold pieces in half (like a book). Unfold and brush the entire paper with sesame oil.

8 Assemble packets one at a time. Layer two or three pieces of lettuce in center of right side of paper to make a bed.

9 Arrange two shrimp and three scallops on lettuce bed. Spoon some additional marinade over top. Sprinkle 3 T. diced red pepper on top.

10 Fold left side of paper over filling and *match* edges. Starting at the edge opposite the folded edge, fold ½" over and crease.

11 Now, fold the other two edges of the packet. Seal tightly and repeat the process to double seal. Make the other three packets.

12 Place packets on baking sheets with edges to catch any juices that may leak from the packets. Bake at 450° for 10 minutes.

13 Plate packets and serve immediately. Provide scallions and toasted sesame seeds so each person can garnish their own packets.

WORKING WITH CHOCOLATE

I'm going to cut to the skinny and tell you what you need to know about chocolate. They say it's a lot like wine, but you won't catch me using any goofy words like "earthy bouquet," or "fruity overtones." Next, I'll show you how to make some incredible decorations.

What is it? Here comes the barebones process for making chocolate.

Beans: Chocolate grows on trees—cacao trees. The beans (called either cacao or cocoa beans) are picked, then left a few days to ferment. Next they're dried and roasted. Roasting does a lot for flavor—just like coffee.

Crushing: After roasting, the shells and "nibs" (seeds) inside are broken. The nibs are crushed into a paste called *chocolate liquor*, which consists of just two things: cocoa butter and cocoa powder. The shells get tossed.

Cocoa butter is a fat that gives chocolate its texture—it makes it melt in your mouth. *Cocoa powder* is where most of the flavor comes from.

Refining: The cocoa powder and cocoa butter are separated, refined (purified), and mixed back together. Then a little lecithin is usually added. It's an emulsifier—something that helps it all blend.

Conching: Next, the mixture is "conched"—mixed, kneaded, and heated so it'll be smooth and creamy. The longer it's conched, the better it gets—some of the very best chocolates are conched for up to a week!

Finally, the chocolate's tempered to make it shiny and hard, *see Box*.

Types: Here's the different types of chocolate you're most likely to find.

Unsweetened chocolate: Unsweetened chocolate is also called bitter or "baking" chocolate. It has absolutely no sugar added, so it isn't "eating chocolate"—it's strictly for cooking.

Bittersweet and Semisweet chocolate: These two are both called "dark chocolate" because of their dark color, strong chocolaty taste, and small amount of sugar—but there's no set definition. The only difference is that semisweet has a bit more sugar.

You can use them interchangeably. And either one is good for the decorations we're making. But for straight-up eating, connoisseurs will go with bittersweet every time.

Milk chocolate: It's just like it sounds—milk's added to the chocolate, which makes it very mild. And some extra sugar usually goes in to make it sweeter than other chocolate.

But watch out. Milk makes it burn if it even *sees* a flame. It's tough to cook with and weak for decorations.

Chocolate chips: Chocolate chips are made to handle high heat—different fats have been added. This is good for baking things like cookies. Other types of chocolate would scorch. But that's all I use chips for. Taste's okay in your better brands, but not nearly as good as fine bittersweet or semisweet chocolate. And consistency won't hold up for decorations.

White chocolate: White chocolate's white because it doesn't have cocoa powder. It *should* have cocoa butter as its only fat, but usually an inferior fat gets substituted. Read the label to make sure you've got the good stuff.

TEMPERING

Tempering is the last stage in making chocolate. The chocolate's repeatedly heated and cooled to make the fat crystals form a certain way. When done right, the chocolate will get hard and glossy when it cools. And tempering also keeps chocolate from blooming right away, *see Page 31*.

Tempering is tough to master. And it's not necessary for what we're doing. Everything we're about to make, plus the Torte on page 42, will keep looking great for several days *without blooming* if just stored in the refrigerator!

POTENTIAL PROBLEMS

Chocolate can be a little quirky. Here's my take on a few potential problems.

Melting: Chocolate burns in a hurry. Break it into small pieces and use very gentle heat, *see Steps 1–2*.

You *can* use a microwave, but keep the power to 50% or less. Heat it for only 30 seconds to a minute at a time. Then stir until it's fully melted.

Seizing: Seizing is when melted chocolate suddenly clumps up into a paste. The top two causes are burning and small amounts of moisture.

It only takes a drop or two of water to make chocolate seize. (But it's perfectly fine in *large* amounts of liquid, *see Page 42*.) You can save seized chocolate by stirring in oil or water, but you'll often ruin the taste.

Blooming: Blooming is when chocolate gets grayish blotches. It's caused by being stored in too much heat or humidity. Experts disagree on taste, but to me, bloomed chocolate tastes just fine.

DIPPING

Chocolate is a natural for dipping. Here's a couple ideas that'll get you going.

TULIP SHELL ▶

It's one thing to dip *food* in chocolate, but a balloon? Absolutely! This is not only fun to make, it's a fantastic container for ice cream or mousse.

see Page 42

FRUIT AND NUTS ▼

Dipping fruit and nuts is a proven winner. Melt the best-tasting chocolate you can find. Add *nothing*. Don't forget dried fruit—apricots are dynamite!

▲ *Seized chocolate.*

▲ *Chocolate that's just starting to bloom.*

MELTING CHOCOLATE

1 Break the chocolate into small pieces for melting—a mallet does the trick. This helps the chocolate melt faster and a lot more evenly.

2 A double boiler works well for melting. But you still have to watch the heat or the chocolate can burn. Stir constantly until melted.

1 Melt 6 to 8 ounces bittersweet or semisweet chocolate. Let it cool a bit (or balloon will pop!). Dip bottom, then lean it toward you.

2 Lean it to four sides to get shape. Don't rush—chocolate needs a few seconds to stick. Place straight up on waxed paper. Refrigerate ½ hr.

3 Squeeze top of balloon, puncture with scissors. Pinch the puncture shut and then start letting the air out *very* slowly.

4 If chocolate's cool enough, the sides will release from the balloon as the air escapes. If it sticks, refrigerate the others 15 mins. more.

CURLS

Chocolate curls are incredibly versatile garnishes—they'll go with all kinds of desserts. My variations put a new spin on a classic idea.

PINSTRIPE ►

These pinstripe curls will flat-out give you contrast. And you ought to see them piled up high on a cake or a pie!

Check your cupboards, or shop around for something that'll make you a good chocolate mold. I've had the best luck with tops from butter dishes, *see Step 1.* Once you've got your first layer poured, refrigerate at least 30–45 minutes, *see Step 2.* The chocolate *must* be hard when you pour the next layer. Otherwise they'll bleed together, *see Step 3.*

Temperature is critical to making all these curls, *see Step 4.* You just have to try a couple to see how the chocolate responds. Cold chocolate's too brittle. Warm it in your hands a second or two until it becomes pliable.

MARBLED ►

Marbled curls have some contrast too—but it's more understated.

This block is quicker to make—no waiting for each layer to harden, *see Step 1.* If you haven't marbled anything before, you'll be surprised how easy this really is, *see Step 2.*

PENCIL ►

If you've seen my Chocolate Espresso Torte, *see Cover and Page 42*, then you know what these pencil curls can do!

Now, I'll 'fess up. These are the most challenging curls to make—not hard, but they do take practice.

If your baking pan is too cold, it'll cause the chocolate to harden before you can smooth it into the nice, even layer you need, *see Step 1.* And temperature is even more important here than with any other curl, *see Step 2.* *That's* what'll make it happen for you!

1 Melt dark chocolate. Now line mold with plastic—it helps you get the block out later. This mold is actually the top from a butter dish.

3 When the first layer of dark chocolate hardens, pour a thin layer of white chocolate. Refrigerate until hard. Pour final layer of dark.

2 Pour a layer of dark chocolate. A clear mold lets you see how much to pour—a little over a third. Refrigerate. Melt white chocolate.

4 Bring chocolate to room temperature. If too cold, it'll be too brittle to curl. Turn block on side, pull peeler toward you to make curls.

1 Melt both chocolates. Fill bottom third of mold with white. Spoon on 1–2 T. dark. Cover dark with white—repeat till mold's full.

2 Swirl through all the chocolate with a skewer. Raise and lower the skewer a few times to swirl through all the chocolate.

1 Melt dark chocolate. With rubber spatula, spread ⅛" layer of chocolate evenly onto bottom of *room temperature* glass baking pan.

2 Let harden at room temperature for 1 to 2 hrs. Use long-bladed, knife. Scrape away from you, with knife at shallow angle, to form curl.

FILIGREE

Filigree is one of the classiest garnishes around—the possibilities are endless.

PATTERN PIPING ▶

It doesn't get any easier than this! Tape down your pattern, tape some waxed paper over it, and start tracing, *see Step 1*. Any number of patterns will work, *see Step 2*. These are gorgeous just sitting on a plate with a nice dessert. Or, if you're industrious, make structures by gluing some together with melted chocolate.

LACE SHELLS ▼

These lace shells are piped with the same tube as the filigree patterns. And don't look now, but—the balloons are back!

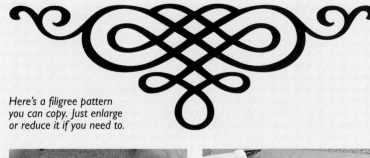

Here's a filigree pattern you can copy. Just enlarge or reduce it if you need to.

1 Fit pastry bag with small writing tube. Fill with chocolate. Tape pattern down, then tape waxed paper over it. Start piping!

2 When done piping, refrigerate until you're ready to use. They'll peel right off waxed paper. This is only the tip of the iceberg!

1 Fill 2 pastry bags: 1 white and 1 dark. Fit with small writing tubes. Melt dark chocolate in bowl. Dip balloon bottoms, and set upside-down.

2 Dipped part is the base. With dark chocolate, make loops from base down sides. Refrigerate, then repeat with white. Refrigerate again.

3 This is just like the Tulip Shells on page 31. Squeeze top, puncture, pinch shut. Slowly release air until the shell releases from the balloon.

LEAVES

There's nothing like the beautiful texture and shape of nicely-made chocolate leaves. And this is another decoration that you can use with almost any dessert.

I've got a few things to point out on this one, though. Paint the chocolate on thick, *see Step 1*. This helps when it's time to peel. Some leaves are poisonous—these rose leaves aren't. And they look great.

When you go to peel the leaves, handle them as little as possible, *see Step 2*. These things melt *so* easy!

1 Melt chocolate—keep warm. Paint *backs* of rose leaves to get good veins. Drape some over spoon handle for curved leaves. Refrigerate.

2 When leaves harden, use a skewer to help peel leaf from chocolate. You want to handle them as little as possible to avoid melting.

Espresso is a dark, strong coffee made by forcing hot water through finely ground, dark-roasted coffee. It takes a little knowledge and the right machine to make

a good (and true) espresso. I tested 20 machines thinking I'd end up giving you my favorite. Wrong. I'm ending up giving you my *six* favorites. And that's OK—they all share the same great features to make true espresso.

Testing: I tested a lot of machines, ranging from $100 to over $1,200. I was after *real* espresso with crema, *see Page 36,* and plenty of steam for frothing. What I found out is that most of what you want in a machine you don't see—it's under the hood!

Pump: The one thing you *must* have is a pump (all my picks do). It's the best way to create the water pressure you need to make great espresso.

Cheaper units ("steam models") pressurize the whole inside of the unit with enough steam to force the water through. This makes the water temperature too high and the pressure too low and inconsistent. You get burnt-tasting espresso with no crema.

And a few expensive models use a piston and a big hand-operated lever to move the water. These babies sure are gorgeous, but they're also inconvenient and hard to use.

Heating: You'll see two main ways of heating the water: a boiler system and a thermal block (or coil). I *much* prefer the boiler, and only found one thermal block unit that I liked (KRUPS).

Thermal block: A thermal block flash–heats water as it's being pumped through. It *can* get water to the right temperature for brewing (195°) and to a decent temperature for steaming (240°). But the more water you run through, the more it seems to fizzle-out. There's no power to spare.

Boiler: A boiler is a little tank that the water is heated in (kind of like a pressure cooker). This is what the big commercial units use. The water's heated to 195° for brewing and anywhere from 240°–300° for frothing!

Here's the key: Any boiler will heat up more hot water or steam than you need. The surplus means extra power that thermal blocks just can't match.

Believe me, testing told the tale. Boilers made more authentic-tasting espressos. And I'll tell you what, they can *really* crank out the steam!

Filter Holder: The heavier the filter holder, the better. Two big reasons: temperature and durability.

▲ *The best filter holders are heavy, like Gaggia's. They'll stay hot and take abuse.*

Temperature is crucial to brewing good espresso, and brewing occurs in the filter. So you want that filter holder to get hot and stay hot—even when you've got it out of the machine to fill it up or to knock out spent grounds.

And think about this—what takes more of a beating? This thing is constantly cranked in and out of the machine, and it's banged around *a lot.* A lightweight filter holder can't

hold up to that kind of wear and abuse. Eventually, it may not even fit securely into the machine any more.

Frothing: Some machines froth milk better and easier than others. But as much as I wanted to give you a hard and fast rule here, I couldn't—all you can do is try 'em out.

▲ *KRUPS' frothing system is the easiest to use, but clean-up's a bear (a lot of parts)!*

My six picks do a good job of frothing or they wouldn't be here. But the Solis and the Saeco are my favorites—tremendous power and easy cleaning. The KRUPS does a great job too—it's just harder to keep clean.

Water Reservoir: Don't listen to any hype over a water reservoir. It just needs to be removable for cleaning once in a while (all my picks are). And capacity isn't such a huge deal either, since any pump machine can be refilled even when it's running.

▲ *What do you look for in a water reservoir? It needs to be removable. Period.*

BRIEL LIDO

Briel's Lido is the least expensive machine to make my list, with an MSRP of $139.99. Best price I found: $99.98.

The Lido does a good job of producing crema, but it's not an aggressive frother. It's a small machine with a clean design. If space is a concern, this may be your machine.

Available from **Zabar's** (800) 697-6301, (212) 496-1234; or **Kitchen Window** (888) 824-4417. Or call **Briel** (888) 274-3555 for your nearest retailer.

SAECO RIO VAPORE ▶

Editor's favorite: Shame on me! I just had to name the "best of the best."

This is everything you'd ever want, and a whole lot of bang for your buck: rock-solid, consistent, easy to use, with a boiler that flat-out cranks. I love to watch it brew into a clear shot glass—the crema just keeps on coming!

The Rio Vapore has an MSRP of $349. Best price I saw: $269.98. Order from **Zabar's**, or call **Saeco** (800) 782-7282 to find a retailer.

SOLIS CREMA SL90 ▶

This machine can be programmed to automatically deliver the same amount of water through the grounds every time. And a lot of parts (boiler!) are made of marine brass. This baby's built to last.

$425 MSRP; best price: $375. Not cheap, but for what you're getting, it's still a good value. Call **Dana-Lu Imports (Solis)** (800) 437-6874 to find a local retailer. Also: **Zabar's**, **Kitchen Window**, or **The Daily Grind** (518) 434-1482.

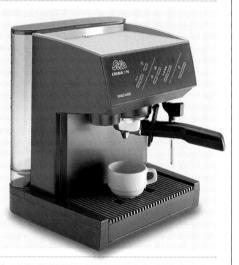

GAGGIA ESPRESSO ▶

This is, *by far,* the very best value I tested—$215 MSRP; $129.98 best price. Why? Gaggia performance. This one can slug it out with the big boys at a fraction of the price.

Pick up the *very heavy* filter holder and you'll know you've got something. And when you taste the brew—you'll know it then, too. Mail order: **Zabar's** or **The Daily Grind**. For a local retailer, call **Gaggia** at (201) 939-2555.

◀ GAGGIA COFFEE CLASSIC

Gaggia can make them gorgeous, too. But this beauty is more than a trophy piece. It's as hard working as it is good looking.

You get even sturdier construction with this Gaggia, and just a bit more power. What can I say about that solid, chrome-plated casing other than: WOW!

MSRP: $399.99; best price I saw: $369.98. Mail order from **Zabar's**, **The Daily Grind**, or **Kitchen Window**. For retailer, call **Gaggia**.

KRUPS NOVO 2000

This is the only thermal block unit to make the cut. Why? It's well made, easy to operate, and froths like mad. And the 2000 surprised me by out-brewing a more expensive KRUPS model!

KRUPS is huge in retail, so finding a Novo 2000 shouldn't be tough. MSRP is $270; best price I saw: $179.98. For a local retailer call **KRUPS** (800) 526-5377. Mail order: **Zabar's** or **Chef's Catalog** (800) 338-3232.

ESPRESSO

So what is good espresso, anyway? It's a combination of four things: quality beans, a great roast, the right grind, and a fantastic brewing process. This leads to

any espresso hound's dream: "crema," that nice, thick layer of brown foam on top of a good espresso. And I'm not talking milk foam just yet—crema comes from the coffee itself.

Then there's taste. Espresso is a lot more than just strong coffee—it's thick-bodied and sort of bittersweet. And the aroma's what'll hook you.

The Bean: Let's face it, espresso is high-quality, full-bore coffee. You want the best possible coffee taste to come through, so use only fresh, high-quality coffee beans.

For all coffee there's only two types of beans: arabica and robusta. Arabica is higher quality 99.9% of the time. Most inexpensive coffee is robusta. Look at the label. If it just says "100% coffee," it's probably robusta—arabica is usually labeled "arabica."

Roast: The longer the beans are roasted, the darker they get, and the more oil that appears on the surface of the bean. The best espresso beans are roasted to a rich, dark brown, with *some* oil on the surface—but not black and oily, *see Q&A, page 41.*

Grind: To get full flavor from the coffee, it has to be ground just right for your espresso machine. I've seen this vary a little from machine to machine, but I'm talking a very fine grind for all machines—between powdered sugar and granulated sugar.

The Brewing Process: The brewing process makes it all happen. First, you've got freshness—it's brewed in single servings. This is HUGE because any coffee's flavor starts deteriorating immediately after it's brewed.

Another thing—pressure is used to force the water through fine, firmly-packed grounds. This means espresso is brewed fast (18 to 28 seconds!). And it takes the right machine to pull it off, *see Wares, pages 34–35.*

The process means intense flavor, too. When you combine water pressure with packed, fine grounds, the water has to travel through *all* of the grounds before it winds up in the cup. You get every bit of flavor this way.

Keys to Brewing: Check out Steps 1–3. With the right coffee and a good machine, there's nothing to it!

1 Fill the filter with exactly the amount of espresso specified for your machine. This helps you get the right extraction of flavor.

2 Press, or "tamp" the grounds into the filter. Twist to smooth the surface. Experience will teach you how hard to tamp.

3 Turn on the pump. A double shot (2–2.5 oz.) should take 18 to 28 seconds. Use a small cup to keep crema from thinning.

But there's one really important thing in brewing to focus on: the relationship between grind and tamping (packing the grounds).

Say your espresso seems to be coming out too fast and winds up "thin-tasting" with little or no crema. Chances are you've got too coarse a grind, you didn't tamp enough, or you didn't put enough coffee in the filter—or any combination of these.

The reverse is also true. If the espresso is just dribbling slowly out of the filter, you probably have too fine a grind, too hard a tamp, and/or too much coffee.

FROTHING MILK

I'll start by debunking a myth—you don't have to use skim milk for frothing. Just about any milk, from skim milk to heavy cream, will froth, but *texture* and how long it lasts will vary. I say, use what tastes good to you.

Start with very cold milk—it froths better. And a stainless pitcher makes the job easier. Once the milk's frothed, use it or lose it. You can't re-froth.

For a lot of froth, keep the steaming wand's tip just under the surface. As froth builds, keep lowering the pitcher. This is called "stretching" (*stretch* the milk to the top of the pitcher).

Last, watch the temperature—milk's easy to overheat (giving it an off-taste). Use an instant-read thermometer and stop frothing at a maximum of 165°. I like to stop at 150°.

1 Fill pitcher no more than halfway. Start machine. Keep tip *just* submerged, and get surface churning. Slowly lower pitcher.

2 Stretch milk toward the top of the pitcher. Stop when you've got plenty of foam and the milk's hot—but not too hot!

ESPRESSO DRINKS

Here are some of the really popular drinks. Keep in mind a single espresso is 1–1½ ounces. A double shot is 2–2½ ounces.

Right now I better take some time to talk about what people seem to get the most confused over: the difference between cappuccinos and lattes.

"Latte" means "milk" in Italian. The drink is a single or double shot of espresso along with 8 to 16 ounces of steamed milk. There's just a thin layer of foam on top.

Cappuccinos have less milk and a lot more foam. The classic ratio is one-third espresso, one-third steamed milk, and one-third foam. So in a 6-ounce cup, you'd get a double shot of espresso, 2 ounces of steamed milk, and a super-thick cap of foam. **AH**

CAFFÈ MOCHA

Chocolate leaves
Dash of cocoa
Whipped cream
Layer of foam
⅓ steamed **milk** plus 2 T. cho**colate** syrup
Double shot **of** espresso

MACCHIATO

AMERICANO

Single shot of espresso with hot water added to fill a 6–8 oz. cup.

Dollop of mi**lk foam**

Double shot of **espresso**

Espresso spoon

CAPPUCCINO

CAFFÈ LATTE

Dash of nutmeg
⅓ foam
⅓ steam**ed milk**
⅓ espr**esso**

Dash of cinnamon

Lots of steamed milk, with a thin layer of foam

Single or double shot of espresso

SPINACH POTATO SOUP

This is a good, hearty soup. But what makes this worth trying, is understanding

how it's thickened. By using a pureed high-starch food, soups can be thickened without adding any unnecessary calories or fat.

Years ago, soups were thickened with béchamel sauce or by adding egg yolks at the end. Limited amounts of roux and beurre manie are used more today.

But for a lower-fat alternative, use a pureed starch like beans, rice, or barley. Starchy potatoes work well, but can make stock grainy.

Caution: Try not to use a food processor or blender to puree hot soups. The hot liquids can fly out and stick to you. Use a food mill or vertical blender.

SPINACH POTATO SOUP *(MAKES 10 CUPS)*
WORK TIME: 15 MINUTES
COOK TIME: 1 HOUR

BOIL:
9 cups Yukon Gold potatoes, peeled, cut into $1/2$" cubes (about 4 lbs.)

FRY AND DRAIN:
6 thick slices bacon, chopped (1 cup)

SAUTE IN 3 T. BACON FAT:
2 cups leeks, sliced
1 t. minced garlic

DEGLAZE PAN WITH:
1 cup chicken stock

ADD AND SAUTE:
8 cups chopped fresh spinach

ADD WITH ALL POTATOES:
2 cups whole milk
1 cup chicken stock
2 t. salt
$1/4$ t. white pepper
$1/8$ t. cayenne

GARNISH: BACON AND LEEKS

OPTION: STIR IN 2 T. BUTTER FOR EXTRA RICHNESS

NUTRITIONAL INFORMATION PER 1 CUP: CALORIES 230; TOTAL FAT 8(G); CALORIES FROM FAT 29%; SODIUM 600(MG)

MAKING THE SOUP

1 Boil potatoes until *al dente* (still a little firm). Drain. Rice half of potatoes. Set aside.

2 Saute bacon in 4-quart saucepan until crisp. Remove bacon. Pour off all but 3 T. bacon drippings.

3 In drippings saute leeks for 5 minutes until soft. Add garlic and saute just until you begin to smell it.

4 Deglaze pan with I cup chicken stock. *Option:* You can use $1/2$ cup white wine, $1/2$ cup stock.

5 Add the spinach and saute just until wilted. You want it to retain its color and some bite.

6 Add milk and remaining chicken stock. Stir in riced potatoes to thicken. Add the seasonings.

7 Gently stir in firm, cubed potatoes. Heat soup until hot—don't boil. Adjust seasonings to taste.

8 Garnish each serving with bacon pieces and sliced leek. A cup serving is only 230 calories!

WHAT'S HAPPENING IN FOOD?

▲ REAL MAPLE SYRUP

Maple syrup is good, but real Vermont maple syrup is great. It's like olive oil. Light Amber "Fancy" is the "extra virgin" of maple syrups. Here's your chance to find out the difference. Order the best from **Couture's Maple Shop**.

Couture's maple syrup comes in three grades: Fancy (if you're lucky enough to get it), Medium, and Dark Amber. Available in sizes from 3.4 oz. up to a gallon. Treat yourself and order it once just to taste the real deal. Call **(800) 845-2733** or **(802) 744-2733** to order or request a catalog.

◀ NEW COOKBOOK

The authors of **Tastes to Astonish** supply you with an array of popular dishes that you can really make. From appetizers to desserts—there's over 200 easy-to-follow recipes. I just wish there were photographs for these great recipes. The Berkley Publishing Group, $14.00.

▼ NEW CALPHALON PANS

I always felt Calphalon cookware had a few design flaws. Recently, they introduced **Calphalon Commercial Nonstick** cookware that corrects these problems.

Its new, long, easy-to-hold, *smooth* handle stays cool because it's stainless steel. This handle is riveted to the body in a special "V" design to also dissipate heat.

The stainless domed lid with easy-to-hold handle is a good design—much better than their flat lids. Finally, **Calphalon Commercial Nonstick** pans are lighter than their other pans. Congratulations, Calphalon. This is well-designed cookware I can recommend.

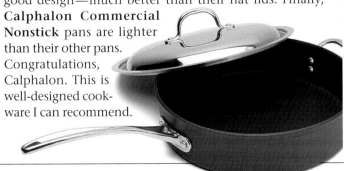

Cuisine

CHARTER VOLUME

Enjoy the <u>entire</u> *Cuisine* collection for **$13.93 off the standard single-issue and binder price!** You get our custom binder, the first six issues of *Cuisine*, and a FREE copy of the Premier issue!

Charter Volume with Binder (CV1B).....$29.95(+S&H)
Charter Volume without Binder (CV1)....24.95(+S&H)
Custom Binder (CB)................................$8.95(+S&H)

BACK ISSUES

Our recipes never go out of style and our back issues are still available for $4.99 each (plus S&H). *Buy 3 or more and pay only $4.50 per issue!*

PREMIER ISSUE: Beef Wellingtons, 6 Unique Appetizers, Turkey Roulade, and Fresh Apple Tart.
ISSUE 1: Seafood Gumbo, White Chocolate Banana Cream Pie, Making Fresh Pasta, and Caesar Salad.
ISSUE 2: Rack of Lamb, 3 Entree Salads, 6 Quick Pasta Dishes, Artichokes, Mashed Potatoes, Goof-Proof Omelet, and Classic Carrot Cake.
ISSUE 3: Barbecued Ribs and Regional Sauces, Grilled Salmon, Pizza on the Grill, Crème Caramel, and Strawberry Shortcake.
ISSUE 4: Spanish Paella, 3 Sandwiches for the Nineties, Grain Salads, Lemon Sorbet, and Blueberry Lattice Top Pie.
ISSUE 5: Crown Roast of Pork, Brown Sauce, Cranberry Sauce & Chutney, French Bread, Bouillabaisse, and Chocolate Cake.
ISSUE 6: Tenderloin of Beef, Cornish Game Hens, Oysters, Cinnamon Rolls, Red Potato Appetizers, Fruit Tart, and Béchamel Sauce.

CUISINE APRON

If you want to look your Sunday best, try the new *Cuisine* apron. Made of "Bull Denim," this apron is made to last. Over 34" long, plus adjustable neck strap. And one small pocket (for instant-read thermometer). In *Red* only.
(701204)..$24.95(+S&H)

**For Credit Card orders or instructions for ordering by mail, please call
1-800-311-3996
and use *KEY: CN07* when ordering.**

Q *I recently read on your web-site about using really good chocolate. It's not available in my local grocery store. Is there a mail-order source where I can buy the good stuff?*

A First, check with specialty food shops in your area. If that doesn't pan out, here are some mail-order sources for my favorite chocolates. But be warned—most require a large minimum order and ship only during cooler months.

New York Cake, (800) 942-2539. Valrhona (2.25 lbs., $19.99). Callebaut (17 oz., $7.99).

Perugina, (800) 272-0500 or (212) 688-2490. Perugina Classic (3 oz., $1.95).

Paradigm Foodworks, Inc., (800) 234-0250. Peter's Nestle Gibraltar (1 lb., $4.50). Lindt Excellence (3.5 oz., $2). Guittard Oro (5 lb., $15). Scharffen Berger (3.3 lb., $33).

People have very different tastes in chocolate, so try them out for yourself to see which is your favorite.

Hold your own taste test—taste different chocolates head-to-head. If you like certain chocolates just tasting them plain, then you'll like how the chocolate will taste in a favorite recipe.

Q *What's the difference between regular paprika and Hungarian paprika? Where do they come from?*

A You're probably most familiar with paprika sprinkled over potato salad or deviled eggs for color. But it's actually a much more important spice than that.

The paprika pepper plant originated in southern Mexico. It was taken to Europe by the Spanish and made its way to Hungary where it's an integral part of their cuisine—it's practically a national treasure.

The peppers used for paprika just don't have one name—it could be tomato peppers or pimientos. "Paprika" is the Hungarian word for "sweet pepper," and has been adopted by many languages.

Over the years, different varieties of paprika peppers have developed. The flavor and color of the spice depends on the peppers used. It also depends on if just the flesh is used, or if the stem, ribs, and seeds are added. The more seeds and ribs that are used, the sharper the paprika.

Paprika is labeled "sweet" or "hot." If it's just called "paprika," it's probably the sweeter variety.

Paprika is produced all over the world. Places like the southwestern United States, South America, and Spain. But Hungarian paprika is considered the best.

All those years of experience with growing paprika and using it to season food every day make a difference. There's no substitute for Hungarian paprika when flavor is important for dishes like Hungarian goulash and paprikash. Other paprikas just don't have the same depth and staying power.

Q *I buy good chocolate when I travel. How long will it keep before going bad?*

A Don't keep milk or white chocolate more than nine months—they contain milk solids that will go bad.

Dark chocolate is harder to pin down. I've heard it'll keep up to ten years, but that's only under ideal conditions.

Chocolate contains fat, so under the wrong conditions, it can turn rancid just like good extra virgin olive oils. If you're not sure your chocolate is good, taste a little. If it tastes bad, it could ruin a recipe—pitch it.

As a rule, buy only as much chocolate as you can use in a few months. Store in a cool, dry place, away from sunlight. The ideal environment is 60–70° F, in less than 60% humidity, but that's not practical for most of us. A cupboard away from any heat sources is your best shot.

Keep chocolate wrapped in foil and plastic, and store it alone—it absorbs odors easily.

Q&A

We'll find answers to your cooking questions, and help find solutions to the unique problems which occur in the kitchen. Any questions? Send your cooking questions to *Cuisine, Q & A Editor,* 2200 Grand Avenue, Des Moines, IA 50312, or contact us through our E-mail address: *Cuisine@cuisinemag.com*

Q *I don't understand coffee roasts—"Italian," "French," and "Dark." Which are good for espresso? Also, what's the best way to store them?*

A Those names can be contradictory. And there's no hard and fast rule for how dark an espresso roast should be. It's a matter of personal (or regional) preference.

The longer beans are roasted, the more oil appears on the surface, and the darker and more bitter they get. Light roasts tend to be more acidic.

For espresso, start with a dark brown roast with some oil on the surface — but not a black roast. Then experiment to find a taste you prefer.

Visit different local coffee shops. They can help you experiment with different roasts. Some coffee shops even roast their own beans. This is the best since coffee beans start deteriorating only after roasting.

And if you don't have a really good grinder, they'll do it for you. Most home grinders can't make the fine, even grind necessary for espresso.

The quality of roasted beans goes down fast, so only buy as much as you'll use in a week. Store in an airtight container, in a cool, dry place — but *not* the refrigerator.

Refrigerators are damp and full of odors that the coffee easily absorbs. Freezing? It's not good, but I do it.

Q *I like whole kalamata olives better than pre-pitted ones. Is there an easy way to pit them myself?*

A There's a couple options. First, you can use a towel. Place whole olives in the towel and press firmly with your hands, rolling the olives to separate them from the pits. This mangles the olives a little, but it gets the job done.

If you're like me and love kitchen gadgets, get an olive pitter. It's easy to remove the pit and leave the olive looking pretty. **Bridge Kitchenware** has one for $5.95, #BCOP. Call (800) 274-3435 or (212) 838-1901 to order.

Q *My grandmother used to make a great custard sauce that had mace in it. What is mace?*

A Mace has been upstaged in the United States by another spice from the same tree—nutmeg.

The ripe fruit of the tropical nutmeg tree splits open so you can see the seed inside. Mace covers the outer shell of the seed like a giant squid attacking a submarine. Nutmeg is the seed kernel inside the shell.

Shown, left to right, are a nutmeg

shell covered by mace, nutmeg without mace or shell, and dried mace.

You can get mace either whole (blades) or ground. Even though it looks neat, mace isn't available "swallowing" up a nutmeg shell as shown. Nutmeg has to be dried outside its shell to reach the highest quality.

Mace is similar to nutmeg, but more subtle. It's good in cakes and puddings, and with fish and poultry.

GLOSSARY

Bloom: Pale gray film, streaks, or blotches that appear on the surface of chocolate when the cocoa butter separates and forms crystals (usually a result of storing in too warm a place). Blooming does not affect flavor or cooking properties.

Devein: To remove the dark brownish-black vein that runs down the back of a shrimp. The vein is really the intestinal tract of the shrimp. In smaller shrimp, the vein can be eaten, but in larger shrimp, the vein contains grit which should be removed.

Hoisin Sauce: Hoisin [HOY-sihn] is a thick reddish-brown, sweet and spicy sauce made from soybeans, garlic, chilies, and various spices. Used as a condiment and flavoring agent in Chinese cooking.

Marrow: A soft, fatty tissue found in the hollow center of an animal's bone—particularly plentiful in the shin and leg bones. Considered a delicacy in Europe, marrow is light and digestible with the same amount of calories as beef fat. It can be cooked in the bone, removed and eaten. Or it can be used in soups and stews for flavor and body.

Mirepoix: A mixture of diced carrots, onions, celery, and herbs sauteed in butter. Mirepoix [mihr-PWAH] is used to season sauces, soups, or stews. It's also used as a bed to braise meats and fish.

Semolina: [seh-muh-LEE-nuh] A grainy, pale yellow flour that is coarsely ground from hard wheats (like durum). It has a very high protein content. Used primarily for pasta dough.

ABBREVIATIONS

t. = teaspoon
T., Tbsp. = tablespoon
oz. = ounce
lb. = pound
Pinch = $1/16$ of a teaspoon
Dash = scant $1/8$ of a teaspoon

CHOCOLATE ESPRESSO TORTE

If it's true about chocolate being an aphrodisiac, then this torte is perfect for Valentine's Day!

CHOCOLATE ESPRESSO TORTE

(ONE 9" TORTE, SERVES 16)
WORK TIME: 15 MINUTES
COOK TIME: 1 HOUR

PLACE IN BOWL:
12 oz. semisweet chocolate, coarsely chopped

HEAT UNTIL BOILING;
POUR OVER CHOCOLATE:
1 lb. unsalted butter (4 sticks)
1 cup (8 oz.) espresso
1 cup dark brown sugar

ADD:
8 eggs, slightly beaten

TORTE, TART, TORTA?

These terms are easy to confuse.

Tart and torte are English names for two different things.

A tart is a lot like a pie. It has a pastry crust and is usually filled with fruit, custard, or both.

A torte is a cake, but there's two kinds. The first, like this one, is a very rich cake made with little or no flour and a lot of eggs. The other is a multilayered cake filled with buttercream or jam.

Torta is both Italian and Spanish. In Italian, it means tart, pie, or cake. It means cake, loaf, or sandwich in Spanish.

MAKING THE TORTE

1 Trace and cut out waxed paper or parchment to fit the bottom of a 9" springform pan. Heat oven to 350°.

2 Place chocolate in a bowl. In a saucepan, bring butter, espresso, and sugar to a boil. Keep stirring until sugar dissolves.

3 Pour butter mixture into bowl of chopped chocolate. Whisk until chocolate is melted and mixture is smooth.

4 Keep whisking as you *very slowly* pour eggs into chocolate mixture. Now, pour the batter into prepared springform pan.

5 Place springform pan in a roasting pan. Add boiling water to roasting pan until water comes halfway up sides of pan.

6 Bake 1 hour. Place on cooling rack. Run thin-bladed knife around inside of pan to loosen torte. Cool, then chill overnight.

Making the Torte

I think this recipe is pretty straightforward. But I do want to hit a few highlights to guarantee success on Valentine's Day.

Mixing and Baking: Start by lining the bottom of your pan with parchment, *see Step 1*. This keeps the cake from sticking.

When you're heating the butter, espresso, and sugar, notice I call for a full 8 ounces of espresso, *see Step 2*. You *can* substitute strong coffee, but the impact's not the same!

And keep on whisking until you get that chocolate mixture nice and smooth, *see Step 3*.

Here's one of the few warning shots I've got for you. In Step 4, you *have* to pour the eggs in *very slowly* while constantly whisking the mixture. This keeps the eggs from cooking.

And don't skip the water bath in Step 5—it helps give you a nice, even cake. After baking, cool it thoroughly before chilling overnight, *see Step 6*.

Glazing: The cake is more stable on a cardboard circle, *see Step 7*. And a pedestal is always best for glazing, *see Step 8*.

Chocolate Glaze

WORK TIME: 10 MINUTES
COOK TIME: 3 MINUTES
MICROWAVE AT 50%:

- 8   oz. semisweet chocolate, chopped
- 12   T. unsalted butter, cut into tablespoons
- 5   t. water
- 1   T. light corn syrup

POUR OVER TORTE

Garnish

- 2   oz. bittersweet chocolate "pencil curls," *see page 32*
- 12   chocolate "leaves," made from rose leaves, *see page 33*
- 12   fresh raspberries

After melting chocolate in Step 9 (overheating will seize it), whisk thoroughly, *see Step 10*. This glaze *must* be completely smooth.

If you have to, tilt the cake to get it covered, *see Step 11*. And don't try to fix minor ripples, they'll just get worse. Only hit uncoated spots, *see Step 12*.

Decorating: Make the curls and leaves a day ahead and chill them. As you're placing the decorations, *see Steps 13–15*, be careful not to melt them with your hands. Use a skewer, knife, or spatula to move and place them.

7 Remove sides from pan. Cut a piece of cardboard to fit torte. Set on top, then invert torte. Place on pedestal.

8 Slide knife between pan bottom and paper to release. Press lightly on cake to smooth out any uneven spots!

9 Combine all glaze ingredients in a bowl. Microwave at 50% power for 3 minutes. Stop and stir after each minute.

10 Whisk glaze until it becomes very smooth. This is important when you start pouring it over the cake.

11 Pour warm glaze over torte, letting it coat sides. Pour fast because that cold torte makes the glaze set up.

12 Use a knife to lightly touch up *only* the uncoated areas. Don't touch anything else or you'll get marks!

DECORATING THE TORTE

13 Place curls in a spoke-like pattern. Use a skewer to keep them from melting. Overlap center.

14 Arrange chocolate leaves in the center of curls. A knife or spatula helps. Overlap them slightly.

15 Finally, place some raspberries in the middle of the leaves. Let a few spill out toward the edges.

MAKING A GRAND FINALE

The best thing about chocolate is experimenting—you can hardly ever go wrong! And if you do, just eat your mistakes. Here, I used several techniques from the chocolate article. Use the balloon trick for making filigree cups. But instead of cups, I made a *delicate* filigree bridge. The raspberry sauce goes great with the torte for color and flavor. I left it tart to offset the torte's richness.

TORTE WITH RASPBERRY SAUCE

Raspberry Sauce goes great with chocolate. This isn't thick like the Blackberry Sauce in Issue 3. Simmer 5 minutes: 3 T. sugar and 1 14-oz. pack of frozen raspberries (no syrup). Use a *fine* mesh strainer to remove seeds.

Chocolate Bridges are easier to make than to handle. Use the balloon trick but don't dip it. Pipe a filigree arch with white and dark chocolates. It'll look like a bow tie from the top. Chill well and handle with care.

Cuisine®

ISSUE No 8
MAR/APR 1998

AUGUST HOME'S

Cuisine
™

AN ILLUSTRATED GUIDE TO CREATIVE HOME COOKING

CRAB CAKES
WITH CHIPOTLE REMOULADE

Also in this Issue:

COUNTRY HAM
LEMON MERINGUE PIE
BEYOND EGGS BENEDICT

Cuisine

Editor
John F. Meyer

Art Director
Cinda Shambaugh

Associate Editor
Charles Smothermon

Senior Graphic Designer
Holly Wiederin

Graphic Designer
Martin Davis

Photo Director
Lark Gilmer

Senior Photographer
Crayola England

Test Kitchen Director
Ellen C. Boeke

Editorial Assistant
Jennifer L. Welter

Electronic Publishing Coordinator
Douglas M. Lidster

Pre-press Image Specialist
Troy Clark

Publisher
Donald B. Peschke

Corporate

V.P. Planning & Finance: **Jon Macarthy**
Subscriber Services Director: **Sandy Baum**
New Business Director: **Glenda K. Battles**
New Business Manager: **Todd Bierle**
Promotion Manager: **Rick Junkins**
Renewal Manager: **Paige Rogers**
Billing Manager: **Rebecca Cunningham**
Asst. Subscription Manager: **Joy Krause**
Production Director: **George Chmielarz**
Production Assistant: **Susan Dickman**
Pre-press Image Specialist: **Minniette Bieghler**
Creative Director: **Ted Kralicek**
August Home Books: **Douglas L. Hicks**
New Media Manager: **Gordon C. Gaippe**
Assoc. Graphic Design Director: **Susie Rider**
Senior Graphic Designer: **Cheryl Simpson**
Controller: **Robin K. Hutchinson**
Senior Accountant: **Laura J. Thomas**
Accounts Payable Clerk: **Mary Schultz**
Human Resource Assistant: **Kirsten Koele**
Customer Service Manager: **Jennie Enos**
Administrative Assistant: **Julia Fish**
Receptionist: **Jeanne Johnson**
Librarian: **Sherri Ribbey**
Special Projects Director: **Saville Inman**
Photo Intern: **Elizabeth Meyer**

Cuisine™ (ISSN 1089-6546) is published bi-monthly (Jan., Mar., May, July, Sept., Nov.) by August Home Publishing Co., 2200 Grand Ave., Des Moines, IA 50312. **Cuisine**™ is a trademark of August Home Publishing Co. ©Copyright 1998 August Home Publishing. All rights reserved. Subscriptions: Single copy: $4.99. One year subscription (6 issues), $24.95. (Canada/Foreign add $5 per year, U.S. funds.) Periodicals postage paid at Des Moines, IA and at additional mailing offices. "USPS/Heartland Press Automatable Poly" Postmaster: Send change of address to **Cuisine**, PO Box 37100 Boone, IA 50037-2100. Subscription questions? Call 800-311-3995, 8 a.m. to 5 p.m., Central Standard Time, weekdays. **Cuisine**™ does not accept and is not responsible for unsolicited manuscripts. **PRINTED IN U.S.A.**

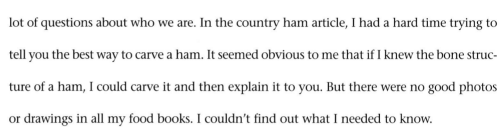

From the Editor:

What do country ham and *Cuisine* have in common? Besides the letter "C," they share a philosophy.

Take a look at the picture on the right—it answers a lot of questions about who we are. In the country ham article, I had a hard time trying to tell you the best way to carve a ham. It seemed obvious to me that if I knew the bone structure of a ham, I could carve it and then explain it to you. But there were no good photos or drawings in all my food books. I couldn't find out what I needed to know.

So with ham in hand, I paid a visit to Dr. Major, my family doctor. He X-rayed it and gave me a quick lesson on my ham's bone structure and popliteal (area behind the knee).

This is where the common philosophy comes in. Not everybody is going to cook a country ham. But you'll probably read about it, and hopefully find out something new and interesting. That's why I went to Dr. Major's office. Country ham isn't just about eating, and *Cuisine* isn't just about recipes—there's more to both of them than *"meats"* the eye. I want you to experience all angles of food. Not just traditional foods, but trends too. I'll always try to make it interesting (and fun) even before you ever set foot in the kitchen.

John Meyer

Real country ham is rich in heritage and taste. I cover all the bases. You'll learn how they're cured and which ones to buy. I'll also show you how to prepare, slice, and serve these special hams.

AUGUST HOME'S Cuisine™

AN ILLUSTRATED GUIDE TO CREATIVE HOME COOKING

GOLF TOWEL KITCHEN HELPER

My kitchen is hectic enough without searching high and low for a towel. When I need to wipe my hands, a golf towel is the answer. Its metal ring clips right onto my belt loop, so it's always at my fingertips.

R.B. Himes
Vienna, OH

FREEZING BANANAS

Many of my recipes call for mashed bananas. I try to use overripened bananas that I've frozen.

But instead of freezing them whole, I peel them first. Then I freeze them in Ziploc® bags. This way, I don't have to wait for them to thaw before peeling. When thawed, I just mash them right in the bag, and there's no mess!

T. Argo
Golden Valley, MN

LOST YOUR MARBLES?

Have you ever ruined a good teapot by boiling it dry? Don't worry about it anymore. Win some glass marbles from a neighborhood kid (or buy some, but that's not as much fun). Then you can put a few of them into your teapot. When the boiling water gets to that dangerously low level, the marbles will rattle an alarm.

A. Knight
Mt. Shasta, CA

EXTRA HERBS?

Recipes often call for only a few tablespoons of fresh herbs. The extra goes bad before I use it all.

So I experimented on several herbs and found that cilantro, tarragon, parsley, and sage freeze great! (Basil turns black, though.)

First I spread chopped herbs on a plate. Then I froze the plate and all. When frozen, I put the herbs inside a Ziploc® bag.

V. Erickson
Paramus, NJ

PEELING SHALLOTS

It takes forever to peel the skin off an onion or shallot because it's dry and tight. So I just soak them in water for 10 minutes to make their skin more pliable. They're much easier to peel.

L. Ciampa
Andover, MA

FROSTING DAM

When I make a filled layer cake, the last thing I want is the jam or pudding to squish out the sides and mess up the frosting. So here's what I do.

Before I put the filling on the bottom cake layer, I pipe a ring of frosting around the top edge of it. This makes a dam to keep the filling in place when I put on the top layer. No more worries about a band of discolored frosting.

D. Tabor
Montpelier, VT

HOLD THOSE LAYERS

Making a layer cake? Insert a straw into the center, then trim it. The layers won't slip around when you frost, and the straw gives you a point in the center to slice to.

J. Columbo
New Port Richey, FL

FREEZING NUTS

My pantry had too many bags of nuts. They eventually turned rancid because of their fat. Now, I store them in the freezer.

J. Kirkgaard
Burbank, CA

TEA INFUSION SPOON

A tea infusion spoon isn't just for tea—it makes a great flour shaker, too. When I'm making bread, I can shake flour over my work surface without dipping my wet, sticky hands into clean flour.

N. Beury
Birdsboro, PA

TOOTHPASTE POLISH

Company was on its way, and I had a tarnished silver sugar spoon, but no silver polish. I'd heard once that toothpaste could be used in a pinch. So I tried rubbing some on the spoon. It worked like magic!

PARSLEY TERRARIUM

Fresh parsley will last for weeks in a jar. Remove the band from stems, but don't rinse parsley. Place it in a clean jar with stems down, replace lid, and refrigerate. Pour off any water that periodically appears in jar.

J. Danko
Henderson, NV

Only real *paste* works—not the gel kind. Just rub some over your silver. Then rinse the toothpaste thoroughly with warm water. Buff with a soft, dry cloth. Your silver's like new!

L. Spike
Guttenberg, NJ

CUTTING MERINGUE

Cutting through meringue is always a challenge. You spent a long time getting that meringue just right so you don't want to mess up all your hard work.

The secret is to dip a sharp knife into hot water. Then cut the meringue with the hot, wet knife.

You can't cut down like with a regular pie—you'll crush the meringue. Instead, first slice lightly across the top of the meringue to get through that initial rubbery layer. The water on your knife dissolves it. The rest should be easy going.

NO BURNT EDGES

Pie crust edges too brown? Make a shield with a foil pizza pan. Cut a hole in the middle so the crust's edge will be shielded from the oven's heat, but the pie's top can still brown. Save shield to use again.

WHISKING

When you have to whisk for a long time (hollandaise) don't *just use* your wrist—not enough muscles for the long haul.

Instead, let your whole arm do the whisking. Look at the photo, the arm is in a natural position and the entire arm is working. A small arm motion results in a large whip movement.

COUNTRY HAM

You want to know what country ham is all about? Well, there's history, tradition, the old South—there's past and there's present. And then there's my favorite thing: The

aroma of country ham frying in a skillet getting ready to be paired up with fried eggs, real stone-ground grits, hot biscuits with sorghum, and plenty of red-eye gravy.

I'll warn you—country ham isn't for everyone. It's saltier, drier, and stronger than the mild, moist ham ("city ham") most people are used to. I cooked some for a few "greenhorns" who'd never had country ham before, and some of them didn't like it at all.

But right now, country ham is almost chic, so plenty of others must love it as much as I do. And keep this in mind—no two country hams taste the same. Every curer has his own way of doing things—saltiness and flavor vary a lot. It's just a matter of finding which country ham *you* like.

How It's Served: Most country ham gets fried up for breakfast and is served with some eggs, grits, and biscuits. Believe me, this is tough to beat.

True connoisseurs bake the ham and serve it as an appetizer! Then there's a *second* meat at dinner—usually poultry. The ham is sliced thin enough to read a newspaper through and is eaten with biscuits, *see Pages 18–19.* The thing is, small amounts of country ham will satisfy.

One more thing: I can't believe I almost forgot this! Any old-timer worth his salt will tell you to get a "left ham"—from the pig's left side.

It's common knowledge that all pigs lay on their right side. This makes right hams tougher than left hams.

Oh, another thing: You can't always trust old-timers. I found out some can be notorious pranksters!

SMITHFIELD—THE ORIGINAL COUNTRY HAM

Country ham got its start way back in colonial Smithfield, Virginia.

Origins: The earliest Smithfield area settlers brought some hogs along from England. These hogs thrived so much that they literally started taking over villages! Settlers had to confine them to an island in the James River—it's still called "Hog Island."

Now, the meat from those hogs needed to be "cured"—made to keep a long time without refrigeration. The Indians were curing venison by rubbing "magic white sand" (salt) into it and then smoking it over a fire.

The settlers knew a thing or two about salt-curing, too—it had been common in Europe for years. I figure the settlers and Indians exchanged a few pointers that made the earliest country hams very special.

Before long, Smithfield turned ham into a business. Soon, Thomas Jefferson prized Smithfield ham. Later on, Queen Victoria became a fan!

Growth Years: As the nation grew, the practice of salt-curing hams spread. But Smithfield stayed on top. It remained biggest and best—why?

The answer most people settled on was peanuts—these hogs ate a lot of them! First, they'd spend spring and summer rooting around the woods for acorns and other wild nuts. Then, after the peanut harvest, they'd go into the fields to root for leftover peanuts. This supposedly made the meat redder, the fat yellower, the taste oilier—and the customers happier.

The Smithfield Law: In 1926, Virginia passed a law to protect Smithfield ham from impostors.

To be a "genuine Smithfield ham," it had to come from peanut-fed hogs raised in Virginia or North Carolina, and it had to be cured in Smithfield.

Today's Smithfield: Today you'll be hard-pressed to find any peanut-fattened hogs, but you can still buy genuine Smithfield ham. The law remains on the books, but it's been changed a little. The hogs don't have to be peanut-fed anymore, and can be raised anywhere. The hams still have to be dry-salt cured and aged *at least* 6 months within the town limits to be "genuine Smithfield."

These days, hams from Smithfield and thereabouts (Virginia and North Carolina) usually share a few characteristics. For one, taste and texture. These hams are among the driest and strongest hams I've ever had. Many aficionados crave (demand!) this taste, but it can really put off a beginner.

Then there's shape. They're often longer and flatter than hams from other parts of the country. A long shank (skinny end) is traditional—fine by me! But some of these hams are flat as a board (mockingly called "banjos"). Unacceptable—I don't care where the ham is from. A ham should have *at least* a plump little rise or "crown" on one side—or I refuse it!

THE REAL SQUEAL: HAM BASICS

Here's the basics you need to know:

What is a Ham? A ham is the cured, smoked, or cooked hind leg of a hog. A "picnic ham" is the cured, smoked, or cooked *front* leg and shoulder, *see Diagram.* Picnic hams are too small for nice, big slices. And they're almost always "cured" (and taste) just like city hams. Here's the scoop on them:

City Ham: City ham is the type of ham everybody's used to. It's what you're going to find in *any* grocery store. The taste is very mild and the texture is moist. It's usually boneless and fully cooked. At times, it can be pretty good.

City hams are injected with a liquid "cure"—a type of salt water and sugar brine. This liquid works through the meat to give it a "ham" flavor. And, this can make it ready for market within 24 hours!

Country Ham: Country hams come in a lot of shapes and sizes. They don't have to come from Smithfield, and don't have to be smoked. They might be long- or short-shanked, and depending on the cure, rubbed with black pepper, sugar, or a secret ingredient.

But they all have this in common: They're *always* cured with dry salt and aged *at least* several months—or even a year or more. No liquid you pump into a ham can ever replace this. Here's why:

When a ham is rubbed with a lot of dry salt and hung up to age, its natural flavor intensifies. This is because the combination of salt and aging works to draw moisture out of the meat. (It shrinks up to 25%!) It's just like reducing a sauce—the more liquid escapes, the more true flavor shines through.

Pork Shoulder, "Picnic Ham"

Whole Ham

Hock, or "shank"

COUNTRY HAM *(SERVES 36)*
WORK TIME: 45 MINUTES
COOK TIME: 2¹/₂ HOURS
COMBINE IN LARGE ROASTER:
1   whole country ham (12–19 lbs.)
    Water
4   apples, quartered
1¹/₂ cups apple juice
1¹/₂ cups Coca-Cola®
¹/₂ cup brown sugar
¹/₂ cup sorghum
¹/₂ cup cider vinegar
FOR THE GLAZE:
1   cup brown sugar
¹/₂ cup dried bread crumbs
¹/₄ cup Coca-Cola®
2   T. port wine
¹/₂ t. red pepper flakes
    Pinch ground cloves

NUTRITIONAL INFORMATION PER 4-OZ.
SERVING: CALORIES 336; TOTAL FAT 18(G); CALORIES FROM FAT 49%; SODIUM 1,296(MG)

GETTING STARTED

You've got some initial preparation once you get ahold of your ham.

Unwrapping: As curious as you may be, don't unwrap the ham until you're ready to *do* something with it. It'll keep at room temperature in the original wrapper for a very long time. Don't disturb this until you're ready.

Chances are, the ham will be moldy when you unwrap it, *see Step 1*. Don't faint, and don't return the ham—there's nothing wrong with it.

Decisions: Now it's decision time. First, you don't *have* to bake the whole ham. (But I'm sure gonna show you how!) If you want to have some steaks for frying, just have them sliced off and leave a big piece for the oven, *see Box below*. The ratio of steaks to "baking ham" is totally up to you.

The other thing is to figure out whether you've got a covered pan that'll hold the ham, *see Step 2*. Sawing off the hock may be all it takes to get it to fit. But another option is to just go out and buy an inexpensive pan—it's really all you need. (I found one for 16 bucks at a hardware store!)

Scrubbing: Put that ham in the sink to contain the mess, *see Step 3*. Scrub it with a brush and vinegar, not soap—unless you find some that really tastes good. Now that sink pays off—rinsing is super-easy, *see Step 4*.

FIRST STEPS—CLEANING

1 A lot of people panic when they first unwrap a country ham and find out that it's moldy. *Most* country hams will have some mold. It's a normal part of the aging process.

2 Make sure you've got a pan (with cover) that'll hold the ham. This pan does *not* need to be expensive! To make the ham on the right fit you could just saw the hock off.

3 The best place to clean a country ham is the sink—it minimizes the mess. Scrub the ham with a clean (new!) scrub brush and plenty of white vinegar. Don't use soap!

4 Be sure to get all the residue rinsed off. You'll want to rinse the ham repeatedly during the scrubbing process to make sure you're getting all of it clean.

CUSTOM-SLICING A COUNTRY HAM

Sometimes I don't bake a *whole* country ham—just a big piece. I'll have my butcher slice the ham for me into hocks, steaks for frying, and a big piece for baking. A lot of butchers will do this for free. Or, with a good saw and a strong arm, you can do it yourself!

I love fried ham steaks, so I had him cut plenty. I'll use the hocks for seasoning some greens. The remaining big piece I'm gonna bake like a whole ham—just the way I'm about to show you.

BAKING AND GLAZING

There's about as many ways of baking country ham as there are boarded-up Stuckey's on the side of the road. Here's the way I do it.

Initial Baking: Take a look at the rack I'm using, *see Step 5*. It lays *perfectly* flat in the pan and raises the ham just a fraction of an inch off the bottom. That's all you need.

Don't get overly concerned with amounts on the baking liquid. This varies with the size of the ham and the pan. My amounts are a good starting point for you, *see Steps 6 and 7*.

The liquid needs to "shimmer"—you want steam and a little bubbling, but no rolling. After an hour's baking, carefully flip it over, *see Step 8*. Then bring the liquid level back up with more apple juice, *see Step 9*.

Temperature: As soon as the internal temperature hits 150°, pull the ham from the oven. This is the most important thing I'm gonna say—go over 150° and that ham will dry out.

Tradition: It's tradition to let the ham cool in the liquid until you can grab it bare-handed, *see Step 10*. This isn't *just* tradition. It's a lot easier to trim the rind and get this ham glazed when it's cool, *see Steps 11 and 12*.

Final Baking: The ham is already cooked all it needs to. Now you just want to put it in the oven long enough to brown the glaze. When it looks done, it's done. There's no point in keeping it in there any longer than you need to—otherwise it'll overcook!

GLAZE
Get all your glaze ingredients stirred together and then look at the consistency. It needs to be thick like the glaze on this spoon to cling well to the ham.

5 Place a shallow rack in a roasting pan. The ham needs to rest *just* off the bottom. This keeps the bottom of the ham from scorching.

6 Pour water into pan until it's about one-third the depth of the pan. You need to leave room for the other ingredients you'll be adding.

7 Add apples, juice, Coke, brown sugar, sorghum, vinegar. Ham should be half covered in liquid. Add more Coke to get level up if needed.

8 Cover and bake at 400° until liquid starts "shimmering." Then reduce oven temperature to 350°. *Carefully* turn ham over after 1 hour.

9 Add more apple juice to keep level halfway up sides of ham. Bake 1 hour longer, *or* until internal temperature reaches 150°.

10 Let ham cool 30–45 minutes—until you can reach in with your hands. Move it to cutting board. Drain all but 1" of the liquid.

11 Combine ingredients for the glaze. Carefully trim rind off ham, making sure to leave a thick layer of fat. Return ham to pan.

12 Rub ham all over with the glaze mixture. Bake, uncovered, at 400° for 20 minutes, or until the glaze is nicely browned.

CARVING

If you don't know the internal structure of a ham, you better go ahead and buy *all* those knives I show you on Page 33 instead of just one—you're gonna wear out a few on all the bones. So learn that structure!

I'm Not Kidding This Time: Remember I kidded you about right hams? You may *get* a right ham. It doesn't make any difference (I swear!), except that my photos and drawings are of a left ham. In a right ham, the bones are exactly the reverse. Don't panic!

I Did It My Way: My way of carving is unique. I don't carve each slice off the *whole* ham—I remove a big saddle of clear meat instead. Once that chunk is on my board, it couldn't be any easier to slice it thin.

Remember, it's *country* ham—the intense flavor goes a long way. My method is the very best way to cut slice after slice of paper-thin bliss. **AH**

STRUCTURE OF A HAM

I remember the first time I carved a ham—it was tough sledding. I had no idea what to expect and kept hitting bone after bone. I'm not about to let that happen to you.

The only thing I could come up with that *really* shows a ham's bone structure is an X-ray. Once I got ahold of that X-ray, we could make some truly accurate drawings.

Go over all the diagrams and photos—before *and* after you get your ham. You'll get it figured out!

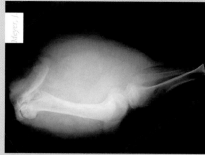

Keep two things in mind. Use skewers to probe the ham for bones and popliteal (tough part behind knee). You'll find out *everything* before you ever make a cut! And second, slice a thin piece off the bottom. This makes for easy cutting.

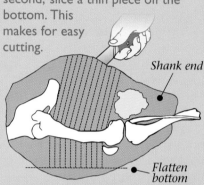

Aitch — Popliteal — Tibia — Femur — Fibula — Patela

Shank end — Flatten bottom

CUT AND SLICE

13 Use skewers to find the bone structure, just like I showed you above. Then flatten the bottom to give the ham a stable place to rest.

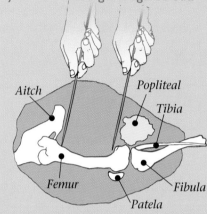

14 Stand the ham up on the flat area you just made. Find the spot closest to the shank end where you can cut right down to the femur.

15 Go to the other end. Use a skewer to find the aitch [pronounced "H"]. Cut down to femur as close to aitch as you can get.

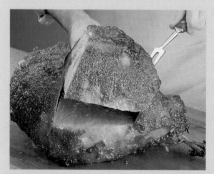

16 All you have to do now is make a horizontal cut just above the femur. This will free up a nice, big saddle of clear meat.

17 Once you've removed the saddle, this thing is easy to work with. On your cutting board, you can slice it as thin as you want!

18 There's another small saddle underneath the ham. Flip it over, find the bones, and remove this saddle just like the other one.

FRIED COUNTRY HAM WITH RED-EYE GRAVY

Sometimes I have a hard time being impartial. Here I go again—pan-fried is my favorite way to eat country ham.

When that ham browns, the flavor becomes even more unbelievable. And if you ever just mouth the words "red-eye gravy" around me, I'm putty in your hands.

Steaks: Forget you ever heard of "paper-thin!" You need a thick slab (*at least* 1/4-inch thick) to stand up to the heat of a hot skillet without drying out and getting hard. And cook it *only* until lightly browned. Thick pieces of fried ham just plain taste better than thick pieces of baked ham!

Skillet: For the best ham and *truly* the best red-eye gravy, use a cast-iron skillet. Maybe there's a reaction between the metal and gravy—who knows? Just trust me—this *is* a fact!

Red-eye: Red-eye gravy got its name because a lot of people used to make it with coffee. Don't ever do this—I tried it, and it's really awful! Use water (and my secret ingredient).

SECRET RED-EYE GRAVY

Here's an old family secret my Grandmother taught me: Add a teaspoon of apple cider vinegar to the gravy while it's reducing. This really kicks it up a notch!

FRIED COUNTRY HAM AND RED-EYE GRAVY

1 Steaks for frying should be thick. But you don't want that rind— cut it off. (I like to leave a little fat. But then again, I don't always lead the best example—do as you see fit.)

2 Heat a cast-iron skillet over medium-high heat before adding ham. The skillet should be dry and hot—no oil. A little sticking is ok— more flavor for the red-eye gravy.

3 Cover the pan while the ham cooks. This seals in flavor and keeps the meat from toughening. (This is controversial—it may lead to my being labeled a heretic!)

4 When the first side's browned, flip the steaks. Re-cover the pan and keep cooking until both sides are lightly browned. Remove the steaks—keep them in a warm place.

5 Leave the pan over medium-high heat. Immediately pour in 1/4 to 1/2 cup water—just enough to barely cover the bottom. Scrape and stir to deglaze. Reduce liquid by half.

6 Making red-eye gravy only takes a couple minutes (it just *seems* a lot longer when you have to wait for this delicacy). Look at the deep color in that ladle—this is living.

SIDE DISHES
for COUNTRY HAM

So, I've talked you into trying country ham. But what goes with it? You might as well go all the way and try some typical Southern side dishes. Most of these side

dishes have been around since early colonial days. Spoon bread and beaten biscuits were always served with country ham. Sweet potatoes, in some form, have long been a companion to ham. And tomatoes? Thomas Jefferson, America's first gourmet, was growing and eating tomatoes when they were still considered poisonous.

If you're a little reluctant about the strong taste of baked country ham, serve these side dishes with slices of milder fried ham, *see page 11.*

Sweet Potato Timbale: Any good southerner worth his salt serves sweet potatoes with ham. The problem is that most of the time, their natural flavor is overpowered by too much sugar and other flavorings.

These individual timbales [tihm BAHL] are made by first roasting sweet potatoes. Roasting is a simple way to intensify flavor because it brings natural sugars to the surface. You'll notice there's no sugar in the recipe. The subtle flavor goes well with the salty ham.

Fried Green Tomatoes: In the South, fried green tomatoes are as common as gnats. To enhance flavor, many cooks brine their tomatoes before frying. But this can make the tomatoes inconsistently salty.

So instead, I salt my slices, let them sit, and then rinse them off. This adds flavor, but eliminates much of the salt and excess water in the tomato. The end results are much more consistent.

Spoon Bread: When serving country ham, there's nothing more traditional than spoon bread. And that's exactly how I left it—traditional.

Spoon bread is a souffle-like cornbread that is so custardy, you have to eat it with a spoon. Thomas Jefferson would be proud of this recipe.

SWEET POTATO TIMBALES

(SERVES 6)
WORK TIME: 25 MINUTES
ROASTING TIME: 35 MINUTES
COOK TIME: 45 MINUTES

PEEL AND CUT INTO 3" CHUNKS:
2 lbs. sweet potatoes

TOSS SWEET POTATOES IN:
1 T. vegetable oil

COMBINE WITH SWEET POTATOES AND PROCESS:
1 cup heavy cream
4 eggs, slightly beaten
3 egg yolks, slightly beaten
1/2 t. orange zest
1/2 t. salt
1/4 t. freshly ground pepper
1/4 t. ground ginger
Pinch of ground nutmeg

DIVIDE AMONG SIX RAMEKINS:
6 T. sorghum
3 T. finely chopped pecans
Orange zest

BAKE TIMBALES IN WATER BATH IN A 300° OVEN FOR 45 MINUTES.

NUTRITIONAL INFORMATION PER TIMBALE: CALORIES 487; TOTAL FAT 26(G); CALORIES FROM FAT 48%; SODIUM 288(MG)

1 Peel sweet potatoes and cut into 3" chunks. Toss potatoes with vegetable oil and spread on baking sheet. Roast at 400° for 35 minutes, until tender, turning potatoes once.

2 In a food processor, combine hot potatoes, cream, eggs, egg yolks, orange zest, salt, pepper, ginger, and nutmeg. Process until mixture is as smooth as possible.

3 Butter six 10-oz. ramekins. Coat the bottom of each ramekin with 1 T. sorghum. Now, sprinkle the sorghum with a teaspoon of pecans and a pinch of orange zest.

4 Fill each ramekin two-thirds full with the warm sweet potato mixture. After filling, gently tap each ramekin on your countertop to settle the mixture.

5 Place ramekins in a large roasting pan so they don't touch each other. *Place pan on oven rack and then fill with boiling water*—halfway up the sides of ramekins. This prevents sloshing!

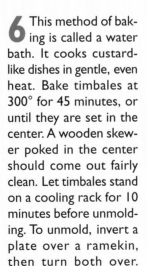

6 This method of baking is called a water bath. It cooks custard-like dishes in gentle, even heat. Bake timbales at 300° for 45 minutes, or until they are set in the center. A wooden skewer poked in the center should come out fairly clean. Let timbales stand on a cooling rack for 10 minutes before unmolding. To unmold, invert a plate over a ramekin, then turn both over. Carefully pull ramekin off timbale, letting sorghum drip onto timbale.

FRIED GREEN TOMATOES
(MAKES 28 SLICES)
WORK TIME: 50 MINUTES
COOK TIME: 25 MINUTES
SPRINKLE WITH KOSHER SALT:
7   green tomatoes, cut into
    $1/2$" thick slices
COMBINE:
$1/2$ cup yellow cornmeal
$1/3$ cup all-purpose flour
$1/4$ cup cornstarch
2   T. baking powder
$1/2$ t. pepper
$1/4$ t. cayenne
STIR IN:
$3/4$ cup cold water
2   egg yolks
2   T. olive oil
*BEAT TO STIFF PEAKS, THEN FOLD
INTO CORNMEAL MIXTURE:*
2   egg whites
FRY IN $1/4$" VEGETABLE OIL.

*NUTRITIONAL INFORMATION PER
2 SLICES:* CALORIES 254; TOTAL FAT
22(G); CALORIES FROM FAT 78%;
SODIUM 237(MG)

1 Layer tomato slices in a bowl and salt both sides. Let stand 30 minutes, then rinse slices under cold water and pat them dry.

2 Here's a twist to traditional fried tomatoes—a cornmeal tempura batter. In a bowl, combine remaining ingredients (except egg whites).

3 Beat egg whites to a stiff peak. With a whisk, stir a small amount into cornmeal mixture to lighten it. Then fold in the remaining egg whites.

4 Pour vegetable oil into skillet to $1/4$" depth. Dip tomato slices in batter and fry slices over medium-high heat until golden brown.

5 Fry tomatoes in batches. It takes 2–3 minutes per batch. Drain on rack over paper towels. Serve with Red Onion Marmalade, *see right.*

RED ONION MARMALADE
(MAKES $4^1/2$ CUPS)
WORK TIME: 25 MINUTES
COOK TIME: 20 MINUTES
CUT IN HALF; SLICE THINLY:
3   red onions (6 cups)
COMBINE IN SAUCEPAN WITH:
2   cups thinly sliced rhubarb
2   cups dried cranberries
$1/2$ cup dry red wine
$1/2$ cup light brown sugar
$1/3$ cup red wine vinegar
$1/4$ cup honey
$1/4$ t. ground cinnamon
    Dash salt
COOK UNTIL THICK.

1 Red Onion Marmalade has a sweet-sour flavor that goes great with both fried tomatoes and country ham. First, thinly slice red onions.

2 In large saucepan, combine onions, rhubarb, cranberries, wine, sugar, vinegar, honey, cinnamon, and salt. Bring to a boil, stirring to dissolve sugar.

3 Reduce heat to medium. Simmer and stir for 20 minutes, or until mixture is as thick as applesauce. Cool and serve at room temperature.

SPOON BREAD *(SERVES 8)*

WORK TIME: 25 MINUTES
COOK TIME: 45 MINUTES

BEAT UNTIL STIFF PEAKS FORM:
4   egg whites
BRING TO BOIL:
3   cups water
GRADUALLY WHISK IN:
$1\frac{1}{2}$ cups yellow cornmeal
WHISK IN:
6   T. butter, sliced
WHISK IN AND COOL:
1   cup whole milk
1   T. sugar
$1\frac{1}{2}$ t. salt
$\frac{1}{2}$ t. pepper
WHISK INTO CORNMEAL:
4   egg yolks
BAKE IN A WATER BATH IN A 400° OVEN FOR 45 MINUTES.

MAKING THE SPOON BREAD

1 Spray eight 5-oz. ramekins with cooking spray. Place them in a roasting pan, evenly spaced but not touching. Heat water for water bath.

2 Premeasure all your ingredients and have them ready. Then, beat the egg whites to stiff peaks. Set aside. Whites will hold until ready to mix.

3 In large saucepan, heat 3 cups water to a boil. Gradually whisk in cornmeal. Stirring constantly, cook over medium heat for 1 minute.

4 Turn off heat. Whisk in butter until melted. Whisk in milk, sugar, salt, and pepper. Let cool 5 minutes. Whisk in egg yolks.

5 Stir a small amount of egg whites into cornmeal mixture with a whisk to lighten it. Then fold in the remaining egg whites.

6 Place ramekins in roasting pan and fill each one to the top with cornmeal mixture. Place the pan on the oven rack.

7 Pour boiling water into the pan halfway up the sides of ramekins. Filling the pan on the rack helps prevent sloshing water into the food or on yourself. Bake at 400° for 45 minutes, or until tops are golden brown and don't jiggle. You *could* test doneness by sticking a wooden skewer into the middle of a spoon bread, but that could deflate it. I had consistently good results with a 45-minute bake time. These are like souffles and shrink fast, so serve immediately.

CURING COUNTRY HAM

Ever dream about what it'd be like to have Babe Ruth show you around Yankee Stadium? Well, for a country ham fanatic like me, having Morris Burger show me

around Burgers' Smokehouse in the Ozarks of Missouri was just that sort of dream come true! It was the past linking up with the present—and the best of both worlds.

Past and Present: You already know the history and tradition of country ham, *see Page 7.* It's special!

But there's even more to it than that. When you sit down to eat real cured and aged country ham, you're tasting something that hasn't changed much in hundreds of years.

If you want to make great country ham, you absolutely have to respect that link to the past.

This is exactly why I couldn't have picked a better place to visit. They not only use, but *revere,* old-time curing methods. These methods haven't changed in generations, and produce the best country ham I've ever tasted.

But remember, I told you past *and present*—there's more. On top of using the old-time method for some hams, they use a little technology on others to help speed up aging. Am I talking about some chemical? No way.

Country hams have to go through seasonal temperature changes to cure. The new method uses refrigeration, heating, and humidity to recreate these natural seasons. By carefully controlling the climate, the curing process speeds way up—other than that, it's the same old way!

People: I *could* jump right into the real ham-curing now. Trust me, there's a lot to say, and I'm antsy to say it. But before I do, I'll tell you that this isn't just about ham, it's about people, too.

Burgers' Smokehouse spans three generations. It began as a hobby for Mr. E. M. Burger. He wanted to cure a few hams for himself and neighbors. They were so good that he decided to cure 1,000 hams—people thought he was nuts. Obviously, he wasn't. Mr. Burger's son, Morris, now runs the place and cures hundreds of times that amount every year.

I enjoyed meeting Morris and his sons. They showed me some old family ham-curing photos and talked about the old days. It was real easy to see their determination to keep the traditional art of ham curing alive.

Walk around the smokehouse and you'll see that same respect for tradition. Some people even go home and cure their own hams in their spare time! Charlie, the curing supervisor, teaches 4-H kids how to do it. He must be a good teacher—come State Fair time, the 4-H'ers take all the ribbons.

Burgers' commitment to tradition is infectious. Combine these people's zeal with the aroma of hickory smoke, and thousands of curing hams, and there's no telling what could happen—I got swept away. Guess who's curing his own country ham?

We're heading to the smokehouse to see *real* country hams curing!

THE CURING PROCESS

Let's go over the traditional long-cure method first. Then I'll point out a few highlights of the modern way.

Salting: Fresh hams are first rubbed all over with a "cure." This is salt, brown sugar, black pepper, and small amounts of nitrites and nitrates.

The salt keeps harmful bacteria from growing, and it draws moisture out of the meat—intensifying flavor. Traces of nitrite and nitrate help protect the meat from botulism and also preserve the color. The other ingredients add a little flavor.

I thought it was interesting that Burgers' country hams are all USDA-inspected. They were the first country ham curer to win this approval.

Wrapping and Bagging: Once rubbed, the ham is wrapped in paper. This holds the cure tight against the meat to give it a chance to work in. The ham then goes into a stretchy mesh bag which helps it keep a plump shape over the long time it will hang.

Hanging: Next the ham is hung up to age in the upper aging room. This room is four stories, floor-to-attic, wall-to-wall ham. When I saw it my eyes bugged right out of my head! A ham spends 9–12 months here, losing about 25% of its weight in moisture.

Shucking: After a couple months the paper is ripped off—"shucked." Then the ham gets put back in the bag to hang and finish aging.

Probing: When the ham is finally ready (up to a year after salting), it gets probed. A small knife is jabbed in and then smelled. If a ham's bad, the knife will smell sour—good thing for the prober this doesn't happen often.

The Key: Let's step back a minute and look at the key to all this: The upper aging room is open to outside air to let the hams go through seasonal weather changes. They *must* have this change in climate to cure.

Seasons of a Ham: Winter is slaughter season—when curing starts. It's cold enough to keep the meat from spoiling before the cure takes.

▲ *The shucking crew hard at it! What a bunch of characters—and great guys. The paper's ripped off and the hams re-hung.*

Then there's spring. Curers call it equalization time, because the warmer temperatures let the salt penetrate all the way to the center of the ham.

Finally, there's "summer sweats." Summer heat finishes the curing and develops the flavor. They say hams hung way up in the attic are the very best—they get the most heat.

New Method: The new method differs in two ways: the climate is controlled and the hams are smoked. Salting, bagging, and wrapping is exactly the same. These are real country hams, with just a *slightly* milder taste. They're done in 4–6 months.

Climate-control: The hams pass through special rooms named for the seasons—winter, spring, and summer. Since the temperatures are kept ideal for curing at each stage (no highs and lows like outside), it speeds things up.

Editor's Letter: This is what I'm talking about in my Editor's Letter. Is Burgers just about ham? Nope, food is an experience. I'm glad I could share the Burgers' experience with you. **AH**

The three smaller photos here show you how a ham is rubbed with cure, wrapped with paper, and then bagged. Now look at the larger photo. They let me crawl up into the attic of the upper aging room so I could look down on four stories of wall-to-wall ham. This was one of the most glorious sights these old eyes have seen!

▲ *The last step is to probe the ham with a small knife. If the ham's bad, the knife will smell powerfully sour.*

BISCUITS

I'm going to tell you right now—make these biscuits. I tried all the techniques and tricks and came up with "the secrets." Use the right flour, keep the dough moist, and don't overwork it.

BUTTERMILK BISCUITS
(MAKES 16 BISCUITS)
WORK TIME: 20 MINUTES
COOK TIME: 15 MINUTES

COMBINE:
2 cups self-rising flour
1½ cups cake flour
2 T. sugar
1 t. salt
½ t. baking powder
¼ t. baking soda

CUT IN:
⅓ cup vegetable shortening

STIR IN:
2 cups buttermilk

SIFT OVER WORK SURFACE AND DOUGH:
½ cup all-purpose flour, divided

CUT BISCUITS WITH A 2½" CUTTER. BRUSH WITH:
2 T. unsalted butter, melted

NUTRITIONAL INFORMATION PER BISCUIT: CALORIES 171; TOTAL FAT 6(G); CALORIES FROM FAT 33%; SODIUM 411(MG)

MAKING THE BISCUITS

1 Heat oven to 475°. Spray two 8" round pans with cooking spray. Combine flours, sugar, salt, baking powder, and soda.

2 With a pastry blender, cut the shortening into the flour mixture until shortening is no larger than the size of a big pea.

3 Stir in the buttermilk completely with a wooden spoon. Let stand 2–3 minutes. The dough will be very wet.

4 Sift ¼ cup all-purpose flour onto the work surface. "Turn out" the dough onto the floured work surface.

5 Sift remaining flour over dough. Flour hands. Turn and fold dough over several times in flour and gently pat to ¾" thick.

6 Using a floured 2½" cutter, cut dough into rounds—don't twist! With a spatula, place cut biscuits into pans (6 per pan).

7 Gently reroll scraps. Don't overwork the dough or add additional flour. Brush tops of biscuits with melted butter.

8 Bake 15 minutes, or until tops are golden. Serve right away. I guarantee, these biscuits will make you go "white-eyed!"

BEATEN BISCUITS

You just learned about country ham. It wouldn't be fair not to teach you about a

true (and old) Southern custom of serving your ham *inside* beaten biscuits.

Before baking powder was available, biscuits were made by beating them until they "blistered." This was done to beat air into them.

Like country ham, beaten biscuits are different. So if you make them, beware.

They're neither tender nor light—closer to a cracker.

Traditionally, beaten biscuits were served when very *special* company came over and often were paired with special meat (country ham).

So how long do you beat biscuits? In the South we say "beat them for 30 minutes—and 45 for company."

SOUTHERN BEATEN BISCUITS

(MAKES 12 BISCUITS)
WORK TIME: 45 MINS.
COOK TIME: 40 MINS.
PULSE IN PROCESSOR:
1   cup all-purpose flour
1   cup cake flour
1   T. sugar
1/2   t. salt
1/4   t. baking powder

ADD:
6   T. lard, cut into pieces
PROCESS:
1/2   cup 2% milk
BAKE IN 325° OVEN FOR 30–40 MINUTES.

Editor's Note #1: True beaten biscuits were made with just flour, lard, and water. I've altered the recipe a little to make them more like a biscuit and less like a cracker.
#2: If you're going to split them for ham, do it while they're hot.

1 Heat oven to 325°. Combine the flours, sugar, salt, and baking powder in a food processor. Pulse for 5 seconds.

2 Add the pieces of lard and process until mixture resembles coarse crumbs. This will take 10–15 seconds.

3 Add the milk and process until dough forms into a ball. Wrap dough in plastic wrap. Let rest for 10 minutes.

4 On an unfloured surface, beat the dough with the smooth side of a meat mallet for 15–30 minutes, until blistered.

5 Fold the dough over occasionally while beating. You will notice that the dough becomes less sticky and stronger.

6 To make each biscuit, pinch off small pieces of dough (walnut-sized) between your thumb and your forefinger.

7 Place pieces on a baking sheet—close, but not touching. Flatten slightly. This evens their cooking surfaces.

8 Prick with the tines of a fork twice. Bake for 30–40 minutes, or until tops begin to color. Serve with country ham!

ASPARAGUS

Most grocery stores have asparagus year round and that's good. But when I start seeing the fresh stuff that has real tight tips and a green color that's so deep, it turns purplish, I know asparagus season (spring) is

here. Asparagus is one of the first fresh vegetables you'll see in the spring. The part we eat is really a young shoot (or spear) from the plant's underground crown of roots. And the word "shoot" describes their growing habits. They shoot up, as much as 10" a day, during their 6–7 week heyday each spring. They'll continue to grow even after they've been harvested.

Regal Personality: Asparagus, like onions, leeks, and garlic, has membership in the lily family. Unlike them, it's achieved the status of a Cadillac. Most of this status is due to its taste—smooth and regally rich.

And, of course, it's *good* for you. Asparagus is one of the most nutritionally-balanced vegetables around. Low in calories, sodium, and a good source of fiber. All the right stuff. It has no fat or cholesterol, as long as it's kept away from the hollandaise—its long-time mate. Status, however, comes with a price. Asparagus rarely travels economy class.

Color: There are three colors of asparagus: green, white, and purple. The most common that we see in the stores is green. Rare white asparagus is essentially a green type which has

never seen the light of day. It grows buried under mounds of soil, and is cut while still underground. Asians and Europeans prefer the white, which tends to be a little bitter.

Purple asparagus is a bit sweeter than green asparagus. It will turn on you though. What was deep purple as a raw vegetable will revert to an ordinary green when cooked.

Selection: Which is better, fat or thin spears? Some claim that the thin ones are younger and therefore sweeter and more tender. Others think that the fat ones are the most tender.

Actually, the size depends on the age of the plant, and there seems to be no clear answer to quality—it boils down to preference. I like the big stuff.

Whatever your preference, select bundles of uniform diameter. Don't mix fat with skinny because they won't have the same cooking time.

Choose spears with tightly closed, dry tips. Stalks should be firm and straight—not wrinkled and rubbery.

Plan to use asparagus as soon as you purchase it. If you have to store it, keep it dry, covered, and in the coldest part of your refrigerator. Wash it just before using.

▲ *Asparagus has **fibrous ends that have to be removed**. You can bend the stalk until the woody end snaps. Or you can make small cuts from the lower end with a knife. When you hit the tender part, it'll yield.*

▲ *To bundle asparagus for boiling or steaming, **align the tips first**. Then wrap kitchen twine around them once or twice. Finish by tying a surgeon's knot. It'll hold securely without bruising the tender stalks.*

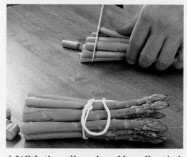

▲ *With tips aligned and bundles tied, **cut the stalks to an even length**. This final cut allows the bundle to stand upright for boiling or steaming, a method which protects the more delicate tips from over-cooking.*

COOKING ASPARAGUS

When it comes to cooking any fresh vegetables less is better. This is especially true for asparagus. Using a light touch is especially true when it comes to cooking time. Here less is definitely more. Asparagus should remain close to its original green color when it's cooked and should never approach an "army green" color. Final texture, likewise, should be crisp and tender, without the slightest hint of "mushy."

There are four main ways to cook asparagus: Boiling, steaming, sauteing, and roasting. Of course, there are other ways, too—like my favorite, grilling. But I'll tell you more about that in a future issue of *Cuisine*.

The four cooking methods are split into two groups: moist-heat cooking and dry-heat cooking.

Moist-heat cooking (steaming, boiling, poaching) is used to bring out the natural flavors of foods. While dry-heat cooking (roasting, sauteing, grilling) intensifies the flavor of food by turning carbohydrates into surface sugars. These sugars then caramelize.

The resulting tastes, while similar, are different. As are the textures. You'll want to experiment with the different methods, *see Boxes below*.

As an Appetizer: Asparagus is more than a vegetable—it can be an appetizer. Consider the Asparagus Crepe, *see Recipe at right*. I created the recipe by inviting in some other recipes from this issue (don't panic, I didn't include the hollandaise sauce). These spicy-rich crepes make great appetizers for a spring buffet. **AH**

COOKING ASPARAGUS

▲*Boiling takes 4–6 minutes. Be sure to bring water to a boil before submerging asparagus. Don't cover the pan. Trapped chemicals from the asparagus turn it yellow. You can also boil in the steamer at right. Don't cover tips with water.*

▲*Steaming in a tall pot is one way to control the doneness of asparagus. The tips, which cook faster than the stems, are farthest away from the heat. Use about an inch of water in the bottom. Steam for about 5 minutes.*

▲*Saute: Heat a small amount of olive oil in your saute pan. Add asparagus spears and cook over medium heat for 3–5 minutes. Shake pan frequently. Season with salt and pepper. For added flavor, sprinkle with soy sauce.*

▲*Roast: Preheat oven to 400°. Put spears onto a baking sheet. Coat with olive oil. Sprinkle with sea or kosher salt and pepper. Roast about 15 minutes, turning a couple of times. When done, they'll be lightly browned and crisp.*

ASPARAGUS CREPE

(MAKES 8 CREPES)
WORK TIME: 15 MINUTES
COOK TIME: 5 MINUTES
COMBINE:
4   oz. cream cheese, softened
3   T. Thai Red Pepper Sauce,
    see Page 31
2   T. blue cheese, softened
1   T. Half & Half
SPREAD EVENLY ON:
8   crepes, *see Page 23*
TOP WITH AND FOLD:
1   lb. cooked asparagus
SPRINKLE WITH AND BROIL:
    Parmesan cheese, shredded
SERVE ON THAI RED PEPPER SAUCE.

1 Mix cream cheese, Thai Red Pepper Sauce, blue cheese, and Half & Half. Spread heaping tablespoon in center of crepe.

2 Position 4 spears of asparagus on crepe with tips hanging over edge. Fold crepe over. Sprinkle with Parmesan.

3 Broil for 2–3 minutes to melt Parmesan. Spoon additional Thai Red Pepper Sauce onto plate, and place crepe on sauce.

CREPE NAPOLEON

Trends travel in cycles. Bell bottoms and platform shoes are back "in." In food, crepes and fondue are making a comeback. And I'm glad. If you're like me, you missed

their big splash in the 70's. (I'm talking about the crepes and fondue).

Crepes are just plain fun, and their versatility has no limits. You already know that crepes don't always have to be sweet—use them for appetizers, entrees, or desserts. And they certainly don't have to be made with just flour and eggs—and then *rolled up* tubular fashion as they were in the past.

Here's your chance to exercise your cooking creativity—and crepes are perfect medium.

What are Crepes? Crepes, as we know them today, are thin, delicate pancakes. But they haven't always been that way. Crepes were first made in Brittany, a northwestern region in France. They were originally eaten as a substitute for bread, using a buckwheat-type flour, water, and salt.

This thick gray crepe evolved into today's delicate crepe made with soft flour, eggs, butter, and milk. Its popularity grew in the mid-1800's when it was predominately used as a dessert.

What is a Napoleon? There are different stories as to the origins of Napoleons. Denmark, France, and Italy all claim some ownership.

My favorite story is an amusing combination of fact and fiction. The French prototype of this pastry was invented long before Napoleon came to power. It was a layered dessert coated with powdered sugar.

The Emperor loved this pastry so much, that he ate too many of them the night before a big battle. Sugar shock set in, altering his battle judgment—Napoleon met his Waterloo the following day. The pastry was blamed and removed from French menus. Disguised with a new icing, it later resurfaced under a new name.

BASIC CREPES

(MAKES TWELVE 8" CREPES)
WORK TIME: 7 MINUTES
REST TIME: 1 HOUR
COOK TIME: 30 MINUTES

COMBINE:
2   cups all-purpose flour
1   t. sugar
      Dash salt

WHISK IN UNTIL SMOOTH:
1   cup club soda
1   cup 2% milk
3   eggs, slightly beaten

WHISK IN AND CHILL BATTER:
5   T. butter, melted

NUTRITIONAL INFORMATION PER CREPE:
CALORIES 149; TOTAL FAT 7(G); CALORIES
FROM FAT 41%; SODIUM 91(MG)

Before we get creative, you need to take "Crepe Making 101." Crepes have been unfortunately labeled as being delicate and difficult to make. This just isn't true—I'll show you.

The Batter: The first step is a good batter. You want the crepes lacy-thin, but strong enough to handle.

This strong but delicate structure is created two ways. First, add soda water to your batter, *see Step 1.* The carbonation helps, but it's the water that plays the major role for lightness.

For strength, let the crepe batter rest at least 1 hour before using, *see Step 2.* This allows the flour and eggs to form a strong bond.

Cooking: Cooking crepes is easy enough once you get in the "zone"—this means making crepes becomes almost automatic after the first few.

Begin by oiling a 10" frying pan, *see Step 3.* A paper towel that's been lightly dipped in vegetable oil works best. You might be inclined to use a nonstick pan, but a regular pan will give you better color.

When the pan is hot (a drop of water will dance on the surface), pour batter into the center of the pan, *see Step 4.* Immediately lift the pan and start to roll and swirl the pan, *see Step 5.* It'll take a few practice crepes before you get the hang of "the swirl."

When the crepe's sides begin to curl, turn it, *see Steps 6 and 7.* As the pan seasons, *see Glossary,* your crepes will slide out effortlessly for flipping and stacking by hand, *see Step 8.*

1 Combine flour, sugar, and salt in a medium bowl. Make a well in the center and add club soda, milk, and eggs. Whisk until smooth.

2 Whisk in melted butter. Cover bowl with plastic wrap. Chill for 1 hour. Right before using, whisk again to remove any lumps.

3 Heat 10" stainless steel skillet over medium-high heat. Before making each crepe, wipe with a paper towel dipped in vegetable oil.

4 Pour 1/3 cup batter into skillet. I filled a 4-oz. ladle about three-fourths full. Don't use too much or the crepes will be too thick.

5 As soon as the batter is poured, roll and swirl the skillet so that the batter evenly coats the entire bottom of the pan.

6 Cook the crepe until the edges start to brown and curl. This takes about 1 minute. Loosen the edges with a metal spatula.

7 Flip the crepe over. This is really easiest if you slide it into your hand, then flip it back into the pan. Be careful not to touch the pan!

8 Cook for another minute, then slide the crepe out of the pan and stack on a plate. Wipe the pan with oil before each new crepe.

(MAKES 2¹/₃ CUPS)
WORK TIME: 10 MINUTES
COOK TIME: 10 MINUTES
WHISK TOGETHER:
2   egg yolks
¹/₄ cup sugar
3   T. cornstarch
¹/₈ t. salt
WHISK IN:
1¹/₂ cups Half & Half
COOK UNTIL THICK; WHISK IN:
1¹/₂ T. unsalted butter
1¹/₂ t. vanilla extract
STIR INTO CUSTARD:
8   oz. mascarpone cheese

1 Off the heat, whisk together egg yolks, sugar, cornstarch, and salt. Work fast—sugar "cooks" the protein in the yolks (scrambled eggs).

2 This mixture is pretty thick, so start whisking in the Half & Half until smooth. Add it gradually to avoid lumps.

3 Stirring continuously, cook custard over medium heat for 10 minutes or until thick. Remove from heat and stir in butter and vanilla.

4 Transfer custard to a bowl. Cool slightly. Whisk in mascarpone cheese until smooth. Cover with plastic wrap and chill (2 hours).

APPLE COMPOTE

(MAKES 2 CUPS)
WORK TIME: 15 MINUTES
COOK TIME: 15 MINUTES
SAUTE IN 3 T. UNSALTED BUTTER:
3   Granny Smith apples, peeled and diced (¹/₄" dice)
ADD AND SIMMER:
¹/₂ cup brown sugar
2   T. fresh orange juice
2   t. lemon juice

Saute diced apples in butter for 8–10 minutes (not quite tender). Add brown sugar and juices. Simmer for 5–8 minutes, or until liquid has reduced to a thick syrup. Keep warm.

APPLE CARAMEL SAUCE

(MAKES 1¹/₂ CUPS)
WORK TIME: 10 MINUTES
COOK TIME: 40 MINUTES
BOIL UNTIL REDUCED TO 2 CUPS;
RESERVE 2 T.:
1   quart apple juice
¹/₂ cup sugar
¹/₂ vanilla bean, split and scraped
ADD AND SIMMER:
¹/₄ cup heavy cream
STIR IN; COOK UNTIL THICKENED:
4   t. cornstarch mixed with
     2 T. reserved reduction
     Pinch of salt

1 In large saucepan, combine apple juice and sugar. Split vanilla bean lengthwise. Scrape out seeds and add seeds and bean halves to juice.

2 Reduce mixture to 2 cups (20–25 mins.). Remove beans and reserve 2 T. mixture. Reduce to simmer and stir in cream. Stir and cook 10 minutes.

3 Mix cornstarch and reserved juice reduction. Add salt. Whisk into saucepan. Simmer for 2–4 minutes, or until sauce is thickened and glossy.

4 To make apple caramel sauce easier to use, let it cool. Then pour it into a squeeze bottle. Chill sauce before use.

BEYOND CREPE NAPOLEON

Now that you know how to make a basic crepe, start being creative with them. Just don't roll them up like a piece of carpet—we had enough of that 20 years ago.

There are a few things I wanted to do with this Crepe Napoleon. First, I wanted to show you that crepes don't always have to be in their expected round shape—I made triangles.

Second, you need to know that once you make the crepes, you can bake, grill, broil, or even steam them.

Third, remember that crepes can be altered by either adding different flavoring to the batter or replacing the flour with other finely ground grains like cornmeal or buckwheat.

Finally, use a variety of fillings or fresh fruits. Be creative! **AH**

see page 23

CREPE NAPOLEONS WITH APPLE COMPOTE AND APPLE CARAMEL SAUCE

(SERVES 4)

WORK TIME: 15 MINUTES
COOK TIME: 5 MINUTES

QUARTER AND BAKE:
4   crepes, *see page 23*

SPRINKLE CREPES WITH:
   Powdered sugar

BUILD NAPOLEONS EVENLY WITH:
2   cups Apple Compote
$1^1/3$ cups Mascarpone Custard
$^3/4$ cup Apple Caramel Sauce

SAUCE PLATES EVENLY WITH:
$^3/4$ cup Apple Caramel Sauce
$^1/4$ cup Mascarpone Custard
     thinned with Half & Half

GARNISH WITH:
   Orange zest
   Mint sprig

NUTRITIONAL INFORMATION PER NAPOLEON: CALORIES 917; TOTAL FAT 39(G); CALORIES FROM FAT 38%; SODIUM 354(MG)

BUILDING A CREPE NAPOLEON

1 Cut crepes into quarters and arrange on cooling rack over a baking sheet. Bake at 400° for 5–6 minutes, or until crisp. Cool crepes.

2 Sprinkle crepes with powdered sugar. Spoon a triangle of apple compote on plate close to one edge. Top with first crepe quarter.

3 Place a small dollop of mascarpone custard on crepe to act as "glue." Set a second crepe on top, slightly offset from the first.

4 Top second crepe with a scoop of custard. Add some more compote and a squirt of caramel sauce. Stack two more crepes on as before.

5 Squirt some caramel sauce on the rest of the plate, following the shape of the Napoleon. This is going to make it look great.

6 Draw three V-shaped lines on the caramel sauce with the thinned custard. Use a skewer to draw through lines—away from crepe.

7 Now, draw through the lines toward the crepe between the marks you just made. This design will make that "Napoleon" icing look.

8 Garnish your Napoleons with a long strand of orange zest and a cluster of fresh mint leaves. Serve immediately before crepes get soggy.

CRAB CAKES

I've been wanting to make crab cakes since the first issue of Cuisine, but it was never the right time. Well, the blue crabs are flocking to shallow waters from their

deep-water winter homes, and I'm fired up to eat some crab cakes.

There's one constant to crab cakes—crab. After that, most every recipe is different, and of course, I've developed my own. I've taken many of the good points of these recipes and rolled them into one killer recipe.

The best crab cakes I've eaten did three things to preserve the crabmeat's taste and texture. First, the meat was not shredded but remained in large pieces. Second, the binder was kept to a minimum. And finally, they weren't oily from heavy frying.

Football fans (especially Chicago) will understand this analogy. A good quarterback ("da crab") will always credit the offensive line ("da binder") with victory. And that's the fact for these crab cakes—the binder lets the sweet flavor of crab stand out.

Mixing: Crabmeat is delicate and shreds in a heartbeat if overmixed. You want *chunks* of crab in your cakes. So it's important to thoroughly mix all the binder ingredients *first* before folding in crabmeat. This minimizes any shredding. No spoons for this step, folding is best done with your hands.

Binder: A good binder should take a backseat to crab. Crabmeat is too expensive and it's flavor is much too sweet and delicate to be covered up with an overpowering binder.

I've seen some cakes bound with cheeses and even mashed potatoes—yuck! Good cakes should have just enough binding ability to barely hold all the ingredients together without producing a heavy hockey puck.

Cooking: There are too many crab cake recipes that bring the binder to a "glue" state. This is so the cakes can take harsh frying—even grilling.

To me, frying absorbs too much fat and imparts an off-taste. These crab cakes are delicate—broiling is just the ticket. And besides, who needs the extra calories from frying? I'm saving them for lemon meringue pie!

TYPES OF CRABS

The type of crab you eat really depends on which coast you live on.

East Coast: The two most popular East-coast crabs are blue and stone.

Blue Crab: Blue crabs are the most popular crab by harvest numbers. They are found all up and down the Atlantic coast and into the Gulf of Mexico, *see Box at right.* When purchasing, it's best to always buy *live* blue crabs.

Stone Crab: Man are these claws good! Stone crabs are found primarily from Miami to Key West. Harvesting conveniently coincides with Florida's tourist season—November through May.

What's interesting is that only the claws are used. When caught, only the larger claw is removed and the crab is thrown back to grow another one (it takes about 18 months). The claws are cooked immediately on the boat and then chilled.

Jonah Crab: Another eastern crab is a Jonah. They hang out in the deep waters of the northeast making them hard to commercially harvest—this drives the price way up. Their claws are similar to a stone crab's.

West Coast: The dominant West-coast crabs are Dungeness and king.

Dungeness Crab: While it isn't harvested in the numbers that eastern blue crabs are, the Dungeness is the most popular crab on the west coast. The meat is similar to blue crab but there's more of it—25% of its body weight is edible meat. Preparation for Dungeness is just like a blue crab.

King Crab: Found in the northern arctic waters of the Pacific, king crabs are known for the firm, white meat in their legs. Like Dungeness, 25% of their body weight is edible meat. Unless you live in Alaska, chances are you'll never see the awesome sight of a live king crab (up to 25 pounds).

Snow Crab: Snow crab is a made-up name because "spider" crab just wasn't marketable. It is almost identical to a king crab, just smaller.

KNOWING YOUR INGREDIENTS: HARD-SHELL BLUE CRABS

Blue crabs live all along the eastern coast, but flourish in the bays and coastal rivers around the Gulf of Mexico and Chesapeake Bay.

These crustaceans are harvested commercially and trail only shrimp and lobster in production. They are not only prolific, but are considered an all-purpose crab. Most crabs are prepared in only one or two ways. King or snow crab *legs* are best split and then broiled or grilled. Stone crab *claws* are cooked right on the boat, then sold already prepared, just waiting for a dipping sauce.

Blue Crab

But blue crabs can be eaten many ways. Their sweet meat is used for soups, casseroles salads, and dips. Or the blue crab's sweet meat can be "picked" and simply dipped into a sauce.

Sook or Female

Jimmy or Male

The only problem I have with blue crabs is the effort it takes to remove their meat. Only about 15% of a blue crab's weight is edible meat.

Names for Blue Crabs: Blue crabs are, of course, either male or female. The male is called a *jimmy* and gets larger and contains more meat than a *sook* or mature female. Jimmies are best for steaming or boiling. You can tell the difference between the two by the "apron" on its underside. The male has a thin "T"-shaped apron while the female has a broader, rounded apron. His claws are all blue, but her claws are red-tipped.

If you look and see a triangular apron, you've got yourself a *sally,* or immature female.

Soft-shelled Crab: No, this isn't a species of crab. It's all about timing. *All* crabs have to shed (molt) their shells as they grow. In the short time between losing its shell and the initial formation of a new one, it's called a *soft-shell* crab. Right before a crab sheds its shell, it's referred to as a peeler. A *peeler* will molt its shell in 3–14 days. And a *buster* is a crab that's in the process of busting out of its shell. Cute names?

PASTEURIZED CRAB

I'm sure there are some cooking magazines that would rather cancel their largest advertiser before using anything other than fresh crabmeat. But unless I'm doing a crab boil, I'm not about to cook and pick 20 crabs to get three cups of fresh meat for crab cakes. I'm heading to the market to pick up some pasteurized crabmeat. Yeah, it's expensive (I paid $20 for a pound), but I made about 10 cakes out of it.

Pasteurized crabmeat is a perfect substitute for fresh—because it *is* fresh! Fresh crab is sealed in cans, then heated just long enough to kill any bad organisms. It's then chilled and can last six months unopened. I prefer crab that's graded lump or backfin. This is the best stuff.

PICKING COOKED CRAB

Picking blue crab and Dungeness crab is a similar process because much of the good meat is in the body.

Best Meat: You're after two things when picking these crabs. The best meat is the large pieces of lump and backfin meat located in the back body chambers. The less desirable claw meat tends to be a little stronger tasting and has a slight brown tint.

Dungeness crab contains a good amount of meat in its legs. But don't bother with blue crab legs. The little bit of meat isn't worth the effort.

Cooking before Cleaning? Blue crabs have to be cooked before picking because the raw meat clings to the shell and shreds if picked. On the other hand, Dungeness can be picked before or after cooking. I couldn't tell much difference in taste between the two. So, I prefer cooking them first just because a quick boil, for a crab, is a little more humane way to go.

BOILING THE CRABS

Live hard-shell blue crabs are great boiled, picked, dipped in sauce, and eaten with a big group of friends.

In the photo at right, I'm using water prepared with a crab boil (a blend of herbs and spices). Use a crab boil when you're going to eat the meat right from the shell.

But if you're picking the meat to use in a recipe (like crab cakes), use salted water (1/2 cup kosher salt per 2 gallons water).

First, rinse the crabs thoroughly under cold running water. If they are especially dirty, you can give them a quick scrub.

Bring the water to a rapid boil. Add cleaned crabs. Cover and bring to a boil, again. Uncover and reduce heat. Simmer the crabs 8–10 minutes.

Crab Boil: You can either make your own boil or you can buy it— Old Bay® makes a good one.

Here's a good starting point. You can adjust from here. In 2 gallons water, add: 5 cloves, 5 bay leaves, 3 T. mustard seeds, 4 red chilis, 3 T. peppercorns, 2 T. salt, 1 T. lemon zest, 1 t. celery seed, 1 t. whole allspice.

"PICKING" THE CRAB MEAT

1 Remove all the legs and the two claws. Use the back of a knife to hit right behind pincers just enough to score the shell. Pull out claw meat.

2 With the crab on its back, pry open the apron with a knife. (This is a female.) With your fingers, pull and remove the apron.

3 Your objective is the body. A blue crab's shell is thin enough to apply pressure on either side and crack it in half. Now, remove the whole body.

4 See the white dead-man's fingers (gills)? Remove these and the hard sandbag that sits in the center. The vein underneath will pull out easily.

5 Split the body in half to expose lump meat in the body chambers. You can take off the thin membrane cover to make meat removal easier.

6 Here is the treasure—lump crab meat! Remove the lump and back-fin meat with a fork or nut picker. Also remove smaller pieces called flake.

FORMING THE CRAB CAKES

I'm going to do something that I don't normally do—go fast. But I think the whole presentation of crab cakes is so important that I want to cram as much as I can in just a little space.

Ingredients: Don't let the ingredient list intimidate you. It's a little long, but there's nothing unusual.

You're starting with what cooks in Louisiana call the "holy trinity"—a combination of onions, peppers, and celery that they use for almost all their dishes. Sauteing the "holy trinity" in butter, "pops" the crab cakes' flavor and gives them some needed color.

Mixing: With all your ingredients ready, combine them thoroughly, *except for the crabmeat*. If you handle the crabmeat too much, it'll begin to shred and fall apart—there'd be no reason to have paid for lump meat.

Use your hands to carefully blend the crabmeat into the mixture. You'll have much better control and a softer touch by using your fingers rather than a cold, hard spoon.

Chilling: After making the cakes, chill them in the refrigerator for about an hour—longer if you want.

Since there's so little binder, chilling gives the binding ingredients that you do use time to fuse together.

Finally, be sure to serve the crab cakes with one of these great sauces. They're a natural with crab.

CHIPOTLE REMOULADE
(MAKES 1 1/4 CUPS)
WORK TIME: 15 MINUTES
COMBINE IN FOOD PROCESSOR;
BLEND UNTIL SMOOTH:
1/2   cup sliced scallions
1/4   cup chopped parsley
2   T. ketchup
1   T. lemon juice
1   T. Worcestershire sauce
1   T. white vinegar
1   T. prepared yellow mustard
1   T. minced garlic
1   canned chipotle pepper
1   T. adobo sauce from canned chipotles
1   t. salt
ADD AND PROCESS UNTIL BLENDED:
1/2   cup mayonnaise
SERVE WITH CRAB CAKES.

MAKING AND FORMING THE CRAB CAKES

CRAB CAKES
(MAKES 10 CRAB CAKES)
WORK TIME: 20 MINUTES
COOK TIME: 8 MINUTES
MELT IN A SAUTE PAN:
3   T. butter
SAUTE IN BUTTER:
"HOLY TRINITY"
1/3   cup red pepper, diced
1/3   cup celery, diced
1/3   cup yellow onion, diced
COMBINE IN A BOWL WITH:
1/2   cup dried breadcrumbs
1/4   cup scallions, minced
1/4   cup mayonnaise
1   egg
2   T. minced parsley
2   t. Worcestershire sauce
2   t. lemon juice
2   t. Old Bay® seasoning
1   t. dry mustard
1/2   t. salt
1/2   t. freshly ground pepper
1/4   t. Tabasco®
ADD AND GENTLY MIX IN:
1   lb. flaked lump crabmeat (3 cups)
FORM CAKES AND CHILL.

NUTRITIONAL INFORMATION PER CRAB CAKE: CALORIES 143; TOTAL FAT 9(G); CALORIES FROM FAT 59%; SODIUM 483(MG)

7 Melt butter in a saute pan. Add the "holy trinity" (peppers, onion, celery) and saute 5 minutes, or until tender. Cool slightly.

8 Combine "holy trinity" with all ingredients, except crab. Gently pick through crabmeat to check for any pieces of shell or cartilage.

9 **Critical:** Use your fingers to carefully blend the crab into the seasoned breadcrumb mixture. This helps preserve large pieces of crab.

▲ In a food processor, combine all remoulade ingredients, except the mayonnaise. Process until the mixture is blended. Then, add the mayonnaise and process until it is uniformly blended.

10 Gently pack crab mixture about 1" thick into a 2 1/2" ring. Don't pack too tightly. Chill in the refrigerator for at least 1 hour.

JICAMA SLAW

(MAKES 4 CUPS)
WORK TIME: 15 MINUTES
COOK TIME: 18 MINUTES

BOIL UNTIL REDUCED TO $^1/_2$ CUP:

- 1 cup fresh lime juice
- $^1/_2$ cup sugar
- $^1/_2$ t. red pepper flakes
- Pinch of salt

WHISK TOGETHER WITH:

- $^1/_2$ cup extra virgin olive oil
- $^1/_2$ cup vegetable oil
- 2 T. minced shallots
- 2 T. minced cilantro
- 2 T. honey
- $^1/_4$ t. salt

TOSS WITH:

- 4 cups peeled and finely shredded jicama, free of water

Editor's Note: You can make additional slaw using finely shredded carrots and vinaigrette.

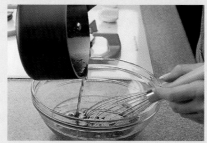

▲ Boil lime juice, sugar, red pepper flakes, and salt to reduce to $^1/_2$ cup. Whisk together with oils, shallots, cilantro, honey, and salt.

▲ For long jicama shreds, cut it into wide chunks that just fit into processor feed tube. Press through fine shredding plate quickly.

▲ Jicama is full of water. To keep your slaw from getting runny, place the shredded jicama in a clean towel and twist to wring out water.

▲ Add a few tablespoons of lime vinaigrette to jicama and toss to coat. Do the same with shredded carrots for a unique, contrasting slaw.

BROILING THE CRAB CAKES AND PRESENTATION

11 Broil cakes for 3–4 minutes, or until browned. Turn them over, gently holding cakes with your fingers so they don't fall apart.

12 Now, finish broiling other side of the cakes for 3–4 minutes. You just want them turning brown and the outside a little crispy.

13 This is what the big time chefs use to apply their sauces—a 69¢ ketchup bottle! Paint your plates with the chipotle remoulade.

14 Place small piles of jicama and carrot slaw near edge. Have all plates painted and "slawed" so they're ready for the hot crab cakes.

15 Finish garnishing with a twisted lime slice and a few pieces of chive. Are your chives floppy? Here's a neat trick. Thread each one from the bottom using thin dried pasta (angel hair or spaghettini). Now step back—this dish is professional stuff!

Notes

THAI RED PEPPER SAUCE
(MAKES 2 1/2 CUPS)
WORK TIME: 15 MINUTES
COOK TIME: 15 MINUTES

BROIL UNTIL BLACKENED:
5   red bell peppers, halved lengthwise, seeds removed

SAUTE:
1 1/2   cups yellow onion, chopped
2   T. extra virgin olive oil

ADD AND SAUTE:
3   cloves garlic, crushed

PROCESS ALL WITH:
1/2   cup fresh lime juice
1/4   cup Thai chili sauce

THIN SAUCE BY ADDING UP TO:
3   T. chicken stock

CRAB CAKES AND POACHED EGGS WITH THAI RED PEPPER SAUCE

1 Cut red peppers in half. Remove the stem, seeds, and veins by pulling them out with your fingers. Place on baking sheet — skin side up.

2 Broil peppers until skin blackens (about 15 minutes). Place in a plastic or paper bag and seal. The steam helps separate skin from flesh.

3 After 10 minutes, remove skins with fingers or knife. Saute onion in oil until slightly golden. Then add garlic and saute 1 more minute.

4 In food processor, combine peppers, onion, garlic, lime juice, and chili sauce. Process until smooth. Add broth one tablespoon at a time.

5 Add only enough broth to make the sauce a thickness you like. You want a smooth sauce, but just don't make it too runny.

6 Spoon this sauce over crab cakes, then top cakes with poached eggs and hollandaise sauce. Garnish with fresh mango. *This is a brunch stopper!*

In case you haven't already guessed, I've been slicing (and eating) an awful lot of country ham lately. It was all the excuse I needed to test out a bunch of slicing

knives. After trying quite a few, I came up with my favorites, *see Page 33*. But before we get into slicers, it'd be a good idea to talk about what to look for in *any* knife.

If you go back to the premiere issue of *Cuisine*, I told you what I like in a chef's knife. A lot of those features apply to slicers, too. Here's what you want to see in any good knife.

The Right Steel: You need high carbon stainless steel. It's resistant to corrosion and sharpens easily to

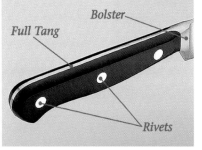

▲ *Here's some of the features I like to see in a high-quality forged knife.*

a razor's edge. But keep in mind that high carbon stainless is very different from *regular* stainless—your *worst* choice. Regular stainless is a harder steel—so hard it won't sharpen worth a hoot.

Forged: Knives are either stamped or forged. A stamped knife is cut out by a machine from a sheet of metal. A forged blade starts out as a steel "blank" (a piece of rough metal) that gets heated and then mechanically hammered into shape. The heating and hammering makes a forged knife heavier, stronger, and better balanced than a stamped knife.

Bolster: The bolster is the wide shoulder between the handle and blade. Just about any good forged knife will have one. A bolster adds weight and control, and makes a knife more comfortable to grip.

Full Tang: The tang is the continuation of the blade into the handle. There are different sizes and shapes. A "full tang" runs the whole length and shape of the handle. This gives you the best balance and durability.

Handle: A handle is either riveted or molded onto the tang. I like rivets a little better—they are stronger. Riveted handles also let you see the tang—you *know* it's a full tang.

Handles come in several materials. I like wood or resin-impregnated wood. They feel secure in my hand because they repel grease.

Some good knives have handles made of molded plastics. These handles tended to fit the shape of my hand better. You can't see it, but they have an ample tang called a rat-tail. For a slicer, this works just as well as a riveted-handled knife.

What's a Good Slicer? I let my testing tell me what a good slicer is all about. I cut plenty of meat—from thick slabs to paper thin—from red meat to fish to poultry.

Oh, and the only difference between "slicers" and "carvers" is that carvers are 8 inches or less; slicers are 10 and over. It's just terminology.

Blade Length: To me, ten inches is the best all-around blade length. Longer blades are often cumbersome. Shorter blades can't cut long slices from large pieces of meat.

Thin Blade: It's easier to cut thin slices with a thin blade. Thick blades have a big taper from top to bottom ("spine" to "edge"). That taper pulls you off-course when you're trying to cut thin slices.

What about cutting thick slabs? You don't need a thick blade for that either. A thin blade will get through just fine—and with less friction.

Type of Tip: Slicers have either a "spear tip" or a rounded tip. I prefer rounded tips because spear tips can easily gouge thin slices. The only real plus to a spear tip is that you can jab it deep to hack out big chunks of meat. I've got other knives that do a better job of that, anyway—it's not what you buy a slicer for.

▲ *You can choose between a rounded or "spear tip." The rounded tip gets the nod.*

Type of Edge: The edge is the key to performance. My picks all have hollow ovals in the blade called Granton Edges® or "Kullenschliff." These things make a knife glide right through meat by introducing air pockets between the blade and the meat. This gets rid of suction and helps lubricate the blade. And don't worry—these knives sharpen just like any other. If you get *anything*, you've got to get this!

Finally, never use a serrated blade on meat. It tears the meat fibers and leaves a trail of ugly marks. Serrated knives are best used on bread.

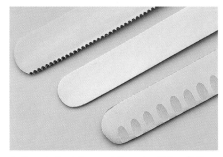

▲ *Serrated, plain, and Granton Edges®, from left to right. Go with "grantons"!*

HENCKELS ▶

This rock-solid Henckels slicer has been with me a long, long time.

Although I've got the molded "Four Star" series handle, this knife is also available with a riveted handle in a hard poly-type material.

I've gotta tell you, of all the molded handles out there, the Henckels Four Star is one of the most comfortable in my hand. This is a fully-forged German knife with the balance and feel you'd want and expect. There's no unpleasant surprises here!

Price range: about $65–75.

GRANTON ▶

My sources say Granton invented hollow ovals. Here's your chance to own an original.

This knife costs half what the others do, but cuts great. You just don't get the beautiful finish, balance, and durability because it's stamped, not forged. If you're after performance at a great price, buy this knife.

The Knife Merchant, *see below,* imports this knife from England. I know of no other source.

Price range: about $35.

WÜSTHOF ▶

Wüsthof is well-known for quality. Every time I've bought one of their top-line knives, it's been good.

The shape of this blade is a little different. Just like my other picks, the blade is pretty thin. But look at how the height tapers slightly from bolster to tip. This makes the knife just a bit more maneuverable.

The Wüsthof also has the smallest handle, which makes it a good choice for people with small hands.

Price range: about $70–75.

MESSERMEISTER ▶

I absolutely love this feel! If you like a heavy, balanced knife with a beautiful finish, look no further.

Craftsmanship is outstanding. And see the piece of metal showing through on the end of the handle? Not only does this help the balance—you can have your initials engraved on it! This knife *does* have the thickest blade, but it's still plenty thin enough for a great slicer. Making paper-thin cuts is just a bit tougher.

Price range: about $70–75.

SALMON SLICER ▶

In my testing, I kept running across salmon slicers. They're so neat I decided to throw this Wüsthof in.

The blade is thin and flexible. Its narrow shape makes sense for cutting super-thin slices of salmon off a big fillet. For one, it's close work and the width lets you see what you're doing. Plus, the cuts aren't usually real long. You don't need a deep blade (like my other slicers) to help you stay on track over long cuts.

Price range: about $100.

▼LAMSONSHARP

Hey, there's no "grantons!"

That's right—and that's why this knife *isn't* one of my picks. But LamsonSharp *is* working on a granton-edge slicer that'll be available this spring or early summer.

LamsonSharp makes quality knives right here in the U.S.A. I use their knives in the test kitchen. I haven't seen the new slicer yet, but I know it'll be good. If you want to hold out for one, call **Lamson** at **(413) 625-6331** for availability.

WHERE TO BUY:

The Knife Merchant, (800) 714-8226, carries all of these knives. **Professional Cutlery Direct, (800) 859-6994**, carries everything but Henckels and Granton brands. I bought knives from both companies and was impressed with the knowledge and service from both. Prices are just to get you in the ballpark—*always* subject to change!

HOLLANDAISE SAUCE

Here's another of the five "mother sauces"—an emulsified butter sauce. Scared? You've tried making it before, but the hollandaise kept separating into an oily mess.

Yes, this is a difficult sauce to make because it's an emulsion. This means you're trying to combine two liquids that don't normally go together—like oil and water. Read the steps carefully and heed the following critical points because there's no room for error. First, have all liquids warm (like a baby bath, 105–110°). Second, don't overcook your egg yolks. Third, whisk steadily in the same direction, *see Tips page 5.* And finally, secure pan and bowl with damp towels.

HOLLANDAISE SAUCE
(MAKES 1³/₄ CUPS)
WORK TIME: 15 MINUTES
COOK TIME: 10 MINUTES

MELT AND CLARIFY:
1¹/₂ lbs. unsalted butter

COMBINE AND REDUCE TO ¹/₂ CUP:
¹/₂ cup white vinegar
¹/₂ cup water

WHISK UNTIL FROTHY AND COOK UNTIL RIBBONS FORM:
4 egg yolks
1 T. vinegar reduction, warm (105–110°)

REMOVE FROM HEAT. WHISK IN:
1 T. whole butter, cold
1¹/₂ cups clarified butter, warm

WHISK IN:
1 T. + 1 t. lemon juice
1 t. salt
¹/₈ t. cayenne

MISE EN PLACE (EVERYTHING IN ITS PLACE)

1 To clarify butter, melt unsalted butter slowly in saucepan. Don't stir. The milk solids (that can burn) float to the top and also settle on the bottom.

2 Skim the foamy milk solids from the top. Without disturbing the settled milk solids, carefully remove all the butter oil to another bowl.

3 Combine ¹/₂ cup water and ¹/₂ cup vinegar. Reduce by half over high heat. I use this reduction rather than stronger-tasting lemon juice.

4 Before you start making the actual sauce, prepare your mise en place. That means you have to get everything ready at your fingertips. Once you get started with this sauce, you can't stop until it's finished. As you can see, I have everything measured out and the towels dampened.

HOLLANDAISE IS AN EMULSION SAUCE

I learned to make perfect hollandaise from several wonderful chefs. As good as those chefs were, they never taught me the "whys" of hollandaise.

Now, I'm going to teach you how. But before I do, I thought you should understand emulsions. So I turned to Shirley Corriher's book, *CookWise*. This is my simplified interpretation of her thorough explanation.

Butter: The butter is an oil that contains large fat droplets. When you make hollandaise, you have to beat the butter so that the large fat droplets become millions of tiny droplets.

Water: Now, you have to keep those tiny fat droplets tiny. So you add a water-type liquid (lemon juice, water, vinegar) to surround each droplet. And that's the problem— keeping those two working together the way they should without doing what comes naturally—separating.

Emulsifier: Enter the emulsifier (stabilizer)—egg yolks. Egg yolks can work with both oil and water so it ends up as the perfect emulsifier.

But that's not quite the end. Read each step carefully because the technique is as important as the why. Thanks, Shirley, I'll take over now. 🄰🄷

CHORON SAUCE
Choron [show RAWHN] is Bernaise sauce tinted with tomato paste. Perfect with beef!
BERNAISE: Make reduction using ⅓ cup white wine, ⅓ cup white vinegar, 3 T. shallots, 1 T. tarragon, 1 t. peppercorns. Strain. Now make hollandaise recipe. Add ¼ cup fresh, chopped tarragon.
CHORON: Add 3 T. tomato paste to the finished Bernaise.

5 Using a balloon whisk and stainless steel bowl (I'm using glass so you can see better), whisk yolks and 1 T. *warm* reduction until pale yellow.

6 Set up double boiler using yolk bowl and saucepan. Don't let water touch the bowl. Whisk over simmering water until yolks ribbon.

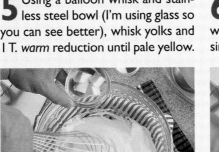

7 Place pan on a damp towel and another between bowl and pan to keep everything steady. Whisk in whole butter to stop yolks cooking.

8 **Critical:** Begin drizzling in *warm* clarified butter, *a few drops at a time*, to temper yolks and butter— bring them to the same temperature.

9 I intentionally let this get too oily to show that there's not enough of the reduction to keep the fat droplets tiny. It's about to separate.

10 When you see the sauce get oily (too glossy) and pull from the sides of the bowl, add *a little* of the warm reduction to "degrease."

11 As mixture loses its sheen and returns to a "flatter" look, add remaining clarified butter in slow stream. Add reduction as needed.

12 With the emulsion finished, add the seasonings. Be sure the lemon juice is room temperature or it could break the sauce.

BEYOND EGGS BENEDICT

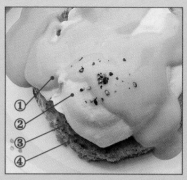

① Hollandaise Sauce
② Poached Egg
③ Ham or Canadian Bacon
④ Toasted English Muffin

EGGS BENEDICT
Eggs Benedict is an American poached egg dish. But don't limit yourself to the standard ingredients listed above. Use the grit cakes on page 38 and slices of country ham—a southern twist to this New York dish.

Ever hear of Breakfast at Brennans? The New Orleans-based restaurant refined breakfast and made it special. My first job was there and it left a positive and lasting

impression on me. I had no idea that eggs could be so much fun.

Brennans brought breakfast and poached eggs to a new level. Diners enjoyed live jazz, sazeracs, milk punch, and fresh oyster appetizers, *see Issue 6*, as they waited for their special entrees. Poached egg dishes like Eggs St. Charles made with fresh sauteed trout, Eggs Nouvelle Orleans [NU-vel OR-lee-ons] with lump crabmeat, and Eggs Sardou. This wasn't just living, it was celebrating.

Breakfast at Brennans is an impression that I won't forget. And I want to pass on a few breakfast ideas to you.

Eggs Benedict: No one is positive about the origin of eggs Benedict. One story claims its roots at New York's Delmonico restaurant. A couple, named Benedict, repeatedly complained that there was nothing new on the menu. They were finally presented with eggs Benedict.

Another claims it was a "secret" cure for a certain stockbroker's (named Benedict) regular hangover. A chef friend heard of the concoction, stole the idea, made a few changes, and put it on his menu. The chef was branded as a "Benedict Arnold," and so the story goes.

No matter how it started, eggs Benedict and poached egg dishes are an American tradition.

Eggs Sardou [sahr DOO], for example, was created in New Orleans for French playwright Victorien Sardou. It's a poached egg dish with creamed spinach, artichoke hearts, anchovies, truffles, and hollandaise sauce.

Now, we're not using anchovies or truffles on either of the two dishes we're making. But we are using the great hollandaise sauce from page 34.

Yes, hollandaise is no angel. It's high in calories. So I altered the recipes to lighten them up (the egg dishes, not the hollandaise).

For eggs Sardou, I jettisoned the creamed spinach and sauteed fresh. The hollandaise works great with the fresh spinach's astringent taste.

The second dish has grit cakes with a sauteed tomato concassée [kon kaas SAY]. Grits are "hot"—they're finally getting the recognition they deserve. Many big-time chefs are using grits to help establish American cuisine (and I couldn't be happier).

If you're looking for the perfect brunch dish, think about these two dishes. Garnish it with a little jazz.

POACHING EGGS

Here are several poaching tricks.

Fresh Eggs: Use fresh eggs. Their whites don't feather in the water.

Vinegar and Salt: Adding vinegar and salt to the water cooks the white faster, preventing feathering.

Boiling Water: When the eggs are first added, the water needs to be gently boiling. This helps set the egg whites quickly.

Saucer: Put egg in water using a saucer. It's easy to spot shells and makes for a gentle plunge.

EGGS SARDOU (MAKES 8 EGGS)

WORK TIME: 30 MINUTES
COOK TIME: 30 MINUTES
POACH AND KEEP WARM:
8   eggs
BRING TO BOIL:
1   cup chicken broth
1/4 cup white wine
2   cloves garlic, crushed
1   t. crushed peppercorns
ADD AND POACH:
8   artichoke bottoms
SAUTE:
1/2 cup julienned ham
1   T. extra virgin olive oil
ADD AND SAUTE:
8   cups fresh spinach, trimmed
1   T. minced garlic
     Salt to taste
ASSEMBLE EGGS SARDOU USING:
1 3/4 cups hollandaise sauce,
     see page 34

NUTRITIONAL INFORMATION PER EGG:
CALORIES 594; TOTAL FAT 61(G);
CALORIES FROM FAT 79%; SODIUM
762(MG)

1 *Make hollandaise first!* For poached eggs, heat water and vinegar to a slow boil (2 T. vinegar to 1 qt. water). Slide egg from saucer into water.

2 When all the eggs have been added, swirl the water around in a circle. This prevents sticking to the bottom. Reduce heat to a simmer.

3 Eggs take from 4–6 minutes to cook, depending on how you like them. Touch with your finger to see how set the yolk has become.

4 Remove eggs with slotted spoon. For a good shape, roll each one in a towel and cut white strands with spoon. You can hold eggs in water.

5 For eggs Sardou, poach artichoke bottoms in saucepan with broth, wine, garlic, and peppercorns. Cook 5 minutes. Saute ham in oil until hot.

6 Turn heat off under poached artichokes; let sit. Saute spinach with cooked ham until slightly wilted. This can be done in batches. Keep warm.

7 When all spinach is wilted, add garlic and saute 2 more minutes. Season to taste with salt. Keep warm. You're now ready to assemble.

8 Spread a bed of spinach on serving plate. Top with two drained artichoke bottoms. Nest a poached egg in each artichoke.

9 Spoon hollandaise over eggs. Garnish eggs with minced chives and red bell pepper. Sliced tomatoes go great with the spinach and sauce.

EGGS WITH GRIT CAKES
(MAKES 8 EGGS)
WORK TIME: 35 MINUTES
COOK TIME: 45 MINUTES
PREPARE AS DIRECTED ON PACKAGE.
SPREAD IN DISH, CHILL, AND CUT OUT:
1   cup uncooked coarse grits
SAUTE:
$1/2$ cup chopped onion
2   T. extra virgin olive oil
ADD AND SAUTE:
4   tomatoes, seeded and chopped
$1/2$ t. salt
$1/4$ t. pepper
TOP GRIT CAKES WITH:
2   T. dried bread crumbs
1   T. shredded Parmesan cheese
ASSEMBLE USING:
8   poached eggs, *see page 37*
    hollandaise sauce, *see page 34*

SOURCES FOR GOOD GRITS
Adams Milling Co. (800) 239-4233
Blackwell Mill (803) 386-3085
Callaway Gardens (800) 280-7524
Hoppin' John (800) 828-4412

EGGS WITH TOMATO CONCASSÉE ON GRIT CAKES

1 Prepare grits according to package directions. Season. Spread grits evenly in a 7"x11" dish that's been lightly coated with cooking spray.

2 Chill grits until they are set (about 1 hour), then cut them into 8 rounds with a 2½" cutter. Place grit cakes on baking sheet.

3 Saute onion in oil for 10 minutes, or until slightly caramelized. Add tomatoes, salt, and pepper. Saute for 5 minutes, until tomatoes are tender.

4 Mix bread crumbs and Parmesan. Broil cakes 2–3 minutes on one side. Turn. Sprinkle mixture evenly over cakes and broil until golden.

5 Place grit cakes on serving plate and spoon some sauteed tomato concassée over them. Let some fall onto the plate.

6 Top the warm tomatoes with poached eggs. Then spoon hollandaise sauce over them. Garnish with fresh melon, grapes, and mint.

◄ BROCCOLI SPROUTS

If you like alfalfa sprouts, you'll love broccoli sprouts. To me, they have 10 times better flavor than bland alfalfa sprouts. They're sharp and peppery and really add something to a sandwich or salad.

But that's not the best part. According to Johns Hopkins University, regular raw broccoli contains a cancer-fighting compound. And these sprouts contain 20–50 times more of this compound than is found in raw broccoli! You'll start seeing these soon in your produce section.

MORE THAN A NEWSLETTER ►

I try to read most of the publications that are about food— there's a bunch! But there are only a few I especially enjoy.

One of them is **The Art of Eating**. It's a quarterly newsletter for people who really want to know the history and traditions behind the food that they love.

Edward Behr passes along these traditions to his readers in a no-nonsense, scholarly way. What makes it so great is each newsletter usually focuses on a specific region. He travels and talks with the people that live there.

Pizza in Naples, Roquefort in France, chocolate in Paris. These are all places you end up learning about. I enjoy the information and knowledge.

To order **The Art of Eating**, call **(800) 495-3944**. Subscription cost is $30. And check out their Web site— www.artofeating.com. It's worth it.

NEW COOKBOOK ►

CookWise: The Hows and Whys of Successful Cooking, by Shirley O. Corriher, is a different kind of cookbook.

This isn't just a collection of recipes. As a food scientist, Shirley uses each recipe as a lesson to show you how ingredients work together. Her explanations of cooking techniques really make sense. I used her book to help you understand our hollandaise on pages 34–35.

Look for Shirley's **CookWise: The Hows and Whys of Successful Cooking** in your local bookstore. William Morrow & Company, Inc.

▲ COUNTRY HAMS

Now that you've heard all about country ham, you probably want to know where to find one. I tried a lot of 'em. Here's my top five.

Burgers' Ozark Country Cured Hams, Inc., (800) 624-5426. This winner is from Missouri. So good, I had to see how they did it.

Tripp Country Hams, (800) 471-9814. Running a close second to Burgers', this Tennessee hickory-smoked ham is aged for 6 months.

Johnston County Hams, (800) 543-4267. A Smithfield-style ham from North Carolina. For the real deal, get their year-old ham. Milder flavored hams (aged 3–6 months) are also available.

S. Wallace Edwards & Sons, (800) 222-4267. Wigwam Brand, aged a full year for intense flavor. This is a good Virginia ham.

The Smithfield Ham and Products Co., (800) 628-2242. The Amber Brand, Genuine Smithfield ham, is the way to go here.

QUESTIONS AND ANSWERS

Q *The recipe for Sweet Potato Tourné in Issue 5 refers to "fresh sage chiffonade." What is "chiffonade"?*

A "Chiffonade" is just a certain way of cutting fresh herbs or leafy vegetables. It's used when an herb's appearance in a dish is important. This French term literally means "made of rags" and refers to how the leaves look after they've been cut—they're thin, shredded strips.

A true chiffonade doesn't have the vein running through the leaf. I don't bother removing the veins in herbs like basil or sage—they're usually tender and not very noticeable. But if I'm using chard or another large-leafed vegetable, I cut the vein out.

To cut chiffonade, stack the leaves on top of each other. (Cutting a bunch of leaves together is quicker than doing one at a time.) Then roll the leaves up into a tube—the direction you roll depends on how long you want the strips. Now, all you have to do is use a chef's knife to slice narrow pieces across the leaves to create the long, thin strips called chiffonade.

Q *A question in Issue 7 mentioned your Web site. Where can I find it?*

A *Cuisine* is in now in cyberspace! Our address is **www.augusthome.com/cuisine.htm.**

There's a cooking forum and everyone is encouraged to participate. Our readers answer other reader's questions! Send in your cooking questions and favorite recipes to share.

You'll also find recipes, tips and techniques, and some of the reviews of kitchen tools from past issues.

Q *My grandma's pie crust was the best. But she used lard. Is it really as bad for me as I've heard?*

A Lard has gotten a bad rap for a couple of reasons. One, it's pork fat. Two, it's pork fat!

Lard's family tree has a bad reputation. Actually, lard is no worse for you than some other fats (like hard margarine). But its baking characteristics are tough to beat. Because lard's melting point is so high, it's able to keep its body longer within baking pastry dough. This made your grandma's pastry flaky.

Q *After reading your terrific article on espresso machines, I went out and bought one. It works great but now it sometimes leaks where I put the filter holder in. What's happening?*

A Leakage could be caused by several things. If coffee grounds get up where the filter holder screws in, it could keep the filter holder from sealing properly. You can use a sponge or paper towel to get up in there and wipe it out.

Your machine could also leak if you've tamped the coffee grounds too much. Or your grinds could be too fine. If the coffee is too tight for the water to flow through easily, it could be forced upward and leak out over the filter's top.

Try cleaning your machine, tamping less, or using a coarser grind. If it still leaks around the filter holder after trying all that, your problem might be more serious. In that case, call the manufacturer's service representative and get their advice.

Q&A

We'll find answers to your cooking questions, and help find solutions to the unique problems which occur in the kitchen. Any questions? Send your cooking questions to *Cuisine, Q & A Editor,* 2200 Grand Avenue, Des Moines, IA 50312, or contact us through our E-mail address: *Cuisine@cuisinemag.com*

Q *I sometimes read about people using cornichons. What is a cornichon?*

A Cornichon is French for "gherkin," the tiny, dark green cucumbers used to make them. (That's a cherry tomato at left to show you scale.) "Corne" means "horn" describing the shape of a cornichon. Cornichons are usually cooked in a vinegar bath and are tangy and tart. Tradition pairs them with rich patés and smoked meats.

Q *I want to make homemade ice cream this summer, but I don't know which machine to buy. What do you suggest?*

A If you have a copy of Issue 4, pull it out. I did a review of ice cream machines in the Wares article. It'll tell you what to look for.

Just in case you became a subscriber after that issue, I'll tell you right now, my favorite was the KRUPS La Glaciere. It's a great machine—you won't go wrong with this baby.

You can call KRUPS to find a retailer near you. The toll-free number is (800) 526-5377.

Q *In Tips from the Test Kitchen, Issue 5, you showed using a wooden spoon to stir seized chocolate. Because wood absorbs moisture, you could be adding to your problem. The moisture in the spoon could make the chocolate seize.*

A You're right. But so are we. If a person were to use an inexpensive spoon, made from loose-grained wood, this *could* cause a problem.

But in the test kitchen, our wooden utensils are made from maple, cherry, rosewood, and olive. They have tight grains that absorb little, if any, moisture—that's why we use them.

Q *Pineapple seems to be "in season" all year long. Since it's picked and shipped still green, how do I select one?*

A The best way to select a good pineapple is by color, smell, and firmness. A ripe pineapple will be firm, heavy, and have a golden color and sweet smell. If it's soft and smells fermented, don't buy it—it's overripe.

You can buy a green pineapple and let it ripen at home, but look at the base first. If it's a little orange or red there, it'll ripen. If it's all green, the pineapple was picked too soon. It'll have a woody texture and will never get very sweet.

Here's a little secret about ripening a pineapple—stand it upside down on the counter. This lets the

sugar in the bottom end flow toward the leafy end. It'll ripen evenly and won't ferment at the bottom. When the pineapple has a golden color and strong, sweet aroma, it's ready to eat.

GLOSSARY

Break/Separate: When two or more ingredients fail to hold together in one uniform state. Hollandaise, for example, can break or separate from a smooth sauce into one that is oily and curdled-looking.

Concassée: [kon kaas SAY] Its root word, concasser, means to roughly chop or pound a food. Concassée is usually made from chopped tomatoes.

Ramekin: [RAM-ih-kihn] A small ceramic or earthenware baking dish. The bottom should be rough (unglazed) to prevent a suction from forming in water bath between ramekin and pan.

Ribbon: When a sauce thickens enough that when lifted, it falls in wide bands. Also, when sauce is thick enough that while stirred with a whisk, it leaves trails that expose the bottom of the pan or mixing bowl.

Temper: To slowly add a hot liquid to eggs or other foods to gradually raise their temperature without making them curdle.

Tempura: [tehm-POOR-uh] Japanese batter-dipped, deep-fried fish or vegetables. Cold water in the batter allows food to steam within hot oil-sealed batter. Creates a puffy coating and makes food cook faster.

Timbale: [tihm-BAHL] A high-sided, drum-shaped mold that can taper toward the bottom. The food baked in the mold is usually a custard-based dish. It's unmolded before serving.

Season: To coat a pan or other metal cooking surface (not non-stick) with oil and then heat it. This prevents sticking by sealing tiny pits in the metal. Soap and water can negate this effect.

ABBREVIATIONS

t. = teaspoon
T., Tbsp. = tablespoon
oz. = ounce
lb. = pound
Pinch = $1/16$ of a teaspoon
Dash = scant $1/8$ of a teaspoon

LEMON MERINGUE PIE

There are three reasons why we're making this Lemon Meringue Pie: crab cakes, country ham, and eggs Sardou! The light meringue and the freshness of tart lemons works! Here's what makes it great.

Crust: I like a traditional crust, no frills. It needs to be flaky and just a little sweet. It also needs to be easy to work with, so there's no splitting or cracking.

Filling: If it's supposed to be a lemon pie, I want to taste *mucho* lemon. A strong tart flavor after a big meal somehow makes you feel better about everything!

Meringue: Two things—it needs to be sweet enough to balance the lemon, and it better be big, big, big! A *little* weeping and cracking is normal—I refuse to get bent out of shape over it!

MAKING THE PIE CRUST

Not only will a good pie crust recipe bake up flaky and delicious—it'll be super-easy to work with, to boot. That's what my recipe is all about.

PIE CRUST

(MAKES ONE 9" DEEP-DISH PIE CRUST)
WORK TIME: 50 MINUTES
REST TIME: 30 MINUTES
COOK TIME: 25 MINUTES

COMBINE:
- $1^1/4$ cups unbleached all-purpose flour
- $1/4$ cup cake flour
- 2 t. sugar
- $1/2$ t. kosher salt

CUT IN:
- $1/4$ cup + 3 T. Crisco® shortening, chilled and diced
- $1/4$ cup unsalted butter, chilled and diced

MIX IN (A LITTLE AT A TIME):
- $1/4$ cup ice water

1 Combine flours, sugar, and salt in a bowl. Add diced Crisco and butter. Cut in with pastry blender until you get pea-sized bits.

2 Mix in ice water 1 T. at a time. Form into ball, then gently press into a disk. Wrap in plastic; chill 30 mins. (or a day ahead).

3 Place dough on floured surface. Lightly dust top of dough. Roll from center out in all directions until it's about $1/8$" thick.

4 Here's the best way to move rolled-out pie dough—lift up edge and roll the pin underneath. Now lift, transfer to dish.

5 Gently fit dough into dish. Trim 1" bigger than dish. Fold edge over to make it smooth. Prick dough all over with fork.

6 Line with foil. Fill up (to top) with dry rice or beans. Bake at 400° for 20 mins. Remove rice and foil. Bake 5 mins. more.

MERINGUE

WORK TIME: 15 MINUTES

COMBINE AND BEAT:

6   egg whites, room temperature

³/₄   t. cream of tartar

Pinch of salt

COMBINE, THEN ADD TO EGG WHITES:

³/₄   cup superfine sugar

1   T. cornstarch

ADD:

1   t. vanilla extract

7 Put the egg whites in electric mixer bowl. Add cream of tartar and salt. Start beating at high speed, using whisk beater.

8 Here's what you're looking for—the egg whites will eventually form stiff peaks. Turn mixer back on and jump into Step 9.

9 While mixing, slowly add sugar and cornstarch mixture a teaspoon at a time. This'll take 6–8 minutes. Add vanilla, stop.

LEMON FILLING

WORK TIME: 20 MINUTES

COOK TIME: 30 MINUTES

COMBINE AND HEAT:

1¹/₂ cups fresh lemon juice (about 5 lemons)

³/₄   cup unsalted butter, cubed

1¹/₂ T. lemon zest

COMBINE:

1¹/₂ cups granulated sugar

¹/₃   cup cornstarch

¹/₄   t. salt

WHISK INTO SUGAR MIXTURE:

4   egg yolks

3   whole eggs

COMBINE LEMON MIXTURE WITH SUGAR AND EGG MIXTURE. COOK AND STIR IN:

1   T. amaretto liqueur

BAKE AT 325° FOR 15–20 MINUTES OR UNTIL GOLDEN.

10 Heat oven to 325°. In saucepan, combine juice, butter, and zest. Cook over medium-high heat until butter melts.

11 Mix the sugar, cornstarch, and salt together in a bowl. Whisk in whole eggs and yolks until smooth.

12 While constantly whisking, slowly but steadily pour the hot juice mixture into the egg mixture. Return to saucepan.

13 Cook over medium heat for 10 minutes, until *very* thick. Stir constantly. Add amaretto, and whisk out any lumps.

14 Take a look at how thick that filling needs to be! Pour it into prepared shell while filling's still hot. Smooth out top.

15 Start topping *immediately*—hot filling helps meringue cook. Seal edges with first layer. Make slight mound in center.

16 For each layer, plop some meringue in the center. Spread evenly toward outside, stopping just inside previous layer.

17 Keep adding layers until all meringue is used—this thing is BIG! Bake in bottom ¹/₃ of oven, 15–20 mins., until golden.

▲ *Let pie come to room temperature before serving or chilling.*

MAKING A GRAND FINALE

While working on this lemon pie recipe, I got a chance to try out all kinds of topping techniques. I favored this application because of its looks and practicality.

Piping a meringue gives you a lot of raised edges. These edges brown up into some eye-catching patterns.

And, this is practical. Each slice has its own design, which makes it easy to cut between every slice.

EASY-CUT MERINGUE

The first step is to fit a large pastry bag with a star tube and fill it up. Now, take the remaining meringue and mound it into a smooth cone on the hot filling. Take a skewer and mark out eight even slices.

Start piping at the top of each slice and work in a zigzag pattern to the bottom. Repeat the process for each slice, leaving just a slight gap between pieces. This is where you'll cut—and it couldn't be easier!

ISSUE No 9
MAY/JUNE 1998

AUGUST HOME'S

Cuisine

AN ILLUSTRATED GUIDE TO CREATIVE HOME COOKING

™

MARGARITA SHRIMP SALAD
WITH AVOCADO VINAIGRETTE

Also in this Issue:
CALIFORNIA ROLLS
GRILLED LAMB CHOPS
NEW YORK CHEESECAKE

Cuisine

Editor
John F. Meyer

Art Director
Cinda Shambaugh

Associate Editor
Charles Smothermon

Assistant Editor
Susan Hoss

Senior Graphic Designer
Holly Wiederin

Graphic Designer
Martin Davis

Photo Director
Lark Gilmer

Senior Photographer
Crayola England

Test Kitchen Directors
Ellen C. Boeke
Sara Ostransky

Editorial Assistant
Jennifer L. Welter

Electronic Publishing
Coordinator
Douglas M. Lidster

Pre-press Image Specialist
Troy Clark

Publisher
Donald B. Peschke

Corporate
V.P. Planning & Finance: **Jon Macarthy**
Subscriber Services Director: **Sandy Baum**
New Business Director: **Glenda K. Battles**
New Business Manager: **Todd Bierle**
Promotion Manager: **Rick Junkins**
Renewal Manager: **Paige Rogers**
Billing Manager: **Rebecca Cunningham**
Asst. Subscription Manager: **Joy Krause**
Production Director: **George Chmielarz**
Production Assistant: **Susan Dickman**
Pre-press Image Specialist: **Minniette Bieghler**
Creative Director: **Ted Kralicek**
August Home Books: **Douglas L. Hicks**
New Media Manager: **Gordon C. Gaippe**
Assoc. Graphic Design Director: **Susie Rider**
Senior Graphic Designer: **Cheryl Simpson**
Controller: **Robin K. Hutchinson**
Senior Accountant: **Laura J. Thomas**
Accounts Payable Clerk: **Mary Schultz**
Human Resource Assistant: **Kirsten Koele**
Customer Service Manager: **Jennie Enos**
Administrative Assistant: **Julia Fish**
Receptionist: **Jeanne Johnson**
Librarian: **Sherri Ribbey**
Special Projects Director: **Saville Inman**

Cuisine™ (ISSN 1089-6546) is published bi-monthly (Jan., Mar., May, July, Sept., Nov.) by August Home Publishing Co., 2200 Grand Ave., Des Moines, IA 50312. **Cuisine**™ is a trademark of August Home Publishing Co. ©Copyright 1998 August Home Publishing. All rights reserved. Subscriptions: Single copy: $4.99. One year subscription (6 issues), $24.95. (Canada/Foreign add $6 per year, U.S. funds.) Periodicals postage paid at Des Moines, IA and at additional mailing offices. "USPS/Heartland Press Automatable Poly" Postmaster: Send change of address to **Cuisine**, PO Box 37100 Boone, IA 50037-2100. Subscription questions? Call 800-311-3995, 8 a.m. to 5 p.m., Central Standard Time, weekdays. **Cuisine**™ does not accept and is not responsible for unsolicited manuscripts. **PRINTED IN U.S.A.**

From the Editor:

One of my favorite articles in each issue of *Cuisine* is what we call our production article. This is where I show you how some of our favorite foods are grown or produced. You might remember some neat ones like curing country hams in Missouri, harvesting cranberries in Wisconsin, or making Vermont maple syrup.

I *stole* the idea while watching one of the home improvement shows. The viewer tags along with the affable host and visits pertinent manufacturers to see how windows, sheetrock, or mantels are made. This made the accompanying projects more interesting.

So now, you and I go on tours, but with one difference—there are *real* and *genuine* people behind each story. On page 20, you see how Vidalia sweet onions are grown and harvested at Bland Farms, one of the largest producers of Vidalias. What you don't see is just what special people all the Blands are. Let me put it this way. Delbert Bland's high school education (along with his wife Sandra) is enough to run Bland Farm's $20 million-a-year operation. After an extensive tour, Delbert asked if I wanted a chew (tobacco), then invited me to his home for the family dinner—he said I could even cook the steaks. It doesn't get more *real* and *genuine* than that. It's this charisma that makes these stories!

John Meyer

I'm not a raw fish fan, but I can eat these California rolls since they they don't have to be made with anything raw. I found them appealing because they are colorful, flavorful and low in calories. I needed this after all the country ham I ate in our last issue!

AUGUST HOME'S Cuisine

AN ILLUSTRATED GUIDE TO CREATIVE HOME COOKING

6
Grilled Lamb Chops
There's nothing better than good lamb chops. I grilled these using a classic technique.

12
Eggplant
Eggplant is a beautiful vegetable with an ugly name. These recipes will make it more appealing.

18
Pita Bread
CLASSIC
There's a big difference between the stuff you buy in the stores and this fresh, hot pita bread.

20
Vidalia Onions
Vidalia onions are a "rite of spring." What makes them so special that we can't wait until they arrive?

22
Vidalia Onion Recipes
Next to eating it raw, here are two recipes that'll show off Vidalia's natural sweetness.

24
California Rolls
They're colorful, healthy, and entertaining. Make them with friends for appetizers or entrees.

34
Seafood Salads
These three seafood salads are perfect for hot weather. They make a great main course.

41
New York Cheesecake
I experimented with hundreds of recipes until I could confidently label this New York cheesecake.

DEPARTMENTS

OVERWHIPPED YOUR CREAM?

I discovered this tip when I let my mixer whip cream too long before checking on it. If you ever overwhip cream, don't throw it out—make butter.

Whipping cream does the same thing as a butter churn, only faster. So, if you ever overwhip your cream, just keep whipping. Don't stop until the cream starts to clump together and gets a faint yellowish color.

Then drain the butter on paper towels, and press out excess liquid. Press the butter into a mold or dish and refrigerate. This butter's fresh-tasting and has no preservatives—it doesn't taste like a mistake at all!

R. Creel
Marietta, SC

FLOSS YOUR CAKE

I used to cut cheesecake with a knife, but the cake always stuck to it. The slices looked just plain awful.

Then I saw your tip about cutting soft cheese with dental floss. It works great for cheesecake too.

Just hold the floss taut and pull it down through the cheesecake. Perfect!

J. Burch
Valparaiso, IN
Editor's Note: You bet, but you still have to use a knife if your cheesecake has a crust.

OUCH—HOT PAN!

Whether I'm in the kitchen cooking alone or with some one else, it's hard to keep track of which pans are hot.

So when I have a hot pan with a hot handle (like cast iron), I wrap a towel around the handle. That way, everyone knows it's hot, and the towel is there when I want to pick up the pan.

CLEANING UP DOUGH

I used to think hot water was *always* better than cold for cleaning. Turns out, that's not the case with doughy, gunked up bowls.

Hot water seems to cook the dough and make it stickier. Cold water cleans the bowl faster with less mess. Dough doesn't ball up and stick to the sponge as much as with hot water.

V. Christensen
Greeley, CO

EASY-OUT ROLLS

I use a springform pan to bake cinnamon rolls. To get the rolls out, I just remove the sides of the pan.

And you know how tops of rolls make neat shapes when the spirals rise during baking? Those shapes don't get flattened like they would if you had to flip the rolls out onto a plate.

K. McGowan
Mountain Center, CA

K. Boattenhamer
San Francisco, CA

WHISK FOLDING

Recipes always say to use a rubber spatula for folding whipped cream or egg whites into other ingredients. A wire whisk works better because it combines ingredients a lot faster without deflating them.

I mix about a third of the whipped cream or egg whites into the other ingredients to lighten them. Then I use the whisk to gently fold the rest of the whites or cream in as usual.

L. Jeter
Garfield, AR

ZIPLOCKED® GRATER

Cheese always sticks to the plate or table it's grated over and makes a mess when I try to pick it up.

I put a large Ziploc bag on the end of my grater. The bag catches all the cheese. No more mess!

J. Killeen
Olathe, KS

EGG HOLDER

When I bake with eggs, I'm always corralling them with other ingredients on the counter so they don't roll off.

Finally, I had enough! I cut apart an egg carton that I keep to hold eggs on the counter until I'm ready for them.

S. Scevers
Abilene, TX

SPLATTER GUARD

Tired of splatters from a hand mixer? Me too—so I made my own shield.

I cut into the side of a paper plate (to slide in the beater legs). Then I cut a small hole in the middle to go around the beater legs. The plate prevents splatters and makes clean up easy.

M. Ehrech
Shelburne, VT

CLARIFIED BUTTER

Use the *oven* to clarify butter. The heat is so gentle that it easily keeps all the milk solids separated.

Put a pound of butter in an ovenproof dish in a 300° oven. The butter separates in an hour. Spoon milk solids off the top to get to the butter. Transfer the butter to a separate container.

R. Buelt
Glendale, CA

PASTA PROBLEM?

My pasta machine clamp doesn't fit my counter top, so I clamp it to a *heavy* cutting board instead. A damp towel under the board keeps it from sliding. And a towel between the clamp and board prevents dents.

J. Ruttenberg
Bloomington, IL

SEND US YOUR TIPS

We'd like to hear from you. Just write down your cooking tip and mail it to Cuisine, Tips Editor, 2200 Grand Ave., Des Moines, IA 50312, or contact us through our E-mail address shown below. Please include your name, address, and daytime phone number in case we have questions. We'll pay you $25 if we publish your tip.

E-mail address: Cuisine@cuisinemag.com
Web site: www.cuisinemag.com

Tips

FROM THE TEST KITCHEN

CHOPPING ONIONS

This is how I chop onions. Most other chefs also use this technique—with one difference. They make a horizontal cut into the onion halves. It puts your fingers at risk and no one's ever given me a good reason for making that extra cut—except that it's how they were taught.

1 Cut off the stem and just a little of the root. Then set the onion up on one of the cut ends.

2 Slice the onion from end to end. Now it's easy to peel. Place peeled halves cut-side-down.

3 Make parallel cuts. ***Don't slice through the root end***—it holds the onion together.

4 Slice across the cuts you just made. The natural sections of the onion fall apart in small pieces.

BALSAMIC SYRUP

Balsamic syrup tastes sweet and looks great. It makes a perfect garnish. Reduce 1 cup inexpensive balsamic vinegar to get about 1/4 cup syrup.

Start on high, but when it's reduced by half, turn the heat to low. Now you really need to start watching—this syrup can get too thick in a hurry.

When the syrup starts to thicken, test it. Remove from heat, put some in a bowl, and stir it. As it cools (1-2 mins.), it should string out from the spoon like cheese on a pizza.

Wave the syrupy spoon in a circle over a plate. The syrup should fling out in strings onto the plate. If it's too loose to make strings, reduce it more.

GRILLED LAMB CHOPS

You'd be hard-pressed to find a better cut of meat than rack of lamb—the cut these chops come from. It's tender and mild, and deserves the very best presentation you

can throw at it. That's why I'm showing you a dramatic full-plated presentation this time—with a cous-cous ratatouille timbale, a thick yogurt "tzatziki" [za-ZEE-kee], and a beautiful, rich date sauce. What makes it all come together is simple—a sprinkle of gremolada and a garnish of mint.

Worthy Technique: I thought long and hard about a cooking technique worthy of this lamb. But I also had to figure in the "X-factor"—in summer, the taste and experience of grilling has me cooking outdoors every chance I get. So I decided on a little innovation—take a classic indoor technique and adapt it to my gas grill!

The Classic Way: You ever watch those cooking shows on TV? You'll see chef after chef sear the meat on the stove (quick high heat), then pop it into the oven to finish it off.

Now, searing browns the meat—this does *amazing* things for flavor.

Just think back to that pan-fried steak we did in Issue 4. (*I* often do!) Back then we used intense, high heat to get some really nice browning.

But the problem is that you can't leave a *thicker* piece of meat (rack of lamb) on intense heat for long—the outside will burn (*especially* if it's marinated) before the center gets done.

The classic technique solves this problem by searing the meat on a cooktop *only* until it gets browned. Then the more gentle, even heat of your oven takes over—it gets the meat perfectly done on the inside without burning the outside.

My Way: I found a way to duplicate the exact same method on my gas grill. (It works on *charcoal*, too.) I'll show you how to do it on page 10. But for now, the bare bones gist is this: By cranking the heat way up on one side and turning it off on the other, your grill becomes just like both stove and oven in one—it all depends on where you put the meat. This is one technique I can't wait to have you try!

MARINATING & TENDERIZING

The lamb we're grilling is naturally fork-tender. But I'm marinating it anyway—just to add a little flavor. You can marinate meat for flavor, tenderness, or both.

Marinating and tenderizing are interesting (and confusing) subjects. The problem is, you can't really figure out one without knowing the other.

Tenderizing: Tenderizing meat is all about breaking down its tough tissues and fibers. There's lots of ways to do this—pounding and grinding are examples. But there's also natural chemicals that can break down meat fibers—I mean enzymes and acids.

Enzymes that come from papaya leaves, figs, and pineapples will tenderize meat. This stuff gets powdered and sold as "meat tenderizer."

As for acids, I'm talking about liquids like vinegar, buttermilk, and wine, to name a few. If meat is exposed to acids for a long time (*days*), tough meat fibers will break down.

But in the end, you can't make filet out of round steak! Extreme tenderizing, *almost every time,* just gives you mushy, dried-out meat—not naturally juicy and flavorful meat.

Marinating: So how does marinating fit in? When there's acid in a marinade, it can both tenderize *and* add flavor—it all depends on how long you leave the meat in it. If you leave it for *hours* (my lamb marinade) it only has time to flavor the meat—not tenderize. If you leave it *overnight* it'll add flavor, plus just a little tenderizing (acceptable). But if you leave it for *days* it'll flavor and tenderize way too much—ruining the meat.

Bottom Line: Marinating is great for flavor. But if you need a lot of tenderizing, you're better off changing *cooking methods*—use long, slow, moist, cooking like the braising we did on Ossobuco in Issue 7. The results are *far* better than trying to turn the meat into something it's not!

GRILLED LAMB CHOPS
(SERVES 4+)
MARINADE TIME: 2 HOURS
WORK TIME: 30 MINUTES
COOK TIME: 20 MINUTES

TRIM AND FRENCH:
2   racks of lamb

FOR MARINADE, COMBINE:
1   cup soy sauce
1/3   cup tamarind sauce
1/4   cup fresh mint, chopped
1/4   cup peanut oil
1/4   cup dark brown sugar
4   cloves garlic, minced
2   t. cumin seeds, toasted
       and crushed
2   t. black pepper

SERVE WITH:
       Ratatouille Couscous
       Timbale, *see page 16*
       Date sauce, *see page 9*
       Tzatziki, *see page 11*
       Gremolada, *see page 11*

NUTRITIONAL INFORMATION PER 3 CHOPS: CALORIES 573; TOTAL FAT 45(G); CALORIES FROM FAT 71%; SODIUM 548(MG)

WHAT TO LOOK FOR

I want to make sure you get the right thing when you go to buy a rack of lamb.

The Meat: First off, make sure you get lamb—not mutton. Mutton comes from sheep two years old or older, and it's pretty tough and gamey. To be marketed as lamb, it has to come from animals younger than two years old.

For me, American lamb (not New Zealand) under a year old is usually pretty outstanding—it's tender, and tastes very mild.

The Cut: The rack is the most tender cut of lamb. That's because it comes from muscles along the back that don't have to do much, *see Diagram.* The less a muscle works, the more tender the meat.

It'll be marketed as "rack of lamb," and have 7–8 ribs. But beyond that, you really have to start being careful. Here's what I mean.

The Trim: How a rack of lamb is trimmed by the butcher couldn't be more important. If he doesn't cut off the chine and feather bones, you're going to be out of luck—carving off chops will be a nightmare.

Take a look at the diagram below on the right—it shows you a whole ribcage and where the chine bones are located. For the photo, above, I went ahead and bought that same

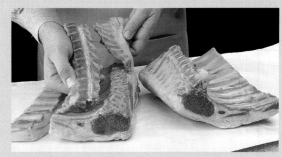

▲ *On the left is a properly-trimmed rack—chine and feather bones removed, and the ribs a nice length.*

ribcage—it's just flipped over, sawn in half, and one half's trimmed.

Now, look at *how* it's trimmed. I'm holding the chine and feather bones. The ribs have been cut to a manageable length. This is what you're after.

There's more trimming left, but I'm about to show you how *you* can do a better job than the butcher would.

Rack of Lamb

Chine bone

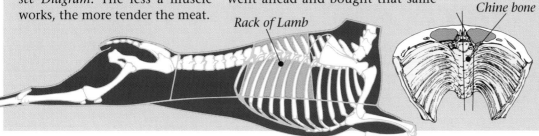

TRIMMING & MARINATING

The last thing I want you to do is take a look at this trimming and get intimidated. Like I told you when we boned out those game hens in Issue 6, just pick up your knife and start in.

Trimming: There's a lot of fat to trim, and you basically want to get rid of it all—down to an "eye" of red meat, plus the bones. Use your knife *and* your hands, *see Step 1*. (Look at Step 5 to see what you're shooting for.)

You're going to notice a very thin membrane over some of the meat—it's called silverskin. To get rid of it, slide your knife underneath it, pull it taut with one hand, and use the knife to slice it off, *see Step 2*.

The rest of the trimming takes nothing more than a little time—cut the fat out from between the bones, and then scrape the bones all the way down to the eye of meat, *see Steps 3–4*.

I grilled some racks that were tied and some that weren't. Tying holds the chops in a nice, round shape while they cook. And cooking makes them *stay* in that round shape—even after you cut the strings. I use a surgeon's knot because it's easy and doesn't slip when you go to tie it off, *see Step 5*.

Marinating: Making the marinade is so simple I'm not going to bore you with it now. I just want to point out that toasting the cumin seeds, *see Step 6*, does make a big difference in flavor—do it! Other than that, just run with it like I show you, *see Steps 7–8*.

TAMARIND

Tamarind is the fruit (these pods) from a tree native to Asia and northern Africa—but it has also been transplanted to a lot of other tropical areas. The pulp from these pods has a sweet and sour, fruity flavor. But the pods are a pain to deal with. Luckily,

...sauce ...Asian ...an markets.

1 Start out by trimming off all the fat. Use the tip of your boning knife to free it up. You can pull a lot of this stuff off by hand.

2 Almost all fat's off now—right down to bones. Next remove silverskin. Work knife under; pull skin taut with other hand as you slice.

3 Now you've got an "eye" of clear meat left attached to the bones. Remove fat between the bones down to eye of meat.

4 Grab a paring knife for this. You're left with membrane and bits of stuff clinging to all these bones. Sorry—you need to scrape it all off!

5 Cut 16 pieces of string, 8–10 inches long. Tie the rack firmly in-between each bone. I'm using a surgeon's knot—couldn't be easier!

6 For marinade, toast cumin seeds in hot, dry skillet. Keep moving them moving all the time (3–5 mins.). They're done when they smell good!

7 Whisk all marinade ingredients together in a bowl. Just make sure the bowl's big enough to hold the marinade plus 2 racks of lamb.

8 Place the racks into the marinade. Make sure all the meat gets covered! Cover and let sit at room temperature for 2 hours.

MAKING THE DATE SAUCE

If you've been with me for a few issues, I'm sure you've already figured out how I feel about sauces—they're absolutely indispensable.

On My Soapbox: A lot of people look at sauces as a time-consuming and unnecessary step—bull! If you want something that's going to capture the heart and soul of what you're making—you go to a sauce.

The right sauce is going to do *everything* for you—bring all your strong flavors together, complement entrees and side dishes alike, and look stunning on the plate. Any sort of plated presentation without a sauce is just plain naked as a jaybird.

My Date Sauce: If you want to see everything I'm talking about first-hand, all you have to do is make this sauce and serve it with the lamb.

This sauce has all the depth and richness it needs to balance the strong flavors that are going to be on that plate. And I made it interesting, too—the dates give it a sweet subtlety. Finally, this sauce couldn't be more gorgeous. Sold? Then I'm done preaching and let's start cooking.

Making the Sauce: One thing I haven't mentioned about this date sauce is that it's easy—which is unbelievable for a sauce this good.

I've got a couple highlights to point out in making the sauce. First, I'm reducing 2 cups of port down to a quarter-cup. That's a *big* reduction that's going to kick in some *big* flavor. But you don't have to use real expensive port for this—save the good stuff for sipping after this meal.

One thing that makes this sauce so quick and easy is the fact that I'm using Demi-Glace Gold™. Using this brand does make a *big* difference. (And no, nobody paid me to say that—I believe in the products I use.)

Once you add the dates, don't cook more than 5 minutes. The dates break down and add too much sugar.

One more thing, butter is *crucial* to finishing this sauce— it makes it rich, shiny and smooth—don't skip it.

DATE SAUCE

(MAKES 2¹/₃ CUPS)
WORK TIME: 5 MINUTES
COOK TIME: 30 MINUTES
REDUCE:
2   cups port wine
HEAT IN A SEPARATE PAN:
¹/₃   cup Demi-Glace Gold™
    (2-1¹/₂ oz. packages), *see WHIF, page 40*
1¹/₃ cups hot water
ADD:
¹/₂   cup coarsely chopped dried dates
WHISK IN:
2   T. unsalted butter

NUTRITIONAL INFORMATION PER TABLESPOON: CALORIES 41; TOTAL FAT 1(G); CALORIES FROM FAT 20%; SODIUM 81(MG)

MAKING THE DATE SAUCE

9 Pour the wine into a 3–4 quart saucepan. Start reducing it over medium heat. It'll take about 20 minutes to reduce down to ¹/₄ cup.

10 While the wine is reducing, bring water to a boil in separate (smaller) saucepan. Whisk in demi-glace. Remove from heat.

11 This is what the wine needs to look like when fully reduced. It gets real bubbly and syrupy as it boils down to final ¹/₄ cup.

12 Whisk demi-glace mixture into reduced wine. Simmer over medium heat about 3 mins.—until it's thick on the back of spoon.

13 Now stir in the dates. The sauce is almost done—just cook it another 5 minutes over medium-low heat.

14 The last thing to do is whisk in the 2 tablespoons butter—one tablespoon at a time. Keep sauce warm while you go to the grill.

GRILLING

This is what I've been chomping at the bit to talk about—grilling.

Like I said right from the start, I'm using a hybrid technique this time around. Here's all the details.

We've talked about gas grills before (Issue 3). My favorites have an "H-burner" design that cooks evenly and gives you two independent burners—a right and a left. You need to have these two independent burners to pull off this technique so you can turn the heat all the way up on one side, and leave it off on the other.

But if you want, you can do this on a charcoal grill—you're just sort of on your own. (I couldn't show you both.) Get plenty of coals red hot ahead of time, then pile them on the left side to simulate burners—left (hot), right (off). From there, follow my steps.

Turn the gas grill on high *on one side* a half-hour ahead. Leave the other side off. Then wrap the bones to keep them from charring, *see Step 15.*

▲ *The racks start out over direct high heat for 2 minutes on each side— enough to brown the outside.*

▲ *The heat stays on high on the other side, but the racks come over here until done—135° internal.*

Grill both racks for 2 minutes a side *directly* over the high heat, *see Steps 16–17.* This is all we need for browning—like a quick sear on the stove. Now, move the racks over to the "oven"—the side of the grill that's off, *see Step 18. Close the lid* to hold in the heat and make it like a real oven.

There's only one thing left that matters—cook the racks until they hit an internal temperature of 135°. This is a nice medium-rare, which is *perfect* for lamb—don't overcook it. The time it takes to hit 135° will vary a lot from grill to grill, so be ready—and monitor the temperature how I show you.

GRILLING

15 Preheat the grill—turn one side all the way up. Wrap the bones in heavy foil. Otherwise, they'll burn to cinders on that hot grill.

16 Lay the racks onto the side of the grill that's going full bore. The high heat on this side is going to brown the racks in no time at all.

17 After 2 minutes, flip the racks over and brown the other side. Be careful not to tear the meat if it sticks. Go another 2 minutes.

ep heat going on one side, move meat over to the robe to monitor the meat. got to close that lid!

19 Insert probe tip in the middle of meat and away from bones. For medium-rare, internal temperature has to hit 135° (about 20 mins.).

20 Remove strings and foil—in that time you just gave it all the resting this meat needs. Strings shape it, *and* show you where to cut!

PRESENTATION

There's a lot to bring together here. Here's how to juggle it all.

Make the tzatziki a day ahead. This gives the yogurt plenty of time to drain (at least 2 hours). Plus, it actually gets *better* overnight.

You can also trim and tie the racks a day ahead, and keep them wrapped and chilled until you're ready to start the 2-hour marinade. The marinade can be made a day ahead, too—just don't start marinating the racks yet.

Start marinating the meat two hours before grilling. While it marinates, make the couscous ratatouille, *see Page 16,* and gremolada. The gremolada needs to be fresh, so don't make it a day ahead.

Begin the sauce a half-hour before grill-time. Keep it warm while you're at the grill—it'll hold.

Now all that's left is grilling— everything else is done and waiting. Go on out to the grill and hit that 135° internal temperature for *perfect* lamb. Then plate it just like I'm about to show you. **AH**

GREMOLADA

MIX FOR GARNISH:

1/2 cup finely chopped fresh parsley

2 cloves garlic, minced

Zest of 1 lemon, finely chopped

Take a look at how I'm peeling that lemon. This makes it a lot easier to cut into strips, and then mince.

TZATZIKI

(MAKES 2 1/2 CUPS)
DRAIN TIME: 2 HOURS
WORK TIME: 10 MINUTES
DRAIN:

2 cups plain yogurt

COMBINE WITH:

1 cup cucumber, seeded & diced

2 T. chopped fresh mint

2 cloves garlic, minced

3/4 t. salt

▲ Put a coffee filter in a strainer, place over a bowl. Add yogurt; let it drain.

▲ Yogurt's ready in 2 hours. Stir in other ingredients. Refrigerate.

I wanted you to see this transformation—the way all the separate elements are brought together.

Unmold the couscous ratatouille timbale onto the plate, like I did on page 16. Then go with the chops. They're almost fanned—so that all the bones arc in the same direction. Now place a little tzatziki up next to the lamb and timbale.

You're ready for the sauce next. There's lots of things to think about in saucing a plate. But for this food and presentation, a couple tablespoons ladled toward the front helps balance the plate visually.

Last, a sprinkle of gremolada ties it all together. Start just behind the tzatziki, go over the sauce and onto the rim of the plate.

COMMON EUROPEAN EGGPLANT

This is the eggplant that's in grocery stores year 'round. The skin is so dark purple it's almost black. It should be glossy, tight and smooth. The thick skin holds its shape when baked but can be tough and bitter on larger eggplants.

BABY (ITALIAN) EGGPLANT

These are miniature versions of the common eggplant and are available during the summer months. They have a thinner skin than bigger eggplants and don't need peeling.

THAI EGGPLANT

I found these when I was shopping at the oriental market for California rolls. They're golf-ball size, green striped, full of seeds and very bitter. In Thailand, they pickle them for a bitter and crunchy contrast in their spicy cuisine.

ASIAN EGGPLANT

These are long, slender and lighter purple than the common eggplant. Since they're thin-skinned, they don't need peeling or purging, *see Page 13*. They're especially good grilled or stir-fried and are firm and slightly sweet.

WHITE EGGPLANT

The *original* eggplant! It gave the vegetable its name because of its white color and oval shape. But they bruised easily in shipping, so a new hybrid was created—with purple, bruise-hiding skin. They're hard to find and expensive, but cook up sweet and firm.

EGGPLANT

My first memory of eggplant is a plate of battered, deep fried slices covered with bland tomato sauce and cheese from a green cardboard cylinder. I don't know if it was

the sauce, the cheese, or just the name "eggplant" that kept me away from it for so long since then.

But now that I'm an adult (sometimes), eggplant has become one of my favorite vegetables. And I don't keep it in a side dish capacity. I use it for appetizers, salads, and entrees.

Eggplant is a pretty interesting beast. It's actually a fruit, not a vegetable. Tomatoes and peppers are in the same family—it's no wonder they go so well with eggplant.

And it's *extremely* popular. Some Middle Eastern cuisines have over 30 ways to prepare it.

Selecting: "Read" the skin when selecting eggplants—it should be glossy, tight, and smooth. The cap should be moist and the eggplant should be heavy for its size.

Storing: Store them at cool room temperature for 1–2 days. Or wrap loosely in plastic or paper and keep in the vegetable drawer of the refrigerator for longer storage. Use in 3–4 days.

Cooking: In these recipes, I cook eggplant four ways—roast, grill, saute, and (my favorite) fry. Let me tell you, this is one versatile vegetable.

I used the common eggplant in all these recipes, but any of the others, except the Thai eggplant, can be substituted with good results.

WORKING WITH EGGPLANT

Eggplant needs some attention before you can start cooking with it.

Peeling: Peeling gets rid of the tough and bitter skin, especially on the bigger common eggplant. A lot of eggplant's bitter qualities can be found just underneath the skin.

But not all eggplants need to be peeled. Baby and Asian eggplants have thin, mild-tasting skins. Or choose smaller common eggplants—they're usually not as bitter.

To peel, use a vegetable peeler or a knife. If using a peeler, I suggest a "Y" peeler. But instead of peeling off long strips (like a carrot), I *saw* back and forth while peeling down.

A sharp knife does the job quickly but with a little more waste.

You can also peel it by first searing eggplant quarters at high heat and *then* peeling them. Skin the eggplant like you would fillet of fish. This way there is absolutely no waste.

▲ *Peel eggplants with a vegetable peeler. Using sawing motion, "saw" off peel.*

▲ *Trim peel off with a sharp knife, slicing down around eggplant.*

Purging: Purging eggplant means to salt the slices. The salt makes the slices sweat out the bitter flavors naturally inherent in eggplant. Purging also firms up the texture so it doesn't fall apart during cooking.

Cooking: Eggplant is naturally spongy and can soak up oil during cooking if you're not careful. I like to just brush it on if I'm grilling or roasting. And I make sure my skillet and oil are ripping-hot if I saute it.

▲ *Sear eggplant quarters at high heat. Cool and "fillet" eggplant like a fish.*

PURGING METHODS

Long ago, eggplant was considered poisonous and thought to cause insanity because it was so bitter.

But back then, salt was considered to have magical properties. So, someone tried soaking eggplant in salt water. The bitterness went away Eggplant's popularity soared.

Salting: The most common method for purging eggplant is to salt and *sweat* it for half an hour.

I like to slice the eggplant into rounds and lightly salt one side of each slice with fine sea salt. I tried using kosher salt but it was too coarse to dissolve into the flesh.

Then, I stack the slices on top of each other on a plate. This way, the weight of the eggplant helps *press* out the juices. Finally, I rinse each slice with cold water to remove the salt and pat dry with paper towels.

You can also cut the eggplant lengthwise in half and make slits in the flesh about 1/2" deep. Salt and drain on a rack, cut side down, for half an hour. Rinse and pat dry.

Searing: I often use high-heat searing as another form of purging to remove eggplant's bitter juices. This is what I'm doing on the right. Besides quickly evaporating the bitter juices, searing also caramelizes (brown) the pieces for extra flavor. This quick cooking method also helps keep the texture firm.

The key is to add the eggplant in batches to a really hot pan. This allows it to caramelize and not steam by overcrowding.

▲ *Searing peeled, diced eggplant at high heat evaporates natural liquids and caramelizes for great flavor.*

▲ *Salt one side of eggplant rounds with fine sea salt. Stack on top of each other on a plate. Drain for half an hour.*

▲ *See the dark liquid on the plate? The eggplant's purged! Rinse the slices and pat dry before using.*

BABA GANOUSH

(MAKES 2 CUPS)
WORK TIME: 15 MINUTES
COOK TIME: 45 MINUTES
ROAST:
2   1 lb. eggplants, sliced
     lengthwise in half
1   T. salt
6   cloves garlic, roasted
2   T. olive oil
TOAST, THEN FINELY GRIND:
$1/2$ t. whole cumin seeds
COMBINE IN PROCESSOR WITH:
$1/2$ cup plain yogurt
2   T. lemon juice
1   T. sesame oil
$1/2$ t. salt
$1/8$ t. cayenne
GARNISH WITH:
     Olive oil and parsley sprigs

NUTRITIONAL INFORMATION $1/4$ CUP:
CALORIES 95; TOTAL FAT 6(G);
CALORIES FROM FAT 50%; SODIUM
161(MG)

MAKING BABA GANOUSH

1 Preheat oven to 400°. Score eggplant halves and sprinkle with 1 T. salt. Drain on rack 30 mins. Rinse, pat dry and roast on rack 25–30 mins.

2 To roast garlic, cut off stem end, drizzle with olive oil. Roast at 400° for 40–45 mins., until soft. Squeeze cloves into processor bowl.

3 Test the eggplant by piercing it with a knife. When done, it should poke through easily, but the eggplant shouldn't be mushy. Cool slightly.

4 Toast cumin seeds in skillet over medium heat (about 5 mins.) Toss to prevent scorching. Grind with mortar and pestle or in clean coffee grinder.

5 Scoop eggplant into processor bowl. Add yogurt, lemon juice, sesame oil, and seasonings. Pulse briefly just to break up eggplant.

6 Stir thoroughly to blend. Transfer baba ganoush to serving bowl. Drizzle with olive oil and garnish with parsley sprigs. Serve with pita bread.

EGGPLANT FRITTERS

(MAKES 8 FRITTERS)

SAUTE IN 2 T. OLIVE OIL:

2   cups eggplant, peeled, diced $^1/_2$"
2   cups diced shiitake mushrooms

COMBINE AND ADD:

1   egg
2   T. milk

COMBINE AND ADD:

1   cup chiffonade of spinach
$^3/_4$ cup grated Parmesan cheese
$^1/_3$ cup grated mozzarella cheese
$^1/_3$ cup bread crumbs
4   cloves roasted garlic, smashed
$^1/_8$ t. cayenne
     Salt and pepper to taste

FOR MARINATED TOMATOES, TOSS:

$1^1/_2$ cup Roma tomatoes, diced
$^3/_4$ cup yellow tomatoes, diced
$^1/_2$ cup slivered yellow onion
$^1/_4$ cup white wine vinegar
2   T. chiffonade of basil
2   t. sugar
$^1/_4$ t. salt

FOR COATING, IN SEPARATE BOWLS:

1   cup all-purpose flour
1   egg + 2 T. water
1   cup bread crumbs

MAKING EGGPLANT FRITTERS

1 Heat oil in large saute pan over medium-high heat. Saute eggplant and mushrooms until golden and just cooked. Transfer to mixing bowl.

2 Combine egg and milk in small bowl. Gently fold into eggplant mixture with spinach, cheeses, bread crumbs, garlic, and seasonings.

3 On parchment-lined baking sheet, gently pack about $^1/_3$ cup eggplant mixture about 1" thick into a $2^1/_2$" ring. Refrigerate at least 30 minutes.

4 In a bowl, combine tomatoes, onion and basil. In small bowl, combine vinegar, sugar and salt. Toss vinaigrette with tomatoes; set aside.

5 Heat $^3/_4$ cup vegetable oil in large skillet over medium heat. Dredge fritters in flour, then egg mixture and bread crumbs.

6 Fry fritters in oil until golden and crisp, about 4 minutes per side. Drain on paper towels. Serve immediately with marinated tomatoes.

GRILLED RATATOUILLE
(MAKES 4 CUPS)
WORK TIME: 30 MINUTES
COOK TIME: 15 MINUTES
BRUSH WITH OLIVE OIL, SEASON AND GRILL:

1	2 lb. eggplant, $^1/_2$" slices, purged, *see page 13*
1	large zucchini, sliced lengthwise in $^1/_2$" slices
1	large yellow squash, sliced lengthwise into $^1/_2$" slices
$^1/_2$	large red bell pepper, seeded, and quartered
$^1/_2$	large yellow onion, sliced into $^1/_2$" discs, skewered

TOSS WITH VEGETABLES:

2	seeded and diced Roma tomatoes
$^1/_2$	cup crumbled feta cheese
2	T. chiffonade of basil
2	T. olive oil
2	T. white balsamic vinegar

GARNISH WITH:
   Fresh basil sprig

MAKING GRILLED RATATOUILLE

COUSCOUS OPTION

1 Preheat grill. Rinse and pat dry purged eggplant. Skewer onions as pictured. Brush vegetables with olive oil; season with salt and pepper.

2 Chop tomatoes and set aside until ready to mix. Grill other vegetables over high heat just until cooked through (10 minutes).

Add $2^1/_2$ cups cooked couscous (prepared according to package directions) to the grilled ratatouille. Toss gently.

3 Cut warm grilled vegetables into $^1/_2$" dice (the warm vegetables will soak up vinegar flavors better). Transfer to a large mixing bowl.

4 Toss vegetables with tomatoes, feta cheese, basil, olive oil, and vinegar. Season with salt and pepper. Garnish with a fresh basil sprig.

To make couscous timbale, spray mold (or a 5 oz. plastic cup) with Pam®. Pack warm mixture into mold and invert onto your serving plate.

STACKED EGGPLANT SALAD

(MAKES 4 SALADS)

WORK TIME: 45 MINUTES
COOK TIME: 15 MINUTES

FOR GOAT CHEESE SAUCE, PROCESS:

3.5 oz. package soft goat cheese
1/4 cup plain yogurt
1 T. chopped fresh parsley
1 T. fresh thyme leaves
1/2 t. salt

FOR VINAIGRETTE, BLEND:

1/2 cup white wine vinegar
1 T. chopped fresh parsley
1 T. chopped fresh marjoram
1 T. fresh thyme leaves
2 T. sugar
1/2 t. salt and pepper to taste

DRIZZLE IN:

1 cup olive oil

DRIZZLE WITH VINAIGRETTE; GRILL:

2 eggplants cut into 12-1/2"
  rounds, purged, *see page 13*
2 zucchini, 1/2" thick on bias
2 yellow squash, 1/2" thick on bias
3 portobello mushroom caps
1 red pepper, 1/2" wide strips
2 hearts of romaine, halved

DOT WITH:

Balsamic syrup, *see Tips, page 5*

MAKING THE STACKED EGGPLANT SALAD

1 Blend goat cheese sauce ingredients in food processor. Transfer to squeeze bottle. Blend vinaigrette ingredients; drizzle in oil in thin stream.

2 Transfer vinaigrette to squeeze bottle. Preheat grill. Rinse purged eggplant and pat dry. Slice vegetables as indicated in above recipe.

3 Drizzle vegetables with some of vinaigrette. Season with salt and pepper. Grill over high heat 10–15 mins. Grill romaine only 2–3 minutes.

4 Slice mushrooms into 1/4" slices. Arrange romaine on plate. Stack some vegetables on an eggplant round. Drizzle with vinaigrette.

5 Next, stack with another layer of eggplant and vegetables. Top with eggplant. Drizzle with vinaigrette. Paint plate with goat cheese sauce.

6 "Dot" plate with balsamic reduction syrup. Assemble additional salads with remaining vegetables. Serve immediately.

POCKET PITAS

(MAKES 8 PITAS)
WORK TIME: 20 MINS.
RISING TIME: 2 HOURS
COOK TIME: 3 MINS.

MIX:
2   cups warm (80°)
    water
1½ t. active dry yeast
1½ t. honey

ADD:
3¾ cups bread flour
¼   cup rye flour
1   T. salt

STIR IN:
2   T. olive oil

KNEAD IN:
1½ cups bread flour

NUTRITIONAL INFORMATION PER PITA: CALORIES 331; TOTAL FAT 5(G); CALORIES FROM FAT 12%; SODIUM 873(MG)

PITA BREAD

There are more kinds of pita breads in the Middle East and eastern Mediterranean than you can shake a stick at. And it's real easy to get sucked into a big debate about which flours and techniques are "authentic."

We're not going there today. Instead, I'm just gonna show you what works for me—what I like to bake and eat!

And if you're still looking for reasons to bake some, let me start out with two: taste and freshness. Dip one of these into some Baba Ganoush, *see Page 14,* and you'll know *exactly* what I'm talking about.

One more thing: This is the easiest and quickest yeast bread recipe I've ever shown you—only 3 minutes to bake. And watching them poof up in the oven is a real kick in the pants!

MAKING THE DOUGH

1 Combine water, yeast, and honey. In separate bowl, combine 3¾ cup bread flour, rye, and salt.

2 Make a well in the flour mixture. Slowly pour in the yeast mixture—keep stirring to combine them.

3 Stir in oil. Add part of remaining flour *just* until dough pulls away from bowl. It's time to knead.

4 While kneading, gradually add remaining flour. To knead, first fold dough in half toward you.

5 Push dough away with heels of hands. Give a ¼ turn. Repeat Steps 4–5 till smooth (about 8 mins.).

6 Place dough in floured bowl, cover, let rise (room temp.) until doubled in size—about 1½ hours.

SHAPING AND BAKING

7 Remove risen dough from bowl and knead for one minute. Use your dough scraper to divide it into 8 equal pieces.

8 Shape pieces into balls by rolling lightly under your hand. Place on floured sheet; cover. Heat oven *and baking stone* to 500°.

9 Let dough balls rest ½ hour. Then roll a ball into an 8" round, about ⅛" thick. From now on, roll one while the other bakes.

10 Using a peel, transfer one (or two if they fit!) to the oven. Bake 3 minutes, and watch 'em poof, making a pocket!

11 After baking, wrap pitas loosely with a towel. The towel keeps the pitas warm and soft until you're ready to dig in.

12 For best flavor, let cool 5 minutes. That pocket makes them versatile—stuff with just about *anything*, or eat them plain.

POCKETLESS PITA

The other day a guy tells me: "Well you *know*, the best pitas don't have pockets." Maybe he's right—this one's for you, pal.

Make the recipe just like I showed you through Step 9. Then take a fork and poke a bunch of holes in the dough *just before* it goes into the oven. I mean a lot of holes! Then bake it as usual.

This hole punching is called "docking." The dough still rises in the oven, but the holes keep it from forming a big balloon like the others. Instead, you get a thick, *even* bread.

ZATAR AND SUMAC—EVER HEAR OF 'EM?

Lately I've been running across all sorts of interesting things. And I hit on this spice blend called zatar that's so intriguing I absolutely had to let you in on it.

Zatar: Zatar is a blend of herbs and spices so important in the Middle East that there's markets that sell *only* zatar and its variations.

Technically, the term "zatar" refers to both a type of herb, and a spice blend. The herb is part of the thyme family, but it's *very* tough to find in this country.

As for the spice blend, I found it through mail order (Penzey's, King Arthur Flour) and at a local international market. The taste of this stuff is a real unique combination of zesty and herby that's plain outstanding with these pitas.

There's about as many variations of zatar as there are Persian rugs stacked in Istanbul. But what *I* found usually consists of thyme, sesame seeds, salt, and sumac (more on sumac in a second). The color of zatar varies a lot, too.

The best way I came up with to use zatar with my pitas was to mix 2 teaspoons of it into ⅓ cup extra virgin olive oil. This makes a fabulous dip for warm pitas. Or, you can take some of that zatar oil and brush it on top of a pita just before it goes into the oven—the taste of it this way is a little more subtle.

Sumac: Sumac, huh? I hear you. You don't run across *this* everyday! (And you really don't want to get it confused with the *poison* sumac tree we have in the U.S.)

Sumac is a key ingredient in zatar because of its tart, lemony sort of flavor. This is a flavor that also works great in a lot of other things. (I'm gonna try some on grilled fish!)

The other thing I want you to notice is the gorgeous color—it's that burgundy you see in the photo.

You can get some sumac from Penzey's, *see Q&A, page 39*, or if you're lucky, from a local market.

VIDALIA ONIONS

Being raised in Georgia, I grew up eating Vidalia sweet onions way before they became a "rite of spring" in markets across the country. Vidalias have an almost

cult-like following. I used to take the spring arrival of Vidalias in stride. But now, as a devout disciple of Vidalias, I can't wait for them to hit the stores and then my dinner plate!

Oh sure, there's several good sweet onions out there like the Texas 1015, the Walla Walla, and the Maui. But I'm partial to Vidalias.

As a kid, I was subjected to a spring ritual of trying the Vidalia "storage du jour" ideas Mom would hear about. To prolong their season, we would wrap them in newspapers, silk stockings, burlap, and even Easter grass. Then, we would store them in different areas of the basement—our version of climate control. Although diligent in our efforts, we were rarely successful in our attempts—seemed Vidalias were a spring delicacy.

Special technology has expanded their availability. The only problem is that there's a limited amount of special soil that Vidalias can grow in.

You first have to understand what a Vidalia onion is. Vidalias come from the Allium family which include leeks, shallots, onions, garlic and chives.

A characteristic of Alliums is that when cut, they can make you cry because of their sulphur content—sulphur naturally irritates the eyes.

Onions are divided into two categories: hot or storage onions and fresh or sweet onions. Sweet onions have low sulphur content.

So now you know what makes you cry when you cut an onion—sulphur. But still, there's more to a Vidalia's sweetness than just the plant. It is raised in soil and fed nutrients that are also low in sulphur.

Vidalia onions are protected by both state and federal laws. There are only 14,000 sandy acres in southeast Georgia that have this low-sulphur soil condition. Even the ground water used in irrigation and fertilizers that are applied are very low in sulphur.

When visiting with Delbert Bland, *see Editor's Letter*, he told me that if you take the same Vidalia seedling and plant it someplace else, it'll grow hot—seems the sulphur is key.

Photo courtesy of: Bland Farms

Photo courtesy of: Bland Farms

THE HARVEST

Vidalias are planted in the fall—from September to February. They grow under perfect climate conditions. The winters are mild (mid 50's) and the springs are moderate (mid 70's), with just enough rain to keep the onions moist and sweet. Heck, most of us would flourish, too, if we had winters like that!

Vidalia Onions are very fragile and must be handled with care throughout harvesting, shipping, and storage. Their delicate nature is caused from the unusual amount of water they retain and their naturally high sugar content—they have more sugar than a Coca Cola!

Harvesting: In early spring, it's Vidalia harvest time. The first thing you encounter is the sweet and pungent smell of Vidalias drying out in the fields. Then, scattered all along the roadside, you begin seeing hundreds of onions that have inadvertently fallen off the harvesting trucks. Yes, I wanted to pick every one up—it was as if an armored car had lost its load. After all, these were Vidalias!

All the harvesting is done by hand because Vidalia onions are so delicate. Migrant workers are hired to do most of the work. They first pull the onions out of the ground and set out them to dry in the Georgia sun. They may lay out in the fields for up to a week, depending on their water content.

After drying, the migrant workers lop off the green part of the onion using heavy shears. They are then gathered in burlap bags and left in the fields until harvesting trucks can pick up the bags and take the onions to the packing plant.

The most awesome sight for me was seeing the thousands of laborers employed to hand-harvest Vidalias. They're an expensive necessity to harvest a huge quantity (100,000 tons) of onions in a short harvest season.

While visiting with Delbert Bland and his father, Raymond, I watched hopeful entrepreneurs show off their automated onion harvesters. As much as the Blands would like to reduce the big payrolls, they've seen nothing yet that can replace gentle human hands.

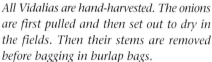

All Vidalias are hand-harvested. The onions are first pulled and then set out to dry in the fields. Then their stems are removed before bagging in burlap bags.

Packing: Vidalias come packed in different ways—bags, boxes and loose. One of Delbert Bland's innovations was to label each onion so you know you're getting a genuine Vidalia. When I buy Vidalias, I look for this.

I also look for Grade A onions. These have no blemishes or soft spots. Inspect your onions carefully—you could end up buying the onions that fell from the harvest truck!

Where to buy Vidalias: As I said, most top-quality Vidalias will come with a sticker. They flood the markets in the spring. Before paying Vidalia prices, inspect them carefully for consistent size and lack of blemishes.

If you have any qualms about quality, mail order them from Bland Farms at 1-800-VIDALIA. But do it quickly. As Delbert Bland says, "You'll only cry when they're gone." **AH**

Placing a label on each Vidalia onion is a marketing innovation that Delbert Bland of Bland Farms started. It's the same idea that Sunkist uses with all their fruit. This gives the consumer confidence that they're purchasing a top quality Vidalia. These stickers are used by most of the reputable growers.

Photo courtesy of: Bland Farms

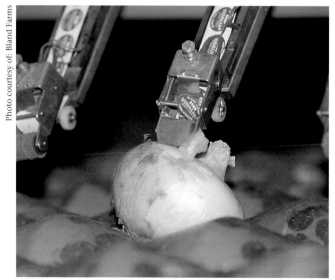

VIDALIA ONION RECIPES

ROASTED VIDALIA SOUP
(MAKES 6 CUPS)
WORK TIME: 15 MINUTES
COOK TIME: 1 HOUR 20 MINUTES

TOSS & ROAST 40 MINUTES AT 425°:
3   Vidalia onions, cut in wedges
2   T. olive oil

ADD, ROAST 20 MINUTES LONGER:
5   cloves garlic, smashed

ADD & REDUCE UNTIL EVAPORATED:
1/2   cup dry sherry

ADD, COVER & ROAST 20 MINUTES:
5   cups chicken broth
2   sprigs fresh thyme
1   bay leaf
    Pinch of red pepper
    Salt to taste

GARNISH SOUP WITH:
    Plain yogurt
    Crushed peanuts
    Sprigs of fresh thyme

NUTRITIONAL INFORMATION PER 1 CUP:
CALORIES 165; TOTAL FAT 7(G); CALORIES FROM FAT 36%; SODIUM 250(MG)

MAKING THE SOUP

1 Cut onions into wedges and put into a roasting pan. Toss pieces with olive oil just to coat them. Roast at 425° for 40 minutes, stirring often.

2 Peel and smash 5 cloves of garlic. Stir these into the roasting pan of onions. Then continue roasting and stirring 20 minutes longer.

3 When the onions and garlic are brown, add sherry. Scrape the bottom of the pan and continue roasting until wine is completely reduced.

4 Add chicken broth, sprigs of fresh thyme, bay leaf, red pepper, and salt. Cover with aluminum foil. Roast for about 20 minutes.

5 Blend soup in small batches (don't over-blend). **Caution:** This can be dangerous (splatters). Firmly secure bowl and lid, then cover with towel.

6 Final texture should be smooth with pieces of roasted onion. Garnish with a dollop of plain yogurt, crushed peanuts and a sprig of thyme.

VIDALIAS STUFFED WITH PEAS IN VERMOUTH CREAM

(MAKES 4 ONIONS)
WORK TIME: 30 MINUTES
COOK TIME: 50 MINUTES

HOLLOW OUT, RUB AND TOSS:

4	large Vidalia onions, core and reserve centers
2	T. extra virgin olive oil
2	t. kosher salt
1	t. white pepper

COOK:

3	cups fresh or frozen peas, cooked until tender

MIX PEAS TOGETHER WITH:

1/2	cup Vermouth Cream Sauce

FILL EACH ONION WITH PEAS. TOP EACH WITH:

2	T. Vermouth Cream Sauce
1	T. fresh chopped peanuts

NUTRITIONAL INFORMATION PER ONION:
CALORIES 283; TOTAL FAT 17(G);
CALORIES FROM FAT 53%; SODIUM
695(MG)

VERMOUTH VIDALIA CREAM SAUCE:

(MAKES 1 1/2 CUPS)

SAUTE IN 2 T. BUTTER:

1	cup Vidalia onion, chopped (reserved from onion centers)

ADD AND REDUCE:

1/4	cup vermouth

ADD AND REDUCE:

2	cups heavy cream
1/8	t. nutmeg

ADD:

1/2	cup blue cheese, crumbled Salt to taste

1 Start by removing the skin from your onions. Level off the root ends so they'll rest flat. Then slice the top 1/3 off each one.

2 Using a spoon, scoop out the center of each onion to within 3 or 4 rings from the outside edge. Save the scooped out onion for the sauce.

3 Coat the onions, inside and out, with olive oil. Season with salt and white pepper. Roast, uncovered, at 400° for 35 minutes.

4 While the onions roast, make the sauce. Saute chopped onions (reserved from Step 2) in butter until they're translucent and tender.

5 Measure and add the dry white vermouth (dry white wine will work just as well). Continue to simmer until wine reduces completely.

6 Stir in heavy cream and nutmeg. Slowly thicken by reducing and stirring until it's about thickness of pancake batter. Add blue cheese.

7 Prepare fresh or frozen peas, and drain thoroughly. In a bowl, mix 1/2 cup of the vermouth cream sauce to peas, gently folding to combine.

8 Fill each roasted onion with pea mixture (about 1/2 cup). Then spoon 2 tablespoons of sauce over each. Top with chopped peanuts.

9 Return the filled onions to the oven and bake them for another 15 minutes or until the peanuts are golden. Serve them right away.

CALIFORNIA ROLLS

If you're like me, the idea of eating raw fish is still a little difficult to swallow. It's true, I like my steaks rare, but at least they're still cooked—a little. A couple of

years ago, I got trapped into going to a sushi bar (actually it was with my boss, Don, so there was no escape short of a car accident). Needless to say I was a little nervous thinking about eating raw sea urchin—I knew I wouldn't be able to keep it down.

Well, Don knew my apprehensions and had fun with me until we arrived at the sushi bar. Meanwhile, I had prepared for the evening by wearing pants with large cuffs—a perfect place for hiding sushi!

Don finally empathized with my dilemma and ordered California rolls for me—sushi "training wheels."

California rolls were created for people like me—there's no raw fish in them and all the other ingredients are familiar. So I can still experience Japanese food and culture without any apprehension—or large cuffs.

What is Sushi: "Sushi" actually refers to the rice—it's special because vinegar is added to it after it's cooked. The tangy flavor complements the subtle flavors of the foods it's with.

Rice is so important to sushi that true Japanese apprentices spend at least a year just making the rice for a restaurant. It's got to be right before a trainee can even pick up a knife.

Some people judge a sushi chef's talent by looking at the grains of rice—if they all lay in the same direction, the chef knows what he's doing.

And sushi isn't necessarily raw fish. Some sushi has smoked salmon or cooked shrimp in it. Japanese children eat "egg" sushi made with a lightly sweetened omelet. I've even seen rolls with tuna salad inside.

Sushi has been reserved as an art form performed by highly trained Japanese chefs. But now, you can just as easily do these California rolls in your own kitchen.

These rolls work for me because they're a good source of inexpensive entertainment. I have friends over and show them how to make their own dinner! They're good-looking, low in calories, and easy to make. No more sushi bar nightmares for me.

The Rolling Mat

The rolling mat is the only special piece of equipment you need for these rolls. It forms the rolls tightly which is really important when you go to cut them. A mat also shapes the rolls into uniform squares and circles.

I bought my sushi mat at an oriental market—it only cost about two bucks. A flexible bamboo placemat

▲ *I reuse my mat so I cover it with plastic wrap each time. There's no sticking when rolling and it's easy to keep clean.*

that I bought at Pier 1 worked almost as well—the slats were just a little big.

Authentic sushi mats are made of skinny bamboo slats tied together with string. They're big enough so a whole sheet of nori fits on it without going over the edges.

Before rolling sushi, I always wrap my mat with plastic to keep it clean and free of possible contamination. This is what I'm doing here at the left.

There's also the possibility the mat has been treated with a toxic stain or paint—this is especially true if it's a placemat. And besides, with the plastic surrounding the mat, the rice won't stick to it when making reverse rolls like I'm doing on page 30.

If the mat does happen to get dirty, wipe it off with a damp cloth. Just don't soak it in water because it can make the bamboo too soft for rolling.

CALIFORNIA ROLLS

(MAKES 12 UNCUT ROLLS)
WORK TIME: 40 MINUTES
COOK TIME: 20 MINUTES
PREPARE:

3 cups rice, uncooked, *see page 26*
3 cups water
6 sheets of nori, halved
3 T. wasabi, *see page 26*

SPRINKLE COOKED RICE WITH:
1/3 cup rice vinegar

TOAST:
1/4 cup white sesame seeds

COMBINE IN A SHAKER WITH:
1/4 cup black sesame seeds

CUT TO UNIFORM LENGTHS:
3 medium king crab legs
1 cucumber, peeled and seeded
1 avocado, halved, pitted and peeled

NUTRITIONAL INFORMATION PER ROLL: CALORIES 230; TOTAL FAT 7(G); CALORIES FROM FAT 29%; SODIUM 385(MG)

KNOWING YOUR INGREDIENTS: NORI AND RICE

California rolls aren't the real thing without two important ingredients: nori and rice.

Nori: Nori is the dark green stuff on the outside of the California rolls. It gives you a base to spread the rice on and then holds all the ingredients inside the roll.

Just because the nori package says seaweed, don't be afraid of it. It's got a grassy, slightly salty taste. But nori's mild flavor really accentuates the mild taste of the California rolls. *And* it's high in vitamins and minerals.

To harvest nori, nets are hung between a series of poles in shallow ocean inlets. When the tide comes in, it brings in the seaweed which clings to the nets. When the tide subsides, the seaweed is gathered and spread on straw mats to dry in the sun.

I scoped out some oriental markets to find nori. Turns out, there's a couple of kinds: toasted and untoasted. And since I couldn't read Japanese, I ended up buying both.

But they're not the same deal. Toasted nori's easier to work with and it just plain tastes better. Save yourself some trouble and buy it that way (it might say "yakinori"). If you can't find it, try a health food store or order it from **Anzen Pacific Corp., (503) 283-1284.**

If you want to toast your own, here's what to do. Using your gas range, turn a burner on high. Hold the sheet about two inches over the flame and parallel to the range top. Move it around for a few seconds until the sheet turns bright green. Toasting one side is enough.

Or you can toast nori in a dry skillet over medium-high heat until light green patches appear. But be careful—it burns easily.

Rice: The right rice *must* be used in California rolls. The obvious choice is sushi rice—it has a high starch content so it's very sticky.

When experimenting, I found that a medium-grain rice works just as well. Besides, the everyday stuff is easier to find. Just don't use a long-grain rice. There's not enough starch to keep the roll together.

The rice has to be *cooked* just right. If overcooked, it's pasty and gummy. Undercooked rice will be crunchy and won't stick together.

I went all out and bought an electric rice cooker. It made perfect rice every time. But no need for this. The stove top worked just as well.

The Japanese have three tricks for good sushi rice. First, they rinse the rice before cooking to remove excess starch which can make it mushy instead of sticky.

After cooking, they "fan" the rice to cool it. This prevents it from getting too soft, and keeps the grains separate and glossy. And finally, they add vinegar to the hot rice for a deep infused flavor.

THE INGREDIENTS

You've heard this before—prepare your ingredients ahead. Once you start rolling, you can't stop.

The rice: Rinsing rice is important, but so is the amount of cooking water. Too much can make the rice soggy and too little can cause burning.

Test the rice for doneness by using your hands like I am in Step 4. "Fan" it right away and be careful not to crush the grains when stirring.

The fillings: Most of my fillings are everyday ingredients. I use common things like carrots, cucumbers, avocado, crab, shrimp, and lobster.

The key here is that they're all fresh. Some other ingredients you might try could be raw fish, peppers, mushrooms, fresh fruits, roast beef, asparagus, or green onions.

A natural flavor that goes great with sushi is wasabi [wah-sah-bee].

It's a root similar to horseradish. This green paste really packs a punch so when rolling, use it sparingly.

Fresh wasabi is expensive and hard to find so I use a powder mixed with water. Buy wasabi at an oriental grocer the same time you buy your mat.

White sesame seeds are easy to find at any grocery store, but I ended up finding the black ones at the oriental market. They taste about the same.

MISE EN PLACE (EVERYTHING IN ITS PLACE)

1 Rub rice between hands under cold running water (like you're scrubbing a shirt). Pour off milky water and rinse until it's nearly clear.

2 Measure water depth, pressing hand flat on rice. Water should come to within an inch of your wrist. Or use 1 cup water to each cup rice.

3 Bring covered rice to a boil over high heat. Reduce to low. Cook 15 minutes. Remove from heat. Keep covered and let sit 15 more minutes.

4 Test for doneness. Water should be completely absorbed. Smear small amount of rice between fingers and look for tiny "kernel" of white.

5 Transfer rice to roaster. Drizzle with 2 T. rice vinegar. Fan to cool while stirring gently. Add remaining vinegar. Stir until cool. Cover.

6 Mix 3 T. wasabi powder with cold water until it's a thick paste and looks like guacamole. Cover with plastic and set aside.

7 Dry-toast white sesame seeds in small skillet over med. heat until golden. Stir to avoid burning. Mix with black seeds; transfer to shaker.

8 Slice cucumber, crab and avocado into slender, uniform pieces. Brush avocado with lemon juice to prevent browning.

9 Fold nori sheets in half along the "grain." Then crease with your fingers. Open and gently tear apart. Notice the rough and smooth sides.

GETTING READY TO ROLL

Make a few practice rolls using just cucumber. There'll be a big difference between your first and second roll.

Working the Rice: Dip your hands in a bowl of ice water while you work with the rice. It'll help keep the sticky rice off your hands—like dusting your hands with flour when baking. But don't get them too wet. The water can make the rice and nori soggy.

Take a look at the nori sheets. There's a rough side and a smooth side. Spread the rice on the rough side—it sticks to it the best.

When you spread out the rice, leave a 1" strip of nori at the top. This is what you'll use to seal the roll.

Now, look at step 13. See how I'm "pulling" the rice to the bottom of the sheet? It's a little awkward—just keep your hand damp. Make sure you spread the rice evenly.

Rolling: Add your fillings and line up the nori at the bottom of the mat. Notice on step 16 that I'm lifting the mat up with my thumbs and holding the fillings in place with my fingers. Roll that bottom edge into the middle, coming over the fillings.

Tuck it in tightly, rolling to the end. The tighter the roll, the easier it will be to cut. Dampen your finger and run it along the nori flap to seal.

Shaping: I'm making square rolls here. The bamboo mat really helps with this. Put a lot of pressure on the roll in Step 17 to get it a tight square.

It's not the end of the world if the roll is uneven—keep reshaping it.

PUTTING IT ALL TOGETHER

10 Lay half sheet of nori on mat, rough side up with a long side toward you. Lightly moisten hands with ice water.

11 Form about ½ cup rice into a log in one hand. Place on upper left side of nori, leaving 1 inch at top. Spread rice across nori.

12 Moisten hands again and evenly pat out rice across nori. Wet hands as needed to keep rice from sticking to them.

13 Secure nori in place with one hand. With other hand, "pull" rice down to bottom edge of the sheet. Fill any holes with more rice.

14 Spread about ¾ tsp. wasabi in a thin stripe down center of rice. Sprinkle rice with sesame seed mixture.

15 Lay fillings across wasabi in single rows. Use small pieces to fill in middle. Leave fillings sticking out both ends.

ROLLING

16 Begin rolling, lifting mat with thumbs. Hold fillings in place with fingers; roll top over them. Roll tightly to the end.

17 Firmly press and squeeze roll into square shape. Use mat to help you. Get roll as tight as possible without tearing the nori.

18 Unroll the mat and check for uneven areas. Reposition the mat and reshape as needed. Set aside for 5 mins. before cutting.

MAKING THE CUTS

The nori gets soft and chewy after a while making it hard to cut. So don't even *think* about trying this with a dull knife. And a serrated knife pulls out the rice and shreds the edges of the nori. A sharp blade is the ticket.

For a clean cut, dip the knife blade in cold water each time. Wipe off any excess water and residue with a towel.

The trick for a smooth cut is using a swift, deliberate stroke. First, lightly score the nori to make an initial cut. The nori tends to be a little tough.

Now aggressively cut all the way through the roll. Don't be wimpy—try to use one slice in one direction. Just don't use a sawing motion.

I use three basic cuts: end, straight and diagonal. You can make some interesting arrangements with them.

It takes practice to get even pieces. I got pretty frustrated at first because the pieces were so uneven—you will, too. I just ended up being a little more creative in my presentation.

END CUT

▲ *Wet and wipe knife blade. Measure in about 1" from the edge of the nori. Score and cut through.*

▲ *Wet and wipe knife again. Line up the cut end with the other end. Score; cut through. Set pair aside.*

STRAIGHT CUT

▲ *Wet and wipe knife again. Score and cut through the middle of remaining roll.*

▲ *Wet and wipe knife. Line up remaining two pieces. Score and cut in half.*

DIAGONAL CUT

▲ *After making end cuts, wet and wipe knife. Position at a 45° angle. Score and cut through as before.*

▲ *Line up the angled piece "back-to-back" with the other, as shown. Wet and wipe knife, then score and cut.*

▲ *Wet and wipe knife again. Score and cut the remaining piece in half. Serve rolls within 1–2 hrs. of cutting.*

PRESENTATION

The Japanese are artists when it comes to presenting food. Simple plates and garnishes let the food speak for itself.

Presentation displays their reverence for nature. Balance and order are most important, yet nothing can look staged.

Japanese food and presentation reflect their philosophy of conflicting extremes—ying and yang. They believe in a natural tension. Crunchy and soft, hot and cool, sweet and sour. Analyze the presentation on the right. Hot wasabi and cool rolls, toasted sesame seed with soft rice, soft avocado paired with crisp cucumbers. These round rolls are presented on a square plate. Are you getting the idea?

DIPPING SAUCES

You won't find these dipping sauces on a Japanese table—their sauces are simpler. One of my favorite true Japanese sauces is simply mixing soy sauce with wasabi—try it.

It only takes a few minutes to put these other sauces together. Leave them at room temperature until you're ready to serve them. You know how soup gets better after it sits for a while? Same thing here—in a couple of days, they're even better! They make a great marinade for meats and poultry.

SPICY SOY SAUCE

COMBINE:

$1/4$	cup water
3	T. soy sauce
3	T. green onion, minced
$1^1/2$	T. rice vinegar
$1^1/2$	T. sesame oil
1	t. sugar
$3/4$	t. Tabasco sauce

PINK PEPPERCORN SAUCE

COMBINE:

3	T. soy sauce
3	T. water
1	T. sesame oil
1	T. seasoned rice vinegar
1	T. minced green onion
2	t. sugar
2	t. chili paste, *see glossary*
1	t. minced ginger
1	t. minced garlic
1	t. crushed pink peppercorns

SWEET AND SOUR SAUCE

COMBINE:

$3/4$	cup seasoned rice vinegar
$2/3$	cup water
$1/4$	cup sugar
$1/4$	cup packed light brown sugar
2	T. dry sherry
2	T. lime juice, strained
2	cloves garlic, minced
1	t. chili paste

HOISIN–SOY SAUCE

COMBINE:

$1/4$	cup water
3	T. brown sugar
2	T. soy sauce
2	T. lime juice, strained
1	T. hoisin sauce, *see glossary*
1	T. dry sherry
1	t. chili paste
2	cloves garlic, minced

HOW TO USE CHOPSTICKS

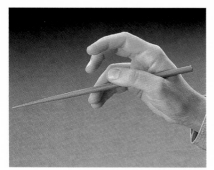

▲ Rest the bottom chopstick firmly in the "crook" of your thumb, pressing it against your ring finger, about $2/3$ from the top of the stick.

▲ Hold the top stick between your thumb, index and middle fingers, like it's a pencil. Practice moving it up and down.

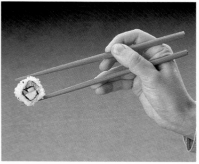

▲ Moving only the top stick, pick up food. Keep bottom stick steady, maintaining pressure with your thumb and ring finger. If this fails, spear it!

PHILADELPHIA ROLL

(MAKES 12 UNCUT ROLLS)
Prepare Rice, Nori, Wasabi and Sesame Seeds, see page 26.

CUT TO UNIFORM LENGTHS:
1   cucumber, peeled and seeded
1   8 oz. package cream cheese
6   oz. smoked salmon

NUTRITIONAL INFORMATION PER ROLL:
CALORIES 263; TOTAL FAT 12(G); CALORIES FROM FAT 40%; SODIUM 363(MG)

This is the roll I talked about earlier when I said the rice was on the outside and the nori was rolled inside. You've already learned the steps—they're just "inside-out!"

There's one difference: spread the rice completely over the nori and don't leave a strip at the top. The sticky rice makes its own seal.

Once you've got the rice spread out over the entire sheet of nori, gently flip everything over so the rice is on the bottom.

1 Slice cream cheese into slender sticks. Trim smoked salmon into thinner pieces, if necessary.

2 Spread rice over nori, sprinkle with seeds and flip over. Add wasabi and fillings. Roll as before.

MANHATTAN ROLL

(MAKES 12 UNCUT ROLLS)
Prepare Rice, Nori, Wasabi and Sesame Seeds, see page 26.

CUT TO UNIFORM LENGTHS:
3   medium king crab legs
1   cucumber, peeled and seeded
1   avocado, halved, pitted and
     peeled
OVER EACH ROLL, SPREAD:
2   T. tobiko (flying fish roe)

NUTRITIONAL INFORMATION PER ROLL:
CALORIES 283; TOTAL FAT 10(G); CALORIES FROM FAT 31%; SODIUM 419(MG)

The orange stuff on this roll is tobiko [toe-bee-ko], or flying fish roe. It's much drier and smaller than some other fish roe. It's also less salty and fishy tasting.

Check your fish market or oriental grocer before calling **Anzen Pacific Corp., (503) 283-1284** to mail-order it in.

1 Spread rice on nori, covering completely. Gently spread tobiko over rice. Sprinkle with sesame seeds.

2 Carefully flip nori over so rice is on the bottom. Spread wasabi on nori, add fillings and roll.

"HAM 'N GREENS" ROLL
(MAKES 10 UNCUT ROLLS)
Prepare Rice, Wasabi and Sesame Seeds, see page 26.

BLANCH:
20   large collard leaves, stemmed
20   asparagus spears
PREPARE:
$^1/_2$ lb. thinly sliced deli ham, cut into $1^1/_2$" ribbons
2   medium carrots, julienned

NUTRITIONAL INFORMATION PER ROLL:
CALORIES 242; TOTAL FAT 6(G);
CALORIES FROM FAT 22%; SODIUM 295(MG)

OK, for all you landlubbers. You like the concept of California rolls, but seafood isn't your bag. Try using collard greens (or any large, sturdy green) instead of nori. Blanch it but *not* to that "army green" stage. Then place the asparagus and ham on the rice. This really works great.

1 Blanch large leaves in boiling salted water, about 2 mins. Plunge in ice water and drain on towels.

2 Lay leaves on mat in opposite directions. Make as square as possible. Add fillings and roll.

SHRIMP ROLL
(MAKES 12 UNCUT ROLLS)
Prepare Rice, Nori, Wasabi and Sesame Seeds, see page 26.

SKEWER, BROIL, THEN HALVE:
1   lb. (16–20) shrimp, peeled and deveined
CUT TO UNIFORM LENGTHS:
1   medium carrot, julienned
1   avocado, halved, pitted and peeled

NUTRITIONAL INFORMATION PER ROLL:
CALORIES 224; TOTAL FAT 7(G);
CALORIES FROM FAT 29%; SODIUM 89(MG)

Shrimp (lobster, too) make a good substitute for crab. What I like most about the shrimp is that you can add a unique, extra flavor by grilling or broiling them. And I didn't have to use too many since I split them down the center. Carrots worked especially well here because of their crunch and color.

1 Skewer shrimp from head through to tail. Broil until pink and cooked through, about 5 mins.

2 Remove skewers and cut shrimp in half lengthwise. Proceed with rolling as you've done before.

Wares

I've never been more brutal on a group of products than I was on these food processors—by the time I got done, the test kitchen was littered with broken and burnt-up

machines. Now, don't get the wrong idea—I didn't ask the machines to do anything their manufacturers said they couldn't handle. But you need to look at a food processor as a work-horse in your kitchen, and only the strong are gonna survive.

When the smoke cleared after my testing (literally!), three machines stood head and shoulders above the rest—still going strong.

Out of those three, I picked a "best of the best"—the Cuisinart. It's my personal favorite, and I'll tell you why in a minute.

But I want you to rest assured—all three of these are strong machines that'll *definitely* do the job.

Why Get One? A food processor can do an awful lot for you, like chopping, mincing, pureeing, slicing, and making emulsified sauces. On some of those jobs *nothing* works better.

Then there's speed and convenience. When I'm in a hurry or working with large amounts, my food processor is almost indispensable—it blazes right through a lot of jobs that are way too tedious and time-consuming to do by hand. And clean-up is pretty much confined to your work bowl and blade. Let's face it, for most of us—this is a tool you gotta have!

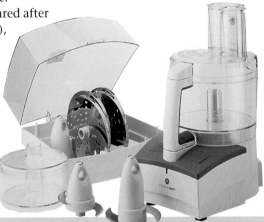 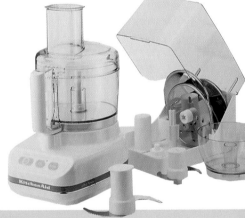

BRAND & MODEL	KITCHENTOOLS FPKT 800	KITCHENAID ULTRA POWER KFP600
WE PAID	$199.00	$199.00
SIZE OF BOWL	9 cups	11 cups
EASE OF USE	The easiest machine to use and clean	Very easy to use and clean—no problems
USEFUL ACCESSORIES	Accessory storage case, discs for grating, thin-, medium-, and thick-slicing, fine and coarse shredding, mini-bowl, dough blade	Accessory storage case with discs for thin- and medium-slicing, fine and medium shredding, mini-bowl, dough blade
WARRANTY	Full 5-year; mfr. repair or replace	Full 1-year total replacement
COMMENTS	This processor absolutely blew me away—it is *so* well thought-out! The KitchenTools line-up is brand new from Black & Decker, and all I can say is: Keep up the good work! The blades are easy and safe to use, and this thing is quiet, smooth, and powerful.	I can speak from experience about this KitchenAid—I've been using one (and loving it) for years. I was even more impressed when I got this new one, because they fixed a *tiny* problem (the cap on the blade). They really didn't have to fix it—that's class!

WHAT TO LOOK FOR

Here's what you want in a processor.

Size: To gauge size, look at the volume of the workbowl. Anywhere from 9–11 cups is a good all-around range. Smaller bowls won't do you any good when you're slicing or shredding large amounts of food—you have to keep stopping and emptying out the bowl. Bigger bowls work fine—it's just that they're usually overkill for me.

Ease of Use: If a machine's tough to figure out, use, and clean, it's gonna wind up at a garage sale some day. Go for a simple design like my three—no extra buttons, spindles, and chutes.

Two things not to get hung-up on—huge feedtubes (the chute on the lid) and lots of speeds. All you need is one speed plus pulse (quick on/off). And yes, big feedtubes *can* be nice, but don't pick a machine just for that!

Accessories: My picks come with enough accessories to do everything you need—you get different discs for slicing and shredding, plus dough blades. Two manufacturers give you a storage case and small workbowl.

Now, lots of accessories are nice, but don't get seduced by them—you're after performance. Get the right machine, *then* worry about what accessories it comes with. You can always buy more stuff—you *don't* want to buy another machine.

Power: As for power, forget any numbers. (I didn't even put them in my chart.) In testing, *supposedly* less-powerful motors (in amps) sometimes outperformed more-powerful ones. Just take this to the bank: My three picks test out (on real food) *tons* more powerful than the competition.

Heavy-duty Construction: I tested both cheaper *and* more expensive machines than my three—none were as heavy-duty. These guys weigh more, are more stable and solid, and are quieter. And my picks all have an automatic shut off to keep the motor from burning up if it gets overworked.

I like the motor to be mounted *under* the workbowl (not to the side)—for power, efficiency, and less noise. A workbowl should be *thick*—compare, and you'll really see a difference.

Good Blades and Discs: You can learn all you need to know about blades and discs just by looking at the food when you're done processing it!

If your discs and blades are up to snuff, the food'll be pureed, chopped, or shredded *evenly*—without a bunch left plastered on the sides of the bowl!

Safety: The safety feature I really want to see (and what all my picks have) is a switch that keeps the motor from running unless the lid is locked into place. This is to keep hands and fingers out of harm's way. But be careful—these boys can still be dangerous.

Warranty: You're plunking down a couple C-notes here to get something that'll last. The manufacturer better back your investment. A full one-year warranty is *minimum* for me.

Cuisinart
This machine won my heart—you're looking at a true champion!

CUISINART PRO CUSTOM 11

$199.00

11 cups

A little tougher to use and clean

Discs for thin- and medium-slicing, a shredding disc, dough blade, and compact (no feedtube) cover

Full 3-yr., 5-yr. motor; repair or replace

This champ is a go-to machine that'll do everything you ask of it. There's no frills here, but that's all right—smooth, rock-solid performance is reward enough for me. This is one machine I couldn't bring to its knees.

THE BOTTOM LINE

There's plenty of good reasons for picking any one of these three machines. But at the end of the day, I'd go with Cuisinart.

Like I told you before, my testing was aggressive. And the toughest thing I asked these machines to do was to knead bread dough. (To tell you the truth, I never use a food processor for bread—your hands and/or stand mixer do a much better job. But what test material!)

All three of my picks gutted-out the kneading test, but the Cuisinart was the strongest—even though its motor was rated in amps as *smaller* than the other two! (See what I mean about numbers?) That kind of power performance makes me think this baby will be around for a long, long time. Plus, the smoothness of its pureeing, slicing, and shredding was simply unbeatable.

I've got one small reservation, though. (Or else I'd just be giving you one machine, not three!)

Cuisinart gives you the very biggest feedtube. This is both good and bad. You can stuff more through it, but it's *so* big they also had to make it safe (a hand could fit in). In the process, they made it much more complicated to use and clean than any other feedtube.

They do give you an extra cover *without* the feedtube for things like chopping—where you don't need a feedtube. It's much easier to use and clean. But one cover should've been enough. Instead of two, I'd rather have more discs and/or accessory case!

3 SEAFOOD SALADS

Hotter weather brings on the need for cooler foods. So I thought that main course seafood salads would solve several problems like lower caloric intake, good taste

and visual appeal. And finally, plating up a meal that could be eaten at either lunch or dinner.

Seafood: I chose seafood because it's in season and can be served either hot or cold. With these salads though, I do try to serve the seafood at least somewhat warm so I get the hot and cold contrast that I find so appealing in salads. Actually, I find *any* contrast interesting in all courses.

You'll notice that I used bitter salad greens. Again, I like the contrast I found between the naturally sweet seafood and the sharper greens.

Salad Dressing: One of the other things I did on these salads was to take common dressings and jazz them up a little. I did this intentionally to show that it's OK (and trendy) for you to move out of the normal range.

On two of the salads, I started with a pretty basic vinaigrette and then added a dominant flavor like avocado or roasted tomatoes. This not only added flavor but also lots of color.

The intense tomato and avocado pulp did one other thing that was a pleasant surprise—it acted as an emulsifier to help join the oil and vinegar.

TUNA AND ITALIAN WHITE BEAN SALAD

(MAKES 4 SALADS)
WORK TIME: 2 HOURS
COOK TIME: 1 HOUR (BEANS & TUNA)

ROAST:
8   Roma tomatoes, sliced $1/2$" thick

FOR WHITE BEANS, COMBINE:
1   lb. dried white beans, rinsed
3   cups chicken stock
$3/4$ cup diced onion
$1/2$ cup white wine
4   cloves garlic, minced
1   bundle fresh thyme ($1/3$ cup)

FOR WHITE BEAN MARINADE, COMBINE:
$1/2$ cup white wine vinegar
$1/4$ cup extra virgin olive oil
2   T. fresh thyme leaves
$1/2$ t. salt
$1/2$ t. black pepper

TOSS WITH WHITE BEANS:
$1^1/2$ cups diced roasted tomatoes
$1/2$ cup thinly sliced red onion

FOR TOMATO VINAIGRETTE, PULSE:
$1^1/2$ cups roasted tomatoes
$1/2$ cup extra virgin olive oil
$1/4$ cup red wine vinegar
2   T. fresh thyme leaves
1   T. tomato paste
5   cloves roasted garlic
1   shallot, diced (3 T.)
$1/2$ t. salt
$1/4$ t. pepper

SEAR IN SAUTE PAN:
1   1 lb. tuna steak
    Cracked black pepper
    Extra virgin olive oil

ARRANGE ON EACH PLATE:
4   radicchio leaves
4–6 arugula leaves

NUTRITIONAL INFORMATION PER SERVING:
CALORIES 1,016; TOTAL FAT 47(G);
CALORIES FROM FAT 40%; SODIUM 225(MG)

1 Slice Roma tomatoes ¹/₂" thick. Place on a rack on a baking sheet and roast slowly at 300° for 2 hours. This intensifies the tomato flavor.

2 Combine beans, stock, onions, white wine, garlic, thyme. Cook 45 minutes or until tender. Drain and remove thyme. Rinse to remove starch.

3 Whisk together vinegar, olive oil, thyme, salt and pepper. Pour ¹/₃ cup over warm beans. Infusing beans while warm enhances flavor. Cool.

4 Dice 1¹/₂ cups (half) of roasted tomatoes and *thinly* slice ¹/₂ cup of red onion. Add this to the cooled bean mixture and set aside.

5 In a processor, pulse remaining roasted tomatoes, olive oil, red wine vinegar, thyme, paste, garlic, shallot, salt and pepper till smooth.

6 Lightly coat tuna with olive oil. Press *cracked* black pepper into both sides. Sear tuna (turn once) in *hot* pan—a minute per side for rare.

7 On a serving plate, layer the radicchio and arugula leaves. Arrange them like the petals of a flower. This is the base of the salad.

8 Now you can begin to assemble the salad. Mound portions of the marinated bean mixture in the center of the radicchio and arugula leaves.

9 Like a piece of meat, wait to slice the tuna just before serving. Then slice it "across the grain." This way you'll get long strips instead of chunks.

10 Using your knife as a spatula, slide 3 slices of tuna off the blade and into position on top of the beans. Arrange "criss-cross" fashion.

11 Top the tuna with the roasted tomato vinaigrette you made in step 5. Let it "river" onto the beans. Don't cover up all the tuna and beans.

12 Drizzle radicchio and arugula with vinaigrette (remaining bean marinade). Then sprinkle salad with cracked black pepper.

MARGARITA SHRIMP SALAD *(SERVES 4–6)*

WORK TIME: 45 MINUTES
COOK TIME: 20 MINUTES

FOR THE SHRIMP, MARINATE:
1	lb.	shrimp (size 16–20)
1	cup	lime juice
1/2	cup	white tequila
2	T.	Triple Sec
1	T.	red pepper flakes
1	t.	kosher salt

FOR SALAD, TOSS TOGETHER:
1	cup	roasted red pepper, diced
1	cup	roasted yellow pepper, diced
1	cup	roasted corn kernels
1	cup	tomato, chopped, seeded
1	cup	canned black beans, rinsed
2/3	cup	red onion, thinly sliced
1/4	cup	chopped cilantro leaves
1	T.	jalapeno, seeded & minced

FOR VINAIGRETTE, BLEND:
1 1/4	cups	light olive oil
1/2	cup	white wine vinegar
1/4	cup	lime juice
1/4	cup	cilantro leaves
1/2	t.	salt
1/8	t.	cayenne pepper
1		avocado, roughly diced

DIP GLASS RIM IN:
Lime juice
Finely chopped cilantro

GARNISH WITH: Baked tortilla strips

PREPARING THE MARGARITA SHRIMP SALAD

1 Mix marinade. Peel and devein shrimp (including tail). Leave tail shells *only* when shrimp is eaten with fingers. Marinate shrimp 1/2 hour.

2 Roast the corn and peppers. Do this on the grill or under broiler. Slice corn from the cob and peel the charred skins from the peppers.

3 Dice the roasted peppers and mix them in bowl together with the corn, tomatoes, black beans, onion, cilantro, and minced jalapeno.

4 For vinaigrette, blend ingredients in processor (except avocado). Add avocado. Pulse just until blended—too much will make it turn oily.

5 Remove shrimp from marinade and grill (you can also saute them). Add hot shrimp to roasted mixture. Toss with 1/2 cup avocado vinaigrette.

6 Dip the glass rim in lime juice and then into *minced* cilantro. Spoon salad into glass. Garnish with baked tortilla strips, lime slice and cilantro.

SCALLOP AND SPINACH SALAD WITH WARM BACON DRESSING (SERVES 4)

WORK TIME: 30 MINUTES
COOK TIME: 15 MINUTES

SAUTE:
1/2 lb. bacon, finely diced

DEGLAZE PAN WITH:
8 oz. white balsamic vinegar

ADD:
1 T. lime juice
1 T. sugar
    Reserved bacon grease
    Cooked bacon
1 t. cracked black pepper

SAUTE IN OLIVE OIL:
24 sea scallops, dusted in flour
1 T. garlic, minced

DEGLAZE PAN WITH:
1/4 cup white balsamic vinegar

HOLLOW CENTER OF:
4 small red potatoes, cooked

ARRANGE ON EACH PLATE:
2 avocado halves, fanned
    Spinach, washed and trimmed

ADD TO EACH PLATE:
6 pink grapefruit sections
4 slices smoked salmon, rolled

FILL EACH POTATO WITH:
    Mixed baby greens and herbs

DRIZZLE SCALLOPS AND SALAD WITH:
    Warm bacon dressing

PREPARING THE SCALLOP AND SPINACH SALAD

1 For dressing, dice and saute bacon. Reserve grease. Deglaze with vinegar. Add lime juice, sugar, grease, bacon, back to pan. Simmer 5 mins.

2 Dust scallops with flour. Saute in a *little* oil over high heat until golden. Remove. Add garlic and deglaze with vinegar. Pour glaze over scallops.

3 Make vase from cored, cooked potato. Scoop out avocado halves and cut to fan. Brush fans with lime juice. Arrange fresh spinach on plate.

4 Place the fanned avocado halves at 12 and 6 o'clock. Then place grapefruit sections at 9 and 3. Put the potato vase in the center.

5 Roll smoked salmon and tuck next to vase. Bundle some fresh baby lettuces and herbs together. Insert the bouquet into potato vase.

6 Finally, add warm scallops to the salad so that they trail out from the potato vase. Lightly coat scallops and salad with warm bacon dressing.

Q *My springform pan leaked when I made the Chocolate Espresso Torte in Issue 8. Do I just have a cheap pan?*

A I used a Kaiser La Forme springform pan in my tests and never had a problem. Since then, I've heard from a couple of readers whose pans leaked. Sorry! But don't worry, you don't have to get a whole new pan.

First, make sure the bottom's in the pan right. It's easy to get it in wrong. Once you're sure it's put together right, test it in some water. If it leaks, use *extra-wide* foil to make a waterproof cup around your pan when you bake in a water bath.

Q *There's all kinds of plastic wrap available. Some stick, some don't—what's the difference? And will any cling to metal?*

A Depending on what I'm using it for, I look for a couple of things in a plastic wrap— cling and durability.

Differences in cling and durability are caused by different kinds of plastic. Saran (polyvinylene chloride) doesn't cling well, but it's the strongest. It'll hold up to a pounding. Reynolds (polyvinyl chloride) clings the best and is the next strongest. Lower-priced wraps (polyethylene) cling OK, but they're thin and tear easily.

There's no plastic wrap on the market that clings to metal, plastic, or wood. It would cost so much to make, it'd put us all in Chapter 11 to buy it!

Q *Can I omit bay leaves in my cooking? These fragrantless leaves don't seem to do much.*

A *Don't* omit. You'll be missing out. Bay is unique— almost minty. Sounds like your leaves are just too old. All dried bay leaves *look* old—they're pale green and brittle. But you should still be able to smell them.

Dried bay leaves will keep a year. If you're not sure how old yours are, test one by breaking it in half. If you can't smell it, you need some new bay leaves.

There's two kinds of bay: Turkish and California. Some people prefer Turkish bay while others like California bay—it's stronger and more pungent, so you might only need to use half a leaf.

Q *My friend told me that pine nuts come from a pine cone. Is she right?*

A Pine nuts *do* come from pine cones. They're so expensive (over $1 an ounce) because they have to be extracted from the cone and their individual shells.

Out of a hundred varieties of pine trees, only about a dozen produce nuts good enough to eat. Most of the ones available in the U.S. are imported—from Europe or Asia.

Spanish and Portuguese nuts are oblong. They have a soft texture and their flavor is very

good, but it's mild—strong-tasting foods can hide their flavor. These are the prettiest pine nuts, and probably the hardest to find—I got some from a local Italian specialty store.

Pakistani nuts (shown) are longer than the Spanish ones. Their flavor is stronger and more oily, and the texture is a little crunchier.

Chinese nuts are triangular, like candy corn, with a brown tip. The flavor is strong, and they're more roasted-tasting and crunchy than all the other pine nuts.

I've found both Pakistani and Chinese nuts in a local grocery store—usually hidden away in the gourmet section.

Q&A

We'll find answers to your cooking questions, and help find solutions to the unique problems which occur in the kitchen. Any questions? Send your cooking questions to *Cuisine, Q & A Editor,* 2200 Grand Avenue, Des Moines, IA 50312, or contact us through our E-mail address: *Cuisine@cuisinemag.com*

Q *I'm curious about something... is orzo a rice or a pasta? How about couscous? It looks like a grain.*

A Yeah, orzo (left) does look like rice, but it's a pasta. It's usually used in soups, but don't let that stop you. Orzo is a great substitute for rice in most dishes, too.

Couscous (right) looks like a grain, but it's really pasta, too. Italy doesn't have a monopoly on pasta—this one's from northern Africa. It's traditionally made by hand from semolina

Q *In Issue 7, you credited images of mace and nutmeg to Penzey's, Ltd. How do I contact them to obtain a catalog?*

A You can call (414) 574-0277. Or, mail your request for a catalog to:

Penzey's, Ltd.
Post Office Box 1448
Waukesha, Wisconsin 53187

Q *Do I really need both candy and deep fry thermometers? Can one be used in place of the other?*

A You only need one thermometer for both candy making and deep frying, as long as you get the *right* thermometer.

The important temperature ranges for candy and deep frying are different. For candy, the range is from 230° to 310°. For deep frying, it's 335° to 375°.

But that's not a problem. You just have to make sure your thermometer's temperature range includes both. Taylor makes deep fry/candy ther-

(that's a coarse yellow flour made from hard wheats). Semolina is dampened and rolled in flour to make tiny beads. These beads are couscous. They can be eaten like rice, or added to soups or salads.

Traditionally, couscous is steamed in the perforated top of a special pot called a couscoussier. Its design is similar to a pasta pot. Meat, vegetables, and spices simmer in the bottom part of the pan. The steam cooks the couscous on top. If you feel like shelling out some bucks for a real couscoussier, give Bridge Kitchenware a call, (800) 274-3435. An 11-quart couscoussier goes for about $140.

Couscous is available in U.S. grocery stores. Just prepare as directed. It couldn't be easier!

Q *In your biscuit recipe in Issue 8, you use self-rising flour and add baking powder and soda. Aren't these in the flour already?*

A Self-rising flour does already have baking powder and salt. Traditional biscuit recipes call for just self-rising flour—no additional soda or powder.

I tried it that way first, and it was OK. But I found that adding baking soda and more baking powder gave me a biscuit that was even lighter, higher, and just plain tasted better.

mometers that are intended for both, and have a range of 100° to 400°.

Candy/deep fry thermometers are available as both mercury and dial. I'll go with mercury every time—it's more accurate than a dial.

Sure, dial thermometers are convenient to use and clean, but they work with a spring and can be off by as much as 8° to 10°. That's especially unacceptable when you're working with something as touchy as candy.

GLOSSARY

Chiffonade: [shihf-uh-NAHD] A French phrase meaning "made of rags." It refers to thin strips or shreds of vegetables and herbs. Several leaves are stacked together and rolled tightly like a cigar. Thin slices are made across the roll.

Chili Paste: A spicy Asian condiment used to season sauces, soups and marinades. Ingredients vary, but the type I use is made from red chili peppers, garlic, vinegar and salt. Most Asian markets and some supermarkets carry it.

Deglaze: After sauteing (usually meats), food and fat is removed and a small amount of liquid is added and stirred to loosen flavorful particles stuck to the bottom of the pan. This makes a great base for a sauce.

Devein: To remove the dark brownish-black vein that runs down the back of a shrimp. It's really the intestinal tract. In small shrimp it can be eaten, but in large shrimp it contains grit that should be removed.

Hoisin Sauce: [HOY-sihn] A thick reddish-brown, sweet and spicy sauce made from garlic, soybeans, chilies, and various spices. Used as a condiment and flavoring agent.

Neufchatel cheese: American neufchatel [noo-shuh-TELL] cheese is slightly lower in calories than cream cheese and contains more moisture.

Japanese Rice Vinegar: A light, sweet vinegar made from fermented rice. *Seasoned rice vinegar* is even sweeter, but you can add sugar to the unseasoned type for a substitute.

Triple Sec: A strong, clear orange-flavored liqueur.

ABBREVIATIONS

t. = teaspoon
T., Tbsp. = tablespoon
oz. = ounce
lb. = pound
Pinch = $1/16$ of a teaspoon
Dash = scant $1/8$ of a teaspoon

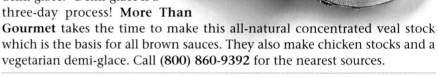

DEMI-GLACE GOLD® ►

Remember this demi-glace from the Premier Issue? It's so good, it's worth mentioning again. I hate cooking shows when the chef says "now just add some demi-glace." Demi-glace is a three-day process! **More Than Gourmet** takes the time to make this all-natural concentrated veal stock which is the basis for all brown sauces. They also make chicken stocks and a vegetarian demi-glace. Call **(800) 860-9392** for the nearest sources.

CARAMEL SAUCES ►

I had this by accident one night. It was so good, I immediately wanted to tell you about it. **The King's Cupboard®** devotes all its time to making 10 great dessert sauces. Take your pick of chocolate and caramel flavors like Cream Caramel, Raspberry Caramel, Bittersweet Chocolate, Mint Chocolate, and Espresso Chocolate.

These dessert sauces have ingredients you can pronounce—no colors or preservatives. Call **(406) 446-3060** to order or to find nearest retailer.

▲ MISTO™ OIL SPRAYER

With the **Misto Oil Sprayer**, you can use any kind of oil you want! You can use your own extra virgin olive oil instead of settling for those flavored nonstick sprays available in stores. No more chemicals—just pure oil!

The Misto sprayer is refillable. It has a non-aerosol pump so you can manually build up pressure. The oil releases in a fine, even spray. Great for grilling, roasting, and basting without the hassle of a brush.

The Misto sprayer is available in either aluminum or stainless steel and holds 3 ounces of oil. To order, call **Sur La Table** at **(800) 243-0853**. Aluminum (Item #18073, $19.95), stainless steel (Item #18354, $24.95).

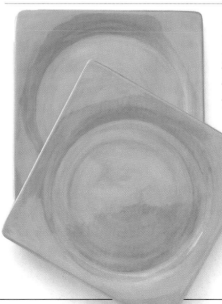

◄ DESIGNER PLATES

Los Angeles Pottery carries some great products from **Laurie Gates Designs**. These plates are one of my favorites. They put me in the mood for summer! The sunny yellow brightens any table, and the square shape is a lot of fun. I just had to use one for the Stacked Eggplant Salad, page 17.

Each plate is handmade, from the square shape to the application of the glaze. They measure $10^1/2$" square—great as chargers or serving plates. Oven, microwave, and dishwasher safe. Call **Sur La Table** to order, **(800) 243-0852**. Item #15535, $19.95.

NEW YORK CHEESECAKE

I can't tell you the number of times I've heard customers ask waiters "Is this real New York cheesecake?" I've had New York cheesecake plenty of times and it's definitely a

legitimate question. But if you're not in New York, it's almost impossible to find the real deal. There seems to be nothing like it in the world.

That was my mission—to make a *real* New York cheesecake. Where did I begin? Well, I first imported 10 different cheesecakes from New York and then sampled each one—tough job!

Then I started experimenting until I matched the best qualities of each one. Here's what I found out.

Filling: The "soul" of New York cheesecake is its filling. There are three characteristics that make good filling.

First, it has to be dense. Most cheesecakes don't come close to being this heavy. You don't use a lot of extra egg whites or lighter "wimpy" cheeses.

Second, because of the large amount of cheese used, it's tangy. You don't have to use a lot of sugar.

Finally, it has to be that "stick to the roof of your mouth" buttery.

Don't even think about the diet here. Just cut a smaller piece.

Just for fun, I tried to find fancy cream cheeses thinking it would add a lot of character—you know, organics, and ones with no preservatives, waxes or gelatins. It ended up that good old Philadelphia® brand was best.

And if you use low-fat Neufchatel, don't be writing me letters saying your cheesecake wasn't great. It needs fat!

Crust: Some have 'em—some don't. I just happen to prefer a crust. So I took the liberty of making one with a little twist—toasted pecans. It's not too complicated or too sweet.

Topping: Actually, not many New York cheesecakes are topped with anything. They are what they are.

So I left mine alone. Almost. I couldn't help adding some fresh berries with a super-simple raspberry and red wine sauce on the back cover. After all, it's almost summer.

Here's my version. And you know what? This cake could find a place in the "Big Apple" just fine.

THE CRUST

Like I said, crust is a matter of preference. Some die-hard New Yorkers wouldn't dream of sinking a fork in a piece of cheesecake with one. And others like their crust to come all the way up the sides.

So I took the safe road and walked the fence. I used a pecan crust on the bottom and a dusting (mainly for looks) of pecans on the sides.

This isn't a wimpy cheesecake. So the toasted pecan crust is bold enough in both texture and flavor to stand up to this flavorful cake. The other crusts just couldn't stand up.

NEW YORK CHEESECAKE

(MAKES 1- 8 INCH CAKE)
WORK TIME: 1 HOUR
COOK TIME: 2–2^1/$_4$ HOURS

COMBINE; RESERVE 2 T:
1   cup graham cracker crumbs
^{1}/$_2$ cup finely chopped toasted pecans

ADD; PRESS INTO BOTTOM OF PAN:
^{1}/$_4$ cup melted unsalted butter
3   T. sugar

CREAM TOGETHER:
7   pkgs. (8 oz. each) Philadelphia® cream cheese, softened
1   cup sugar
1   T. vanilla

ADD ONE AT A TIME:
4   eggs

BLEND IN:
^{1}/$_2$ cup sour cream

BAKE AT 300°.

CAKE PANS

If there's one similarity in all the New York cheesecakes I sampled, it was the height. You know what height can do to a dish—wham! This New York cheesecake should be sky-scraper high!

If you've made cheesecake in the past, you more than likely used a springform pan so you could remove the cake easily. But we're making a New York cheesecake and all the springform pans I could find just didn't have tall enough sides. Besides, they were all too wide (9 or 10 inches across). I wanted plenty of height with a smaller diameter.

My cake pan is basic but special, too. It's 8 inches across and a whopping 3 inches high! And there's no way this baby will leak in a water bath with this solid bottom.

But if you do use a springform pan (10x2^1/$_2$"), *make sure* the bottom fits tightly. Then wrap wide, heavy-duty foil around the bottom and up the sides to prevent water from penetrating into the cake. I bought both these pans from **Sur La Table**, (800) 243–0852.

PREPARING THE CRUST

1 Preheat oven to 350°. Toast pecans on baking sheet for 15 min., or until golden. Cool. Reduce oven temperature to 300°.

2 Grind cracker crumbs and pecans in food processor until fine. Set aside 2 T. Add butter and sugar to processor. Pulse to blend.

3 Spray sides and bottom of cake pan with Pam®. Trace and cut out round of parchment to fit pan. Line bottom with parchment circle.

4 Spray parchment and sides again. Make sure the pan is greased well so the cake doesn't stick to the sides and crack during baking.

5 Sprinkle reserved 2 T. crumbs around sides of pan. Tilt and tap pan to distribute crumbs evenly. It'll be a light dusting of crumbs.

6 With rubber spatula, press remaining crumb-butter mixture onto bottom of pan. Begin heating water for water bath.

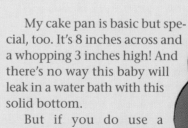

MAKING THE CAKE

This is pretty straightforward stuff. But you need to know a few things.

Mixing: I made sure I tried mixing this cake with a hand mixer. I wanted to make sure all this cream cheese could be blended without burning up your hand mixer. I didn't want you stopping just because you didn't have a bruiser stand mixer. The key is to use room temperature cream cheese.

Baking: I've used water baths before for baking custards. Starches are sometimes added to egg mixtures to prevent them from curdling when baking. Since there is no starch (flour or cornstarch) in this cheesecake, it needs the gentle heat of a water bath to join the egg and milk proteins. This cheesecake is just a very heavy custard and needs the same treatment.

A water bath also keeps the sides and bottom from burning during the long baking time.

When baking time is up, remove the cake. It won't seem done because it'll have a jiggle in the middle (about the size of a tuna can). Don't worry. You've heard me talk about residual heat? There'll be plenty of heat to finish the job after 2$^1/_4$ hours of baking.

MAKING THE CAKE

7 In large mixing bowl, cream together cheese, sugar and vanilla until smooth. Add eggs, one at a time, beating well after each addition.

8 Scrape down sides and bottom of bowl frequently during mixing so that no lumps remain. Add sour cream. Mix just to blend.

9 Pour batter into prepared pan which is set in a roasting pan. Smooth top. Be sure cake pan is taller than roaster or the cake will steam.

10 Set roaster in oven on rack positioned in middle. Pour hot water into roaster to come 1"–1$^1/_2$" up the sides of the cake pan.

11 Bake at 300° for 2–2$^1/_4$ hrs. or until top is golden and cake is set around edges. It'll be jiggly in the center but will cook while it cools.

12 Remove cake from roaster and set on cooling rack. Run knife around sides to loosen. Cool to room temperature. Refrigerate overnight.

13 To unmold, run knife around sides again. Place inverted plate on cake and flip. Rap plate on counter and lift pan, shaking gently to release.

14 Remove parchment from crust. Place serving plate on crust and invert again. Carefully remove top plate.

15 To serve, dip a thin-bladed knife in hot water and slice. Wipe blade clean and dip again after each cut.

MAKING A GRAND FINALE

TOPPING A CHEESECAKE

For the glaze you'll need: a 14 oz. pkg. frozen red raspberries, 1 cup red wine, $1/3$ cup sugar, and a 10 oz. jar red currant jelly. Combine berries, wine and sugar in saucepan over med. heat. Crush thawed berries with back of spoon.

Strain raspberry juice through fine sieve; discard seeds. Return juice to saucepan. Simmer over med. heat about 25 mins., until reduced to $1/2$ cup and very syrupy. Whisk in currant jelly until melted. Cool to room temp.

Pour about $1/4$ cup cooled glaze on cheesecake. Spread lightly, leaving a $1/2$" margin around edge. Randomly arrange 3 cups assorted fresh berries on top. Serve immediately. Extra sauce is great on ice cream!

ISSUE No. 10
JULY/AUG 1998

AUGUST HOME'S

Cuisine
™

AN ILLUSTRATED GUIDE TO CREATIVE HOME COOKING

TAMALES
WITH RED CHILE SAUCE

Also in this Issue:
TEXAS BRISKET
3 QUESADILLAS & SALSAS
GRILLED PINEAPPLE UPSIDE-DOWN CAKE

Cuisine

Editor
John F. Meyer

Art Director
Cinda Shambaugh

Assistant Editor
Susan Hoss

Senior Graphic Designer
Holly Wiederin

Graphic Designer
Martin Davis

Senior Photographer
Crayola England

Test Kitchen Directors
Ellen C. Boeke
Sara Ostransky

Contributing Editor
Saba S. Tian

Editorial Assistants
Jennifer L. Welter
Stephanie Neppl

Electronic Publishing
Coordinator
Douglas M. Lidster

Pre-press Image Specialist
Troy Clark

Publisher
Donald B. Peschke

Corporate

V.P. Planning & Finance: **Jon Macarthy**
Subscriber Services Director: **Sandy Baum**
New Business Director: **Glenda K. Battles**
New Business Manager: **Todd Bierle**
Promotion Manager: **Rick Junkins**
Renewal Manager: **Paige Rogers**
Billing Manager: **Rebecca Cunningham**
Asst. Subscription Manager: **Joy Krause**
Production Director: **George Chmielarz**
Production Assistant: **Susan Rueve**
Pre-press Image Specialist: **Minniette Bieghler**
Creative Director: **Ted Kralicek**
Photo Director: **Lark Gilmer**
August Home Books: **Douglas L. Hicks**
New Media Manager: **Gordon C. Gaippe**
Assoc. Graphic Design Director: **Susie Rider**
Senior Graphic Designer: **Cheryl Simpson**
Controller: **Robin K. Hutchinson**
Senior Accountant: **Laura J. Thomas**
Accounts Payable Clerk: **Mary Schultz**
Human Resource Assistant: **Kirsten Koele**
Customer Service Manager: **Jennie Enos**
Administrative Assistant: **Julia Fish**
Receptionist: **Jeanne Johnson**
Librarian: **Sherri Ribbey**
Special Projects Director: **Saville Inman**
Intern: **Adriel Lage**

Cuisine™ (ISSN 1089-6546) is published bi-monthly (Jan., Mar., May, July, Sept., Nov.) by August Home Publishing Co., 2200 Grand Ave., Des Moines, IA 50312. **Cuisine**™ is a trademark of August Home Publishing Co. ©Copyright 1998 August Home Publishing. All rights reserved. Subscriptions: Single copy: $4.99. One year subscription (6 issues), $21.94. (Canada/Foreign add $6 per year, U.S. funds.) Periodicals postage paid at Des Moines, IA and at additional mailing offices. "USPS/Heartland Press Automatable Poly" Postmaster: Send change of address to **Cuisine**, PO Box 37100 Boone, IA 50037-2100. Subscription questions? Call 800-311-3995, 8 a.m. to 5 p.m., Central Standard Time, weekdays. **Cuisine**™ does not accept and is not responsible for unsolicited manuscripts. PRINTED IN U.S.A.

From the Editor:

Last month, the Boy Scouts of America invited our staff to attend a seminar about rope tying. Now obviously, this is something they know how to do well—and I have no clue about knots other than tying a "granny knot". But it was a day out of the kitchen, so I went with a good attitude.

It turned out to be more than tying knots—it was about progressive learning. I first learned about the different names of rope ends. Then I was taught how to tie some basic knots and was explained their uses. We then learned how to lash two sticks together. By the end of the day, with the basic knowledge of knot tying and lashing, we were able to build a twenty foot stick bridge that could hold eight adults!

Why am I telling you this? I try to do the same thing with you—but with cooking. I'm teaching you basic techniques that you can apply to many forms of cooking. *Cuisine* isn't about recipes (the bridge), it's about technique (the knots). So, in the Brisket article, *see Page 24*, when I spend three pages on just the grill and fire, you can understand you're learning about the basics of smoking—the brisket just happens to be a great reward.

John Meyer

*In **Cuisine**, I always like to show you how to present regular food in some fun ways. This is what I did with the Caribbean Quesadilla, although this quesadilla isn't exactly run-of-the-mill stuff. Since people "eat with their eyes," presenting it this way, makes a pretty spectacular plate.*

AUGUST HOME'S Cuisine

AN ILLUSTRATED GUIDE TO CREATIVE HOME COOKING

Tips

HANDS ON FIRE?
My hands really burn when I work with chiles. But I can't grip my knife very well wearing rubber gloves.

So I keep a bottle of vinegar or alcohol nearby. Rubbing a little on my hands after chopping chiles cures the burning.

B. Viel
Perris, CA

HERB GRILL BRUSH
It's summer and my grill is in high gear. Something I like to do when I grill is make a basting brush from fresh herb sprigs.

It's easy—just tie several long herb sprigs (I like rosemary) around a wooden chopstick with a piece of cotton string.

As you baste on the sauce, the herb brush also "bastes" herb flavor on the fish, meat, and vegetables.

When you're finished, pull the sprigs off the chopstick and toss them back on the grill. They smell great as they burn.

R. Craig
Tampa, FL

RIPENING AVOCADOS
To quickly ripen rock-hard avocados, punch holes in a paper bag and add the avocados—plus an apple. Close the bag and leave at room temperature 2–3 days.

The apple gives off a gas that makes fruits ripen more rapidly.

S. Black
Brighton, CO

STORING ASPARAGUS
To keep asparagus several days, cut off the butt ends and stand them upright (unwashed) in a container. Add an inch of cold water and cover with a plastic bag. Refrigerate. Refresh the water as needed.

M. Evans
Lake Oswego, OR

FLOURING WITH COCOA
Whenever I dust a pan with flour for chocolate cake or brownies, I get a white film on the outside of the cake after it bakes. So, I use cocoa to "flour" the pan instead.

M. Childs
Reeds Spring, MO

MELTING CHOCOLATE
It's easy to scorch chocolate trying to melt it on the stove. But by giving it a hot water bath, I get consistently good results.

Just put chocolate pieces in a Ziploc® bag and drop it into a bowl filled with hot (not boiling) water. In a few minutes, the chocolate will be perfectly melted.

D. Rosenberg
Fenton, MI

MULTI-PURPOSE PASTA INSERT
Chicken soup lovers: make bone removal easy. Cook that bird in a large pasta pot with an insert! When the broth is done, just lift out the insert. It catches the meat and bones but leaves all the broth behind in the pot. No more fishing for stray chicken bones!

M. Papillo
Norma, NJ

FRESHER POTATOES

Tired of white tentacles sprouting from your sack of potatoes? They'll stay fresh and firm longer if you store them in a bag along with an apple. The apple gives off a gas that prevents potatoes from sprouting.

S. Horibe
North Miami Beach, FL

KEEPING BERRIES

To keep berries fresh days after picking or buying, I don't wash them—even a gentle rinse crushes and bruises berries, spoiling them faster. Instead, I put them in a colander and store in the refrigerator.

D. Diekmann
Dillon, CO

WATER STRAWS

I like to decorate my cakes with fresh flowers from my garden. It makes a great showpiece—as long as the flowers don't wilt!

To keep them fresh, cut a 3" piece from a drinking straw. Bend one end up and tape it. Then fill the straw ³/₄ full with water and stick the flower stem in.

Arrange the flowers on the cake. The flowers will stay fresh and won't wilt by the time I serve the cake.

J. Majors
West Woodbury, VT

FREEZING SPINACH

If a recipe calls for chopped, cooked spinach, I freeze fresh spinach ahead of time. Then all I have to do is crumble the brittle, frozen spinach. It saves me having to pull out and clean my cutting board and knife.

R. Beaudin
Bangor, ME

Tips

PERFECT GRAPEFRUIT SECTIONS

To section a grapefruit, cut off the top and bottom just to the pulp. Stand it on one end and cut away all the peel and bitter white pith, following the curve of the fruit.

Now, slice out a segment by cutting next to the membrane on one side of the segment, all the way to the middle of the fruit. Cut it again on the other side of the segment and lift it out. Repeat all the way around the fruit.

PUTTING OUT THE FIRE

More info on quelling chile fires. I called the National Hot Pepper Association. They told me that it is the capsaicin oil concentrated in the

veins and seeds that causes the problems. Water (including teas and soft drinks) and sucking in air only intensifies the problem by spreading the hot capsaicin oil.

They suggest using foods that can absorb the oil. Next time your mouth catches on fire, reach for dairy products like milk, yogurt, or ice cream. Or try low-moisture fruits and starches like bananas, rice, or bread.

SEND US YOUR TIPS

We'd like to hear from you. Just write down your cooking tip and mail it to Cuisine, Tips Editor, 2200 Grand Ave., Des Moines, IA 50312, or contact us through our E-mail address shown below. Please include your name, address, and daytime phone number in case we have questions. We'll pay you $25 if we publish your tip.

E-mail address: Cuisine@cuisinemag.com
Web site: www.cuisinemag.com

Photograph: Scott Little; Food Styling: Janet Pittman

TAMALES

Thinking about tamales, I knew I wanted to improve on what most of us have had in the past—tamales that were heavy and tasteless. Well, focusing in on one

tamale is like saying I'm going to teach you how to bake bread. There's too many breads, each with their own origin, made with different leavening agents and flours. Same for tamales.

There was a big difference between my perception and tamale reality. Three myths were quickly dispelled.

Myth 1: *I always thought that tamales were heavy and considered the main course in a meal.* Actually, tamales are very light because so much air is whipped into the fat. I also found out that small tamales can make great appetizers. And many chefs sweeten them and turn them into desserts.

Myth 2: *Tamales are filled with only shredded pork or beef.* Not true! They can be filled with anything. I had them filled with duck, lobster, scallops, and chicken. But some of the best tamales I ate were vegetarian. They had fillings like mushrooms, black beans, green chiles and cheese.

Myth 3: *The filling is the most important part of a tamale.* Wrong. Tamale-makers spend more time on the dough than the filling. It becomes an art and trademark of a good tamale maker. While the filling *is* important, it's considered almost secondary to a flavorful light corn dough.

With my past tamale knowledge shattered to pieces, I came back with two problems—what type of tamale to make and which fat to use.

Basic Tamale: There are so many regional variations of tamales, I didn't want to confuse you. The only way to handle this is the *Cuisine* way.

I'm going to show you how to make a basic tamale and then come back to specific regions in later issues. For now, it's basic training for you.

Lard: All tamales are made with corn dough, *see Masa*, and a fat. True tamales are made with lard (rendered pork fat)—this is the second problem.

I struggled with telling you to use lard because of its bad reputation. I've decided not to use it for a couple of reasons—taste and acceptance.

Good-tasting lard which gives off a rich roasted pork taste, is hard to find. You could render it yourself, but it stinks up the whole house!

And then the term "lard" has such a bad connotation. For now, I'd rather see you having fun making tamales and not fretting about cholesterol.

Wrappers for Tamales

There are two ways to wrap up tamales for steaming—dried corn husks and banana leaves.

Corn Husks: For our tamales, we're going to wrap and form them in dried corn husks that you'll make pliable by soaking in boiling water. The main reason for using the dried husks is that they're available in most grocery stores—especially in Mexican markets (if you're fortunate enough to have one in your city).

If your store carries dried peppers, look for the corn husks there. Melissas and Friedas are two well-known brands. The dried husks don't impart much taste, but for a little "herbier" taste, try using fresh green husks.

Banana Leaves: You can also use banana leaves to wrap your tamales. Mexico's southern regions prefer to use banana leaves because they infuse an earthy-grassy flavor into the masa. Banana trees flourish in this area and the leaves are common in recipes.

If you can find banana leaves in a Mexican or Asian market (they come fresh or frozen), they first have to be made pliable for folding.

Remove the large vein from the center and then cut 12" squares out of the leaves. Either steam them for 20 minutes or pass them over an open flame until they become soft and shiny as their oil is excreted. Fold them as you would pliable corn husks.

Knowing Your Ingredient: Masa

For me, I consider tamale dough more important than the filling. A good dough should be light and very flavorful—not like some of the heavy gut-bombs you may have regretted eating in the past.

The main ingredient to tamale dough is corn. Once you get the hang of making a good dough, you can start experimenting with flavors by using peppers (for the heat and flavor), herbs, cheeses, or even wrapping the tamales in green corn husks or banana leaves.

But before we get to the dough making, you need to know what the dough is made from. There arethree terms you need to know—masa, fresh masa, and masa harina.

Masa: Masa [MAH-sah] is the Mexican word for corn dough used to make tamales. It's made from either fresh masa or masa harina. Basic masa contains a form of fat (like butter, shortening, or lard)and a leavening agent (baking powder). The masa is then whipped until it's fluffy and airy to make a light tamale dough. Flavors can also be added to the masa before shaping the tamales.

Fresh Masa: Fresh masa is corn tortilla dough and can be purchased from a Mexican market or a tortilla factory (if you live near one). To make masa, you have to use fresh masa or masa harina.

Fresh masa is made from corn that's first sun- or fire-dried. It's cooked and then soaked overnight in water mixed with "slaked" lime.

"Slaked" lime is nothing more than calcium hydroxide (pickling lime). If you try making fresh masa at home, use *only* pickling lime from the grocery store. Other limes like agricultural lime or calcium oxide are extremely caustic.

After the corn is rehydrated in the slaked water, it's then ground to make the unflavored fresh masa.

Masa Harina: Masa harina [ah-REE-nah] is the dried version of fresh masa. Since fresh masa can spoil quickly, drying it after it's rehydrated, gives masa harina a long shelf life. And this is why we're going to use it for our tamales. Masa harina is easy to find, can keep a long time in storage, and makes a pretty good tamale.

Tamales with Red Chile Pork *(Makes 16 Tamales)*

Work Time: 1½ hours
Cooling Time: 2 hours
Cook Time: 3 hours

For the Pork Filling—
Sear in 1 T. Oil:
2   lbs. pork shoulder, cubed

Add and Simmer:
½   yellow onion, peeled and cubed
1   dried New Mexico pepper, stemmed and seeded
6   cloves garlic, smashed
    Water to cover

For the Chile Sauce—
Cover with Boiling Water:
4   oz. dried New Mexico chiles,

Puree Chiles with:
1   cup chile water (from soaking New Mexico chiles)
1   cup beef broth
2   T. minced garlic
1   t. dried oregano

Simmer Chile Puree with:
4   t. sugar

Combine and Simmer:
2   cups prepared pork, shredded
¾   cup prepared chile puree

For the Masa —
Beat until Light:
1⅓   cups chilled vegetable shortening
2   t. baking powder

Slowly Add:
4   cups masa harina
2½   cups chilled low-salt chicken broth, divided
2½   t. salt

For the Corn Husks —
Cover with Boiling Water:
42   dried corn husks, separated

Steam Tamales 1½ Hours or Until Husk Pulls Easily from Masa.

Nutritional Information per Tamale: Calories 366; Total Fat 24(g); Calories from Fat 58%; Sodium 498(mg)

PORK FILLING AND SAUCE

Before making the tamales, you first have to make the filling and sauce. You *always* do this first so both the filling and sauce have time to cool completely before rolling the tamales. If it's not completely cool, you could create bacteria by keeping all the ingredients too long in the "danger zone" (between 45° and 140°).

One neat thing about tamales is that you can fill them with anything—chicken, beef, mushrooms, seafood. For our recipe, we're using pork.

Pork Shoulder: Pork shoulder works well for this recipe because it's lean with plenty of taste.

First, brown the pork in a very hot saucepan, *see Step 1.* Even though you're going to boil the meat, searing tends to add extra flavor.

Next, add the onions, chiles, and garlic. Cook and stir for a few minutes. Then add the water and simmer until the meat starts to fall apart (about 1¹/₂ hours). Remove the meat to a mixing bowl, *see Step 2.*

Finally, start to shred the meat by pulling it apart with two forks, *see Step 3.* Shred the meat completely so you don't have the surprise of a big chunk of meat in your tamale.

Red Chile Sauce: To make the chile sauce, first saute the chiles in a hot skillet, *see Step 4.* This starts to plump them as their oil is extracted.

Next, remove the seeds and stems, *see Step 5,* and cover the peppers with boiling water for about 20 minutes.

When softened, puree the chiles, beef broth, garlic, and oregano until smooth, *see Step 6.* For extra "pepper" flavor, add some of the water that the peppers soaked in.

Now, over low heat, cook the chile puree with a little sugar for 10 minutes, *see Step 7.* This thickens the sauce and gets rid of any remaining raw taste.

Finally, cook the sauce and meat so the flavors can meld, *see Step 8.*

1 Sear the cubed pork shoulder in 1 T. oil. Add the onion, New Mexico chiles, and garlic. Now add enough water to cover.

2 Cover the pan and bring to a boil. Reduce the heat and simmer for 1¹/₂ hours. Remove the meat and discard the cooking liquid.

3 Using two forks, begin to shred the meat. Hold one fork stationary, and shred with the other. The tines do all the work for you.

4 Over medium heat, toast (saute) chiles 3–4 minutes. Press down with a spoon, turning once. Chiles will plump and smell toasty.

5 Cool chiles. Remove stems and seeds. Place chiles in a bowl. Cover with boiling water until softened—about 20 minutes.

6 Drain chiles, reserving 1 cup of the liquid. Puree soaked chiles, chile water, beef broth, garlic, and oregano until smooth (2–3 minutes).

7 In medium saucepan, simmer chile puree and sugar over low heat. Stir frequently, until sauce has thickened (about 10 minutes).

8 Combine the shredded meat and ³/₄ cup of the chile puree and cook briefly so the flavors blend. *Chill* this mixture *thoroughly.*

MAKING THE MASA

After thinking about it, I thought it best that you use masa harina to make the tamales for two reasons. Most grocery stores stock it. But more importantly, it'll make a good, consistent dough. There's just too much moisture variation in fresh masa.

Fat: The key to good tamale dough is whipping the fat to incorporate air into it. This is what makes tamales light. But beware! Beating can make the dough too warm. It's just like pie crust. Too much heat can melt fat droplets, resulting in heavy doughs.

Beat the shortening in a mixer for about three minutes, *see Step 9.* Keep feeling the mixing bowl to make sure the fat isn't getting too warm.

Now, slowly blend the harina into the fat, *see Step 10.* When it's fully blended, add the broth (reserve ¹/₂ cup), *see Step 11.* Continue beating to incorporate as much air as possible into the dough.

Float Test: To determine if you have enough air in the dough, try the float test, *see Step 12.* The dough balls should float in cold water if the dough has been adequately whipped. If the balls sink, continue whipping a few minutes more and test again.

Next, add remaining broth, salt, and other flavorings you want. The extra broth will make it the consistency of cookie dough, *see Step 13.*

Chill the dough so the fat sets up for shaping and cooking, *see Step 14.* While dough is chilling, prepare the cornhusks for rolling, *see Steps 15–17.*

PREPARING THE MASA

9 Beat chilled shortening and baking powder until light in texture (about 3 minutes). A stand mixer outfitted with a paddle works great.

10 Continue beating while you slowly add the harina. This traps air into the dough making the tamales light. Scrape the bowl often.

11 With the mixer still running, slowly pour in 2 cups chicken broth. If you pour *too* quickly, the broth will splatter everywhere.

12 To make sure you've incorporated enough air into the dough, drop a small dough ball into cold water. It will float if it's ready.

13 Beat in the remaining ¹/₂ cup broth. You should have the consistency of cookie dough. Taste the dough and season with salt.

14 Place the dough in a bowl covered with plastic wrap and refrigerate for at least 1 hour. It's much easier to work with if it's cold.

THE CORN HUSKS

15 Separate the corn husks and discard ones with holes, large tears, or discoloration. Place the husks in a large, deep bowl.

16 Pour boiling water over the husks to cover. This process will rehydrate the husks and make them more pliable.

17 Weight the husks with a plate to keep them submerged. Let them sit for at least 30 minutes. Set to the side until ready to use.

WRAPPING AND STEAMING

I know several ways to wrap tamales—and I know several different wrappers that can be used. But I found using two cornhusks that have been soaked in boiling water the easiest and most foolproof. This method gives you plenty of space to make the tamale and it also makes the actual shaping process pretty easy.

Cornhusks: Use two cornhusks with the narrow ends opposite each other. This configuration allows plenty of room to form a dough rectangle.

Wrapping: When I first started making tamales, I found that many people left one end of the cornhusk open which exposed the tamale. Well, I'm kind of a neatnik—I like both my ends tied in a tight little package.

Securing each end gives you a more even tamale shape. It forms a nice cylinder and closes the ends so they are symmetrical.

Wrapping both ends also forces you to tie each end. This allows the tamale to cook more evenly.

Steaming: I found steaming is the best way to cook tamales evenly. Here's what you have to do.

With both ends formed and secured, stand the tamales vertically in a steamer or large sauce pot without crowding them. You want steam to be able to circulate around them. So they don't touch each other, stuff cornhusks between each vertical tamale.

Finally, steam them long enough (about 1 1/2 hours) so they peel away easily from the cornhusks.

WRAPPING AND STEAMING

18 Pat husks to remove excess moisture. Tear thin strips for ties. Overlap two husks (about 3") so that narrow ends are opposite.

19 Dip your hands in cold water (just to moisten) and pat 1/3 cup of masa onto husks. Form a 4x6" rectangle with the masa.

20 Spoon 2 T. meat filling evenly down the center of the masa. Note: Be sure to leave a border on all four sides for the next step.

21 Fold the long sides of the husks gently over the filling. Using the husks, roll the dough over the filling to enclose it on all sides.

22 Overlap the long sides. Shape and roll it tightly. Fold up the narrow ends towards the middle. Now, roll the tamale over to tie.

23 Using the strips you tore earlier, wrap a tie around the tamale and the folded end. Secure with knot. Repeat with the other end.

24 Place the tamales upright over 2" of gently boiling water. Add extra husks to fill in spaces. Cover and reduce heat to simmer.

25 Steam 1 1/2 hours. Uncover and let stand 10 minutes before serving. Tamales will be firm and should pull easily away from husks.

26 Use the remaining steamed husks for the "boats". Tie off both ends tightly with a strip of husk. They make great salsa holders.

PLATING

I really wanted to spend a little time with you on plating and presentation. It's such a major part of food—and what better way to demonstrate this than to dress up the common tamale.

Think about the ingredients you use in making tamales and the indigenous products of the region. This is what I want you to use to garnish your plate.

Look at all the photos. I've used fresh cornhusks, various fresh and dried peppers that I thought were pretty, nopales (cactus paddles), sauces we've made, tropical fruits, and of course, flowers. See Cathy's edible flowers article on pages 38–41. **AH**

SALSA VERDE *(MAKES 3 CUPS)*
BLANCH 2 MINUTES:
12	medium tomatillos

PROCESS UNTIL COARSELY BLENDED:
3	jalapenos, seeded and sliced
2	t. chopped fresh cilantro
2	t. fresh lime juice
1	clove garlic, crushed
1	t. kosher salt

Think of basic Mexican ingredients and combinations. Remove some of the green husks off fresh corn and use them as a bed. Make a sauce boat out of a husk like I did on Step 26 (use fresh or dried husks). Find some good-looking peppers (I used red jalapenos) and cut out long points from the ends to form flowers. Soak in ice water so the tips spread like the green onion fans we did in Issue 2 on page 15. Fill pepper flowers with queso fresco (crumbly cheese available in Mexican markets), the cornhusk boats with tomatillo sauce, then the gaps with the tomato salsa from page 17.

GUACAMOLE *(MAKES 2 CUPS)*
MASH WITH A FORK:
2	avocados, peeled and pitted

STIR IN:
2	T. sour cream
4	t. fresh lime juice
3	t. jalapeno pepper, seeded and minced
3/4	t. kosher salt
3	drops Tabasco®

You already have the red chile sauce made from page 8. Pool it in the center of the plate and make a line of sour cream around it using a squeeze bottle. Using a toothpick, pull the sauce through the sour cream to make the burst. Fill the cornhusk boat with guacamole. Garnish with a daylily, cilantro, and peppers.

ITEMS NEEDED FOR EACH PLATE:
	Black bean salsa, *see Page 17*
2	nopales
1/2	mango for fan
1	cornhusk boat
1	rose, *see Edible Flower article, pages 38–41*
1	side of lime

This is one of my favorites because it's so simple yet it packs a big visual punch. Make a bed using nopales, *see below*. Then fill a cornhusk boat with the black bean salsa on page 17. The red and black makes a perfect contrast to the deep green of these cactus paddles.

Now, add a sliced mango fan. This is a great complementary flavor—especially with the black bean salsa. Garnish with a lime (slice only a third off the side—it's a hot new trend!), and add a rose.

NOPALES

Nopales [noh-PAH-lays] are the fleshy leaves (called paddles) on the nopal cactus. But before I get into trouble, they're not leaves at all but the stem from the nopal cactus—they just resemble leaves. The nopal cactus bears a fruit called prickly pears.

The pears are juicy and edible but so are the paddles. The thorns have to be shaved off (vegetable peeler) before eating. They're then sliced and simmered in water until tender.

QUESADILLAS

Photograph: Scott Little; Food Styling: Janet Pittman

CARIBBEAN QUESADILLA

(MAKES 4 QUESADILLAS)
WORK TIME: 40 MINUTES
COOK TIME: 20 MINUTES

FOR QUESADILLA "HOLDERS", CUT:
1   fresh, ripe pineapple

FOR AIOLI, BLEND IN FOOD PROCESSOR:
2   ripe avocados, peeled, pitted ,and cut into chunks
3   T. lime juice, strained
3   T. chopped fresh cilantro leaves
1   T. seeded, minced jalapeno
1   T. minced garlic

SLOWLY DRIZZLE IN:
1/2   cup light olive oil
     Salt and cayenne pepper to taste

FOR FILLINGS, PREPARE AND SET ASIDE:
11/2   cups cooked, cleaned King crab meat, torn or cut into chunks
1   cup diced red bell pepper
1   cup bias-cut green onions

BLEND TOGETHER AND SET ASIDE:
11/2   cups soft, mild goat cheese
2   t. adobo sauce *(see Glossary on page 37)*

HEAT IN SAUTE PAN:
1   T. vegetable oil

IN SAUTE PAN, LIGHTLY FRY:
4   10-inch spinach tortilla wraps or flour tortillas

SERVE WITH:
     Pineapple-Pepper Salsa, see Page 16

NUTRITIONAL INFORMATION PER QUESADILLA:
CALORIES 619; TOTAL FAT 33(G); CALORIES FROM FAT 47%; SODIUM 1,326(MG)

One thing a lot of restaurants do these days is "tweak" traditional dishes and update them for today's tastes. Well, I decided to do some "tweaking" of my own with

these quesadillas [keh-sah-DEE-yah]. I ate quesadillas in all kinds of restaurants, from Mexican food chains to Latin dance clubs. But nothing stood out as being truly special.

Most of the quesadillas tended to be more like a Mexican grilled cheese sandwich. Tortillas being the bread with mild white cheese in the middle (usually a little chicken is added).

While this "bread and cheese" thread is woven into all my quesadillas, the real fun is tweaking the different tortillas, cheeses and fillings.

Tortillas: Tortillas come in as many colors and flavors as you can dream up. Just in one store here, I found yellow, red, white, green, and blue. You find them as "wraps" in the refrigerated section of your grocer. Any tortilla will do.

Cheese: Who says you have to use Monterey Jack cheese all the time? Smoked Gouda was a natural with the smoky flavors of grilled portobello quesadillas. And the mild goat cheese didn't overpower the delicate crab meat in the Caribbean quesadilla.

Fillings: The sky's the limit when it comes to quesadilla fillings. Here, I broke it down into three fillings—seafood, steak, and vegetables. None require huge amounts of preparation time—they can easily be done ahead.

Aioli and Salsa: I'm starting to find that the really good quesadillas are served with an aioli and fresh salsa.

No more big ice cream scoops of sour cream and guacamole. Flavorful, colorful aiolis and salsas can now grace your quesadilla plates, bringing them to a new level of acceptance.

1 To make the quesadilla "holders", cut the top off the pineapple and halve it lengthwise. Then cut each half into thirds.

2 Lay a wedge of pineapple flat side down so it won't roll around. Make three 45° angle cuts across the top, but don't cut all the way through.

3 "Notch" each 45°cut by making a 90°cut a little to the left of each cut. Slice down to where the cuts meet and remove the small piece.

4 Puree avocado, lime juice, cilantro jalapeno, and garlic until smooth. With processor running, drizzle in olive oil. Season with salt and cayenne.

5 Prepare the crab, pepper, and onion for the quesadillas; set aside. For the goat cheese spread, stir adobo sauce into softened cheese.

6 Preheat vegetable oil in large saute pan over medium-high heat. Evenly spread about ⅓ cup goat cheese mixture over each tortilla.

7 Place a tortilla in the hot pan. Spread about ⅓ cup crab over half the tortilla. Sprinkle with ¼ cup onion and ¼ cup pepper.

8 Cook until tortilla is golden brown on the bottom but still soft enough to fold over, about 3–5 mins. Fold the unfilled side over the fillings.

9 Carefully turn the quesadilla over using a large spatula—I flip fast, using my free hand to help. Some filling may fall out—just tuck it back in.

10 Cut the quesadilla into thirds. Arrange a pineapple wedge on each serving plate and use a squeeze bottle to "paint" on the aioli.

11 Tuck a quesadilla triangle into each notch in the pineapple. Adjust them so they "fan" out like a deck of cards.

12 The Caribbean flavors of this quesadilla are perfect with the Pineapple-Pepper Salsa on page 16. It's also great with grilled salmon.

STEAK QUESADILLA

(MAKES 4 QUESADILLAS)
WORK TIME: 1 HOUR
COOK TIME: 30 MINUTES
MARINATE ¹/₂ LB. FLANK OR SKIRT
STEAK FOR 30 MINUTES IN:

- ¹/₃ cup fresh lime juice
- ¹/₄ cup olive oil
- 1 T. minced garlic
- ¹/₄ t. cayenne pepper

FOR BLUE CHEESE AIOLI, BLEND:

- 1 cup mayonnaise
- 1 T. minced garlic
- 1 t. lemon juice
- ¹/₂ t. salt
- ¹/₈ t. cayenne pepper

ADD AND PROCESS UNTIL SMOOTH:

- ¹/₃ cup crumbled blue cheese

ASSEMBLE WITH:

- 2 cups Monterey Jack cheese, shredded
- 1 red pepper, grilled, peeled, cut in strips
- 1 yellow pepper, grilled, peeled cut in strips
- 4 8-inch flour tortillas
  Saute in lightly oiled pan

MAKING THE STEAK QUESADILLAS

1 I like marinating meat in plastic bags—no mess or clean up. Add marinade ingredients and steak; let sit at room temperature 30 minutes.

2 Blend the mayonnaise, garlic, lemon juice and seasonings in food processor. Add blue cheese; blend until smooth. Transfer to squeeze bottle.

3 Preheat grill. When hot, grill peppers until charred, about 10 minutes. Steam in plastic bag until cool. Peel, seed and cut into strips.

4 Grill steak 5 minutes on each side. Rest 5 minutes to distribute juices. Slice at an angle, against the grain, ¹/₄" thick. Heat oil in large saute pan.

5 Add tortilla to pan and sprinkle with ¹/₂ cup cheese. Lay steak and peppers strips on one half. Turn other half over fillings when cheese melts.

6 Remove quesadilla from pan when browned. Cut into thirds. Serve with Blue Cheese Aioli and the Two Tomato Salsa from page 17.

GRILLED PORTOBELLO QUESADILLA

(MAKES 4 QUESADILLAS)

WORK TIME: 30 MINUTES

COOK TIME: 30 MINUTES

FOR THE ROASTED RED PEPPER AIOLI,
PUREE IN BLENDER:

2   large red peppers, grilled, peeled, seeded and diced

3   cloves garlic, coarsely chopped

ADD TO PEPPER PUREE AND BLEND:

1   cup mayonnaise

$1/4$ t. salt

$1/8$ t. cayenne pepper

FOR GARLIC OIL, COMBINE:

$1/2$ cup light olive oil

1   T. minced garlic

ASSEMBLE WITH:

2   cups fresh baby spinach leaves

$1^1/3$ cups grated smoked Gouda

$1^1/3$ cups seeded, diced tomatoes

4   large portobello mushroom caps, brushed with garlic oil, grilled and sliced

4   10-inch vegetable tortilla wraps

8   cups mixed baby greens

$1/3$ cup salad vinaigrette

Photograph: Scott Little; Food Styling: Janet Pittman

MAKING THE GRILLED PORTOBELLO QUESADILLA

1 Preheat grill. When hot, grill peppers until charred, about 10 minutes. Steam in plastic bag until cool. Peel, seed and roughly dice.

2 Puree peppers and garlic in blender. Add mayonnaise and seasonings and blend until very smooth. Transfer aioli to a squeeze bottle.

3 Mix together oil and garlic and set aside. Prepare the spinach, cheese, and tomatoes and set aside. Brush portobellos with garlic oil.

4 Grill mushrooms on both sides until cooked through (about 4 minutes each side). Thinly slice. Brush one side of tortillas with garlic oil.

5 Place tortilla on grill, oiled side down. Sprinkle with cheese. Add spinach, mushrooms and tomatoes. Start with the spinach so it wilts.

6 Grill until browned. Toss greens with your favorite vinaigrette and serve quesadilla with Red Pepper Aioli and Black Bean Salsa on page 17.

Photograph: Scott Little; Food Styling: Janet Pittman

SALSAS

There's nothing that says "summer" more than fresh salsas. With all the great produce flooding the grocery stores and farmer's markets these days, I just enjoy

wandering up and down the aisles conjuring up different combinations. The hardest time I had here was limiting the choices to just three recipes.

And salsas aren't just for tortilla chips anymore. A spoonful with a piece of grilled fish or meat adds amazing flavor and color—without a lot of extra work or calories. And, of course, they're a perfect fit next to the updated Quesadillas on pages 12–15.

Foods should have contrasts. I made sure these salsas had different elements that created plenty of "tension"—cilantro with spicy chilies, sweet peppers and tart lime, soft pineapple against crunchy jicama.

You won't find these salsas anywhere near the jars of red sauce and tortilla chips at the grocery store. Their fresh taste puts them where they belong—on your table.

PINEAPPLE–PEPPER SALSA
(MAKES 4 CUPS)
WORK TIME: 20 MINUTES
PEEL AND TRIM:
1   cup fresh pineapple, diced
PEEL AND JULIENNE:
$^1/_2$ cup jicama, julienne
TOSS WITH:
$^1/_4$ cup purple onion, slivered
$^1/_4$ cup red pepper, diced
1   T. fresh lime juice
$^1/_2$ t. habanero, seeded and minced
$^1/_2$ t. salt
$^1/_8$ t. cayenne pepper
2–3 drops Tabasco®
JUST BEFORE SERVING, MIX IN:
$^1/_2$ cup banana, diced
1   T. fresh cilantro, chopped
1   T. fresh mint, chopped

NUTRITIONAL INFORMATION PER $^1/_4$ CUP:
CALORIES 21; TOTAL FAT 0(G); CALORIES FROM FAT 6%; SODIUM 74(MG)

COOL IT!
The same sulphur compound that makes you cry when you cut raw onions is responsible for the "burn" you get when you eat them raw. Cool it by rinsing the cut onion in cold water. Drain it well before adding to the salsa.

MAKING PINEAPPLE-PEPPER SALSA

1 Trim the peel off a fresh pineapple. Cut into quarters, remove core and dice to make 1 cup. Peel jicama and julienne to make $^1/_2$ cup.

2 Combine pineapple, jicama, onion, red pepper, lime juice, spices, and Tabasco. Remove seeds and membrane from habanero; mince and add.

3 Just before serving, add diced banana, chopped cilantro, and chopped mint. Toss gently and serve immediately.

1 Seed tomatoes by cutting across their "equator" and squeezing out the seed pockets. Dice and place in a bowl.

2 Add rinsed onion to tomatoes. Quarter a jalapeno pepper, trim out the seeds and mince. Mix with other salsa ingredients.

TWO TOMATO SALSA

(MAKES 3 CUPS)
WORK TIME: 20 MINUTES
MIX TOGETHER:

1	cup red tomatoes, seeded and diced
1	cup yellow tomatoes, seeded and diced
3/4	cup white onion, diced and rinsed

3	T. fresh cilantro, chopped
2	T. fresh lime juice
1	T. light olive oil
2	t. jalapeno, seeded and minced
2	t. fresh garlic, minced
1/2	t. sugar
1/2	t. salt
1/8	t. cayenne pepper

BLACK BEAN SALSA

1 Bring water, beans, garlic, and thyme to a boil. Cover, reduce heat and simmer 40–45 mins. until soft but not mushy. Drain.

2 Roast red peppers. Cool, peel and dice. Roast and mince habanero. Add to other salsa ingredients. Then, toss gently.

BLACK BEAN SALSA

(MAKES 4 1/2 CUPS)
WORK TIME: 20 MINUTES
COOK TIME: 40–45 MINUTES
BRING TO A BOIL, COVER AND SIMMER:

3 1/2	cups water
1	cup dried black beans
3	cloves garlic, smashed
3	sprigs fresh thyme

COOK UNTIL BEANS ARE SOFT BUT NOT MUSHY. DRAIN IMMEDIATELY, REMOVE GARLIC AND THYME; RINSE. SET ASIDE TO COOL.

TOSS BEANS WITH:

3/4	cup yellow onion, diced, rinsed
3/4	cup roasted red pepper, diced
1/2	cup tomato, seeded and diced
2	T. fresh cilantro, chopped
1	T. fresh thyme, chopped
1	T. fresh lime juice
1	T. white balsamic vinegar
1	T. light olive oil
2	t. minced garlic
1/2	t. roasted habanero, minced
1/2	t. salt

BROWNIES

Everyone has a recipe for the best brownies, and they also have different ideas what a brownie should be like. Cakey, fudgy, moist and light, dense and chewy, frosting, nuts—the concepts go on and on.

And of course, I have my own ideas which I'll share with you. If called on to do so, brownies need to be able to stand on their own. Deep chocolate flavor, a texture that won't crumble in your mouth (actually, a little roof-sticking is good), and a thin crust on top.

From here, you can start adding toppings if you want. Or do what I did on the back cover and make a fancy $8.00 dessert with it.

BASIC CHOCOLATE BROWNIES
(MAKES 1- 9X13" PAN)
WORK TIME: 30 MINUTES
COOK TIME: 22–25 MINUTES
MELT AND SET ASIDE:
12 oz. semisweet chocolate, broken up
$1\frac{1}{2}$ cups sugar
12 T. unsalted butter, cut into tablespoons
WHISK TOGETHER:
1 cup all-purpose flour
$\frac{1}{4}$ cup cocoa, sifted
2 t. baking powder
$\frac{1}{4}$ t. salt
BEAT UNTIL FOAMY:
4 large eggs, room temp.
2 T. instant espresso powder, *see Page 37*
1 T. vanilla
BAKE AT 350° 22–25 MINS.
IN PREPARED 9X13" PAN.

1 In double-boiler, stir chocolate, sugar, butter over simmering water. Remove bowl. Cool to room temperature.

2 Preheat oven. Spray bottom and sides of baking pan with Pam®. Cut and place parchment paper and spray again.

3 As chocolate cools, measure $\frac{1}{4}$ cup cocoa and sift into bowl containing flour, baking powder, and salt. Whisk.

4 Beat eggs, espresso powder, and vanilla until foamy, scraping once. Beat in cooled chocolate mixture, scraping once.

5 Sprinkle small amount of flour in chocolate mixture and fold. Repeat. Add remaining flour. Fold in until no flour appears.

6 Spread batter evenly in pan. Bake in center of oven 22–25 minutes or until a toothpick inserted in center is barely moist.

7 Remove from oven and cool completely. Run knife around edge of pan. Place rack on top of pan and invert. Peel paper.

8 Invert again onto cutting surface. With a sharp knife, trim off edges and cut brownies into 2" squares.

BROWNIE POINTS

- I just like using a simple aluminum baking pan for most of my baking (including these brownies). *For me*, there are too many variables with other materials. Glass cooks too hot, the insulated pans can cook unevenly along the edges, and the darker pans bake edges and bottoms faster than the center. Besides, the simple aluminum pans are the least expensive.
- A hand mixer works just as well as a stand mixer.
- To store brownies, wrap tightly in plastic wrap at room temperature. Chilling the plain brownies tends to dry them out. However, refrigerating the ganached brownies is okay. The ganache protects the cake part and the ganache holds up better when chilled.
- Brownies freeze well, but tend to be denser.
- Melted butter intensifies the fudgy flavor.
- Beware of overbaking. When you insert a toothpick and it comes out barely moist, they're ready.

Ganache [gahn-AHSH] is a rich chocolate icing that is used in several ways. It can glaze, frost, fill or pipe by changing the ratio of chocolate to cream, chilling, or whipping. Use ganache as a glaze to dress up a basic brownie.

CHOCOLATE GANACHE

(MAKES 1 CUP)
COOK TIME: 5 MINS.
COOL TIME: 30–60 MINS.
HEAT UNTIL SIMMERING:
$^2/_3$ cup heavy cream
POUR CREAM OVER:
4   oz. bittersweet chocolate, broken into pieces
WHISK UNTIL SMOOTH.

A Few Ganache Tips

Use a good chocolate: Good chocolate contains a high percentage of cocoa butter—you'll taste the difference.

Don't use chips: Plain chocolate chips have extra fats to prevent melting.

Don't over-whisk the cream and chocolate: Overbeating creates air bubbles that are difficult to remove. These bubbles will show up in the finished glaze. This ganache is intended to be *very* smooth and shiny.

1 For different shapes, use cookie cutters. This makes smooth sides. Place upside down on wire rack over tray or wax paper.

2 Bring cream to simmer, pour over chocolate. *Gently* whisk until smooth. Let set at room temperature 30–60 minutes.

3 Press in any rough edges on your brownie shapes to make smooth surface. Stir ganache and pour over top of brownie.

4 With an offset knife (any flat knife will do) smooth out pooled ganache over top and edges. Work on one brownie at a time.

5 Refrigerate the glazed brownies at least two hours to set the ganache. Bring to room temperature before serving.

BROWNIE TOPPINGS

Here are a few general topping directions:
Toast (really saute) chopped nuts in $^1/_2$ T. unsalted butter over medium heat for 3–4 minutes until golden. Place peanut butter, caramel sauce or chocolate pieces into corner of Ziploc® bag. Press air out before sealing.

Place in bowl of hot tap water for 5 minutes. Snip a tiny corner off bag. Place cut brownies on a cooling rack (keep space between them) with wax paper under the rack . Working quickly, use a back and forth motion to drizzle over all the cut brownies. Now, add the nuts.

PEANUT/PEANUT BUTTER
$^1/_2$ cup rough chopped peanuts, toasted
$^1/_3$ cup creamy peanut butter

PECAN/CARAMEL
$^1/_2$ cup rough chopped pecans, toasted
$^1/_3$ cup caramel sauce

MACADAMIA/WHITE CHOCOLATE
$^1/_2$ cup rough chopped macadamias, toasted
1   oz. white chocolate, broken into pieces

CHOCOLATE MINT
2   oz. bittersweet chocolate, broken
$^1/_2$ t. peppermint extract
(Chocolate may be cross-drizzled.)

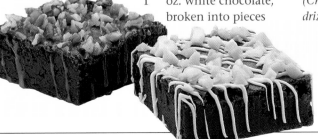

◄ COOKING SCHOOL IN A BOX™

There are a lot of articles about Mexican cooking in this issue, and I introduced you to several new ingredients. Culinary Alchemy puts many of them together for a great gift (be sure to include a *Cuisine* subscription!) The Mexican Spice Kitchen™ is beautifully packaged and includes 27 ingredients to create 30 authentic Mexican dishes. It also comes with a cookbook, *Cooking with the Chiles and Spices of Mexico*, that includes 56 recipes and foods of Central Mexico — dry sautes, slow simmered meats, roasted vegetables, toasted seeds, nuts, and spices. Each ingredient is individually packaged and carefully labeled.

To order, call **Culinary Alchemy Inc.** directly at **(800) 424-0005** or **Fancy Foods Gourmet Club, (800) 576-3548,** Item #GS470 $39.00.

▼ INGENIOUS IGNITORS

Have you ever tried to light that grill, smoker or fireplace only to burn your hand and singe part of your arm? Here are two great solutions! The **Olympian Electric Match** and the **Extra-Long Flexible Gas Match**.

The electric match is 13" long and works on a "C" battery (included). The flexible match is 15" long with a flexible nozzle that bends into any shape you need. It's fueled by butane and a "AA" battery (included). Great for those hard-to-reach places and sparks for thousands of ignitions.

Both ignitors are available through **Chefs™ Catalog** at **(800) 338-3232.** Olympian Electric Match, Item #7869 $19.99; Extra-Long Flexible Gas Match, Item #3417 $39.99.

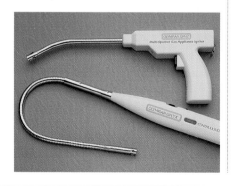

◄ WECK® CANNING JARS

These jars have it all! Wide, easy to fill glass jars with decorative shapes. Snap-on (reusable) clips instead of rims and rings that tend to rust. The jars stack easily and are a breeze to open. Plastic covers are included for use after the jars are opened. Each order includes a *Weck Home Canning Guide* with easy-to-follow steps.

To order, call **Sur La Table (800) 243-0852.** Item #12390 ($\frac{1}{5}$ liter) $14.50; #17226 ($\frac{1}{2}$ liter) $16.95; #12392 (1 liter) $16.95; and #12389 ($\frac{1}{2}$ liter bottle) $16.95.

▼ CERTIFIED ORGANIC TEAS

The **Republic of Tea®** has done it again! This California-based company answered the strong consumer demand for organics with its line of 11 organic teas. The list includes four black teas, one oolong, three green, and three caffeine-free herbal blends. The new line of organic teas is packaged in the distinctive tins of The Republic of Tea.

Each of the teas is hand-picked and grown without the use of chemicals and synthetic fertilizers.

Order it from **The Republic of Tea** at **(800) 298-4 TEA**.

CHILES

There's no doubt about it, chiles are hot. From the mildest to the most fiery, these peppers are finding

their way into our food. And we're loving it! I've been growing dozens of different chiles and cooking with them for nearly 20 years. Yes, I do a little gardening on the side.

But, first, let's get the terminology straight. So far I've used the words chile and pepper. And there are lots of other words I could use such as chile, chili, chili pepper, paprika, and Capsicum [KAP-sih-cuhm]. They all refer to the plants and pods of the genus *Capsicum*. They got the genus name from the Greek word *kapto*, meaning "to bite", and most peppers sure do have a bite to them! You can call them what you want. From here, I'll refer to them as chiles or peppers.

Shapely Peppers: Did you know there are over 200 types of chiles? And each type has many varieties!

Most peppers, both hot and sweet, are properly named *Capsicum annuum*. With so many different peppers, how do you begin to tell them apart?

Unlike most other vegetables and fruits, peppers are grouped by shape. Within that grouping there may be many different varieties that you can grow in your garden or find in the market. For example, one group is wax peppers. Sometimes called banana peppers, they tend to be large, with a cone-like shape, and the tips are bluntly pointed. Within that group are different varieties, such as "Santa Fe Grande", "Sweet Banana", and "Hungarian Yellow Wax".

The peppers you see on the next pages are actually pepper groups. I've picked the best eating and most common peppers that you can find easily.

Selecting Chiles: When buying fresh peppers, look for ones with bright colors. And then feel the chiles. You want them firm. You don't want any with soft spots or wrinkles.

Generally speaking, peppers tend to intensify in both flavor and heat (or sweetness) as they ripen and turn color. Most peppers start out green on the plant, and *then* turn color as they ripen. You know people who can't eat green bell peppers because they get indigestion? It's because the peppers haven't ripened yet. They're in essence, eating an unripe vegetable— so, of course, they're more prone to get indigestion. If they ate ripened red or yellow bell peppers, they'd probably avoid an upset stomach.

Storing Chiles: Fresh chiles will keep about a week in the vegetable bin of your refrigerator. Try those new ventilated vegetable storage bags— they can add a few extra keeping days.

By the end of summer, I've usually produced more fresh peppers than I can eat. I don't have the time to make them into sauces, or roast and freeze them. So I dry them. Wearing rubber gloves, use a large embroidery needle and heavy cotton thread to string the chiles. Then hang them in a well-ventilated room to dry. It takes about 2 weeks for them to dry.

But don't make the same mistake I did. I didn't realize the needle carried the heat of the pepper directly to my fingers. My fingers burned for weeks from this sneak attack. And I thought I was being careful!

Beat the Heat: Capsaicin is the chemical that gives chiles their fire. It's most concentrated around the stem, in the inner membranes (ribs) and seeds. If you like the pepper flavor but want to avoid the intense heat, use a paring knife to cut out these parts.

Always wear rubber gloves when handling chiles. I bought a supply of disposable gloves at my pharmacy.

When working with peppers, avoid touching any part of your body—especially your nose or eyes. If you start to burn, neutralize the area with vinegar or lemon juice. Just don't use soap and water. Capsaicin is an oil and will only spread with water to make things worse.

HOW HOT IS HOT?

The heat of peppers is measured in Scoville Heat Units. These are measured by testing peppers using high-performance liquid chromatography. Simply, it's a relative heat index for chiles.

You'll notice that for each pepper, there is a range of heat. That's because not every pepper of the same type measures the same. Cayennes grown in my garden may be hotter than those grown in yours, and even those from one plant to another may vary in intensity, depending on the parentage of each of the plants.

The range of heat is from 0 (sweet bell peppers) to 300,000 Scoville Heat Units (the very hottest habanero). But the scale goes up to 1,000,000. There isn't a pepper (so far) that's gone beyond the 300,000 barrier. With genetic engineering (breeding peppers for heat), it's just a matter of time. I pity the man who even thinks about eating one of these hornets.

SCOVILLE HEAT UNITS

Wax	0–40,000
New Mexican	500–2,500
Ancho/Poblano	1,000–1,500
Pasilla	1,000–1,500
Jalapeno	2,500–10,000
Serrano	10,000–20,000
Cayenne	30,000–50,000
Tabasco	30,000–50,000
Exotics (Thai)	30,000–100,000
Habanero	80,000–300,000
None Yet	300,000–1,000,000

EXOTICS - THAI [TI]

Thai is one kind of exotic pepper. They're thin-fleshed and small, only about 1 to 1 1/2 inches long and 1/4 inch in diameter. When ripe, the color ranges from green to red. Don't let the size fool you, they pack a lot of heat. Unlike some other peppers, the heat doesn't disperse in cooking. They're often used dried, a favorite in southeast Asian cuisine and stir-fries.

JALAPEÑO [hah-lah-PEH-nyoh]

Jalapeños are named for Jalapa, the capital city of Veracruz, Mexico. Their smooth skin changes from dark green to scarlet as they ripen. Sometimes they have a thin, edible "netting" around them, called "corkiness". There's nothing wrong with them.

Jalapeños grow about 3 inches long and 3/4 to 1 inch in diameter, with a rounded tip. Despite their heat, they are one of the most popular chiles (the hot seeds and veins are easily removed). Most groceries carry fresh jalapeños, or you can find canned ones. They are excellent filled with cheese or meat. Stuff them with Jack cheese, then roll in egg and bread crumbs. Fried, they make great appetizers.

CHIPOTLE [chih-POHT-lay]

Chipotles are smoke-dried jalapenos, sort of the equivalent of pepper jerky.

I haven't mastered the drying technique, so I buy chipotles. Like any dried pepper, their reddish-brown skin is wrinkled. Their smoky flavor is quite distinctive, somewhat sweet with a chocolately taste. Chipotles are pretty easy to find in supermarkets and all Mexican markets carry them.

You can also find them canned—they are the main ingredient in adobo sauce (you see me use them in many of our recipes). Pickled, they are often served as an appetizer.

WAX

Wax peppers, also known as banana chiles, are relatively large, growing 3 to 5 inches long and 1 1/2 inches in diameter. Their conical, tapering shape ends with a blunt point.

They're one of the tamest of all the chiles. Some don't have any heat, while others have more of a bite. Their flavor is kind of like a tangy melon and somewhat mild, depending on variety. They are a beautiful creamy yellow color.

"Santa Fe Grande", "Sweet Banana", and "Hungarian Yellow Wax" are all varieties of wax peppers you might see.

Use wax peppers in salads for color and a little tang. You can also find them as pickled peppers.

One of my favorite combinations is to saute wax peppers with a few slices of jalapenos (and a little habanero if I'm looking for a real kick). Then I add this mixture to sliced sausage and scrambled eggs.

PASILLA [pah-SEE-yah]

Pasillas are more commonly seen dried than fresh (they're called chilaca when fresh). They get their name from the Spanish word that means "little raisin". The blackish-brown color gives rise to their other name—chile negro. They grow from 6 to 8 inches long and 1 to 1 1/2 inches in diameter. Pasilla's rich flavor and medium pungency are great in sauces, especially in traditional Mexican moles. I grind them to a powder for fresh fruit salsas.

HABANERO [ah-bah-NEH-roh]

Habaneros are among the hottest chiles. Native to the Caribbean, Yucatan, and northern South America, they range from pale green to bright orange when ripe. They're shaped like a miniature lantern.

Habaneros have a fruity aroma and distinctive fruit-like taste (this is why they're so good in sweeter dishes).

Commercially, they're made into very hot sauces. You can usually find both fresh or dried habaneros in most markets.

Habaneros are often confused with Scotch bonnet chiles, which are also extremely hot. Scotch bonnets range in color from yellow to orange to red. They're used most often in jerk sauces and Caribbean curries.

SERRANO [seh-RRAH-noh]

Serranos are small, only about 1^1/$_2$ inches long with a slightly pointed end. The smooth skin turns from bright green to scarlet to yellow as it ripens. They're hotter than jalapenos. Many groceries and Mexican markets carry fresh serranos. If you can't find them, look in the canned food or ethnic food aisle, where you'll likely find them canned, pickled or packed in oil.

Serranos are commonly used to season guacamole and pico de gallo salsa. In the spring, I make a fiery salsa with chopped cucumbers, cilantro, Vidalia onions, and young green serranos. It adds a fresh and surprising afterburn to grilled hamburgers!

Dried serranos are called chile seco, and can be found whole or powdered.

NEW MEXICO

This type of pepper was called Anaheim, but now "Anaheim" is only one of the many varieties of New Mexico peppers. These peppers have been cultivated in New Mexico for over 300 years.

The pods range from 4 to 12 inches long, ending with a blunt point. They start out green and turn a glorious red when ripe. New Mexico chiles are used both green and ripe. You can roast and peel them, or they're great stuffed.

Dried, they're called chile pasado. These are the chiles that are traditionally allowed to remain on the plant until leathery, then tied into ristras (or strings), and dried in the sun.

TABASCO [tah-BAHS-koh]

This is another species of pepper, *Capsicum frutescens*. Originally grown in Mexico, they were transplanted to Louisiana, where they were cultivated for making Tabasco sauce. The demand was soon greater than the supply. Now they're grown commercially in Central America, but still processed in Louisiana. The pods are small, up to 1^1/$_2$ inches long and ^{3}/$_8$ inch wide. The young pods may be yellow or green, but they mature red. Besides their use in hot sauce, tabascos are used fresh in salsa or used dried in stir-fry dishes.

POBLANO [poh-BLAH-NOH]

Poblanos are dark green to reddish-black chiles whose flavor varies with color—the darker the pepper, the richer and sweeter the taste.

They grow 4 to 5 inches long and 2^1/$_2$ to 3 inches wide, with a tapering body (like a pointy bell pepper). You can find poblanos fresh in Mexican markets and some supermarkets in summer and early fall, or canned year round. These mild peppers are best cooked. They're traditionally used to make chiles rellenos.

CAYENNE [KI-yehn]

Cayennes are brilliant red when ripe, growing from 2 to 5 inches long and about ^{1}/$_2$ inch in diameter. They're often wrinkled with a pungent taste. You usually find them dried rather than fresh, or in their most common form— powdered (cayenne pepper).

Cayenne is excellent to add heat and flavor to soups and sauces. The immature (green) cayennes can be used in salsas.

Usually, the dried red pods are ground into powder or crushed into flakes. Louisiana hot sauce (not Tabasco) is traditionally made with cayenne peppers.

ANCHO [AHN-choh]

Anchos are dried poblanos. Their name means "wide," referring to their broad, heart-shaped pods.

Smaller than the fresh poblano, they're about 3 to 4 inches long. They range in color from brick red to dark, mahogany brown. The taste is sweet and fruity. In fact, they are the sweetest of the dried chiles and most commonly used dried chile in Mexico. Mulato is a type of dried poblano that is used in making mole (a Mexican sauce with chocolate and several chiles).

Photograph: Scott Little; Food Styling: Janet Pittman

TEXAS BRISKET

I wanted to smoke brisket for a long time, but needed some help. When I asked for advice, everyone gave me a different opinion. I got my fill of that real quick.

There was only one solution—head for Texas where I could be filled with more advice (and brisket) than my mind and body could hold.

In Texas, I was introduced to something truly special—plenty of smoky, tender brisket. It came piled high on white bread with cole slaw and a little more sauce. And I figure this will be as close to heaven as I get before actually passing on.

The Brisket Guys: The guys who know Texas brisket have been around smoke and fire for so long their skin is permanently infused with smoke. That's not all bad. In Texas, smoke in your skin is as honorable as the stars and ribbons on a general's uniform.

I visited with the best brisket smokers in the business—Harry Collins at **The Salt Lick**; Jose Guerrero at **Donn's Bar-B-Que**; Bobby and John Mueller of **Louie Mueller Barbecue**; and Art Blondin of **Artz Ribhouse**. They're all in and around Austin—the mecca of smoked brisket. Look 'em up, if you get the chance.

The Brisket Lessons: I have barbecue in my blood, but I don't have brisket blood. So the first lesson I learned is that good brisket takes time—a *lot* of time. They all taught me that "low and slow" temperatures work pure magic, transforming big, tough hunks of brisket into tender, smoky pieces of heaven.

Lesson two is that flavor comes from three different areas—the rub, the mop, and the smoke.

The rub is a blend of dry spices that's "rubbed" onto the brisket before smoking. There are all different rubs but all of them can be applied just before smoking (unlike a marinade).

A mop is a liquid that's "mopped" on while smoking. It not only gives the brisket flavor, but provides moisture during the long smoking process.

And finally, there's smoke—the flavor that comes from different hardwoods you burn with the charcoal. But too much smoke destroys brisket.

This hardwood smoke creates the prized deep pink "smoke ring" that surrounds a perfectly smoked brisket.

Take a look at the photo above. This is what you're shooting for—tender brisket that's slightly charred but juicy, with a perfect smoke ring. You can almost smell the smoked brisket.

SMOKING RULES OF THUMB

Indirect Heat: Whether you use a smoker or a grill, use indirect heat. Smoking brisket this way, away from the coals, means maximum smoke time resulting in moist, tender meat.

Temperature and Time: I tried different temperatures and times. I found a temperature of 225° for four hours worked best. Longer smoking at lower temperature tended to dry out the meat. Hotter temperatures with shorter times resulted in a tougher, burned brisket.

Smoke: The smoke from burning wood is what really flavors the brisket.

There's some trendy options out there like grapevines, old wine casks and whiskey barrels—but the small amount of flavor they give brisket isn't worth the trouble or expense.

Mesquite and hickory are the traditional woods used to smoke brisket in Texas. But other hard woods, like oak or pecan, are great. Soft wood, like pine, burns too hot and leaves nasty resin deposits—don't even try it.

TEXAS BRISKET *(30 SERVINGS)*

WORK TIME: 1 HOUR
COOK TIME: 4 HOURS
TRIM:
1   whole brisket (8–10 lbs.)
RUB WITH:
3/4   cup Rub Mixture, *see Page 28*
SMOKE FOR 4 HOURS, BASTING EVERY HALF HOUR WITH:
1   recipe Mop Sauce, *see Page 28*
SERVE WITH COWBOY BEANS, CORN CAKES, AND RED CHILE PEPPER SAUCE.

NUTRITIONAL INFORMATION PER 5-OZ. (+2 T. SAUCE): CALORIES 521; TOTAL FAT 36(G); CALORIES FROM FAT 62%; SODIUM 1,775(MG)

WHAT IS BRISKET?

Brisket is a cut of meat not many people know much about. If you've eaten corned beef on St. Patrick's Day, you've had "pickled" brisket.

What is brisket? The brisket is the chest muscle of beef cattle underneath the first five ribs. It's a small section of meat compared to other parts of the animal. But you're not cutting this into smaller steaks or roasts. It's *all* brisket.

Location of the Brisket: Look at the diagram, above right. Since the brisket is so close to the front legs, you can bet that the muscles get a good workout—just standing and walking around builds them up. The more exercise, the tougher the meat. It also means there's a lot of tough connective tissue.

But that's not all bad. The exercised muscles contain myoglobin, an oxygen-holding compound. This oxygen creates a flavorful piece of meat. Think of a chicken. The legs work harder than the breast. While the legs are tougher, they're also much more flavorful. Brisket's tenderness will come from the slow smoking process.

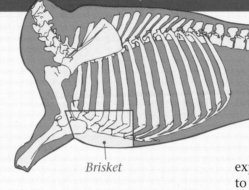

Brisket

Anatomy of a Brisket: At first, I was a little intimidated by this giant hunk of meat. But once I knew the parts, I felt better working with it.

Look at the whole brisket pictured below. See the thick and thin ends?

That thick end is called the *point* or *second* cut. It's marbled with fat on the inside and has a thick cap of fat covering it on top. Flavor all over the place! But a lot of times it's trimmed away from the rest of the brisket and ground into hamburger meat.

The thinner *flat* or *first* cut, on the right, is what's left. This is what you're likely to find in the store as "brisket," and is the section used to make corned beef. It's not nearly as fatty but the developed muscles of the cut sure do make for some flavorful meat.

What to buy: So after all that explaining, I'm going to tell you to buy the *whole* brisket—both the point and flat cuts. Here's why:

A whole brisket gives you the best of both worlds: the fat of the point cut renders as it smokes, basting the meat with flavor.

And the tough muscle of the flat cut turns fork-tender since it smokes for hours. You just can't beat this combination.

I went to a small butcher shop to buy the whole brisket. Ask for it specifically—usually it's bought whole from producers and then trimmed down into the two cuts.

But make sure they leave that fat cap on! Anybody worth their "Cowboy Beans", *see Page 30,* will smoke the whole brisket. And besides, it makes great sandwiches for a week.

Whole Brisket (point and flat cuts)

Brisket (flat cut only)

BUILDING A BETTER FIRE

You're going to *smoke* this brisket and building a "low and slow" fire is the first step to a tender piece of meat.

The Grills: Normally, I use a gas grill, but I learned (the hard way) it's not for smoking brisket. I had to use wood chips in a smoker box. The smoke flavor was way too mild.

I had better luck smoking on a charcoal Weber. The chunks of wood went directly on the coals and gave me plenty of smokiness.

But then there was the Oklahoma Joe pictured on the right. No, this isn't a plug for Oklahoma Joe. I paid full retail for this—about $600. But a good smoker is worth every penny.

This "Joe" is the trick for *serious* smoking. Thick steel walls help maintain a low, even heat. The offset fire box creates plenty of smoke and there are two dampers for circulation. And be sure to buy the optional temperature gauge—it's definitely worth the extra $30 to monitor the chamber.

Oklahoma Joe's Smoker

Temperature gauge

Fire box

LIGHT THE FIRE

If you're serious about smoking, then start with the right charcoal. I use hardwood lump charcoal instead of the perfectly shaped briquettes. It's burned hardwood left in its natural state and it has no chemical additives.

Hardwood charcoal burns hotter and cleaner than briquettes. It's also easy to start—no need for lighter fluid. I found it where they sell barbeque supplies.

I hate the taste and smell of lighter fluid (it seems to permeate the meat). So, I use a starter stick. It's wax and compressed sawdust. They start quickly, burn about 10 minutes, and don't get blown out in a gust of wind. Buy them at the supply stores, or mail order from **Futures Unlimited Inc., (888) 326-8906.**

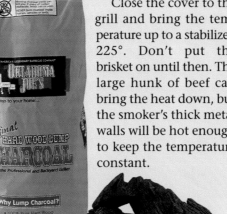

GET IT "LOW AND SLOW"

Getting a fire that's "low and slow" means you'll need to baby it for a time to build up the heat in the smoker.

I'll show you how to build a fire on Page 27. The key to a good fire is keeping the air flowing around the coals. Open all vents and doors when you light up for the best circulation.

When the coals are covered with gray ash and the embers begin to glow, add the hardwood to create smoke.

Close the cover to the grill and bring the temperature up to a stabilized 225°. Don't put the brisket on until then. The large hunk of beef can bring the heat down, but the smoker's thick metal walls will be hot enough to keep the temperature constant.

GIVE IT FLAVOR

The brisket's *soul* comes from smoke. Nothing, not even rubs or mops, can beat the taste of smoke.

Use hardwood in chunks (about the size of your fist) or small logs depending on the size of your smoker. Chips are okay for smaller jobs, like fish, but totally impractical here for long smoking.

Then there's the debate about aged wood vs. green wood. Aged wood (aged at least 6 months) is drier and burns more evenly than freshly cut green wood. Green wood contains too much resin (sap) which burns too hot and creates too much smoke.

Again, you can buy hardwood from the barbeque supply store. Or find it in your backyard. Try hickory, cherry, pecan, apple, maple, or oak—just not pine!

LIGHT MY FIRE

Sure, this Oklahoma Joe is pretty special. But it's got some basic features you can apply to any kind of grill.

Smoking Chamber: The chamber needs to be big enough (with cover closed) to hold *at least* one whole brisket *and* allow for good smoke circulation. My chamber is 29"x15"x8".

Fire Box: The offset fire box makes the Joe perfect for indirect cooking methods, like smoking. The food is cooked *away* from the heat source which prevents flare ups and hot spots. It also can maintain a low heat.

Door and Stack Vents: Both the stack vent and door vent combine to make a dual damper system that can really control the temperature in the smoker. If the fire gets too hot, adjust either vent to a smaller opening. Open them wider for more heat.

Drip Bucket: The drip bucket catches fat drippings from the brisket so you don't have a mess underneath your grill. This is a must.

Stack vent

Smoking chamber

Drip bucket

Door vent

FUELING YOUR FIRE

1 Since it was windy the day I smoked this brisket, I notched one end of the starter stick. The notched end stayed lit better.

2 Stack some hardwood charcoal in one corner of the firebox. Light the notched end of a starter stick and place it in the charcoal.

3 Spread out the coals when they're covered with gray ash and glowing. Add more charcoal and close the cover, but keep the vents open.

4 When your fire's about 150°, add some smoking wood. Close the smoking chamber to trap the smoke; keep the vents open for circulation.

5 Stir the coals around to keep the heat even. Add more hardwood and adjust the vents so the temperature stays consistent.

6 Alternate between charcoal and smoking wood when stoking the fire. Charcoal is best to increase the heat; get more smoke by adding wood.

RUB, TRIM AND MOP

Getting a brisket ready for smoking isn't exactly rocket science, but it does require a little preparation.

The Rub: Rubs are a mix of seasonings that are "rubbed" into foods before cooking. They're usually dry, but can also be a paste by adding crushed fresh herbs or oils.

Rubs form a crust during cooking that pack a lot of flavor. They range from mild to very hot. Each barbeque master has their own recipe—some very complex and others as simple as just salt and pepper. Mine is in between—the cumin makes it unique.

The Trim: The first thing you'll want to do with this whole brisket is trim off the thick fat cap that covers it. Don't! It'll baste the meat and keep the brisket moist while it smokes.

Okay, trim off a *little* of the fat—down to a 1/4" layer. Any extra is trimmed off after the brisket's smoked.

The Mop: Don't go running to your broom closet. In barbeque-speak, this "mop" is a very thin sauce—it gets the name from the tool used to "mop" the sauce on the meat.

Sure, you can use an everyday basting brush. But I like using a small *cotton* mop. Don't get grossed out, but I buy cotton toilet mops from the grocery store. They're the perfect size.

Every barbeque expert has their opinion on mops—both when to mop and what ingredients to use.

What you want is a thin acidic sauce—like a marinade. Minimize ingredients with sugars (to prevent burning) and try to achieve taste from acids like vinegar, mustard, or citrus.

Because of the long smoking process, I mop every half hour.

RUB MIXTURE
(MAKES ABOUT 1 CUP)
WORK TIME: 5 MINUTES
IN A SMALL BOWL, COMBINE:
- 1/4   cup kosher salt
- 2   T. ground black pepper
- 2   T. granulated garlic
- 2   T. cayenne pepper
- 2   T. cumin seeds, lightly crushed

7 Lightly crush cumin seeds in a mortar and pestle to release their oils. Mix together with other rub ingredients and set aside.

8 Feel around the "fat cap" for any really thick areas and trim some of it down—you want about a 1/4" layer of fat covering the top.

9 Turn the brisket over and feel for more excess fat. Trim it down to 1/4", but don't dig into the meat—this fat will really keep it moist.

10 "Rub" both sides of the brisket with 3/4 cup rub mixture, working it into every nook and cranny. Set the brisket aside.

11 To make anchovy paste for the mop sauce, smear 6 or 7 anchovy filets against a cutting board with the back of a knife.

MOP SAUCE
(MAKES 8 CUPS)
WORK TIME: 10 MINUTES
IN A LARGE BOWL, COMBINE:
- 3   cups apple cider vinegar
- 1   cup sugar
- 1/2   cup Red Chile Sauce, *see Page 7*
- 1/2   cup molasses
- 1/2   cup Worcestershire sauce
- 1/4   cup yellow mustard
- 1/4   cup soy sauce
- 3   T. Rub Mixture, *see recipe this page*
- 2   T. anchovy paste
- 1   T. tomato paste

WHISK IN:
- 3   cups extra virgin olive oil

YOU CAN RESERVE 2–3 CUPS SAUCE FOR SERVING.

NUTRITIONAL INFORMATION PER 2 T.: CALORIES 115; TOTAL FAT 10(G); CALORIES FROM FAT 77%; SODIUM 315%

12 In a large bowl, mix together all the mop ingredients. Whisk in olive oil and set aside 2–3 cups of it to serve with the brisket.

NOW YOU'RE SMOKIN'!

Remember reading in Greek mythology about the sirens luring sailors with melodious voices, causing their ships to crash into the rocks? When you smell this brisket smoking, you'll understand the temptation of sneaking slices of brisket before its finished. The "sirens" of smoke will draw you to the beef—but be strong! Hold out!

Starting the Smoking: Start smoking the brisket by putting it on the grill with the fat side down. This starts to soften and render the fat so it immediately begins to baste the meat when you turn it over.

As the smoke and heat penetrate the less fatty top side, it seals the rest of the meat to keep moisture in.

Mop and Turn: After 30 minutes, mop the brisket and turn it, keeping the thinner end away from the heat. Mop the other side and close the lid. Keep doing this every half hour.

Is It Done Yet?: Smoke an 8–10 pound whole brisket for four hours.

The outside of the meat will be black—charred-looking. But that's a good thing—this "char" tastes great. And inside it'll be moist and flavorful.

Right under the charred exterior, you'll find that deep pink smoke ring. This is a mark of distinction and accomplishment. It means you've applied the right amount of smoke.

Some people mistake the smoke ring for undercooked meat. Not so. It's the meat's natural reaction to the nitrogen oxides that are given off when hardwood burns.

Slicing: Before slicing, let the brisket rest 15 minutes to let interior juices flow towards the drier surface. This is a natural process—liquids *always* take the path of least resistance.

There will still be some fat on the outside although most of it will have been rendered during smoking. I leave mine on, but you can trim yours.

Brisket's grain runs in different directions. Change slicing positions so you always cut against the grain.

Begin at the tip end and slice at an angle, about 1/4" thick. Slice until you hit the fat pocket in the middle of the brisket. Turn it around and slice the other side, like I did in Step 20. **AH**

13 When the smoker's at 225°, put the rubbed brisket on the grill, fat side down, with the thinner end away from the heat source.

14 Set aside 2–3 cups mop sauce for serving with the finished brisket. After an hour, "mop" the brisket with some of the sauce.

15 Turn the brisket over and mop the other side. Do this every half hour for 3 more hours to add moisture and flavor to the meat.

16 Adjust the temperature in the smoker with the vents. A thermometer in the smoker will help you keep things "low and slow."

17 After 4 hours of smoking, remove the brisket from the smoker. Rest it for 15 minutes before trimming off excess fat.

18 Start slicing at the tip, against the grain of the meat and at an angle. Thinner slices will be more tender. And look at that smoke ring!

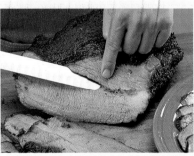

19 I wanted to show you this pocket of fat in the middle of the brisket. It melted and basted the *inside* of the meat during smoking.

20 When you hit the middle of the brisket, turn it around— the meat grain changes direction. Keep slicing on the other side.

COWBOY BEANS

COWBOY BEANS

(MAKES 10 CUPS)

WORK TIME: 15 MINUTES
COOK TIME: 3¼ HOURS

WASH, BOIL, THEN SOAK FOR 4 HOURS:

4 cups assorted dry beans (pinto, lima, garbanzo, and red beans)

SAUTE IN 2 T. VEGETABLE OIL:

1 lb. lean pork, cut into chunks

ADD, COOK UNTIL CARAMELIZED:

1 large onion, sliced
2 dried ancho peppers, stemmed, seeded, and sliced
3 cloves garlic, smashed

DEGLAZE PAN WITH:

½ cup chicken broth

STIR IN:

3½ cups chicken broth
1½ cups canned crushed tomatoes
1 cup brown sugar
2 T. Worcestershire sauce
1 T. yellow mustard
1 t. dry mustard

BAKE 2 HOURS, ADD:

¾ cup white vinegar

UNCOVER AND BAKE 1 MORE HOUR.

MAKING BEANS

1 Rinse and sort dried beans. Put them in a non-reactive pan. Fill with water (2" above beans). Bring to a boil, then turn off. Let soak 4 hours.

2 On high heat, saute pork chunks in 2 T. vegetable oil. When brown, add dried peppers and onions. Cook until caramelized (well-browned).

3 Add crushed garlic, but don't let it burn. Deglaze pan with ½ cup chicken broth, scraping the pan to remove flavorful bits of meat.

4 Add brown sugar, Worcestershire sauce, yellow and dry mustards, crushed tomatoes, and drained beans. Add chicken broth. Stir.

5 Bring everything to a boil. Then cover and put into a 300° oven for two hours. Stir the pot every 30 minutes. Be sure to stir the bottom.

6 Add ¾ cup vinegar. Continue baking, uncovered, one more hour. Note: Don't add the vinegar until the last hour—your beans won't soften.

CORN CAKES

Photograph: Scott Little; Food Styling: Janet Pittman

CORN CAKES
(MAKES 8 CAKES)
WORK TIME: 15 MINUTES
REST TIME: 30 MINUTES
COOK TIME: 4 MINUTES EACH

ROAST AND PREPARE:
1 cup corn, cut from 2 roasted ears
$1/2$ cup roasted red pepper, peeled and diced

CUT:
2 T. jalapeno peppers, minced

COMBINE:
1 cup all-purpose flour
$1/3$ cup corn meal
1 t. salt
$1/2$ t. baking soda
$1/2$ t. baking powder
$1/2$ t. black pepper

MIX WITH DRY INGREDIENTS:
$3/4$ cup milk
$1/3$ cup buttermilk
2 egg yolks
$1 1/2$ T. melted butter

LET BATTER REST 30 MINUTES.

SAUTE CAKES IN:
   Vegetable oil

MAKING CORN CAKES

1 Roast or grill sweet corn and red pepper until both are blackened. Slice corn from the cobs to measure 1 cup. You can use frozen corn.

2 Sweat roasted peppers in plastic bag for 10 minutes. Then peel away the charred skin, without washing. Remove veins and seeds. Dice.

3 Cut jalapeno peppers into quarters. Remove stem, seeds, and veins. *Mince* the jalapeno quarters to measure at least 2 tablespoons.

4 Mix dry ingredients in bowl. In another bowl, combine milks, egg yolks, melted butter. Blend with dry ingredients. Add corn, chiles, peppers.

5 After the batter rests for 30 minutes, heat oil in skillet. Pour $1/3$ cup of batter to form each cake. Saute until lightly browned.

6 Flip each corn cake and saute other side. Serve cakes hot with brisket, sour cream, and some red chile sauce. This is eating!

PRESSURE CANNING

I usually have a department in Cuisine called "Wares" which talks about kitchen equipment. But since this is when all that good fresh

produce is available to us, I thought it would be fun to talk about something different—canning.

But there's a problem. Techniques and timing change depending on what you're canning. Varying acidic levels, altitude, and recipes affect results. To avoid all these variables, we're only going to can tomatoes.

I'm sure some of you have "generational" canning knowledge. But some techniques have changed over the years. Think of this as a refresher course to update your skills. For those of you just starting out, follow these techniques carefully. It's a lot of fun.

GENERAL INFORMATION

Before you get going, you need to know some general information.

Methods of Canning: There are two kinds of canning methods: hot-water canning and pressure canning.

Hot-water canning (or water-bath canning) is when you process the jars in a large covered cooking pot outfitted with a rack (like a cooling rack). Jars are totally submerged in water and simmered for a period of time. This method is used for highly acidic foods like tomatoes, pickles, and fruits. The temperature can only get up to 212°F (boiling temperature).

Pressure canning is the second method which requires some special equipment. Low acidic foods (like most vegetables) are packed into jars, then placed in a *pressure canner*. When the special heavy lid is securely fastened, the canner processes food under pressure (240–250°F). Don't pressure can with a pressure *cooker*!

Packing Methods: There are two ways to pack produce into jars — cold pack (also called raw pack) and hot pack.

The cold or raw packing method is used to place unheated, freshly-prepared foods into hot jars. Boiling liquid is then poured over the food.

With cold packing, it's easier to arrange produce in the jar, but I found the food tended to shrink and float.

For hot packing, food is simmered first, and then loosely packed into hot jars while still warm. Boiling water or any hot residual cooking liquid is added to fill to the proper headspace.

While the hot pack is harder to handle, it has its benefits. Cooking removes much of the air from the food so there's less shrinkage during processing. It seems to seal in flavor and color of the food much better than the cold pack method. Finally, because of the heat, the vacuum seal is better which increases the shelf life.

Headspace: Headspace is the space between the very top lip of the jar and the food or liquid. The proper amount of headspace creates a tight vacuum seal. No matter what canning or packing method you use, it's important to follow the directions for leaving the appropriate amount of headspace. This is vital and varies with each recipe, *see Chart page 35.*

Cleanliness: Cleanliness is the most important factor in canning. Bacteria can easily develop. Be sure to keep all dish towels, work surfaces, equipment, *and* your hands perfectly clean. Monitor this carefully.

Altitude: If you're canning in a high altitude area (over 1000 feet above sea level), you need to adjust both your processing time and gauge pressure. Most recipes are written for altitudes of less than 1000 feet—good recipes should have an altitude adjustment. If not, call your county extension service or look at the chart on page 35.

Removing Air Bubbles: Once you've placed your food in the jars, it's important to remove trapped air bubbles that have formed inside the jar.

Air bubbles will float to the surface during processing. This can cause too much headspace and reduce the strength of your seal.

Remove bubbles with a clean, non-metallic utensil. Use a plastic knife, plastic spatula, or like I do, a wooden skewer. Using anything metal could scratch the glass and result in weakening the jar's integrity. With so much pressure, the jar could break.

Jars: Canning jars are specially designed for strength and pressure. Use only jars designated for canning. Avoid commercial-type jars such as mayonnaise, peanut butter, jelly, or pickle jars. They don't have the structural ability to withstand the pressure.

Lids and Rings: One final note. While the screw-on rings can be used more than once (provided they aren't rusted), the flat lids cannot. They've been treated with a sealing compound that is good for one-time use only.

KNOWING YOUR EQUIPMENT

Most of these canning items shown are available at your local hardware, grocery, or department store.

Pressure Canner: A pressure canner is a specially-made heavy pot which has a lid that can close steam in tight. It looks and acts similarly to a pressure cooker. But as I said earlier, they are not interchangeable.

A *pressure canner* is bigger and can hold large quart jars without crowding them. It regulates the amount of pressure that forms inside by a simple pressure gauge which fits over the "petcock" vent on the lid.

There are two types of pressure gauges: weighted and dial. *Weighted gauges* have three holes for different pressures. The amount of pressure is controlled by weight so nothing mechanical can go wrong. They are very precise and require no "annual check-up" like the more complicated dial gauges do.

The vent tube in the lid is called the *vent port* or *petcock*. When the vent port is covered, pressure and temperature rise inside the canner. Check the vent occasionally to make sure it's not clogged up. If it's blocked, pressure can build up inside the canner releasing the *safety valve*. Run a thin wire or thread through to clean it.

Not all pressure canners have *gaskets*. If yours does, be sure to clean it after each use. Then replace it once a year just to be on the safe side.

The last part of your canner is the *rack*. This elevates the jars above the bottom of the base allowing steam to circulate around the entire jar.

For $60, this was a fun and worthwhile investment for me.

Now that you know about a canner, here are some more items that you'll need.

Jars: Use only standard canning jars. Kerr, Ball, and Weck are good brand names that are well-known.

Check jar rims for chips or cracks which can prevent the jar from pressure sealing to an airtight state. Irregularities can cause food to spoil in 24 hours!

For recipes requiring processing under 10 minutes, it's necessary to sterilize your jars and lids.

To sterilize, place jars in a large saucepan and cover with water. Bring water to a boil and maintain for a full 10 minutes. Keep jars and lids in the hot water until ready to use.

Don't think your dishwasher can sterilize. Mold and fungus spores are killed at around 212°—most dishwashers only hit about 140°.

For recipes that are processed over 10 minutes, wash in hot water with a mild detergent. Rinse thoroughly. Sterilization is not needed because of the long exposure to heat during processing. Keep the clean jars and lids submerged in hot water or in a 180° oven until ready to use.

Lids and Rings: The self-sealing tops consist of two pieces. A flat metal lid and a metal screw ring.

Lids: The flat lid has a trough, which is filled with a colored gasket. This gasket is coated with a sealing compound. When jars are processed, the lid gasket softens and covers the sealing surface allowing air to escape but not enter. As the gasket cools, it forms an airtight seal.

Like anything rubber, time and exposure can age a gasket. I buy only the amount I'll need for one season. *Never re-use a lid. The sealing compound on the lids only works once.*

Rings: You *can* reuse the metal rings that are used to secure and seal the lids during processing. They're for sealing and not storing. The rings are removed from the jars after the cool down (12–24 hours). Just make sure they're not rusted or dented.

Jar Lifter or Canning Tongs: Canning tongs are a handy little piece of equipment. They're used to remove the hot jars from the pressure canner—and believe me, these jars are hot! You'll need a pair of these. By putting pressure on the handles, the jar lifter pinches the neck of the hot jar with its rubber-tipped ends.

Canning Salt: If you choose to add salt, pure canning salt or pickling salt is what you want to use. Regular table salt contains a filler that can cause cloudiness. Salt is for flavoring only in canned foods and doesn't have to be used—it is not a preservative in the canning process.

Other Items: I'm not going to bother telling you how these items work, but you'll need them. They are: wide-mouth funnel, bamboo skewer, timer, clean towels, and a good 'tude.

Jar Lifter or Canning Tongs

Canning Jars

Wide-mouth Funnel

Lid   Gasket Compound   Ring or Band

Weighted Gauge

Vent port or Petcock

Rack

Lid   Safety Valve

Gasket   Base

PREPARING THE TOMATOES

Now that you're armed with some general canning information, I'm going to "baby step" you through processing all those summer tomatoes.

While I told you that acidic foods (like tomatoes) have been traditionally processed using the hot-water method, recent research shows that pressure canning will result in a higher quality product. This is what we're going to do with tomatoes.

Preparing the Tomatoes: Sort the tomatoes, discarding ones with cuts or bruises. They should be firm, ripe and all about the same size.

Allow 2½–3½ pounds for one quart. Wash tomatoes in cold water and then remove their skins as I'm doing in step 3. Remove the stem and any tough core. You can leave the tomatoes whole or cut in half.

Then use the hot pack method—cook them first. This brings out their fresh flavor and keeps the bright color.

Acid Level: To prevent bacteria, you have to hit the right temperature. Achieving the right acid levels is just as critical. While tomatoes are naturally acidic, there are new hybrids that have been genetically engineered to contain less acid.

Extra acid has to be added. Use bottled lemon juice (not fresh) or citric acid to each jar before processing. To be safe, buy litmus paper from the drug store. A reading below 4.0 is required for the proper acidity level.

PREPARING AND FILLING THE JARS

1 Examine the jars, and rings carefully. Wash the jars and rings in detergent, rinse thoroughly and place in a 180° oven until ready to use.

2 Place the canning lids in boiling water for 2–3 minutes. Remove from heat but leave them in the hot water until needed.

3 Cut an "X" in the base of each tomato. Blanch tomatoes in simmering water until peel splits. Plunge into cold water, then peel and core.

4 Quarter tomatoes and place in a saute pan. Heat quickly to a boil and cook for 5 minutes. Add 2 T. of bottled lemon juice per quart jar.

5 Fill jars with hot tomatoes using the wide-mouth funnel. Keep adding the tomatoes, pressing lightly, to fill empty spaces with juice.

6 Be sure to leave ½" headspace for each jar. This is measured from the top of the jar to the top of the food or its liquid.

7 Jiggle a wooden skewer up and down around the inside of the jar to remove trapped air bubbles. Adjust the headspace as necessary.

8 Wipe the jar rims inside and out with a clean, damp cloth. Place the lid, gasket side down, onto the jar rim. Center the lid.

9 Place a ring over the flat lid and tighten it just to the point of resistance. Do not overtighten—a good seal is created from the vacuum.

PRESSURE CANNING

Place the cooking rack in the pressure canner. Add 2–3" of hot water (check the manufacturer's directions) and 1 T. vinegar. The vinegar prevents discoloration of the interior. Place filled jars on rack making sure there's room for steam to circulate between each jar. Then fasten canner lid securely.

Leave the weighted gauge off the vent port. Turn the heat on high until steam flows from the vent port. Let the steam escape through the vent port for 10 minutes. Then place the weighted gauge on the vent port. For these tomatoes, it's set on 10 lbs.

Reduce the heat so that the canner maintains a steady pressure—the gauge will rock periodically (check manufacturer's directions on how often the gauge should jiggle or rock).

Start timing now. When the timed process is completed, turn off the heat and let the canner release its pressure by cooling down naturally.

After the canner has released its pressure (no more steam is coming from the vent port), remove gauge. Wait 2 minutes and remove the lid.

Take out each jar with lifters and place gently on a towel or rack. Leave at least 1" space between jars. Cool at room temperature for 12-24 hours.

As the jars cool, the contents contract, pulling the lid firmly against the jar to form a vacuum. You know you've done a good job by the looking at and listening to the lids. They'll be concave and make a sharp "ping" sound when tapped with a spoon. **AH**

10 Position the rack in the canner and place filled jars on it. Make sure there's space for steam to circulate between each jar.

11 With weight removed, turn heat to high and vent the canner for 10 minutes. Place the weight on 10 lbs. and start timing.

12 Reduce heat so weight "rocks" per canner instructions. When done, let cool, remove weight and wait 2 minutes. Remove lid.

13 With a "jar lifter" remove the jars to a rack leaving 1 inch of space between jars. Cool for 24 hours, then remove *only* the rings.

14 To test the seal, tap the lid with the back of a spoon. It should make a clear "pinging" sound and the lid will be concave.

15 Wipe off the lids and jars, then rinse and dry. Label each jar with the date and contents. Store canned foods between 50°–70°.

TOMATO TYPE	PACKING METHOD	HEADSPACE	DIAL GAUGE	WEIGHTED GAUGE	TIME (PINTS/QUARTS)
Crushed	Hot	1/2"	11 lbs.	10 lbs.	15 mins.
Whole or Halved (packed in water)	Raw or Hot	1/2"	11 lbs.	10 lbs.	10 mins.
Whole or Halved (no added liquid)	Raw	1/2"	11 lbs.	10 lbs.	25 mins.
Whole or Halved (packed in tomato juice)	Raw or Hot	1/2"	11 lbs.	10 lbs.	25 mins.
Tomato Juice	Hot	1/2"	11 lbs.	10 lbs.	15 mins.
Tomato-Veg. Juice Blend	Hot	1/2"	11 lbs.	10 lbs.	15 mins.
Sauce (unseasoned)	Hot	1/4"	11 lbs.	10 lbs.	15 mins.
Sauce (seasoned)	Hot	1/2"	11 lbs.	10 lbs.	15 mins.

ALTITUDE CHART

The chart at left is for altitudes below 1000 feet. Use this chart for higher altitudes.

ALTITUDE (IN FEET)	WEIGHTED GAUGE	DIAL GAUGE
1,001–2,000	15	11
2,001–4,000	15	12
4,001–6,000	15	13
6,001–8,000	15	14
8,001–10,000	15	15

The processing times will remain the same.

Q *I was excited to see the New York Cheesecake featured in Issue 9. I followed the recipe exactly, but had extra batter. What went wrong?*

A Gina from New York and other loyal readers called me about their problem. My head's hanging so low in shame, I can hardly type this apology.

I *inadvertently* gave you the wrong pan dimensions—the right size should've read 8" across by $3^1/2$" high, not 3".

In an attempt to redeem myself, I've reworked the recipe to fit the smaller pan. Only the filling measurements and baking time are adjusted. The crust is the same.

I am very sorry for the mistake. But think of it this way—now you have two great cheesecake recipes!

NEW YORK CHEESECAKE

(MAKES 1- 8 INCH CAKE)
PAN SIZE: 8"x3"
WORK TIME: 1 HOUR
COOK TIME: $1^1/2$–2 HOURS

COMBINE; RESERVE 2 T.:
1   cup graham cracker crumbs
$1/2$ cup finely chopped toasted pecans

ADD; PRESS INTO BOTTOM OF PAN:
$1/4$ cup melted unsalted butter
3   T. sugar

CREAM TOGETHER:
6   pkgs. (8 oz. each) Philadelphia® cream cheese, softened
$3/4$ cup sugar
2   t. vanilla

ADD ONE AT A TIME:
3   eggs

BLEND IN:
$1/3$ cup sour cream

BAKE AT 300° FOR $1^1/2$–2 HOURS.

Q *I would like to use a fresh vanilla bean in place of vanilla extract in my recipe. What's the ratio I should use?*

A Pam Penzey at Penzey's, Ltd. spices and seasonings gave me some great vanilla bean and vanilla extract information.

In most recipes, you can replace 1–2 teaspoons vanilla extract with half a vanilla bean. (Use a whole bean for denser recipes like cheesecake.) Split the bean in half lengthwise, scrape out the tiny black seeds with the back of a paring knife and add both directly to the batter.

With heavier cookie doughs, the bean flavor doesn't mix in evenly—it's best to use the liquid extract in that case.

Q *What's the deal with skirt steak— where does it come from, and why is it so expensive?*

A Skirt steak belongs to a small group of meat cuts known as "butcher steaks"—there's just one or two of each of these cuts per animal. The butcher would take them home instead of selling the few he had.

Well, he really lucked out because the skirt steak is one of the most flavorful cuts of meat you can get.

Skirt steak is the diaphragm muscle of a steer that controls breathing. It's a long, flat piece of meat that looks sort of like a belt. Which brings me to the most well-known skirt steak dish—fajitas [fah-HEE-tuhs]. It means "little belt" in Spanish.

The popularity of fajitas (and the fact that there are only two steaks per steer) makes it tough to find in supermarkets—all the restaurants get it first.

But if you do find some skirt steak (I buy mine at a Mexican market), it'll seem inordinately pricey for a tough cut of beef. It's simple economics— supply and demand.

Q&A

We'll find answers to your cooking questions, and help find solutions to the unique problems which occur in the kitchen. Any questions? Send your cooking questions to *Cuisine, Q & A Editor,* 2200 Grand Avenue, Des Moines, IA 50312, or contact us through our E-mail address: *Cuisine@cuisinemag.com*

Q *I've seen several recipes that call for instant espresso powder. What is it and where can I find it?*

A Instant espresso powder is just a freeze-dried espresso grind of coffee that works the same as instant coffee—just add water. It's really convenient when you need a caffeine jolt but don't want to get out the espresso machine.

Normally, I don't mess with instant coffee. But this espresso powder has its advantages—it dissolves easily, so you can flavor sauces, ice creams and baked goods without adding watery espresso. And the concentrated flavor means you don't have to use much for kick.

Find the instant espresso powder in the instant coffee section of your grocery store.

Q *I love the recipes in Cuisine, but I'm a little reluctant to try those using raw eggs—shouldn't we be concerned about salmonella?*

A According to the National Egg Council, the recent outbreaks of salmonella poisoning are really focused in on institutional type cooking and not home use.

Actually, the percentage of eggs that carry salmonella is very small—only about 1 in 10,000. If there *is* salmonella present in an egg, there's usually not enough of it to make a healthy adult sick. But you still need to take precautions.

Proper refrigeration, safe cooking techniques, and common sense fight salmonella bacteria best.

Store all eggs and egg-based foods in the refrigerator. Warm environments are the perfect place for the bacteria to build up.

Cook eggs thoroughly—the American Egg Board recommends cooking eggs to at least 160°. Buy eggs from a reputable source or a grocery store with large turnover. And pitch eggs with cracked shells.

When I call for fresh eggs, I'm teaching a traditional technique. If you're reluctant, use an egg substitute—it's perfectly acceptable.

Q *What is the difference between Blackstrap molasses and plain molasses? Do they taste different?*

A Molasses is a by-product of sugar refining. The juice is squeezed from sugar cane and then boiled

down to a syrup. Sugar crystals form during boiling—they're removed and processed into granulated sugar. The remaining dark liquid is molasses.

There's three kinds of molasses—light, dark, and blackstrap. Light molasses is the syrup that remains after one boiling. It's sweeter (because there's more sugar left in the liquid), thinner and lighter in color.

The second boil produces dark molasses—less sweet, thicker, and darker than light molasses. It's what I used in the brisket mop sauce on page 28.

Blackstrap is from the third, final boil. It's bitter, very thick and dark. Some feel it's higher in nutrition than the others, but it's main use is in cattle feed.

EDIBLE FLOWERS

Seems that flowers are popping up everywhere, not just in gardens anymore. They're in salads, on cakes, even served as hors d'oeuvres. With all this blooming food

Photograph: ©Cathy Wilkinson Barash

around, John wanted to introduce you to the flavor and beauty of edible flowers. And although he appreciates flowers in his food, they aren't a part of his culinary heritage. So, he asked me, Cathy Wilkinson Barash, to share my expertise about these delightful blooms with him and you.

I've been eating flowers since I was a small child. Got in trouble for doing that because my parents didn't know that the flowers I had nibbled in the garden (roses, calendulas, daylilies, and pinks) were indeed safe.

Over the years my interest in edible flowers continued. I was dismayed by a lack of documented information. So, I decided that if I couldn't find a good book with cultural information on flowers as well as recipes on how to use them, I would write one myself. In 1993, my book, *Edible Flowers from Garden to Palate*, was published.

It may seem that edible flowers are a relatively new culinary embellishment. Fact is, people have been eating flowers for millennia. The ancient Romans not only strewed their dining rooms with rose petals, they used them in cooking. Seems that the peasants had been using rose hips (the fruit from a rose) for a long time, and then the noblemen discovered that the rose petals were pretty tasty. Of course, if you eat the flowers, then no fruit can form, so this was a major point of contention.

The Chinese document using flowers in food even longer. As many as 4000 years ago, they were eating chrysanthemums and daylilies.

Daylilies are still used today in Chinese cuisine. I'll bet you've eaten a daylily and not even known it—they're a standard ingredient in hot and sour soup. Next time you have it, examine what's in the bowl. White tofu, white chicken or pork, slices of bamboo shoot, and the long, thin, slightly fibrous dried daylily flower. They're available in Oriental markets as "golden needles."

TEN RULES

The world of edible flowers is full of beauty and wonder. Yet there are also some hazards. So to help you avoid any problems, I've come up with this list of rules. Obey them and you'll enjoy the positive benefits of flowers in your food. Disobey them, and you could be in for a nasty experience (anything from a headache or nausea to serious poisoning).

1. Eat only those flowers you can identify as safe and edible. One problem I have with many edible flower books is that they have no color photographs (mine has ID shots for each of the 67 flowers listed).

The other is they just talk about flowers in general terms without using their proper (botanical) names. Since common names vary from region to region, they can be misleading. For instance, gillyflower can refer to both Dianthus and Matthiola. Dianthus, also commonly known as pinks, are edible, while Matthiola, or stocks, are not and can make you sick.

2. Don't assume that a flower is edible because it's on a plate of food. Know what you're eating at restaurants or at a catered affair. Be especially wary of flowers on wedding cakes. Unfortunately, some cooks use flowers not understanding safety or flavors (see Rule #1).

I've been to restaurants where a dish was served with non-edible, or even poisonous flowers! When this would happen, I'd explain to the server that while the dish is beautiful, the flowers aren't edible. Not knowing, they'd offer up Rule 3 thinking organic means safe.

If you or your waiter aren't absolutely sure, don't eat the flowers—put them in a vase on the table!

3. Eat only those flowers that have been grown organically. Plants tend to concentrate chemicals from the soil. You don't want to eat ones that have been grown using anything but safe and natural fertilizers.

4. Don't eat flowers from florists, nurseries, garden centers or public gardens. You have no idea how these plants were grown and what chemicals (insecticides, hormones, or fertilizers) may have been used on them.

Cut flowers from florists are the worst—many are grown in South America using chemicals that are now outlawed in this country. And once they arrive at the florist's, they are put in water with preservative—nothing you want to ingest.

5. Eat only the petals of edible flowers (see the illustration below). Remove and discard the pistil and stamens before eating. There are some exceptions to this rule—flowers that are really tiny (those that you'd need magnifying glasses and tweezers to see and remove the offending parts). These include edibles such as lilacs, lavender, thyme, and anise hyssop. Pansies, violets, and Johnny jump-ups are also exceptions. (I can hardly find the pistils and stamens on them with a magnifying glass!)

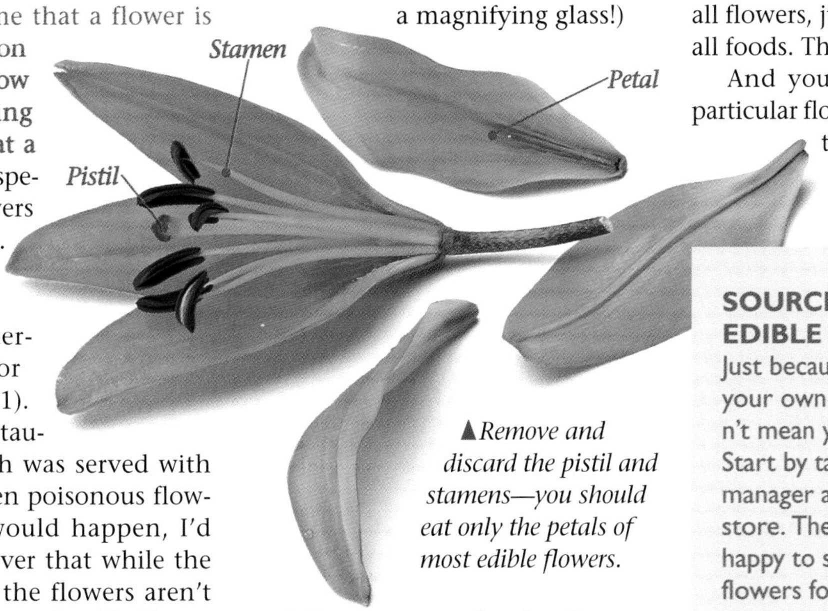

Stamen

Petal

Pistil

▲ *Remove and discard the pistil and stamens—you should eat only the petals of most edible flowers.*

6. Don't assume that just because a flower smells good it is edible—most flowers are inedible. In fact some are poisonous. Some sweet-smelling but potentially deadly flowers are lily-of-the-valley, wisteria, heliotrope, and Carolina jasmine (here's where we get to the common name thing again. The true jasmine is edible, yet night jasmine is poisonous—three different plants botanically).

7. Don't eat flowers if you have hay fever, asthma, or allergies. Even though you remove the pollen-bearing parts, you could still antagonize any of these conditions by ingesting flowers. Better safe than sorry.

8. Don't eat other parts of the plant unless you know them to be safe. Even though the flowers may be delicious, the leaves, stems, or roots may be toxic. For example, elderberry flowers are delicious (safe when cooked, or brewed into wine; never eat them raw), but the stems and leaves of the shrub are toxic.

9. Don't eat flowers picked from the side of heavily trafficked roads. This is common sense. These flowers would be imbued with the chemicals from car and truck exhausts—also from weed control sprays.

10. Introduce flowers into your diet gradually—in small quantities and one variety at a time, the same way you'd introduce a baby to new foods. You may not like the flavor of all flowers, just like you may not like all foods. That's okay.

And you may be sensitive to a particular flower, like some people are to strawberries or shellfish. Again, my old adage—better safe than sorry.

SOURCES FOR EDIBLE FLOWERS

Just because you don't grow your own edible flowers doesn't mean you can't enjoy them. Start by talking to the produce manager at your local grocery store. The store will often be happy to special order edible flowers for you. And don't overlook local horticultural and botanical groups as good possible sources.

Mail order sources are:

Earthy Delights:
(800) 367-4709

Mariposa Farms:
(515) 236-5740

Diamond Organics:
(888) 674-2642

FLOWERS FOR FLAVOR

Flowers go beyond mere beauty. Is there anything else you can add to a dish, besides saffron or turmeric, that gives such color? Like any herb or spice, edible flowers add flavor to food. The range of flavors are:

LICORICE: anise hyssop and fennel
BEAN-LIKE: redbud and tulips
BITTER: calendula, chicory, mums, English daisy, and sunflower
CITRUSY: citrus and tuberous begonia
FLORAL: apple, clove pink, honeysuckle, lilac, pea, pineapple guava, rose, and scented geranium
FRUITY: chamomile and rose of Sharon
HERBAL: basil, borage, cilantro, dill, marjoram, oregano, rosemary, sage, signet marigold, and thyme
MILD: hibiscus, okra, and roselle
MINTY: bee balm, Johnny jump-up, pansy, and mint
ONIONY/GARLICKY: chives, garlic chives, nodding onion, society garlic
PERFUMED: jasmine, lavender, linden, and violets
SPICY/PEPPERY: arugula, broccoli, mustard, nasturtium, and savory
SWEET: dandelion, most daylilies, elderberry, red clover, pineapple sage, sweet woodruff, and yucca
VEGETAL: squash and zucchini

FLOWERS FOR COLOR

Since flowers come in every color of the rainbow, you can have fun planning a meal with them. Coordinate the food to match your clothing, the color of your dining room, or just your favorite color.

Flowers make food elegant. You can turn family fare into company food—even tuna salad! Toss in some chopped tulip petals, thyme, rosemary, or pansies. Then, make the big splash by serving it in a large edible flower such as a tulip, daylily, or hibiscus.

A good way to introduce friends and family to edible flowers is to chop them finely and toss into a mixed green salad dressed with a *simple* vinaigrette. Then, garnish the salad with several whole flowers. Flowers can save calories, too. With their distinctive tastes, you don't have to use as much salad dressing. You can just enjoy the flower's flavors.   —*Cathy Wilkinson Barash*

▲ CALENDULA

Also known as pot marigold, calendulas should not be confused with true marigolds (*Tagetes* spp.), which taste yucky. (That's why we use botanical or Latin names to properly identify the plants). They're also called poor man's saffron—the yellow or orange petals, when chopped, give the same color and slightly acrid flavor to foods that the expensive spice does. I like to cook rice with chopped calendulas and a little butter. You can dry calendula petals for out of season use; keep them in jar in a cool, dry place.

▲ VIOLET

Violets are lovely woodland plants with sweet-smelling, violet-flavored blooms (yes, a lot of edible flowers taste just like they smell—lilacs and roses, to name a few). They are most often white or lavender in color. The old-fashioned, dainty blooms are traditionally candied. Try boiling them with sugar and water to make a syrup that is great on pancakes, or drizzled over orange slices. Or, use it for baking to add an indescribable hint of flavor to a chocolate cake.

▼ ROSEMARY

Rosemary flowers, like those of many herbs, are more mildly flavored than the leaves, with a hint of sweetness. The tiny flowers are pale to deep blue. They make a superb, palate-cleansing sorbet. Their flavor is good with chicken or pork; chop them and use them in a marinade, or sprinkle the meat with them before sauteing. Finish the dish by deglazing the pan with rosemary vinegar.

▼ DAYLILY

Although each flower lasts for only one day (or night; yes, there are night-blooming daylilies), each of the buds on the stem blooms sequentially. Pick the fattest bud (tomorrow's flower) and steam, stir-fry or bake it—the flavor varies and can be like green beans or eggplant. Once the flower's open, you're in for a treat. Taste a petal—the base is crunchy and often sweet. I make sorbet and serve it in a daylily "cup." I also stir-fry the petals or just toss them in a salad for a terrific, slightly sweet crunch. With thousands of different daylilies, you'll find a range of flavors... a few are even peppery.

▲ NASTURTIUM

Nasturtiums are the most widely recognized of all edible flowers. They range in hues from red to orange to yellow, with a delectable peppery flavor. Eat one by itself—the first sense you have as you chew it is sweetness, then the spicy, peppery flavor comes out. (And, don't bite off little bits of the flower, pop it all in your mouth!)

For a neat-looking salad, make two dressings. First, plate baby greens on a clear glass plate. Blend nasturtium flowers with olive oil in a blender and drizzle this emulsion on the salad. Then, blend the leaves (also edible with the same peppery flavor) with white wine vinegar, and drizzle this onto the plate. Garnish with whole flowers and leaves. Enjoy!

▲ PANSY

Pansies are so personable with their cute, colorful faces and minty flavor. You can eat the entire flower and the sepals (the green parts that hold it together). Don't eat too many; they have a diuretic effect. I toss them into fruit salads or make simple hors d'oeuvres by spreading some whipped cream cheese (with flowers chopped in it) on a cracker and top it with a pansy blossom.

▼ SAGE

It wasn't until I tasted my first blossom that I truly fell in love with sage. They're the blue to purplish flowers that grow on the stalk above the leaves. The flower's flavor is sweeter and more delicate than the leaves. It combines well with fresh orange, red onion, and bulb fennel to make a colorful salad. My absolute favorite thing to do with sage flowers is to make sage brochettes. Dip a 4 to 6 inch length of the flower spike into a tempura batter (recipe in my book) and then fry. The result is crispy and delicious—a taste treat like no other.

Photograph: ©Cathy Wilkinson Barash

▼ ROSE

Nothing is quite as sweet as a rose. Yet, not all roses taste good. The old-fashioned ones are more flavorful than many modern hybrids. The thorny beach rose (*Rosa rugosa*) is one of my favorites, which also include "Double Delight", "Fragrant Cloud", "Gertrude Jekyll", "Flower Carpet Red", and "Mirandy". Rose petal syrup is traditional in middle eastern cuisine—good baklava is drizzled with it. Open-faced rose butter tea sandwiches are elegant.

Photograph: ©Cathy Wilkinson Barash

Photograph: ©Cathy Wilkinson Barash

▲ TULIP

This spring I invented a double Dutch treat—tulip petals dipped in melted Dutch chocolate. Refrigerate until the chocolate sets, then fold the tulip in half (only half is dipped in the chocolate to allow the beauty of the flower to show) and pop it into your mouth. Yum! Tulip's flavor varies from bean to pea-like. They're a great addition to tuna fish salad—chop or chiffonade the petals and add to your favorite tuna salad recipe. For an elegant presentation, spoon the salad into a large tulip (pistils and stamens removed) on a bed of lettuce. A meal fit for a king!

Photograph: ©Cathy Wilkinson Barash

▲ CHIVES

I couldn't be without chives in my garden. I love the pinkish-lavender pompon flowers. When young, they have a sweet oniony taste and quickly mature to a grown-up onion flavor. Always break the chive head into individual flowers—the whole flower can be the equivalent of an entire bulb of garlic. Chives are great in marinades. Sprinkle a few extra flowers over meat or vegetables while grilling. I use chives in any dish instead of onion—they add more zip and, of course, add the element for which we prize flowers—color.

GRILLED PINEAPPLE UPSIDE-DOWN CAKE

Photograph: Scott Little; Food Styling: Janet Pittman

GRILLED PINEAPPLE UPSIDE-DOWN CAKE

(SERVES 8)

WORK TIME: 30 MINUTES
COOK TIME: 35–40 MINUTES

GRILL:

1 fresh pineapple, cut into $1/4$" slices

WHISK TOGETHER:

$1^1/_2$ cups all-purpose flour
1 T. cornmeal
$1^1/_2$ t. baking powder
$1/2$ t. salt

CREAM TOGETHER:

8 T. unsalted butter, at room temperature
1 cup sugar

BEAT IN:

4 large egg yolks
2 t. vanilla

MIX WITH DRY INGREDIENTS:

$1/3$ cup whole milk
$1/3$ cup cream of coconut*

FOLD INTO BATTER:

4 large egg whites
2 T. sugar

LINE $10^1/_2$" IRON SKILLET:

3 T. unsalted butter
$1/3$ cup light brown sugar
7 slices grilled pineapple

** Use **cream of coconut** and not coconut milk. The cream of coconut is sweeter.*

Pineapple Upside-Down Cake is one of my all-time favorite desserts. But there's always a problem with them—they don't have enough "goop" around the pineapple. To me, that's what

you want with this cake. I thought the problem would be easily solved by doubling the pineapple, butter, and brown sugar. I was wrong.

Well, back up. I was almost wrong. The gooey caramel part I wanted turned out great, but it destroyed the delicate cake underneath. The cake part absorbed too much moisture and syrup, and ended up collapsing the cake. After 18 unsuccessful attempts, I gave it up. I tried a different approach for the caramel.

Rather than having the cake create its own sauce, I *minimized* the sauce so it wouldn't overpower the light cake or natural sweetness of the grilled pineapple.

I made Cajeta instead. Cajeta [kah-HAY-tah] is a Mexican caramel sauce made with goat's milk. Just because it has goat's milk, don't turn up your nose. It's easy to make and tastes great (not goaty). Typically, cajeta is paired with desserts not as sweet as itself, so it goes great with this cake.

PREPARING PINEAPPLE

1 Slice fresh pineapple. I keep the core in place to hold shape. Remove disks. Save juice for sauce.

2 Grilled pineapple is special. Grill rings over medium heat a total of 5–7 minutes, turning once.

3 Preheat oven to 350°. In a mixing bowl, whisk together the flour, cornmeal, baking powder, and salt. Set aside.

4 With mixer on medium, beat butter until it is smooth and creamy. Now, gradually add sugar. Beat for 2 minutes.

5 Add egg yolks and vanilla. Beat to incorporate, scraping sides once. Stir cream of coconut. Measure and combine with milk.

CAJETA SAUCE

(MAKES 1¹/₄ CUPS)
COOK TIME: 1 HOUR
BRING TO BOIL:
3   cups goat's milk
³/₄   cup sugar
1   T. light corn syrup
1   vanilla bean, cut into
    four pieces
REMOVE FROM HEAT, ADD:
¹/₄   t. baking soda, dissolved in 1 T. water
STRAIN, FINISH WITH:
1¹/₂ t. dark rum
1¹/₂ t. pineapple juice

6 With mixer on *low*, alternate adding dry ingredients with combined milk mixture. Begin and end with dry ingredients.

7 Beat egg whites on medium until slightly foamy. Gradually add sugar. Increase speed to med-high until soft peaks form.

8 Stir 1 cup of beaten egg whites into batter. Gently fold in remainder of whites until they are fully incorporated into batter.

1 Heat goat's milk, sugar, syrup, vanilla bean to a boil. Add baking soda and water—mixture will foam.

9 Spray bottom and sides of cast iron skillet with Pam®. Melt 3 T. butter in skillet. Sprinkle with brown sugar—press to level.

10 Place grilled pineapple in skillet by first placing 1 ring in center, then arranging 6 outer rings slightly overlapping.

11 With pineapple rings set in the skillet, pour in the batter. Spread so that it is smooth. Bake at 350° for 35–40 min.

2 Cook on medium heat. Stir frequently. Reduce until it turns to light caramel syrup (about 45 minutes).

12 Cake is done when a toothpick that is *fully* inserted into center, comes out dry. Stick it in all the way to check entire depth.

13 Remove skillet from oven. Immediately run knife around the edge of pan to prevent the sides from sticking.

14 Immediately invert onto serving plate. Cool 5 minutes. Serve with warm cajeta and *unsweetened* whipped cream.

3 Strain sauce to remove vanilla beans. Stir in rum and pineapple juice to finish. Serve warm sauce with cake.

Photograph: Scott Little; Food Styling: Janet Pittman

MAKING A GRAND FINALE

I call this my $8.00 dessert. I got this idea one night when I went to a fancy cajun restaurant. The chef served *three* warm beignets (it's kind of a New Orleans doughnut) on a fruit coulis. The dessert plate was dusted with powdered sugar and cocoa and garnished with orange zest. They were charging $8.00 for a doughnut dessert and couldn't make them fast enough!

That's what we're doing here. You're dressing up the great brownies from page 18, and making a fancy $8.00 dessert out of them. Heck, you can even use a mix and dress them up!

BUILDING THE $8.00 BROWNIE

Mango Coulis: Make ⅔ cups mango coulis by blending 1 peeled and cut mango with 1 T. lime juice. Put coulis in a plastic squeeze bottle. Cut another mango and a kiwi into slices. Wash and dry fresh raspberries.

Paint the Plate: Paint the plate with ganache (use technique, page 19). Use a paper plate to practice. Center ganached brownies on plate. Dust with powdered sugar. Place coulis dots, sliced fruits, and raspberries.

AUGUST HOME'S

Cuisine

AN ILLUSTRATED GUIDE TO CREATIVE HOME COOKING

™

FRENCH BISTRO FOOD
CASSOULET: White Bean Casserole

Also in this Issue:
BRAISED SHORT RIBS
PÂTE À CHOUX: Eclairs
BRIOCHE: Rich Egg Bread

Cuisine

Editor
John F. Meyer

Art Director
Cinda Shambaugh

Assistant Editor
Susan Hoss

Senior Graphic Designer
Holly Wiederin

Senior Photographer
Crayola England

Contributing Photographer
Dean Tanner
Primary Image

Test Kitchen Directors
Ellen C. Boeke
Sara Ostransky

Contributing Editor
Ann Crowley, PhD

Editorial Assistant
Stephanie Neppl

Intern
Adriel Lage

Electronic Publishing
Coordinator
Douglas M. Lidster

Pre-press Image Specialist
Troy Clark

Publisher
Donald B. Peschke

Corporate
V.P. Planning & Finance: **Jon Macarthy**
Subscriber Services Director: **Sandy Baum**
New Business Director: **Glenda K. Battles**
New Business Manager: **Todd Bierle**
Promotion Manager: **Rick Junkins**
Renewal Manager: **Paige Rogers**
Billing Manager: **Rebecca Cunningham**
Asst. Subscription Manager: **Joy Krause**
Production Director: **George Chmielarz**
Production Assistant: **Susan Rueve**
Pre-press Image Specialist: **Minniette Bieghler**
Creative Director: **Ted Kralicek**
August Home Books: **Douglas L. Hicks**
New Media Manager: **Gordon C. Gaippe**
Assoc. Graphic Design Director: **Susie Rider**
Senior Graphic Designer: **Cheryl Simpson**
Controller: **Robin K. Hutchinson**
Senior Accountant: **Laura J. Thomas**
Accounts Payable Clerk: **Mary Schultz**
Human Resource Assistant: **Kirsten Koele**
Customer Service Manager: **Jennie Enos**
Administrative Assistant: **Julia Fish**
Receptionist: **Jeanne Johnson**
Librarian: **Sherri Ribbey**
Special Projects Director: **Saville Inman**

Cuisine™ (ISSN 1089-6546) is published bi-monthly (Jan., Mar., May, July, Sept., Nov.) by August Home Publishing Co., 2200 Grand Ave., Des Moines, IA 50312. **Cuisine**™ is a trademark of August Home Publishing Co. ©Copyright 1998 August Home Publishing. All rights reserved. Subscriptions: Single copy: $4.99. One year subscription (6 issues), $21.94. (Canada/Foreign add $6 per year, U.S. funds.) Periodicals postage paid at Des Moines, IA and at additional mailing offices. "USPS/Heartland Press Automatable Poly" Postmaster: Send change of address to **Cuisine**, PO Box 37100 Boone, IA 50037-2100. Subscription questions? Call 800-311-3995, 8 a.m. to 5 p.m., Central Standard Time, weekdays. **Cuisine**™ does not accept and is not responsible for unsolicited manuscripts. PRINTED IN U.S.A.

From the Editor:

It wasn't too hard to figure out what to put into the fall issue of Cuisine—comfort food. If you're like me, you never tire of it, and the recipes that conjure up memories of slow-cooked meals at grandma's house are endless.

I don't think anything says comfort food better than a French bistro—it seems to be the birthplace of real comfort food. French laborers and aspiring artists would consider the family-owned bistros a second home where they could socialize in a warm atmosphere, and get a "homestyle" meal at a reasonable price.

Don't make the mistake of considering bistro fare comparable to what we know as classic French cooking. There are no complex sauces and fine wines here. Bistro food is basic, characterized by slow-cooked dishes, prepared ahead of time, and served quickly. Hearty foods like roasts, casseroles, stews, and soups are typical, but now newer bistros are starting to put their modern spin on traditional dishes.

And that's what this issue is about—bistro food. Some traditional dishes made the old way and others with a little twist. I hope they all warm you up as it gets cooler.

John Meyer

*In this issue of **Cuisine**, I show you how to make braised short ribs with a French twist. You probably thought short ribs were just inexpensive stew meat. Well, they are. With a little flare, they'll turn into a special entree. Mine are flamed with brandy and served in a bourguignonne sauce on a bed of purple potatoes.*

AUGUST HOME'S Cuisine

AN ILLUSTRATED GUIDE TO CREATIVE HOME COOKING

TIPS AND TECHNIQUES

BEYOND PIZZA

Instead of using a knife that crushes my brownies, I cut them with a pizza cutter. It makes nice cuts and lets me trim off the crumbly edges that stuck to the pan. It's easy to make straight, even brownies. I can even cut them hot while in the pan.

E. McKeon
Glendale, CA

MINCING FRESH HERBS

When I have to chop or mince fresh herbs, I always use kitchen shears.

I place the herbs in a glass, stick my shears inside, and cut the herbs into the size I want without bruising them.

I. Shapiro
Folsom, CA

FROZEN GEL PACKS

I was taught to chill the bowl to whip cream faster and increase its thickness.

Once, I was in a hurry and grabbed a frozen gel pack from my freezer. I put it under my mixing bowl, then whipped the cream. It worked like magic. Best of all, the packs are reusable!

A. Persico
Bismarck, ND

COOL IT!

My grandpa taught me a "cool little trick" for whipping cream. Fill a large bowl with ice water. Pour the cream in a smaller bowl and set it in the ice water. Anchor both bowls with your hand and beat with a hand mixer. Easy!

R. Hodgson-Jensen
Bellingham, WA

ICE CUBE FAT SKIMMER

Sometimes I don't have time to chill my sauces so I can skim the fat. I found a quick way to remove it from gravy, stock, and stews.

I cut a large piece of cheesecloth and fill it with ice cubes. The amount of ice will depend on the amount of stock or gravy you are working with. Then I tie the cheesecloth with a piece of string to secure the cubes.

Dunk the cheesecloth into your stock or gravy. The fat will solidify and stick to the ice bag when it comes in contact with it.

S. Kugelman
Toms River, NJ

PROPER PLACESETTING

At a recent dinner party, I noticed that my knife was on the left side of my plate.

This simple rhyming method will help children (and adults) set the table properly: "The silverware had a fight. The knife and spoon were right, so the fork left." Here's another way to remember: the words knife and spoon have five letters, as does the word right. Fork and left both have four letters.

K. Bland
Gove, KS
Editor's Note: I thought this was a nice tip. For the holiday issue, I'm doing an article on proper table settings. —John

FREEZING BLUE CHEESE

When I have leftover blue cheese, I just throw it in the freezer in a sealable bag. The frozen blue cheese is always ready to go on top of salads and other dishes.

When it's frozen, the cheese breaks off easily. It can also peel off in curls using a vegetable peeler or paring knife.

S. Stansfield
Sussex, NJ

MAKING INSULATED COOKIE SHEETS

Insulated sheets bake evenly, but due to the price, I made my own. I took two conventional cookie sheets (the same size) and put a penny at each corner of one. I placed the other on top to create an air space.

H. Ferris
Alameda, CA

REFRIGERATING SPICES

Refrigerate red pepper spices, like chili pepper or cayenne. It helps keep the flavor of the ground spices fresh and their color bright. Don't let the spices sit out of the refrigerator for very long, though. If they warm up, condensation could create moisture in the bottle and ruin the spice.

R. Gregory
Lebanon, TN

SHARPENING SHEARS

My mother taught me a simple way to sharpen my kitchen shears: I just cut a piece of steel wool. Once I was in a pinch and grabbed a Scotch-Brite™ pad. They both work great.

J. Patrice
St. Paul, MN

FREEZING LEMON SLICES

To add a little zing to your drinks, use frozen lemon slices. Lemons (and limes) freeze in perfect condition. Not only do they add flavor, they keep beverages cooler too! I always keep slices of each in the freezer for beverages — water, iced tea, beer, or soda.

L. Coomes
Kirkland, WA

PEELING PEARL ONIONS

Pearl onions are about the size of a grape and have a mild flavor. They can be cooked (they are often creamed) and served as a side dish, pickled, or used as a condiment or garnish.

I've paired these little "pearls" with mushrooms for the Bourguignonne Sauce, *see page 32.*

Because they're so small, it can be a tedious job to remove their papery skin. To make this job a little easier, plunge the whole onions in boiling water for 1 minute — just to loosen their skin. Remove from the boiling water and drain. Trim off the root ends with a paring knife and gently squeeze to slip off the skins.

CREME FRAICHE

Use your own creme fraiche [krehm FRESH] instead of sour cream. It's richer tasting and won't break when blended with hot foods, like sour cream tends to do.

To make your own, combine 1 cup heavy cream, 2 T. buttermilk, and 2 t. lemon juice in a glass bowl. Cover and let stand at room temperature for up to 24 hours, until thickened. It can keep up to a week in the refrigerator. You'll want to cover it tightly.

SEND US YOUR TIPS

We'd like to hear from you. Just write down your cooking tip and mail it to Cuisine, Tips Editor, 2200 Grand Ave., Des Moines, IA 50312, or contact us through our E-mail address shown below. Please include your name, address, and daytime phone number in case we have questions. We'll pay you $25 if we publish your tip.
E-mail address: Cuisine@cuisinemag.com
Web address: http://www.augusthome.com

CASSOULET

Even though you may not know a word of French, you'll know what cassoulet is all about—casserole. But cassoulet isn't your typical culinary cop-out. It's been a

French mainstay for centuries. In the family tree of casseroles, cassoulet [ka-soo-LAY] is at the top—the great-granddaddy of franks and beans.

Mention the word "casserole" and people roll their eyes. Cassoulet is not even close to dinners made with leftovers mixed with cream of mushroom soup. Well, cassoulets are "hot" right now, sharing the limelight with other "comfort foods" like rice pudding, mashed potatoes, and short ribs.

Cassoulet was born in southwestern France as a make-ahead dish. Most homes weren't equipped with ovens, so housewives would bring their cassoulets to the local bakery in the morning. There, they would bake in the cooling bread ovens for hours.

Cassoulet grew into standard fare on bistro menus. It epitomizes what bistro cooking is all about—basic, slow-cooked comfort food that uses local ingredients. Nothing fancy—just good eating that reminds you of food that might have been made by your mom or grandma. It's a popular menu item on most French bistro menus, and I couldn't pass up the opportunity to give it a try here.

The Cassoulet Trinity: There has always been debate surrounding what authentic cassoulet is. I don't have a definitive answer, but I can tell you there are three *sacred* characteristics.

White Beans: Dried white beans *are* cassoulet. Without them, it wouldn't exist. The very process of making a cassoulet dictates a long cooking time—canned beans can't hold up.

Meats: For every cassoulet, there are different meats and sausages claiming to be the authentic combination. Pork, lamb, anything that flies, and all types of cased sausages are acceptable.

Crust: The bread-crumb crust on a cassoulet is an important part of the cooking process. It's "turned" into the cassoulet several times, naturally thickening while absorbing flavor.

CASSOULET WITH DUCK

(SERVES 8–12)

WORK TIME: 3 HOURS
COOK TIME: 5 HOURS

DICE AND SWEAT IN 2 T. OLIVE OIL:
1½ cups carrots, diced
1½ cups yellow onions, diced
1½ cups celery, diced
1½ cups parsnips, peeled and diced

DEGLAZE WITH:
1 cup dry white wine

ADD TO VEGETABLES AND SIMMER:
3 cups dry white beans
6 cups chicken broth
Bouquet Garni, *see below*

BLANCH, PEEL, SEED, AND CHOP:
6 tomatoes

GRATE (1½ CUPS PULP):
4 tomatoes, halved and seeded

SEASON AND BROWN:
1 4-lb. duck, cut into 8 pieces

IN 2 T. DUCK FAT, BROWN:
1½ lbs. unseasoned fresh bratwurst

SEASON AND BROWN IN BATCHES:
1½ lbs. lamb stew meat chunks

PROCESS THEN DEGLAZE PAN WITH:
1 cup chicken broth
10 garlic cloves

COMBINE AND TOP CASSOULET WITH:
2 cups unseasoned bread crumbs
½ cup chopped fresh parsley
½ t. salt
⅛ t. pepper

ARRANGE ON TOP OF CASSOULET:
3 tomatoes, each cut into 6 wedges
8 fresh thyme sprigs
Browned bratwurst

GARNISH WITH:
Gremolada, *see Page 10*

NUTRITIONAL INFORMATION PER SERVING:
CALORIES 810; TOTAL FAT 45(G); CALORIES
FROM FAT 49%; SODIUM 480(MG)

BOUQUET GARNI

A bouquet garni [boo-KAY gahr-NEE] is a bundle of herbs and spices either tied together, or wrapped in a piece of cheesecloth and then tied in a pouch. Keeping things together this way makes for easy removal after cooking.

But if you don't have any cheese-cloth, try tying everything in a large coffee fil-ter—it works just great.

1 Spread dried beans on a baking sheet and sort through them to remove any stones, dirt, or shriveled beans. Then rinse and drain.

2 Prepare the vegetables—I like to dice them fairly large. This way, they retain some of their shape during the long cooking time.

3 For blanching and peeling, cut a small "X" on the bottom of 6 tomatoes. Dunk in boiling water 30 seconds then plunge in ice water.

4 Peel skin from tomatoes. Cut them in half across their "equa-tors;" squeeze out the seeds. Trim out the core; chop into a large dice.

5 Cut 4 unpeeled tomatoes in half crosswise and squeeze out seeds. Grate the cut sides on a large-holed grater to make tomato pulp.

6 Heat 2 T. olive oil in a large soup pot. Add vegetables. Cover and sweat about 15 minutes. Deglaze with wine and simmer 1 minute.

7 Assemble the *bouquet garni*. Add the rinsed beans and 6 cups chicken broth so that the broth covers the beans. Bring to a boil.

8 Tie *garni* to handle. Reduce heat, cover, and simmer 30 mins., until beans start to get tender. They'll still be firm. Drain, reserving liquid. Cool.

KNOWING YOUR DUCK

Duck is just one poultry option in cassoulet. If you're not familiar with it, here's some things to know.

Breeds: The most common breed of domestic duck, and the one I use, is called Pekin, or Long Island. Others, like Muscovy and Moulard, are bred to be leaner and are more expensive. The strong, gamey flavor of wild duck will overwhelm this dish—avoid it.

Characteristics: One of the main characteristics of duck meat is that it's all dark—there's no white breast meat like there is on a chicken. That's because these birds fly, using their breast muscles more. This exercise increases the amount of oxygen in the blood, darkening the meat. Chickens, on the other hand, only use their legs for movement, so their breast is white and the legs are dark.

Another characteristic of duck is its fatty skin—plenty of it. You can, of course, trim some off. But the best thing to do is brown the duck before adding it to the cassoulet, like I'm doing in Step 19. This'll render most of the fat out so it doesn't pool at the top of the cassoulet. Now you're left with flavorful meat, just slightly higher in calories than other poultry.

Cutting: Cutting duck into pieces is just like cutting chicken. Their architecture is the same. Just follow the instructions at the right.

Three utensils make the procedure a breeze: a boning knife cuts through the delicate meat; a chef's knife is good for separating joints; and poultry shears cut through small bones and cartilage. Be sure they're sharp.

FINDING DUCK

A clipper ship captain brought the country's first domesticated ducks to Long Island, NY from China in 1873. They've been bred there ever since.

Today, several other states produce duck, and it's fairly common to find whole frozen duck in the grocery store. Make sure the packaging is well-sealed, and don't refreeze thawed birds. Fresh duck should have a plump breast and tight, creamy colored skin. If you can't find one, order from **D'Artagnan**, (800) 327-8246.

TRIMMING THE DUCK

9 Thaw the duck, if frozen. Rinse and pat dry. With the breast side down, cut along both sides of the backbone—from "stem to stern."

10 Turn the duck over and pull leg and thigh away from the body. Cut through skin down to the joint, trimming close to duck's body.

11 With your hands, pop the thigh out of the hip joint. Cut between the joint with a boning knife to remove leg and thigh.

12 Use your fingers to find the indentation between leg and thigh. Cut through this joint with a chef's knife and separate the pieces.

13 Cut off the breast meat with a boning knife, down both sides of the breastbone. Keep the knife against the breastbone.

14 With shears, cut out the breastbone where the meat attaches to the bone. Cut to the center of the neck.

15 Open up the body and cut out the backbone. Cut through both sides of the ribcage, removing as many ribs as possible.

16 Detach wings from breasts, leaving about a third of the breast attached to wing piece. Trim off wing tips and excess fat.

BROWNING AND DEGLAZING

Just like the short ribs on Page 30, I brown the cassoulet meats first for color and flavor. Plus, it renders some of the fat, especially with the duck.

"Browning" Points: Some points about browning (searing) are worth repeating. You'll hear more about them on page 30. But here's the gist.

To brown any food, you need to apply high heat to it, so proteins and sugars turn brown as they cook.

When meat hits a hot pan, surface moisture immediately evaporates. All that's left are those proteins and sugars. When they break down, you get a flavorful, brown crust.

The first step to getting that crust is using the right pan—something big so you don't crowd the meat, and something heavy that retains heat.

Nonstick pans aren't for searing. They don't brown well, and the high heat could warp them or damage the lining. Save them for omelets.

Second, get your pan hot (but not smoking) before adding the meat. Too high a heat can cause scorching that could deliver an off-taste.

Don't bother using oil to brown. You're going to first brown the duck. That rendered duck fat in the pan is enough to brown all the other meats. It'll also provide extra flavor.

Finally, it's perfectly fine to brown the meat in batches. Overcrowding creates steam, which turns the meat gray instead of brown.

Deglazing: Deglazing is a flavorful way to clean your pan. There's tons of flavor in those bits on the bottom.

You can deglaze with any liquid, but I'm use something a little different here—chicken broth pureed with garlic. This'll clean out your sinuses!

Traditionally, the sausages were simmered in garlic and lard. I spared you this step and decided that chicken broth was a better alternative.

SAUSAGE VARIETIES

There are thousands of sausage varieties in markets, butcher shops, and through mail order. You can use almost any type in cassoulet, from garlic pork to chicken-apple to lamb. When choosing a type of sausage, look for one that's fresh (that is, not dried), and in natural casings. Here's a few you might want to try:

Bratwurst [BRAHT-wurst]: a German sausage made from pork and veal with mild seasonings.

Italian Sausage: Italian sausage comes in two styles—hot and sweet. Both have garlic and fennel seed. The hot style is too spicy for cassoulet—you want the sweet sausage.

Kielbasa [kihl-BAH-sah]: also called Polish sausage, kielbasa comes unsmoked or smoked and is seasoned with garlic. It comes in long links, so cut it into 5" lengths for the cassoulet.

PREPARING THE MEATS

17 In a food processor, process 10 garlic cloves until finely chopped. Add 1 cup chicken broth and process until blended. Set aside.

18 Heat a large saute pan over high heat. Liberally season duck pieces and lamb chunks with salt and freshly ground pepper.

19 Sear the duck in batches, skin-side-down. Cook until golden; remove. When finished, pour off all but 2 T. fat; return skillet to burner.

20 Add sausages to skillet and cook until browned, turning once. You don't have to cook them through. Remove sausages; set aside.

21 In the same skillet, brown the lamb in batches. Don't crowd the pan. Remove browned meat and sear another batch.

22 Return all lamb to skillet and deglaze with garlic-broth mixture. Bring to a boil; simmer 1 minute, scraping up bits from the bottom.

Like the paella in Issue 4, the cassoulet has its own special cooking vessel with a history based on fact and lore.

The Cassole: A cassole [cas-SOHL] is the clay pot the cassoulet's cooked in—it was the first casserole dish. And, just like casserole, cassoulet gets its name from the dish it's made in.

An authentic French cassole is made of clay and looks like a short terra cotta flower pot that's been glazed only on the inside.

Originally, potters "half-glazed" their cassole dishes to save a few francs. Housewives (the first cassoulet cooks) liked the unglazed outside because it was easier to grip, and so the tradition stuck.

I use a large clay dish from Spain. It's not as deep as a French cassole, but it is wide—14" across. Order it from Sur La Table, (800) 243-0852.

But don't worry if you don't have a clay pot. You can use any large, heavy cooking pot—no problem. And I do mean large, at least four quarts— my cassole is 4$^1/_2$ quarts. Since you'll be "turning" the cassoulet as it bakes, the more room you have, the easier it will be to maneuver.

A cassole should have plenty of surface area—the wider the better. This exposes the cassole's ingredients to more heat, causing evaporation and thickening. This helps form that crust.

Assembly: Assembling cassoulet isn't that tricky, but it does have to be done in the right order so that none of the ingredients get overcooked.

While you can make the cassoulet all in the same day, I prefer to brown the meat and cook the beans a day ahead. This gives the flavors a chance to blend (and makes less work for me).

If you do make it a day ahead, brown all your meats and sausage. Build the cassoulet up to Step 20. Do not add the sausage, tomato wedges, or bread crumbs at this point—you'll add them in stages after the duck and beans have cooked for an hour.

You might want to make your own bread crumbs—do this before cooking the cassoulet. Use any stale white bread (I use day-old French bread that I get pretty cheap from the bakery).

Although you initially layer most of the ingredients in the cassoulet, I want you to first mix the lamb, beans, and tomatoes (pulp and chunks) together in a mixing bowl. That way, all these smaller elements are evenly dispersed throughout the cassoulet.

And don't fret over this whole assembly deal. This is a casserole. It'll end up pretty jumbled up, anyway.

ASSEMBLING THE CASSOULET

This gremolada provides a needed contrast to the rich duck. Make it the day you're serving the cassoulet.

GREMOLADA
MIX AND REFRIGERATE UNTIL READY TO USE:
- $^1/_2$ cup finely chopped fresh parsley
- 2 cloves garlic, minced
  Zest of 1 lemon, finely minced

Using a sawing action, shave off the outer peel (not the white pith). Cut the peel into strips, and then mince.

17 Process slices of dry French bread to make bread crumbs. Combine crumbs with chopped parsley, salt, and pepper. Set aside.

18 Remove *bouquet garni* from beans. Combine beans with the lamb-garlic mixture, tomato pulp, diced tomatoes, and salt and pepper.

19 To assemble cassoulet, spread half the beans in the cassole. Place 4 pieces of duck on top. Repeat layer using remaining beans and duck.

20 Pour reserved bean liquid over the cassoulet. You may need to add more chicken broth so liquid is within $^1/_4$" of the top of dish.

BAKING THE CASSOULET

Something special happens when this cassoulet is baked. And it's not just that your house smells so good.

The Crust: One hallmark of a good cassoulet is a golden brown crust of bread crumbs covering the top.

Tradition dictates that you "turn" the cassoulet during cooking—that just means the crust is broken and stirred back into the pot. More crumbs are added and it bakes some more, until the crust forms again.

But I don't do this just to uphold tradition. There's good reason for it— the bread crumbs soak up the juices so the cassoulet isn't runny or soupy.

The exact number of turns is a matter of debate. Traditionalists insist on at least seven. I found this produces a cassoulet that is way too dry. So, I'm breaking tradition—twice is plenty. The cassoulet isn't soupy, but it's not loaded with crumbs, either.

Adding Sausage: Cassoulet is traditionally turned seven times… and sausage is supposed to be cooked with all the other ingredients. Not here.

Add the browned sausages after the second turn. This way, they don't dry out during the long cooking time. I also arrange fresh tomato wedges on the top for color and extra flavor.

To really bump things up, I sprinkle a little gremolada on each serving, *see opposite page*. Die-hard cassoulet fans might look down their noses at this. But the freshness of the parsley and citrus zest contrast well with the rich flavor of the duck. **AH**

21 Sprinkle ⅔ cup bread crumbs on top of cassoulet. Place dish on baking sheet and bake at 375° for 1 hour. "Turn" crust into beans.

22 Sprinkle "turned" cassoulet with another ⅔ cup bread crumbs. Continue baking cassoulet for another hour.

23 While cassoulet is baking, cut two tomatoes into wedges, about 6 per tomato. Pick out some sprigs of thyme for the top.

24 "Turn" down cassoulet a second time. I add the reserved sausage and tomatoes now—this way, the sausages don't dry out.

25 Add some fresh thyme sprigs and sprinkle the top with remaining bread crumbs. Return to the oven and bake 1 more hour.

26 The cassoulet is done when top crust is crispy and bubbly. Spoon beans and some of each meat on plates; sprinkle with gremolada.

CASSOULET VARIATION

In France, cassoulet varies from city to city. And each city claims theirs as the only "true" cassoulet. Most of the hoopla comes down to the meats. I narrowed it to sausage, duck, and lamb, but you don't have to go down that road.

Sausage: Every cassoulet includes some kind of sausage. In one city, they use a garlic sausage called Toulouse. I had some shipped in and it was really good. If you can find it, use it.

Just for fun, I tried using lamb sausage, but it was too dry for my taste. I went with simple pork bratwurst, but there's nothing wrong with using good veal, chicken, or turkey sausage.

Poultry: Duck and goose are the most common kinds of poultry in cassoulet. I know I'm asking you to stretch your wings a little (pun intended) and try it with duck. But if you're still a little wary, the cassoulet is great with chicken, too.

Lamb: I really like lamb, so I jumped at the chance to use it here. If you don't like lamb, pork or beef make good substitutes. Be sure it's meant for stewing—leaner cuts, like loin, will dry out or shred.

Bottom Line: No matter what meats you choose to use, the bottom line to this cassoulet is flavor. There's no point in using something if you don't like it. And if three meats seems indulgent, just use two—a poultry and a sausage.

BRIOCHE

If I lived in France, every afternoon would include a trip to a secluded neighborhood bakery for fresh brioche. Spread with "real" butter and marmalade, I'd eat it

with a hot cafe au lait. France is out of reach for now, so my kitchen will have to satisfy any of my gastronomical fantasies. I can get pretty close with this brioche recipe.

Brioche [BREE-ohsh] isn't your typical long, crusty French bread. It's a yeast bread made with butter and eggs. It's very rich. The top bakes to a golden, shiny crust with a knot.

The sides form their own distinctive fluted shape (from molds).

Brioche is so delicate and tender, it's considered more of a cake than bread, usually eaten on coffee breaks or with chocolate in the afternoons. Do you recall Marie Antoinette's response to rebelling peasants? "Let them eat cake!" Yes, she was referring to brioche—obviously not our recipe.

BASIC BRIOCHE

(MAKES EIGHTEEN $3^1/2$" BRIOCHE)
WORK TIME: *Make dough one day ahead (it requires overnight refrigeration), plus 2 hours before baking.*
BAKE TIME: 20-23 MINUTES
COMBINE FOR THE SPONGE:
$1/4$ cup warm water (110-115°)
$1^1/4$ t. active dry yeast
$1^1/4$ cups bread flour
5 T. cold water (60°)
INCORPORATE WITH SPONGE:
4 cups bread flour
8 large eggs, cold
$1/2$ cup sugar
1 t. yeast dissolved in 2 T. cold water (60°)
$1/2$ t. salt
SLOWLY ADD:
$3/4$ lb. unsalted butter, chilled, diced
FOR GLAZING:
1 egg, beaten

NUTRITIONAL INFORMATION PER BRIOCHE:
CALORIES 323; TOTAL FAT 18(G); CALORIES FROM FAT 51%; SODIUM 99(MG)

What's the Secret? The secret to good bread is making the proper dough. It becomes a careful combination of science and art. Brioche is no different. The final product should have a tight-grained, soft-textured interior, and it should be very tender.

Like cake, brioche's tenderness comes from the eggs and butter. The soft texture comes from the unusual amount of moisture in the dough.

But getting a tight grain was a problem for me. Many batches turned out with larger holes like other breads I had made in the past. I realized the solution was in the kneading. It had to be kneaded for a *long* time.

I started with a food processor, but found that the dough was just too much for the motor. It kept stalling.

Then I tried kneading the dough by hand, but with so much effort, I found that I kept stalling too. And the final brioche just wasn't as light.

Finally, out came my stand mixer. I found the dough could reach a silky smooth consistency on low speeds. It's the number of revolutions (not the speed) that produces the very tight grain because the gluten really has time to develop a fine mesh. I couldn't be more pleased with the results.

STARTING OUT

Before baking any bread, you have to understand the ingredients and how they work with each other.

Flour: I used bread flour, and here's why. Bread flour has a higher protein content than other flours. This is important because the proteins in the flour connect with each other, grab the water, absorb it, and form gluten sheets. These gluten sheets trap air and gas made by the yeast. As the gas expands, the dough rises.

Protein controls gluten. The higher the gluten, the stronger and more elastic the dough. With all the butter and eggs in brioche, you definitely need a high-gluten flour to give it structure. Use lower-protein flours (cake flour) for pies, cakes, and muffins.

So how can you tell what the flour's gluten (protein) level is? You can't. In all the cookbooks I've read and all the baking classes I've attended, they have recommended using flour with a gluten level between 11.5–12.5%. That's great and I'm glad I know it, but not one of the bags of flour I bought shows that.

Flour companies make all types of flours with different gluten levels. In general, they are: cake, all-purpose, and bread flour. Where and when their wheat is grown dictates gluten levels within these types. For example, all-purpose flour from the South has a lower gluten content than an all-purpose flour from the Midwest.

What does all this mean? Try them out for yourself. For brioche, use flour labeled "bread flour." It will have a high gluten level. I used King Arthur bread flour because it has a higher gluten level than comparable flours.

Remember, this is a science. To measure accurately, pour the flour into your measuring cup. Then level with a knife. Don't settle it by tapping. This compacts the flour.

The Sponge: So now you have the right flour capable of making a tight gluten mesh. But it's kind of like owning a sports car with no gas. Your flour needs fuel to make it go (rise).

You can create the gas (it really is a gas—carbon dioxide) two ways. First by mixing the yeast with water, letting it activate, and then adding it to the flour. This is called the direct method.

Or you can create a "sponge." A sponge is made by mixing just a portion of the total flour, water, and yeast together. This mixture sits at room temperature to ferment, and then it's mixed with the rest of the ingredients to make the final dough.

Why the sponge? When it came right down to it, the brioche just tasted better! A slow rise produces better tasting bread. It's what aging is to wine. Since there's less yeast, the dough takes longer to rise creating a deeper, more aromatic bread.

BRIOCHE MOLDS

Brioche molds have flared, fluted sides. They come in many different materials and sizes. As you can see in the Wares article on page 16, the end results can vary slightly depending on the material you use. I use 3½" molds made out of tinned steel for my brioche. They cost about $1.25 each. You can pay about 50% more and get nonstick molds, but it's not worth it to me. Besides, they tended to bake the bottoms a little darker. If you're careful with the egg-wash, the brioche will pop out easily with the less expensive tinned molds.

Most cookware stores carry them, or call **Sur La Table** at (800) 243-0852, Item #3747.

MAKING THE SPONGE

1 Mix yeast into warm water. Let sit for 5–10 minutes. It will dissolve and "swell." If it doesn't, it isn't active. Start over with new yeast.

2 Use dough hook to combine yeast mixture, flour, and 5 T. cold water. Scrape as needed. After it's combined, mix another minute.

3 Dough will be stiff and sticky. Place in a large bowl and cover with plastic wrap. Let sit at room temperature to ferment for 3 hours.

4 The sponge really goes to town during the 3-hour fermentation. It's sticky, so use a plastic scraper to remove. Check out the aroma!

MAKING THE DOUGH

Have patience now, this dough takes a little time to develop. The pay-off will come when you break into that classic, light, fine texture of brioche.

Development of Dough: Use the dough hook to mix the sponge and all ingredients (except the butter) on the lowest speed until incorporated.

Now, bump up to the next speed and mix for 15 minutes. This kneads the dough and develops a mesh of gluten to trap the sponge gases. The dough will be loose and soft but have a lot of strength. This intensive mixing produces brioche with a tight crumb structure instead of big holes.

Adding the Butter: Gluten development stops when the butter is added, so it goes in last. Add the chilled butter. It should be soft enough to press but still cool. Each piece does not need to be fully incorporated before adding more butter.

Rising: Rising is a growing process. As yeast grows, it converts the flours' starches into alcohol and carbon dioxide. This is called fermentation, producing a strong, flavorful dough.

Cover the dough to keep it moist. It will nearly double in size after one hour of fermentation. Do this at room temperature (75–80°). There's no need to look for a "warm place" to let it rise. Turns out the ideal atmosphere for fermentation for both the sponge and the dough is right in the kitchen.

Fermentation is a continual process. It begins with the sponge and continues through the "ovenspring" or rapid rising that occurs during the first few minutes in the oven. When the dough reaches 138°, the yeast is dead and fermentation stops.

PREPARING THE DOUGH

5 Mix together sponge, flour, eggs, sugar, salt, and dissolved yeast on lowest speed of mixer until no flour is visible. Scrape as needed.

6 Mix on second lowest speed for 15 minutes. Dough will become smooth and very elastic. It'll pull away from side of bowl by end of mixing.

7 While mixing, press and add butter bits (sugar-cube size), one at a time. Take about 8–10 minutes to do this. Then, mix 4 more minutes.

8 Transfer dough to a large, flour-dusted bowl. Cover with plastic wrap. Let rise for 1 hour at room temperature. Remove wrap gently.

9 Use a plastic scraper to remove dough to a lightly floured work surface. It's a big blob of airy, beautiful dough and feels just great.

10 Dust dough and hands with flour. Gently pat (this degasses it) into a loose, rectangle shape (about 14"x16"). Dough has a nice, puffy feel.

11 Scrape under dough to lift end and gather into hands. In one movement, lift and stretch dough to fold 1/3 over. Repeat on other end.

12 Using the same motion, fold dough from the top down, and then from the bottom up. The scraper will help you lift it into the bowl.

13 Turn dough seam-side down and place in flour-dusted bowl. Dust top with flour, cover tightly with plastic wrap and refrigerate overnight.

SHAPING AND BAKING

Brioche can be made in many shapes and sizes, but I'm sticking to the classic "brioche à tête" which means with a head (that's the topknot).

Shaping: Lightly press out dough with the flat of your hands. There is no specific size because all you want to do is divide the dough in half.

Cut the dough in half (never tear dough because it destroys the gluten mesh). Now, cut each half into 9 pieces, as I'm doing in Step 15.

With the dough on a hard surface, roll each piece into a ball. Do this carefully. Hold the side of your hand firmly against work surface, but don't press the top of the dough. Use your fingers to *corral* the dough ball around its sides. Now, move your hand in a circular motion. It's the counter surface that does the shaping—not your hands. After each rolling, scrape to remove any residual dough left on the surface. Cover the balls loosely with plastic wrap. Let the dough rest 20 minutes, and lightly roll ball again. Now it's time to create the topknot.

Topknot: Lightly dust surface and the side of your hand with flour. About one quarter of the way down from the end, press the side of your hand firmly onto the ball (like you're giving it a karate chop). Using a sawing motion, quickly roll the ball to make a knob. If dough sticks, flour surface or hand a little more. Dough is now pear-shaped with a topknot.

But the topknot has to be firmly secured to the base, or it'll blow off during baking. To do this, place dough into individual brioche mold (lift it by topknot). Then, pull knot up with one hand and press flour-dipped fingertips firmly to the bottom of the mold to form a crater around the neck of the knot (the knot never leaves the base). Now set the knot back in.

Place filled molds on cookie sheets and brush with eggwash. Don't get egg on tin or it'll be hard to unmold. Tent with plastic wrap, let sit for 20 minutes, brush again, and bake.

Baking: Bake 20–23 minutes, until deep golden brown on top (bottoms will be lighter). If the tops brown too quickly, tent with foil to finish baking.

14 The next day, remove dough from bowl (again with the scraper). Dust hands and surface with flour. Lightly press dough out.

15 Cut dough in half. Divide each half into 9 pieces—about 3 ounces each. ETE (estimated time of eating)— about 2 hours out.

16 On clean surface, carefully roll each piece of dough into a ball (see Shaping). Cover loosely with plastic wrap and let rest 20 minutes.

17 Lightly flour surface. Dip side of hand in flour. A quarter of the way down ball, press firmly. Saw and roll almost all the way through.

18 Lift ball by knot into a mold sprayed with Pam®. Dip two fingertips in flour. Stretch the neck of the knot with your other hand.

19 Firmly press floured fingertips to bottom of mold. Repeat all around neck. This will help hold your topknot on. Set topknot in.

20 Brush brioche with eggwash. Tent with plastic wrap for final 20-minute proof (dough will rise to fill mold). Brush again with eggwash.

21 Bake 20–23 minutes on middle rack of an oven preheated to 375°. Transfer to cooling rack and eat immediately!

BAKING SHEETS

Last month, I was invited to Maytag Appliances to see what they were up to other than washing machines. Their reputation for getting clothes cleaned is almost an American institution. So when I heard they were

concentrating on cooking appliances, my interest really piqued. But you're not going to hear about any of their new concepts from me—I'll let their advertising department handle that.

One of the things Maytag was demonstrating was how their ovens were designed to bake evenly with the racks at any level of the oven (a definite advantage when baking multiple sheets of cookies).

This was pretty cool, but what I found more interesting was that they experimented with different types of cookie sheets. With all the baking we do in our test kitchen, it was eye-opening to see the results of different bakeware. So I thought it would be fun to run the same experiment for you, and let you see the results. It may help you buy the right bakeware and, as the results "pan out" (no pun intended), may save you some money.

I'm showing you this test for one simple reason—to make sure you get the results you want when baking.

The Test: The test was pretty simple. I took one recipe for cookie dough (white chocolate macadamia nut, to be exact) and baked it on a variety of sheets. You can see the difference in the finished products.

The Players: I sampled from a big universe of baking sheets, then chose a stack of nine to show you. They were divided into three categories: insulated, cookie sheets with sides (jelly-roll type), and the more typical cookie sheets without sides. Each category had a few nonstick pans.

The Results: The three categories of baking sheets provided surprising results. The insulated sheets shined through in the easy removal department, however they proved to be more of a pain when it came to cleaning — do not immerse in water. The cookie sheets with sides produced more even results, but the cookies were a little dry. The sheets without sides performed similarly to the insulated pans, although they seemed to overbrown the cookies a bit.

Overall, I found the design of an effective cookie sheet had little to do with the insulation or the sides. I found that the coloring is a much more important factor. The lighter and shinier the pan, the closer the outcome to what I was expecting—that is, a golden, moist cookie.

The pans with the darker coating gave me much darker cookie bottoms and tops, and not as much softness in texture as the shinier pans. As a matter of fact, one of the least expensive sheets consistently gave me the most satisfactory results (Lincoln Wearever Aluminum). I also tested cake pans and ended up with the same results.

Now, I'm not saying any of these pans are bad, but I think I'll save my money for other kitchen toys. This seems to be one area where price does not equate with quality. **AH**

EXTRAORDINAIRE™
Cookie Sheet: 16" x 14"
We paid: $18
Material: Nonstick coating on heavy gauge steel; insulated.

BAKER'S ADVANTAGE
Cookie Sheet: 17" x 13"
We paid: $16
Material: Nonstick coating on heavy aluminum; insulated.

WEAREVER AIRBAKE®
Cookie Sheet: 14" x 16"
We paid: $9
Material: Aluminum; insulated.

BAKER'S ADVANTAGE
Cookie Sheet: 17^{1}/$_{4}$" x 11^{1}/$_{4}$" x ^{3}/$_{4}$"
We paid: $11
Material: Nonstick coating on steel.

WILLIAMS SONOMA
Half Sheet Cookie Pan: 18 x 13 x 1"
We paid: $25
Material: Ceramic nonstick coating on aluminized steel.

LINCOLN WEAREVER
Bun Pan: 18" x 13" x 1"
We paid: $5
Material: 18-gauge aluminum.

CALPHALON®
Cookie Sheet: 14" x 17^{1}/$_{2}$"
We paid: $24
Material: Nonstick coating on heavy-gauge aluminum.

WILLIAMS SONOMA
Cookie Sheet: 16" x 14"
We paid: $19
Material: Nonstick ceramic coating on aluminized steel.

FOX RUN CRAFTSMEN
Cookie Sheet: 13^{1}/$_{2}$" x 11"
We paid: $8
Material: Stainless steel.

ONION SOUP GRATINÉE

Photograph: Scott Little; Food Styling: Janet Pittman

MAKING A BROWN STOCK

1 Wash the shanks first. Then roast for 30 minutes at 400°. Apply a coat of tomato paste for color.

2 Place vegetables under the meat and roast 40 minutes. Direct contact with pan "browns" them.

3 After browning, place contents of roaster in stockpot large enough to hold meat and vegetables.

4 Fill pot with water to cover ingredients. Add all herbs and peppercorns. Start to simmer—not boil!

5 Now put empty roasting pan on burner. Deglaze with wine, reduce by half, and add to pot.

6 Constantly skim the impurities—(blood, fat, and albumin). They can cause a cloudy stock.

7 After 3–4 hours of slow simmering, the stock is ready. It will be a rich mahogany color. Now, carefully strain all the stock through a fine-mesh strainer. But let the stock drip through naturally. If you mash the vegetables, the stock will turn cloudy.

On a classic menu, you'll often see soup as just one of many courses. But in a bistro, soup is often considered a meal

in itself. This onion soup is not only a French classic but is very characteristic of bistro cuisine. It's simple and it's cooked for a long time. The smooth taste comes from the natural flavors of the ingredients. Gratinée [grah-tee-NAY] refers to the topping of cheese that's browned in the oven.

The Stock: I use brown stock in onion soup because it adds flavor and makes the soup more robust. But the fact is, you can get good results from any stock including water—I've made it with low-sodium *canned* beef broth, and it was great. The large amount of slowly caramelized onions delivers most of the flavor.

BROWN STOCK

(MAKES 8 CUPS)
WORK TIME: 20 MINUTES
COOK TIME: 3–4 HOURS
ROAST:
6   beef shanks, washed (about 5 lbs.)
COAT WITH:
1/2 cup tomato paste
CONTINUE ROASTING WITH:
2   stalks celery, chopped
2   carrots, chopped
2   onions, chopped
1/2 leek (green part only)
2   cloves garlic
REMOVE TO STOCKPOT.
COVER WITH WATER, ADD:
1–2 bay leaves
2   sprigs fresh thyme
1   bunch fresh parsley
1   t. peppercorns
DEGLAZE ROASTING PAN
WITH AND ADD TO STOCKPOT:
2   cups dry red wine

ONION SOUP

The real flavor of classic onion soup comes from the caramelized onions. This is a long process (up to 1½ hours) and can't be rushed.

Caramelizing: For good caramelized onions, use a *heavy* saute pan—you don't want hot spots that could possibly burn the onions.

Place the sliced onions in a covered pan and sweat them until the big pile reduces and becomes clear.

Remove the lid and let the onions cook slowly. Be sure to stir them often. What's happening is that the carbohydrates in the onions are breaking down into sugar as heat is applied. These sugars then turn a rich brown color (the same reaction when white sugar is heated, melts, and turns to caramel). The deeper brown the onions get, the richer the flavor.

Wine and Sherry: I use a dry white wine not only to add flavor to the stock but to cut the sweetness of caramelized onions. And for extra body in the stock, try adding a little sherry. No, it's not French, but it goes great with the melted Gruyère cheese that finishes the soup. Try it!

FRENCH ONION SOUP

(SERVES 6)

WORK TIME: 30 MINUTES
COOK TIME: 3 HOURS

SWEAT AND CARAMELIZE IN 8 T. UNSALTED BUTTER:

12 cups yellow onions, thinly sliced (3–4 lbs.)
½ cup chopped garlic

ADD AND REDUCE:

1 cup dry white wine
⅓ cup dry sherry

ADD AND SIMMER:

3 T. all-purpose flour
6 cups brown stock
   Bundle of fresh thyme
   Salt and pepper to taste

LADLE INTO BOWLS. TOP WITH, THEN BAKE:

12 slices dry French bread
3 cups Gruyère cheese, shredded
½ cup Parmesan cheese, grated

NUTRITIONAL INFORMATION PER SERVING: CALORIES 998; TOTAL FAT 45(G); CALORIES FROM FAT 40%; SODIUM 959(MG)

Finishing: With the reduction completed, add flour and cook briefly. You'll be surprised at how much body this little bit of flour gives the soup. Be sure to cook it a few minutes to remove the starchy taste. Now, add the stock and herbs and finish cooking.

MAKING THE SOUP

8 In large covered skillet, sweat thinly sliced onions in butter for 20 mins. over medium heat.

9 Add chopped garlic. Cover and continue cooking for an additional five minutes.

10 Remove the cover. Cook onions over medium-low heat for 1½ hours until caramelized.

11 Add the wine and sherry. Turn up heat to reduce wines until evaporated (about 10 minutes).

12 Add flour and stir. Cook to remove the starch of the flour (about 1–2 minutes).

13 Stir in the brown stock. Add thyme, salt, and pepper. Simmer soup for 40 minutes.

TOPPING THE SOUP

Hang on to your béret, because I'm going against the delicate approach to French cooking. Check out the copious amount of Gruyère cheese I'm using in Step 15. There's only one thing better than that warm pull of cheese from the soup top—those baked-on cheese "crisps" clinging to the outside!

14 Ladle soup into ovenproof bowls on baking sheet. Top each with 2 slices of dry French bread.

15 Combine cheeses. Sprinkle ½ cup over top of each soup bowl. Pile it on right up to the edge.

16 Bake bowls of soup in 475° oven for 15 minutes or until cheese is browned and bubbly.

Photograph: Scott Little; Food Styling: Janet Pittman

MUSSELS
(MAKES 4 FIRST-COURSE SERVINGS OR 2 ENTRÉE SERVINGS)
WORK TIME: 40 MINUTES
COOK TIME: 15 MINUTES
COOK:
1½ cups dry white wine
½ cup shallots, minced
2 T. garlic, minced
ADD AND SIMMER:
1 cup heavy cream
½ t. curry powder
ADD, THEN COVER:
32 mussels, cleaned
REMOVE MUSSELS. ADD:
¼ cup unsalted butter
FINISH WITH:
¼ cup minced parsley
¼ cup sliced green onions
POUR OVER MUSSELS AND SERVE.

NUTRITIONAL INFORMATION PER FIRST COURSE SERVING: CALORIES 502; TOTAL FAT 37(G); CALORIES FROM FAT 65%; SODIUM 401(MG)

MUSSELS

There is a classic French dish called mussels marinière. Typically prepared with shellfish, most often mussels, marinière sauce is a simple combination of white wine,

fresh herbs, and butter—what's not to like with these ingredients?

When I started experimenting with this recipe, I knew I wanted to teach you this classic dish. But I began making several variations to the marinière [mah-reen-YEHR] sauce. I found out quickly from my informal panel of tasters that they liked a variation much more than the classic. The difference? Cream and curry.

Of all the variations I made, the panel of mussel afficionados always chose the dishes made with cream as their favorite. They said it smoothed out any overpowering flavors and created "harmony" in the dish. I liked what I was hearing. Anytime I can create harmony in any phase of my life, I'm going with it.

But what I really found unusual was the surprise ingredient I added that the panel overwhelmingly selected—curry. I only added a small amount so it didn't dominate the sauce. (Curry tends to overpower.) It was just enough to give an extra richness to the sauce.

And the color! The sauce turned a beautiful creamy yellow that went with everything—the green and black shells, the salmon-colored meat, and the fresh green herbs. It all worked.

The other neat thing about this recipe is that you can eliminate the cream and curry and end up with the classic mussels marinière (it's what I originally wanted to show you). With either recipe, you won't be disappointed if you're a mussel lover.

WHICH MUSSEL TO BUY?
The two most common mussels you'll run across are green-lipped and blue.

The most common is the blue mussel which isn't blue but black. This small mussel thrives mainly off the coast of New England and in the Mediterranean.

Green-lipped mussels are from New Zealand. Because of their larger size, they're often used for stuffing, but are great steamed. These days, most all mussels are cultivated to ensure their safety.

STORING AND SELECTING

Mussels should be handled with as much care as fresh oysters.

Storing: Mussels are best if eaten the same day you buy them, but you can store them up to three days.

Don't clean mussels before storing—this can shorten their shelf life. Refrigerate them on a bed of ice in a perforated container. Place ice *under* the mussels so that when it melts, the water drips onto a tray and not onto other shells (which could contain bacteria). This water could contaminate any live mussels below.

Selecting Good Mussels: Mussels should be alive—if they're dead, pitch them. Sometimes a mussel's shell is open. Tap it. It'll close within 30 seconds, if it's alive. Discard unusually heavy mussels (they're full of sand), and mussels with cracked shells. Finally, don't use mussels that rattle when you shake them. This means the mussel has died in its shell. **AH**

1 Store mussels *on* ice in a colander so melted ice can drain away from mussels. Cover with a damp towel and refrigerate up to 3 days.

2 Scrub shells with a stiff-bristled brush to remove mud and sand. As they're cleaned, place in ice water to flush out any sand in the mussel.

3 Mussels usually "gap" (shells are slightly open). This is the way they filter water. If open, tap it. The live ones will close their shells.

4 Remove the mussels' beards by pulling them off with your fingers or a pair of pliers. (See the Q&A on page 35 for more details.)

COOKING THE MUSSELS

5 Cook shallots and garlic in simmering wine over medium-high heat until they are translucent. This is known as "sweating."

6 Stir cream and curry powder into pan. When it is heated through, add the cleaned mussels. Cover the pan so the mussels can steam.

7 Steam mussels for a few minutes, until their shells open wide. Remove steamed mussels to a bowl. Discard any that did not open.

8 Whisk butter into sauce to thicken and smooth it. This is called "mounting" the sauce with butter. It gives it a nice rounded flavor.

9 Turn the heat off under the pan. Finish the sauce by stirring in the parsley and green onions just before you're ready to serve it.

10 Spoon the curry-cream sauce over mussels. Serve immediately. Just dig the mussels out of their shells with a fork and dip in the sauce.

BISTRO SALAD BAR

Let me reassure you—this bistro salad bar isn't like the ones you're used to. Are you familiar with the concept of Chinese dim sum? This is where waiters wheel carts

to your table and you choose from all types of different foods—kind of a mobile buffet. Many of the French bistros I visited had the same concept but just with salads. I thought you could have fun with the same idea.

You don't need any carts for these salads to pull off this traditional concept. It's a fun, different presentation.

Composed Salad: In France, a combination of three or four smaller salads is called a "composed salad." I like the idea of having several contrasting elements on a plate—textures, colors, and tastes. Not so much to be distracting, but plenty of things to keep it interesting. And definitely not the same old iceberg lettuce.

"Real" French Dressing: Don't be too disappointed hearing this, but a real French dressing is a vinaigrette—a delicate balance between a good oil, an acid (like vinegar or lemon juice), and seasonings.

The classic vinaigrette ratio is three parts oil to one part vinegar. But I found it too bland. It's fine for more delicate leafy greens, but these salads need more of a hit. So I ended up with a higher ratio of acid (3:2) for these vinaigrettes. You can still use them on leafy salads, but you'll probably want to go back to a more classic ratio.

Since there aren't many ingredients in these vinaigrettes, second-rate products stick out like a sore thumb. Buy the best vinegars and oils you can. I found Champagne vinegar in a local specialty food shop. If you can't find any, substitute a high-quality white wine vinegar. And *always* use the freshest herbs available. I promise, you'll taste the difference.

BASIC VINAIGRETTE

(MAKES 1½ CUPS)
WORK TIME: 10 MINUTES
COMBINE IN BLENDER:

½	cup white wine vinegar
¼	cup minced shallots
2	T. sugar
1	T. Dijon mustard
1	t. salt
⅛	t. freshly ground pepper

ADD IN A STEADY STREAM:

¾	cup extra virgin olive oil

WHISK IN:

¼	cup chopped fresh parsley
2	T. chopped fresh chives
2	T. fresh thyme leaves

The toughest part to a good vinaigrette is combining (*emulsifying*) the oil and vinegar so they stay together.

The best way to emulsify these vinaigrettes is in a blender. The oil is incorporated better and the *emulsification* holds longer (no floating oil).

To help the *emulsion* process, I use Dijon mustard as an *emulsifier*. It binds the oil and vinegar together and helps blend all the other flavors.

These vinaigrettes stay emulsified pretty well. But if they separate, whisk to blend, or put them back in the blender and mix for 10–15 seconds.

MAKING A VINAIGRETTE

1 Shallots are a staple in French cooking. Mince them like onions—make lengthwise cuts from root end, then cut across.

2 In a blender, combine vinegar, shallots, sugar, mustard, salt, and pepper. Mix on a medium speed until well blended.

3 Oil and vinegar stay emulsified better when mixed in the blender. With the motor running, add the oil in a slow, thin stream.

4 I whisk in the chopped herbs by hand. This way, they don't get blended into a paste. They stay intact and look like "herbs."

POTATO SALAD WITH MUSSELS

This potato and mussel salad is a French classic. At first, I wasn't sure about the combination of potatoes and seafood. But the briny flavor of the mussels is great with the neutral potatoes and tangy vinaigrette.

Be sure to add the vinaigrette while the potatoes are still warm—this helps them soak up the flavors.

A baking sheet works great for mixing—the potatoes cool quickly and don't break apart when tossed.

Add the mussels just before serving. Acids from the vinaigrette, "cook" them and make them tough.

And if mussels aren't your thing, feel free to leave them out. This salad is great without them.

(MAKES 4 CUPS)
WORK TIME: 30 MINUTES
COOK TIME: 20 MINUTES
*BRING TO A BOIL IN SALTED WATER
AND COOK UNTIL TENDER:*

2	lbs. new red potatoes, sliced ¼" thick

DRAIN; DRIZZLE WHILE HOT WITH:

1½	cups Basic Vinaigrette, *see above*

JUST BEFORE SERVING, ADD:

½	lb. steamed mussels, *prepare as on p. 21, omitting cream and curry*

GARNISH WITH:

2	T. chopped fresh parsley

1 Cover potatoes with cold salted water and bring to boil. Reduce heat. Simmer until tender (about 15 mins.). Drain and layer on pan lined with parchment. Drizzle hot potatoes with vinaigrette. Bring to room temp.

2 Steam mussels and remove from their shells. Just before serving, toss mussels with cooled potatoes and transfer to serving platter using parchment to avoid breaking potato slices. Garnish with chopped parsley.

Photograph: Scott Little, Food Styling: Janet Pittman

MUSHROOM-GOAT CHEESE SALAD

With this salad, lightly cook the mushrooms in the vinaigrette. This eliminates that spongy texture and "raw" taste of fresh mushrooms.

When you add the little bit of goat cheese to the warm vinaigrette, it melts to make a great creamy dressing. This salad tastes best served at room temperature.

(MAKES ABOUT 3 CUPS)
WORK TIME: 30 MINUTES
COOK TIME: 10 MINUTES
SIMMER IN SHERRY VINAIGRETTE:
$^1/_2$ lb. crimini mushrooms, cleaned, halved or quartered
REMOVE FROM HEAT. TOSS WITH:
$^1/_2$ lb. shiitake mushrooms, stems removed, thinly sliced
$^1/_2$ lb. oyster mushrooms, trimmed, sliced
COOL 5 MINUTES, THEN ADD:
$^1/_4$ cup chopped fresh parsley
$^1/_4$ cup chopped fresh thyme
2   T. soft goat cheese:
TOP WITH GOAT CHEESE ROUNDS

SHERRY VINAIGRETTE
(MAKES 1$^1/_4$ CUPS)
COMBINE IN BLENDER:
$^1/_4$ cup fresh lemon juice
$^1/_4$ cup dry sherry
$^1/_4$ cup minced shallots
2   T. sugar
1   T. Dijon mustard
1   t. salt
$^1/_4$ t. freshly ground pepper
ADD IN A STEADY STREAM:
$^3/_4$ cup extra virgin olive oil

I Because mushrooms soak up water, I wipe them clean with a damp paper towel. You can also use a soft-bristled brush to clean.

2 Prepare sherry vinaigrette and heat to a simmer in a large saute pan. Add criminis; cook 2–3 mins. Off heat, add remaining mushrooms.

3 Cool mushrooms 5 mins. Toss with fresh herbs and 2 T. goat cheese. Transfer to serving dish with slotted spoon. Top with goat cheese rounds.

Leave the lid off the pot when you blanch the green beans (or any other green vegetable). They give off a gas which turns them "army green" if the cover is left on.

(MAKES 4–6 SERVINGS)
WORK TIME: 40 MINUTES
COOK TIME: 5 MINUTES
BLANCH, COOL, AND PAT DRY:
1¹/₂ lbs. green beans, stemmed
TOSS WITH:
³/₄ cup Champagne Vinaigrette
IN ANOTHER BOWL, TOSS:
1 large beet, peeled, spiral cut
¹/₂ cup Champagne Vinaigrette
    Juice of one orange
SPRINKLE PLATED BEETS WITH ORANGE ZEST. TOP WITH BEANS AND CUCUMBER CREME FRAICHE.

CHAMPAGNE VINAIGRETTE

(MAKES 1¹/₄ CUPS)
Prepare as for Basic Vinaigrette, except substitute champagne vinegar for white wine vinegar and omit the chives.

1 For cucumber creme fraiche, combine 1 cup creme fraiche (see page 5), 1 minced cucumber, 3–4 drops Tabasco, and salt to taste. Chill.

3 Toss beans with ³/₄ cup vinaigrette. Zest one orange; set aside. Spiral-cut beet (see page 36). Toss with orange juice and ¹/₂ cup vinaigrette.

2 Blanch green beans (5 mins.) in boiling salted water until bright green and barely tender. Plunge in ice water to stop cooking. Drain; dry.

4 Spread a bed of beets on a serving plate and sprinkle with zest. Top with dressed beans and garnish with Cucumber Creme Fraiche.

Bistro food is considered hearty and much of it is prepared with some type of smoked pork. This cabbage salad is no exception. The smoky bacon flavor works great with the cabbage and apple cider vinegar.

This salad must be served right away while it's still warm and the flavor is at its peak. You don't want the bacon fat solidifying when cool.

(MAKES ABOUT 4 CUPS)
WORK TIME: 30 MINUTES
COOK TIME: 20 MINUTES
FRY:
¹/₂ lb. thick-sliced bacon, chopped
SAUTE IN BACON BITS AND GREASE:
1 small green or Napa cabbage, cut in thin shreds (8 cups)
1 small red cabbage, cut in thin shreds (8 cups)
TOSS WITH:
1¹/₄ cups Apple Cider Vinaigrette, *see above right*
¹/₄ cup chopped fresh parsley

APPLE CIDER VINAIGRETTE

(MAKES 1¹/₄ CUPS)
WORK TIME: 10 MINUTES
WHISK TOGETHER:
²/₃ cup apple cider vinegar
2 T. minced shallots
2 T. brown sugar
1 T. Dijon mustard
1 t. salt
¹/₄ t. freshly ground pepper

1 The bacon grease replaces the olive oil here. Fry bacon over low heat until fat is rendered, but bacon is not crisp (about 15 minutes).

2 Add both cabbages to pan and cook, turning constantly, until lightly wilted (2 minutes). Cabbage should still be a little crunchy.

3 Transfer cabbage to large mixing bowl and toss with Apple Cider Vinaigrette and parsley. Serve immediately. It's great on grilled sausages!

SHIITAKE MUSHROOMS

Shiitake Mushroom Photographs: Jim Carney

▲ *An ironwood tree is considered a"weed," and not good for lumber.*

What do you conjure up in your mind when you think about how mushrooms are grown? Perhaps a dark, damp underground cavern or basement? Well, maybe

some are, but not the popular shiitake mushrooms—they're grown on stacks of wood! This whole process is very interesting, so I wanted to share it with you. And since we're cooking with a lot of mushrooms this issue, I thought the timing was perfect.

I went to the Eagle Bluff Learning Center in southeast Minnesota, where they have been experimenting with growing shiitake mushrooms since 1983. Seems that the Chinese have been cultivating shiitake for thousands of years. But it wasn't until the Japanese began marketing them thatthey took off in popularity here.

As many of our farmers began to struggle financially in the early '80's, they started looking for alternative revenue sources. Since many farms included large stands of hardwood trees (cut hardwood is a natural host for shiitake), researchers checked out the feasibility of raising shiitake.

The Wood: To determine the most effective hardwood for the job, over 50 species of shiitake were tested on 10,000 logs. The ironwood tree (it's considered a "weed tree" and of no lumber value) was the clear winner. It had the correct chemical makeup needed for growing shiitake.

▲ *Over 130 holes are drilled in each log to prepare it for the mushroom spawn.*

► *Holes are filled with spawn (inoculated), then plugged with melted cheese wax.*

Ironwood's physical characteristics also lends itself to prolific shiitake production for several reasons. First, the logs can be reused up to six times before they can no longer produce mushrooms. Because of the tree's naturally small stature, the cut logs used are easy to handle (they're moved up to 25 times per cycle). And finally, its bark is thin enough to let the mushrooms pop through easily.

Inoculation: To start, a seed material (called spawn) is grown in a laboratory under sterile conditions. Then the spawn is mixed with sterile sawdust and sold to the growers.

The growers drill holes around the logs. Normally, there are five rows of holes ($1/2$" x 1") along the 40-inch length of log (about 130 holes). With a metal plunger, the spawn is forced into the holes ("inoculation") and then each hole is sealed with melted cheese wax to protect the spawn from contamination and dehydration.

Root Development: In order for the spawn to start developing roots, the inoculated logs are brought into an environmentally controlled building. Adequate shade, moisture, temperature, and time are essential for growing shiitake. They're stacked in a criss-cross fashion which lets warm, moist air circulate around the logs. During this six-month dormant period, the mushroom spawn grows roots that are called "mycelium." This white, thread-like web grows up and down (lengthwise) with the grain of the wood as it literally digests the log and obtains its nutrients.

Fruiting: When the mushrooms begin to grow on the log, it's called "fruiting." To activate the fruiting process after the dormancy period, the logs are soaked in large pools of water for 24 hours. They are then racked in an upright position and kept in a warm room. During the next 5 to 7 days, the mushrooms will develop and pop through the bark of the log in clusters. This happens so quickly, you can almost see them grow. The logs have to be picked several times during the week.

▲ *To allow for air circulation, logs are stacked in a criss-cross manner during their dormancy period.*

► *To start the fruiting (mushroom growing) process, logs are soaked in large water tanks for 24 hours.*

Recycling Logs: After the mushrooms have been picked, the logs are stacked for a resting period of two months. At the end of this resting time, they are again ready for another cycle. Each log can be used for growing mushrooms 4 to 6 times in a year and will yield 3 to 4 pounds each cycle. By the last fruiting, the nutrients in the logs are totally digested by the mycelium. However, they are not just thrown out. The now featherlight, decomposed logs (they are as light as balsa wood at this point) are used for firewood to heat the fruiting and holding rooms.

Harvesting and Selling: Each shiitake is carefully picked by hand. They are placed in shallow boxes with air holes to allow for circulation.

Immediately after picking, the mushrooms are refrigerated, shipped out to market, and used or sold within four to seven days.

What's the significance in such a short selling period and why am I telling you this? You've probably had mushrooms go "slimy" on you in the refrigerator, so you know they don't have a long shelf life—after all, they are a fungus.

I thought it was interesting that growers don't activate the fruiting process until they have a buyer for their crop. If there isn't a market for shiitake, the grower will postpone activating the fruiting process by not soaking the dormant logs. He will simply let the logs rest an extra week or two until a market has been established for his crop.

It's just amazing to me how kind nature can sometimes be to us if we only listen to her.

▲ *After soaking, the logs are racked in an upright position and kept in a warm room. Within a week, the shiitake begin to pop out in clusters along the length of each log. The newly emerged shiitake have tan to light-brown colored tops with small white spots—kind of like Bambi.*

Flavor: Shiitake have a distinctive "meaty" flavor, and are strong enough to hold up in any dish. But only the caps can be eaten. The stems are merely an extension of the host wood, and are too tough and "woody" to eat. They are, however, full of flavor and good for stocks and soups.

Selecting and Storage: Look for shiitake that are firm and dryish (but not leathery) with domed caps that slightly curl under.

Unfortunately, most shiitake are sold to us packed in plastic. Since they are full of water, they tend to sweat, creating a little sauna. This shortens their shelf life dramatically.

When you buy shiitake (or any mushroom) remove any plastic film and let air circulate around them in your refrigerator. Use them right away or keep (*maybe*) up to three days. **ᴀʜ**

▲ *The end view of a log shows how the mycelium digests the wood for nutrients.*

BRAISED SHORT RIBS

Photograph: Scott Little, Food Styling: Janet Pittman

What's that saying? "The more things change, the more they stay the same." Nothing could be more true than for short ribs. Growing up, I ate plenty of them

because they were such a cheap cut of meat (you know the typical "growing up poor" stories). Well, I didn't walk to school in the snow, but we did eat plenty of inexpensive cuts of meat.

After leaving home, I left the tough cuts behind and indulged myself on more tender cuts of meat.

Now, I enjoy both the tender and tough cuts. The tougher cuts require longer cooking and more skill to bring out their great flavor. And this is just what bistro cooking is all about—slow cooking with simple ingredients. Just like you had growing up.

That's what we're going to do with short ribs—take inexpensive meat, cook it correctly, and present it so that it can be served even at a dinner party. Yes, you heard me correctly. Short ribs are back in vogue. Many hot new bistros springing up in big cities prepare short ribs just one day a week. It becomes a much-anticipated event.

The Secret: The secret to good short ribs is braising. This long, slow, cooking process uses "moist-heat" created by a little liquid and a tight fitting lid. It can be done either on top of the stove or in the oven.

Simply put, meat is divided into two basic categories—tough and tender. Tougher cuts of meat (meats that have little or no fat running through their muscles because they get plenty of exercise) should be cooked in a moist environment. This "moist-heat" cooking (braising and stewing) provides plenty of time for tough cuts to absorb flavor while breaking down the connective tissues in the muscles.

On the other hand, tender cuts of meat (muscles that don't get much exercise, like steaks), have thin veins of fat running through them (marbling). As this fat cooks at high temperatures, it melts to make the meat flavorful and tender. Dry-heat cooking (grilling and roasting) works best for these cuts since there's no need for added flavor or tenderness.

TECHNIQUE: BRAISING

Braising is a French, moist-heat cooking technique which is used primarily for larger, tougher meats and vegetables. Small amounts of liquids are added to a deep pan which is covered and cooked slowly at low temperatures (about the boiling temperature of water—212°). This is done either in the oven or on top of the stove. The ingredients are never entirely covered by liquid (stewing) as this tends to boil them rather than creating the gentle steam characteristic of a braise.

To understand braising, you have to understand the structure of meat and its reaction to heat.

Cooking: When cooking meat, you're extracting water (and flavor) from the muscles. You can see this easily when frying chicken. When you put raw chicken into hot grease, it creates large, turbulent bubbles (from all the water coming out). As it cooks, the bubbles become smaller and less frequent. That's because there's less and less water remaining. All meat reacts the same way.

Meats are made up of muscle fibers, connective tissues (collagen), fat, and water. As meat cooks, water in the muscle fibers and collagen begin to evaporate causing them to tighten, constrict, and squeeze out water from the meat.

Tough and Tender Cuts: As I said before, meat can be divided into two categories—tough and tender. Tender cuts of meat, like steaks, have fat running between their muscles fibers called marbling. As tender cuts of meat are cooked, water is extracted but replaced by the melting fat. This flavors and rehydrates the meat.

But tougher cuts don't have the benefit of the self-basting marbling. Enter the braise. When cooked long enough, collagen eventually melts and the muscle fibers relax. Collagen turns into a flavorful, rich gelatin which not only flavors the meat but also the braising liquid. The vacated space created by the melted collagen along with the relaxed muscles then allows the flavors to be reabsorbed.

BRAISED SHORT RIBS
(SERVES 6)
WORK TIME: 30 MINUTES
COOK TIME: $2^1/_2$–$3^1/_2$ HOURS
SEAR IN $^1/_4$ CUP OLIVE OIL:
10   beef short ribs
       (approximately 5 lbs.)
REMOVE RIBS, ADD:
2   cups celery, cut in 1" chunks
2   cups onion, roughly chopped
1   cup carrots, cut in 1" chunks
$^1/_2$ cup shallots, roughly chopped
$^1/_4$ cup garlic, roughly chopped
HEAT, ADD, THEN IGNITE:
$^1/_3$ cup brandy or Cognac
ADD AND REDUCE BY ONE-FOURTH:
1   cup dry red wine
ADD AND BRING TO SIMMER:
    Beef ribs
3   cups beef stock
4   sprigs fresh thyme
2   bay leaves
COVER AND BRAISE. REMOVE RIBS, STRAIN SAUCE, AND CHILL.

NUTRITIONAL INFORMATION PER SERVING:
CALORIES 459; TOTAL FAT 28(G); CALORIES FROM FAT 55%; SODIUM 120(MG)

WHAT ARE SHORT RIBS?

Short ribs are rectangles of beef ranging in length from 2–3 inches. They are made up of layers of meat and fat with a rib bone running through the middle. Because of the location of this cut of meat, short ribs are tough and require proper cooking to make them tender.

Short ribs come mainly from either the chuck or plate section of the ribs. But occasionally, they are trimmed from ends of the prime rib (just above the plate).

From the Chuck: Short ribs from the chuck tend to be a little more meaty but also a little chewier and less tender than those from the plate area. That's because the chuck area (shoulder) gets a good workout during its lifetime so there's less marbling to make them tender. If you get chuck short ribs, prepare to cook them a little longer to make the meat more tender. Braising is the only way to cook chuck ribs.

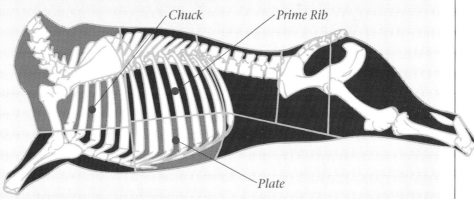

Chuck   Prime Rib   Plate

From the Plate: Ribs cut from the plate area make better short ribs because they are more tender (that area doesn't get much exercise). They're not as meaty as chuck ribs, nor do they contain as much fat.

You usually don't see plate short ribs during the warmer summer months. Braising isn't a favorite summer cooking process so most of these tender ribs are cut longer and sold for barbecuing.

Other Names: In order for us all to talk the same language about cuts of meat, the meat industry has come up with a system called the *Uniform Retail Meat Identity Standards.*

So, when you go to the market, you should find short ribs labeled either Beef Chuck or Plate Short Ribs (indicating origin of rib). But you might see unapproved names like English, Flanken, or Braising Ribs. Don't obsess, they're all good.

BROWNING

The first step in braising is to brown the meat and vegetables.

Browning: You may think that browning (searing) meat tends to retain the meat's juices—not true. The fact is, browning only retains moisture because the muscle fibers and connective tissues haven't had a chance to constrict and squeeze out the water.

What "true browning" does do is intensify the flavor of both the meat and sauce. It also begins to introduce a rich brown color to the liquid that will become the sauce.

Browning meat is simple if you follow these rules. Don't crowd the meat or vegetables. If you get too many items in a pan, they tend to steam (turn more gray than brown). It's okay (even preferred) to brown in batches.

Use a high heat but not so high that the fat or oil smokes. You want it browned—not blackened. Scorched fat and oil can be overpowering. Brown the meat on all sides. Remember, browning creates flavor.

Finally, most meats require little or no oil. You notice I'm not flouring the ribs because it takes too much oil to brown them. Besides, the flour can cause an unpredictable result (in thickness and smoothness).

WHAT IS COGNAC?

Cognac is a type of brandy, meaning that it has been distilled from wine. Simply put, all Cognac is brandy, but all brandy is not Cognac. Specifically, Cognac is a refined brandy. It's produced from a base wine made mainly from the Ugni Blanc grape. It's distilled twice, which produces a clear 70% distillate. Then the aging begins in special oak barrels. The Cognac absorbs the tannins and flavors of the oak, but gets its smoothness from up to 50 years of aging and evaporation. Yes, evaporation— known as "the angel's share."

1 Prepare your mirepoix. Cut celery, onion, carrots, shallots, and garlic into rough chunks. These only flavor the sauce then get strained.

2 In a large, deep pan, heat ¼ cup oil over medium-high heat. Add short ribs and sear all sides. Don't turn too soon. Let them brown.

3 After the short ribs are well-browned on all sides, remove them to a platter. Set them aside and keep them warm.

4 Add all the chopped vegetables to pan. Reduce the heat a little and sweat the vegetables. You want them tender and a little browned.

5 Place brandy (you don't *have* to use Cognac—save that for sipping) in a measuring cup and microwave it on high for 30 seconds.

6 **This is dangerous.** Add brandy to pan. Ignite it with a long match to remove the alcohol. You may want to experiment using 2 T. at a time.

7 After the brandy is burned off (cover pan with a lid to put out the flame, if needed), add the wine. Reduce the wine by one-fourth.

8 Add the ribs, beef stock, fresh thyme sprigs, and bay leaves to the pan. Bring to a boil. Now, it's ready to go into the oven to braise.

BRAISING

As I told you earlier, braising is a slow, gentle process in which you're trying to break down the muscle fibers and incorporate the gelatin (melted collagen) into the the braising liquid.

The bottom line is that you're trying to get a tough cut of meat tender enough to be easily pierced with a fork or a skewer, like I'm doing in Step 11. If you think about it logically and apply some basic science principles you learned in high school, braising all makes perfect sense.

First of all, you want to create steam in the pan. Why? Steam is gentle but hotter than hot, dry air or hot water. So it figures that you have to keep the liquid at a slow boil (just over 212°) to create steam. You can achieve this by setting your oven anywhere between 250–300°.

But that's a 50° swing in temperature. What do you set it at? While any temperature in that range works, I suggest that you set it at the lowest temperature. Just enough to provide a slow, rolling boil. Why? The key to braising is the steam. The longer you let the meat braise in the pan without disturbing the steaming process, the more tender the meat will become.

If you braise ribs at the higher end of the temperature spectrum (closer to 300°), you'll have to lift the lid to turn the meat more often to prevent scorching. The more you lift the lid, the more steam (heat) is lost and the broader the temperature fluctuations. You want this to be a slow, steady cooking process.

9 Cover the pan. Place in a 250–300° oven. You want the liquids in the pan just to maintain a simmer (a slow bubble).

10 Turn the short ribs every 30 minutes. This ensures even cooking. Cook for about 2–3 hours in this gentle manner.

11 Test short ribs for doneness. A skewer inserted in the meat should slide in easily and the meat should be pulling from the bones.

12 Remove short ribs from the pan. Let them cool completely. Then cover the ribs and refrigerate them.

13 Strain the vegetables from the sauce. The vegetables have done their job (added flavor), so discard them. Chill the sauce.

14 After the sauce has chilled, any fat will have risen to the top and solidified. You can easily lift it off the sauce in large pieces.

BOURGUIGNONNE
I'm preparing the short ribs in a classic "cuisine of Burgundy" style. Burgundy is a region in France known for its great cooking. And *à la bourguignonne* [boor-gee-NYON] refers to a cooking preparation in which meats (usually beef) are braised in red wine. The dish is then finished with small mushrooms and tiny onions. So our braised short ribs are a great take off on the classic *boeuf bourguignonne*.

I'm using three basic mushrooms that are easy to find at the market. Don't fret if you can't find them—the small white mushrooms work great, too.
Crimini: Also known as brown, Italian, or Roman mushrooms. They're tan to dark brown and have an earthy flavor. They hold their shape when cooked.

Oyster: A very delicate flavored and textured mushroom. I use these for their graceful, fluted caps. Only cook these for a short time.
Shiitake: These have a meaty flavor with a firm texture. Perfect in strong sauces. Unlike other mushrooms, their stems are inedible and should be cut off.

BOURGUIGNONNE SAUCE

(SERVES 6)
WORK TIME: 25 MINUTES
COOK TIME: 40 MINUTES

COMBINE FOR BEURRE MANIE:
1/4   cup all-purpose flour
1/4   cup butter, room temperature

SAUTE IN 3 T. BUTTER. SET ASIDE:
1/2   lb. white pearl onions, peeled
1/2   lb. red pearl onions, peeled
1/2   lb. oyster mushrooms
1/2   lb. crimini mushrooms
1/2   lb. shiitake mushrooms, trimmed

SAUTE IN 2 T. BUTTER:
3/4   cup minced shallots

ADD; THICKEN WITH BEURRE MANIE:
1   cup dry red wine
      Sauce from braised short ribs

NUTRITIONAL INFORMATION PER SERVING:
CALORIES 464; TOTAL FAT 27(G); CALORIES
FROM FAT 52%; SODIUM 449(MG)

FINISHING

I'm taking a little different approach to finishing our short ribs to make an unusual but flavorful presentation.

Onions and Mushrooms: First, you're going to saute whole pearl onions and a variety of mushrooms. The trick here is not to overcook them. You want them tender while maintaining their shapes and color. Remember, they'll continue to cook when you add them to the hot sauce.

Thickening the Sauce: Rather than flouring the ribs in the beginning to create a sauce, I prefer to thicken the sauce at the end. This way I can strain the sauce easily, remove unwanted fat, and then adjust the thickness the sauce after the reductions and natural gelatin extraction.

I really like how a beurre manie thickens this sauce. Beurre manie [burr mahn-YAY] means "kneaded butter" in French. It's equal parts flour and butter that are kneaded together until it feels like a soft pie pastry. Beurre manie is added a little at a time to produce just the right thickness.

Purple Potatoes: I just thought this would be a fun presentation— purple mashed potatoes, see next page. Don't worry, they taste just like regular potatoes. Trust me, there won't be any lull in the dinner conversation when you serve these babies! *AH*

15 Make beurre manie by combining flour and butter. Blend it with your fingers until uniform. It should feel like soft pastry dough.

16 Blanch onions for 1 minute in boiling water, then peel (see page 5). Cut stems from shiitakes. Clean remaining mushrooms.

17 First saute peeled onions in 3 T. butter for 2 minutes. Then add all the mushrooms and saute just until tender. Set aside.

18 In large pan, saute shallots in 2 T. butter until tender. Add red wine and reduce by half. Then add defatted sauce from braised ribs.

19 After liquid has come to a slow boil, whisk in walnut-sized pieces of beurre manie. Cook until sauce is desired thickness.

20 Now, place ribs in the hot sauce and simmer until ribs are heated through (10–15 mins.). Add the mushroom-onion mixture.

21 To serve, make a bed with the purple mashed potatoes on a warmed dinner plate. Spread the potatoes about 1/2 inch thick.

22 Top mashed potatoes with short ribs, onions, and mushrooms. Spoon sauce over top. Garnish with fresh thyme sprigs.

MASHED PURPLE POTATOES

(SERVES 6)

WORK TIME: 15 MINUTES

COOK TIME: 20 MINUTES

COOK, DRAIN, AND RICE:

7   cups purple potatoes, peeled and cut into 1½" chunks

STIR IN:

1   cup warm half & half

4–6 T. unsalted butter, room temperature

Salt to taste

NUTRITIONAL INFORMATION PER SERVING: CALORIES 277; TOTAL FAT 12(G); CALORIES FROM FAT 40%; SODIUM 608(MG)

We've made mashed potatoes before, but this is something different. If the purple bothers you, try Yukon Golds for a golden color.

Here are the simple rules for good mashed potatoes. Use starchy potatoes (waxy like white and red don't absorb the cream and butter well). After boiling them, dry them in the pan to remove any excess water. Then, rice them through the smallest holes possible. This will prevent lumps. And finally, use *warm* half & half and butter to maintain the temperature of the potatoes.

PURPLE POTATOES

These South American novelty potatoes are popular with hot new chefs. Originally they were developed by Ag schools to mark boundaries in fields where other potato varieties were sown. They are sweeter and starchier.

PREPARING THE MASHED POTATOES

1 Peel and cut purple potatoes into large chunks. Place cut potatoes in a large pot. Add cold water to cover by 1–2 inches.

2 Bring water to a boil. Then simmer for 15–20 minutes, or until potatoes can be pierced or broken easily with a fork.

3 Drain potatoes and put them back into the pot. Return them to the hot burner for a few seconds to dry them. Stir so they don't burn.

4 Fill up a ricer with potatoes. Squeeze the levers together, pushing the riced potatoes through. Repeat until all potatoes are used.

5 Stir in half & half and the butter. Make sure they are not cold so you don't cool down your potatoes. Add a little salt to taste.

6 Stir potatoes until butter is melted and everything is smooth and well combined. Serve immediately. The color turns bluer as they cool.

Q *Explain what baking in the "upper" or "lower" third of the oven means?*

A Most ovens have room for 4–5 racks. They can be divided into thirds with each third having two rack positions. Let me explain. *Generally*, the top two racks are used for broiling. Many racks at the very top, don't slide in all the way keeping the oven door ajar. This prevents the broiler from getting too hot and fluctuating. Don't use this for baking.

The bottom two racks (lower third) are near the intense heat (this acts like a stove burner). These are used when you need fast heat for breads, or to finish sauteed items (like thick fish or chops).

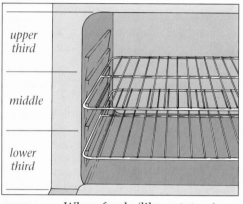

upper third

middle

lower third

When foods (like potatoes) are baked in the top two racks (upper third), you're roasting to brown. Heat naturally rises then bounces off the oven ceiling to brown food.

But the most commonly used middle two racks allows moderate, consistent heat to circulate evenly around the food. This area provides golden browning and even baking.

Q *I buy bags of ready-to-use salad greens. The instructions on the bag say that the greens are washed and ready to use. But recently I've heard that this isn't true. What's correct?*

A Wash it. You can't expect things grown in the ground to be completely free of bacteria. It's normal. Studies show there are levels of a harmless bacteria in bagged salads, but there have been no confirmed reports of illness related to them.

Even if a bag indicates it's been "prewashed" or is "ready to eat," you're better off washing it anyway. Your greens will also be crisp and tastier after a bath.

Q *I know you recommend using fresh herbs when preparing your recipes. But sometimes I can't get fresh herbs. What is the equivalent measure when using dried herbs instead of fresh ones?*

A If you have to use dried herbs, substitute about 1/3 as much dried herbs for fresh since dried herbs are three times stronger than fresh. All the moisture has been removed from dried herbs and their flavor is much more intense. Do you remember eating beef jerky as a kid? Pretty potent stuff! Dried herbs work the same way. So if you're making marinara sauce, go ahead and substitute 1 teaspoon dried basil for 1 tablespoon of fresh.

Q *I've heard about the hazards of using a wooden cutting board (bacteria breeding grounds) and the benefits of using plastic instead. With all the concern about E. Coli bacteria, is plastic really any safer than wood?*

A Seems wooden cutting boards are the way to go. Recent studies indicate wooden boards are the better choice for safe food preparation.

When purposely contaminated with organisms, such as Salmonella, 99% of the bacteria on the wooden board died within three minutes, while all the bacteria on the plastic board was still alive and kicking.

Bacteria on plastic cutting boards has nowhere to go because plastic is non-porous—it sits on the surface. But bacteria on wooden boards absorbs into the woodgrain and eventually dies. This excludes wooden boards which contain deep cut marks.

If you think you're safe because you own an anti-bacterial cutting board, think again. The EPA says those aren't effective against the same organisms. But don't expect your wooden board to clean itself. Wash thoroughly with *hot, hot, hot,* soapy water after each use.

We'll find answers to your cooking questions, and help find solutions to the unique problems which occur in the kitchen. Any questions? Send your cooking questions to *Cuisine, Q & A Editor,* 2200 Grand Avenue, Des Moines, IA 50312, or contact us through our E-mail address: *Cuisine@cuisinemag.com*

Q *What are beards on mussels? Are they edible? Why do you need to remove them?*

A The beard, which feels like soft steel wool, is made of proteins secreted from the mussel. It hardens on contact with salt water. These long filaments, called byssus threads, are incredibly strong and are used to cling to rocks and pilings. This anchors the mussels in their feeding grounds so they aren't swept away by strong currents. Don't remove them until ready to cook the mussel or they'll die.

▲ *To remove the beards, pull them with your fingers toward the small end of the shell. Or you can gently pull with pliers.*

Q *In your Premier issue, you made Beef Wellington in frozen puff pastry. I want to make this recipe, but I'd like to prepare the tenderloins and wrap them in pastry the day before. Is this okay to do? Will it get soggy? Are there any special procedures involved?*

A Sure, you can make Beef Wellington in advance. The puff pastry won't get soggy since you chill the meat after searing. This allows time for the juices to "set" and be absorbed back into the meat as opposed to being extracted during cooking. But their shelf life is not without limits. It's best to serve them within 24 hours.

Refrigerate the Wellingtons as soon as all the ingredients are chilled and they're wrapped in the puff pastry. Bake them directly from the refrigerator—this keeps them from overcooking.

Q *What is a shallot? Can I substitute an onion for a shallot?*

A Shallots are a member of the onion family, but aren't baby onions, as their small size might indicate. Shallots are shaped more like garlic with a small head containing several cloves. Their taste is a slight cross between an onion and garlic with a less intense onion flavor. Yes, you can substitute an onion for a shallot, but you won't get the milder flavor of the shallot.

Q *What is "brown butter" and how do I make it?*

A Brown butter is known to the French as beurre noisette [burr nwah-ZEHT]. It's in the same family as beurre rouge and beurre blanc. It's just another kind of butter sauce.

Beurre noisette (literally hazelnut butter), refers to melted butter that's cooked until it's a light brown color, similar to that of a hazelnut.

Brown butter is usually served with lighter foods like fish, eggs, white meats, and vegetables.

To make brown butter, heat whole butter slowly over a low heat until it's an amber color and gives off a nutty aroma. Too high a heat and the milk solids in the butter will burn. Once browned, 4 oz. of butter is finished with 2 t. of vinegar or lemon juice, then capers or parsley is added.

GLOSSARY

Emulsify: [eh-MUHL-suh-fy] The process of binding hard-to-combine ingredients, like water and oil. The final blended product is called an *emulsion* which can last from a few minutes to a few days depending on the *emulsifier*, the item that binds the two hard-to-combine ingredients. Common emulsifiers are mustard and egg yolks.

Mirepoix: [mihr-PWAH] A combination of vegetables used in sauces, soups, and stews or as a bed for braised foods. Used for flavor, the mirepoix may not be used in the final product. Common vegetables used are onions, carrots, and celery.

Mount: A technique where small pieces of cold, unsalted butter are whisked into a sauce just before serving. Mounting gives sauces texture and flavor as well as a glossy look.

Render: The melting of animal fat over low heat so it separates from any connective tissue. This tissue turns crisp and brown (known as crackling) and the clarified (clear) fat is further processed by straining.

Ricer: A kitchen gadget that looks like a big garlic press. This device, also called a potato ricer, forces cooked foods like turnips and potatoes through tiny holes, resembling rice.

Sweat: When foods, usually vegetables, are cooked over low heat in a small amount of fat (usually butter), drawing out juices to remove rawness and develop flavor.

Vermouth: [ver-MOOTH] A dry or sweet white wine which has been fortified and flavored with herbs and spices.

ABBREVIATIONS

t. = teaspoon
T., Tbsp. = tablespoon
oz. = ounce
lb. = pound
Pinch = $1/16$ of a teaspoon
Dash = scant $1/8$ of a teaspoon

ASPARATION ►

It looks like a cross between broccoli and asparagus, but it's *actually* a new hybrid that's a cross between broccoli and *gai lon*, a type of Chinese kale. It has tiny broccoli florets growing on long, thin, tender stems—which don't need to be peeled. The flavor is similar to asparagus and broccoli, only sweeter and milder.

This vegetable can be used much like broccoli, either cooked or raw. Asparation is still new on the market, so check your local grocery store or ask them to order it for you. It's worth a try!

▲ SPIRAL SLICER

For 45 bucks, this little shredder is well worth the price to me. It solves a lot of my garnishing problems by easily making strands and spirals out of almost any vegetable.

Four different blades vary the thicknesses to create elegant ribbons. I used it for my beets on page 24. And I can't wait to fry potato ribbons for a garnish or a nest like the big-time chefs do. The fiberglass stand is a breeze to clean up. The shredder is available through **Sur La Table** at **(800) 243-0852**, item #3890.

◄ PLUGRÁ BUTTER

Every once in a while, a product just stops me in my tracks, and this is it. Plugrá is an unsalted European-style butter, made in the U.S. It has 2% more fat than most American butters and less water. You don't think 2% is much? Wait till you taste this stuff.

Previously sold only to restaurants, it's now available at some grocery and gourmet stores. Available in 1-lb. and 8-oz. bricks. Also try Plugrá's heavy cream. To die for! For **Plugrá** sources, call: in Pennsylvania, **(800) 228-8837**; outside PA, **(800) 535-5371**.

◄ ARANWARE COLLECTION

This is quality earthenware made in the historic city of Derry, Ireland. Available in a beautiful cream color, each piece is decorated with centuries-old Aran Isles stitch patterns that symbolize Irish life of old. The Diamond stitch for success, the Cable stitch for good luck and safety, and the Basket stitch for abundant catches from the sea and a bountiful table of today.

The collection is available in a beautiful 10" pie plate, 13$\frac{1}{2}$" oval baking dish, 12" x 9" rectangular baking dish, 4$\frac{1}{2}$-pint round casserole with lid, and a salad/pasta bowl. Prices range from $25–$56. All pieces are microwave-, oven-, freezer-, and dishwasher-safe. Call **Ross-Simons** at **(800) 556-7376** to order (code: KICAWC), or call **Kara Pottery Co.** at **(800) 430-2008** to find a store near you.

CHEESE SOUFFLÉ
WITH MUSHROOM SAUTE

CHEESE SOUFFLÉ

(SERVES 6)

WORK TIME: 20 MINUTES
COOK TIME: 30 MINUTES

BUTTER SOUFFLÉ DISH; SPRINKLE WITH:

3   T. grated Parmesan cheese

FOR BÉCHAMEL, SIMMER AND STRAIN:

1   cup 2% milk
$^1/_2$ small onion
1   bay leaf
$^1/_2$ t. whole peppercorns
2   whole cloves

PREPARE A ROUX FROM, THEN WHISK IN MILK MIXTURE:

2   T. unsalted butter
2   T. all-purpose flour
$^1/_2$ t. salt
$^1/_4$ t. white pepper
      Dash ground nutmeg

WHISK INTO BÉCHAMEL SAUCE:

2   whole eggs
3   egg yolks

FOLD INTO MIXTURE:

6   egg whites, beaten with $^1/_8$ t. cream of tartar until stiff
1   cup shredded Gruyère cheese

NUTRITIONAL INFORMATION PER SERVING:
CALORIES 226; TOTAL FAT 16(G); CALORIES FROM FAT 63%; SODIUM 477(MG)

Making soufflés is scary. You have to hold your breath and walk on tiptoes to keep them from falling, right? Then they still fall. Well, get over it! The scariest thing about making a soufflé is the anticipation. I avoided

making one for years because I didn't want to fail. Then I finally did one. Pffttt! What's the big deal?

Let's get one thing straight. Soufflés fall. Once you accept this, you're halfway home. Heck, the word soufflé means "to breathe." Imagine it exhaling a big sigh as it falls.

A soufflé is the egg at its most dramatic. Stiffly beaten egg whites puff to create a rich but airy treat. Its top is browned but the inside is moist.

I'm showing you the classic cheese soufflé here. There are three main components to keep in mind.

The Base: The base for a soufflé is what carries its flavor and gives it substance. The classic base is a béchamel sauce. Egg yolks are added for more body. Bases can also be made of vegetable purees or pastry cream.

The amount of flour used to thicken the base is key. You want enough to give you some stability, but not so

much that the soufflé is heavy and cakelike. If the base is too thick, the egg whites can't lift it.

I wanted to make a soufflé that you could get from the oven to the table before it falls in on itself. Adding whole eggs to the egg yolks in the base helps to "set" the soufflé, giving you just a touch more stability.

Egg Whites: Egg whites are what make soufflés rise—and fall. I get detailed with them on the next page.

The Cheese: Since you can't use a lot of cheese (it would weigh the soufflé down), you need one with a lot of flavor. Gruyère is perfect. This firm Swiss cheese has a distinct, nutty flavor that really comes through. Shred it finely, though, so it stays suspended by the egg whites.

THE KEY: EGG WHITES

The success of your soufflé depends almost entirely on how well you handle the egg whites. They are what give the soufflé its height.

Beating: Soufflés puff way up because air trapped inside beaten egg whites expands when heated in the oven—like lots of little balloons. The whites should be beaten to stiff, glossy peaks, so they are still moist enough to stay elastic when baking. Then the soufflé will rise high and stay inflated long enough to get it to the table.

Overbeaten whites look dry and grainy. They've lost their elasticity, so they won't expand much. Ever try to stretch an old, dried up rubber band? It breaks. Same deal with egg whites. The result is a short, heavy souffle.

It's easy to overbeat egg whites, so you have to pay attention. I read that beating an additional egg white into overbeaten whites can save them. I tried it, but I wasn't happy with the results. Better to start over with new whites if it happens to you.

Adding cream of tartar to egg whites helps prevent overbeating. Cream of tartar stabilizes the whites, so it takes longer to overbeat. You only need $1/8$ teaspoon for 6 whites.

Temperature: Let your egg whites come to room temperature before beating them. I compared chilled and room temperature egg whites, and the room temperature whites had much more volume, resulting in a higher soufflé. I thought the chilled whites might give a more stable soufflé, but it didn't seem to make much difference. I'd rather go for a higher, more dramatic soufflé than gain 30 seconds of deflating time.

Folding: Okay. You've gotten your egg whites whipped up to a nice, fluffy foam. Now, don't undo all that good work when you fold them into the base. First, lighten up your base by stirring a big scoop of whites into it with a whisk. You want to mix them in thoroughly, but be gentle so the mixture stays foamy.

Next, scoop half of the remaining whites onto the base. Sprinkle half of the cheese over top. Partially fold the whites and cheese in. To do this, plunge a rubber scraper through the whites to the bottom of the pan, then pull it toward you, bringing the base up and over the whites. Do this just a few times. Fold in the remaining whites and cheese the same way.

Don't worry about folding the whites in completely. It's *much* better to under-fold this mixture than to totally work in the whites. Any lumps of whites will puff up like big marshmallows in the soufflé. Remember, every time you stick that rubber scraper into the whites, you deflate them. Lightly fold to get a bumpy, interesting top to your soufflé — nice.

PREPARING THE BASE

1 Brush 2-quart soufflé dish to top edge with softened butter. Coat completely with Parmesan cheese. (Don't smear it.) Heat oven to 375°.

2 Separate eggs by passing the yolks from hand to hand, letting the whites slip through your fingers. The yolks won't break if you're gentle.

3 In a small saucepan, heat milk to simmer with onion, bay leaf, peppercorns, and cloves. Let stand off heat for 15 minutes to infuse. Strain.

4 In a larger saucepan, make a roux by melting butter over medium-low heat. Whisk in flour. Cook for 2 minutes, whisking constantly.

5 Gradually whisk strained milk mixture into roux. Cook until sauce is thickened, stirring constantly. Add salt, pepper, and nutmeg.

6 Mix together whole eggs and yolks. Off the heat, gradually whisk egg mixture into béchamel sauce. Mix until smooth. Set aside.

FOLDING IN EGG WHITES

7 Beat egg whites with cream of tartar until they have stiff, glossy peaks. Overbeaten whites look dry and grainy.

8 Add a large scoop of egg whites to sauce mixture and stir in completely. This lightens your sauce so you can fold in the rest of the whites.

9 Gently fold in remaining whites and cheese, half at a time. It's better to leave a few patches of whites than to fold until they are deflated.

10 Carefully pour batter into prepared soufflé dish. 1" in from the dish's edge, score the top. This prevents "blow-outs" over the edge.

11 Bake soufflé on the middle rack of the oven for 25 to 30 minutes, or until browned on top and soufflé jiggles only slightly.

12 To serve, use a large fork and serving spoon back-to-back to pull soufflé apart. This keeps it from getting crushed and overly deflated.

MUSHROOM SAUTE

Saute each mushroom type quickly over high heat, *just* until browned. Don't overcook. Separate cooking keeps individual flavors and textures.

Place each batch of mushrooms on paper towels and lightly salt them. They've only just started to weep, so this allows extra moisture to drain.

In the same skillet over medium heat, saute shallots and garlic in butter until tender. Add the Vermouth and reduce for a couple of minutes.

Return all mushrooms to skillet and toss until heated through. Season to taste with salt and cayenne. Add minced herbs just before serving.

MUSHROOM SAUTE
(MAKES 4 CUPS)
WORK TIME: 20 MINUTES
COOK TIME: 25 MINUTES

SAUTE EACH TYPE OF MUSHROOM IN 1 T. OLIVE OIL; SALT AND DRAIN:

- 6 oz. oyster mushrooms
- 6 oz. shiitake mushrooms, stems removed
- 6 oz. small crimini mushrooms
- 6 oz. portobello mushrooms, sliced

SAUTE IN 3 T. UNSALTED BUTTER:

- $1/2$ cup minced shallots
- 2 cloves garlic, minced

ADD AND REDUCE:

- $1/4$ cup dry Vermouth

ADD MUSHROOMS; STIR IN:

- $1/4$ cup minced fresh chives
- $1/4$ cup fresh parsley, chopped
  Salt and cayenne pepper to taste

NUTRITIONAL INFORMATION PER $2/3$ CUP:
CALORIES 196; TOTAL FAT 15(G); CALORIES FROM FAT 67%; SODIUM 221(MG)

PÂTE À CHOUX

Photograph: Scott Little, Food Styling: Janet Pittman

What's in a name? When I started making pâte à choux for profiteroles, I couldn't scrounge up volunteers for a taste test. Obviously, there was a language barrier.

So I changed my tactics and asked for volunteers to taste-test chocolate eclairs and cream puffs. The response was overwhelming. These are desserts everyone has heard of. Not only did the testers eat well, but they got a little French lesson thrown in the deal.

A French Lesson: Pâte à choux [paht-uh-SHOO] is French for "paste of cabbages." In cooking terms, it's a thick, sticky pastry that's baked to make several types of dessert. Two of these desserts are profiteroles [pro-FIHT-uh-role] and eclairs [ay-KLAIR]. They both have the pastry that, when baked, forms a hollow shell—perfect for holding all kinds of creams.

Pâte à Choux: Let's get back to that strange translation of "paste of cabbages." Take a look on page 42, Step 11. When you bake profiteroles, they look like little heads of cabbage.

Pâte à choux is made from flour, butter, eggs, and water. It's looser than other pastry doughs and can't be rolled out. Instead, the paste is piped into shapes and baked.

Pâte à choux is pâte à choux *only* until it's piped and baked. Then it's not a paste anymore and the names change, depending on the shape.

Profiteroles: Profiteroles are miniature cream puffs (about 2 inches). Fill them with ice cream or pastry cream.

Croquembouche: A croquembouche [kro-kuhm-BOOSH] consists of several layers of profiteroles stacked into a tiered cone. Usually the profiteroles are dipped into caramel and become crunchy—hence the literal translation, "crisp in the mouth."

Eclairs: Eclairs are similar to profiteroles except they're long rather than round. Eclair means "lightning bolt," a reference to their length.

How it Works: Choux works because of steam. There's not leavener, like baking powder, to give dough "lift." Here, it's just eggs and heat.

Flour provides structure for the paste. The moisture from the eggs evaporates in the hot oven creating steam. Like a steam engine, the steam is energy creating power to push. In this case, steam is pushing against the pastry walls creating a hollow shell—prime real estate for pastry cream.

MAKING THE PÂTE À CHOUX

Starting the Choux: Preheat your oven and mark the baking pans, *see Step 1*. Have these ready to go. Once you make the paste, you want to bake it right away. You get the most "lift" from eggs that've just been beaten.

Bring the water, butter, sugar, and salt to a boil in a saucepan, *see Step 2*. Then add the flour all at once and mix with a wooden spoon, *see Step 3*. A wooden spoon is strong enough to handle the thick paste.

Return pan to heat to dry out the paste a little, *see Step 4*. This evaporates moisture so you can add more egg.

Remember, the eggs are what give the pastries "lift." So, the more eggs you can add without getting it too thin, the higher and more hollow the profiteroles and eclairs will be.

Adding the Eggs: Adding the eggs requires a judgement call. You might not need to add all the eggs depending on humidity and egg size.

Whisk one egg in a dish and keep it to the side for later, *see Step 5*. Then, start adding the eggs, one at a time, blending completely before adding another. Don't get frustrated. The paste won't want to absorb the egg. Persistence! Stir slowly. Then beat vigorously as each egg is incorporated until it becomes smooth and shiny.

The "V" Test: After adding the fourth egg, use the "V" test to check the paste's consistency. If it makes a "V" shape as it falls off the spoon, you hit the mark, *see Step 6*. If it's too stiff, add a little of that beaten egg you stashed away and test again.

PÂTE À CHOUX
*(MAKES FORTY-EIGHT 2"
PROFITEROLES OR SIXTEEN
3$\frac{1}{2}$" ECLAIRS)*
WORK TIME: 40 MINUTES
BAKE TIME: 25–30 MINUTES
COMBINE:
3/4 cup water
6   T. unsalted butter, diced
1   T. sugar
1/4 t. salt
BRING TO A BOIL; STIR IN:
1   cup all-purpose flour
COOL; ADD, ONE AT A TIME:
5   eggs
***PIPE ON PREPARED BAKING
SHEETS, BRUSH WITH EGG WASH,
AND BAKE IN PREHEATED OVEN.***

PREPARING THE PÂTE À CHOUX

1 Mark greased and floured baking sheets with an inverted pastry tip (1 inch), spacing 1½" apart. Place rack in middle of 400° preheated oven.

2 In a saucepan, combine the water, butter, sugar, and salt. Bring to a boil over medium heat, stirring occasionally to melt the butter.

3 As soon as it boils, remove the pan from the heat and add the flour all at once. Stir until it forms a ball around the base of the spoon.

4 Return to low heat and dry the paste out slightly, stirring constantly, about 30 seconds. A dry film will form on the bottom of the pan.

5 Cool the paste 10 minutes. Whisk one egg in a dish and set aside. Stir in remaining eggs, one at a time, beating thoroughly after each one.

6 To test the consistency, lift some paste with the spoon—if you don't get this "V" shape, add a little of the beaten egg, stir, and test again.

PIPING AND BAKING

I know using a pastry bag scares some of you—I was, too, at first (years ago!). It's easy once you get the hang of it. But don't worry about perfect piping here—remember, the profiteroles are supposed to look like little cabbages.

The Pastry Bag: For these pastries, I use a 14" plastic pastry bag with a 1/2" plain pastry tip fitted in the bottom.

Fill with paste by first putting the bag into a tall glass, *see Step 7*. So the paste doesn't drip out prematurely, try this trick. Tuck some of the bag into the top of the tip when filling—like tucking your pants leg (at the calf) into the top of your boot.

Now, gently shake the batter down into the tip. This eliminates air pockets, preventing piping "explosions."

Twist the top of the bag closed where the paste ends. Hold the twisted part in one hand and steady the tip with the other. You're ready to pipe.

Piping Profiteroles: To pipe profiteroles, hold the bag over the middle of a marked circle on a baking sheet.

With the tip close to the pan (but not touching it), squeeze paste into the circle. *Apply even pressure from your hand at the top of the bag.* Squeeze until the circle's filled, *see Steps 8 and 9*. To release, stop squeezing and *then* lift the tip up and away.

Piping Eclairs: Pipe eclairs with the tip at a 45° angle to the baking sheet, not touching the pan. Squeeze out paste until it's 1" across. Keep piping as you slowly pull the tip toward you, *see Piping Eclairs*. Release like you did the profiteroles.

Eggwashing: Eggwash gives the profiteroles and eclairs a shiny glaze. I dab the egg on with my fingers, *see Step 10*. This way, you don't drip too much on the baking sheet which can make the pastries stick.

Baking: Start baking the pastries at 400° so they're quick to puff out. Then lower the heat to 350° to dry them out. Move to a higher rack if the bottoms get too dark. Bake until golden all over, *see Step 11*. If they are underbaked, the profiteroles will collapse.

Cool on a rack before filling, *see Step 12*. Or freeze them in Ziplocs®, so you can fill them later.

MAKING PROFITEROLES AND ECLAIRS

7 I put the pastry bag into a tall glass when I fill it—this way, both my hands are free to spoon in the paste. Fill the bag about half full.

8 Position the tip at a 90° angle in the middle of a circle, about 1/4" above the baking sheet. Gently squeeze out paste to the fill circle.

9 Don't move the tip while you pipe—let the batter fill the circle. When it's filled, stop squeezing, then gently lift the tip up and away.

11 Bake at 400° for 15 mins. Reduce heat to 350° and bake 10–13 mins. more, until golden. The sides should be dry and not soft.

PIPING ECLAIRS

For eclairs, squeeze out paste until about 1" wide (across). Then pull the tip back towards you, squeezing as you go.

When eclair is about 3 1/2" long, stop squeezing the bag and release the tip up and away from you.

10 With your fingertips, use the extra beaten egg to gently smooth out the curlicues on top of the profiteroles.

12 Transfer pastries to a cooling rack. Cool completely and fill. Or freeze, defrost, then crisp in 325° oven for 15 minutes before filling.

PASTRY CREAM AND GLAZE

That hollow middle is just waiting for something to fill it. Wouldn't you know, I have just the thing.

Pastry Cream: Pastry cream is like pudding. It's a great filling for fruit tarts, spreading between cake layers, or eating straight from the bowl.

This is *vanilla* pastry cream. It's intense flavor comes from using both the vanilla bean and extract. Split the bean and scrape out the tiny seeds, *see Step 13.* Mix the seeds and pod with the sugar, flour, yolks, and salt.

Whisk the warm milk and egg mixture over medium heat until it thickens, *see Step 14.* Whisk constantly to prevent scorching and bring to a boil for 1 minute—this "cooks out" the flour's starchy taste. The flour stabilizes the yolks so they won't curdle.

Transfer to a bowl and stir in the butter and vanilla. Press plastic wrap directly on the cream to prevent a "skin" from forming, *see Step 15.*

Chocolate Glaze: This chocolate glaze gets its gloss from the water and flavor from top-notch chocolate.

Have you had trouble with chocolate before? Relax. There's nothing tough about making this sauce. The water tends to stabilize it. Simmer chocolate, sugar, and water in a pan until it coats a spoon, *see Step 16.* Then whisk in the butter. Cool the glaze a little to prevent excess dripping.

Filling and Glazing: So they don't get soggy, fill and glaze the profiteroles a few hours before serving.

Normally, profiteroles are filled with a pastry bag outfitted with a small tip. But a squeeze bottle works best for me. Find a "natural" hole in the side or top of a profiterole, *see Step 17.* Fill with cream until it's heavy or the cream starts oozing out. Dip the pastry tops in the glaze, *see Step 18.* Or check out the back cover for a fancy dessert presentation. **Ah**

VANILLA PASTRY CREAM
(MAKES 2 1/2 CUPS)
WORK TIME: 10 MINUTES
COOK TIME: 20 MINUTES
WARM IN MEDIUM SAUCEPAN:
1   cup heavy cream
1   cup whole milk
WHISK IN; COOK UNTIL THICK:
2/3   cup sugar
1/2   cup all-purpose flour
10   egg yolks
1   vanilla bean, split, seeds removed
     Pinch salt
OFF HEAT, STIR IN:
1/4   cup unsalted butter, diced
2   t. pure vanilla extract

CHOCOLATE GLAZE
(MAKES 1 1/2 CUPS)
WORK TIME: 5 MINUTES
COOK TIME: 12 MINUTES
COMBINE AND SIMMER:
8   oz. bittersweet chocolate, finely chopped
1/2   cup sugar
1/2   cup water
OFF HEAT, WHISK IN:
2   T. unsalted butter

MAKING THE PASTRY CREAM AND GLAZE

13 In a saucepan, warm the cream and milk. Split the vanilla bean lengthwise and scrape out the seeds with back of a paring knife.

14 Combine sugar, flour, yolks, vanilla seeds and pod, and salt. Whisk into milk and cook over medium heat until thick, about 5–8 mins.

15 Transfer cream to a bowl and whisk in the butter and vanilla extract. Cover with plastic, pressing it right on the cream. Chill thoroughly.

16 For the glaze, simmer chocolate, sugar, and water over medium heat until it coats a spoon. Off heat, whisk in butter, then cool.

17 I use a squeeze bottle to fill the pastries—find a "natural" hole, or poke one in the top or side. Fill with cream until they feel heavy.

18 Dip the tops of the pastries into cooled chocolate glaze, letting the excess drip back into the bowl. Return to rack to set glaze.

MAKING A GRAND FINALE

Photograph: Scott Little; Food Styling: Janet Pittman

PROFITEROLE PYRAMID

For the Apricot Sauce: Combine in a saucepan one 10 oz. jar apricot preserves, 2 T. brandy and 1 split and scraped vanilla bean. Whisk over low heat until the preserves are melted, about 5 mins. Strain and set aside.

Sticking the Profiteroles: To prevent profiteroles from sliding, put a dab of chocolate sauce from page 43 on the bottom of each one. Now they'll stick to the plate to make stacking into a little pyramid easier.

Spooning the Sauces: Spoon the apricot sauce around base of each pyramid. Warm it briefly if it's gelled and hard to spoon. Then drizzle warmed chocolate sauce over the tops of pyramid to form rivers down the sides.

Cuisine

ISSUE No. 12
NOV/DEC 1998

AUGUST HOME'S

Cuisine ™

AN ILLUSTRATED GUIDE TO CREATIVE HOME COOKING

CRANBERRY NAPOLEON
WITH CABERNET SAUCE

Also in this Issue:
CALZONES
ANTIPASTO PLATTER
TORTELLINI & RAVIOLI

Cuisine

Editor
John F. Meyer

Art Director
Cinda Shambaugh

Assistant Editors
Susan Hoss
Kelly Volden
Ellen C. Boeke
Sara Ostransky

Senior Graphic Designer
Holly Wiederin

Contributing Designer
Nancy Roll

Senior Photographer
Crayola England

Contributing Photographer
Dean Tanner
Primary Image

Test Kitchen Director
Kim Samuelson

Editorial Assistant
Stephanie Neppl

Electronic Publishing
Coordinator
Douglas M. Lidster

Pre-press Image Specialist
Troy Clark

Publisher
Donald B. Peschke

Corporate
V.P. Planning & Finance: **Jon Macarthy**
Subscriber Services Director: **Sandy Baum**
New Business Director: **Glenda K. Battles**
New Business Manager: **Todd Bierle**
Promotion Manager: **Rick Junkins**
Renewal Manager: **Paige Rogers**
Billing Manager: **Rebecca Cunningham**
Asst. Subscription Manager: **Joy Krause**
Production Director: **George Chmielarz**
Production Assistant: **Susan Rueve**
Pre-press Image Specialist: **Minniette Bieghler**
Creative Director: **Ted Kralicek**
August Home Books: **Douglas L. Hicks**
New Media Manager: **Gordon C. Gaippe**
Assoc. Graphic Design Director: **Susie Rider**
Senior Graphic Designer: **Cheryl Simpson**
Controller: **Robin K. Hutchinson**
Senior Accountant: **Laura J. Thomas**
Accounts Payable Clerk: **Mary Schultz**
Human Resource Assistant: **Kirsten Koele**
Customer Service Manager: **Jennie Enos**
Administrative Assistant: **Julia Fish**
Receptionist: **Jeanne Johnson**
Librarian: **Sherri Ribbey**
Special Projects Director: **Saville Inman**

Cuisine™ (ISSN 1089-6546) is published bi-monthly
(Jan., Mar., May, July, Sept., Nov.) by August Home
Publishing Co., 2200 Grand Ave., Des Moines, IA
50312. Cuisine™ is a trademark of August Home
Publishing Co. ©Copyright 1998 August Home
Publishing. All rights reserved. Subscriptions: Single
copy: $4.99. One year subscription (6 issues), $21.94.
(Canada/Foreign add $6 per year, U.S. funds.)
Periodicals postage paid at Des Moines, IA and at
additional mailing offices. "USPS/Heartland Press
Automatable Poly" Postmaster: Send change of address
to Cuisine, PO Box 37100 Boone, IA 50037-2100.
Subscription questions? Call 800-311-3995,
8 a.m. to 5 p.m., Central Standard Time, weekdays.
Cuisine™ does not accept and is not responsible for
unsolicited manuscripts. PRINTED IN U.S.A.

From the Editor:

I don't know about you, but for me, the holidays need a little "spicing" up. Be assured, I'll still be in the kitchen with my daughter roasting turkey and making dressing. All this talk about "family values" makes the kitchen a great forum for the family to share quality time and traditions.

But I've also conjured up some interesting twists to the holiday meals. You bet we're using turkey and cranberries—just in a different way. This issue is slanted toward Italian cuisine—everybody's favorite. I've made three great dishes using turkey tenderloin rather than veal. This flavorful piece of white meat is sold separately from the breast and can be used just like more expensive cuts of veal and pork. Beginning on page 30, you'll find some Italian-inspired recipes that are quick and low in calories. And yes, there's even a roasted turkey entree made with cranberries. And I'll show you how a professional chef might plate these dishes. It's the holidays so you can be a little fancier than normal!

So enjoy your new turkey dishes, but most of all, enjoy the holidays with your friends and family. I look forward to sharing another year of cooking with you.

In the future, we'll roast a turkey and come up with some neat side dishes for the holidays. But for now, I'm taking an Italian twist. It seems to be everybody's favorite and a welcome relief from all the typical holiday foods. Try these three turkey dishes—they make great dinners and can easily be prepared ahead.

AUGUST HOME'S

Cuisine

AN ILLUSTRATED GUIDE TO CREATIVE HOME COOKING

THIMBLES TO PROTECT FINGERS

I love using hard cheeses as opposed to the shredded stuff in the store. But I always nick my finger tips when I grate them.

So, I cover two or three of my fingers with metal thimbles. Now, I can grate much faster and closer.

D. Brown
Lindsay, NE

STORING MUSHROOMS

Mushrooms never stay fresh long enough for me to use them all. But I found a way to prolong their lives.

First, clean the mushrooms with a paper towel or brush. Then clean and dry the container that they came in. Put a dry paper towel in the bottom and fill with mushrooms. Cover the mushrooms with a damp paper towel and then plastic wrap. Secure with a rubber band.

This keeps my mushrooms fresh for 5–7 days.

E. Toro
Suwanee, GA

FREEZING ONIONS

I cannot keep the tears from pouring when I cut raw onions. No matter what I do, my eyes always burn and tear up. But I found a way to keep them dry.

About half an hour before I need the onions, I just throw them in my freezer, unpeeled. When I slice the onions after taking them from the freezer, my eyes are clear and dry.

J. Steiner
Polson, MT

HULLING STRAWBERRIES

Use a straw to easily remove the hull from strawberries.

After I wash the berries, I take a straw and push it up from the bottom point of the strawberry. The hull and stem will come out on end of the straw, leaving a perfectly hollowed out strawberry.

E. Overholt
Portage, MI

DATING EGGS

I can never tell which eggs in my refrigerator are fresh or boiled. I also tend to forget how long ago I boiled the eggs.

Now, I write the date that I boiled the egg right on the eggshell using a crayon or a wax pencil.

This way, I know that the egg is hard boiled as well as how long it's been in the refrigerator.

H. Donaldson
Marco Island, FL

TENTING RISING ROLLS

I made your brioche from Issue 11 and found a way to let the dough rise without plastic wrap getting stuck to the dough.

I set the brioche dough (or any rising rolls for that matter) on a cookie sheet. Then I place a wine glass, upside down, in the middle of the sheet. I drape plastic wrap over the base of the wine glass and tuck and secure on all sides of the cookie sheet. The glass creates a protective tent over my dough.

Now I can keep the wrap from sticking to the dough without ruining the top of my rolls and brioche.

P. Merrill
Buffalo, NY

FRESH CUTTING BOARDS

Even after cleaning with hot, soapy water, my wooden cutting board still had a pungent odor. I tried bleach, but wanted a better smell on my board.

I take a slice of lemon and rub it vigorously against my wooden board and rinse with cold water. Now my cutting board is clean and smells great.

S. Peterson
Sacramento, CA

BAY LEAF DEFENSE

Bay leaves and chili pepper pods are non-toxic and repel troublesome insects that try to invade beans, pasta, and other dried food products. To deter pests, just place a pod or leaf in the storage container.

And don't worry—the flavors of the bay leaves or chili peppers don't mix with those of beans or pasta.

J. Evers
Jackson, MS

PRODUCE AIR BAGS

My fresh vegetables and fruits used to look beaten up by the time I got home from the grocery store.

Instead of taking it out on the sacker, I decided to remedy the situation. I place my produce in the store's plastic bags, inflate the bags by blowing air in and sealing them.

This helps prevent my fruits and vegetables from being bumped around.

J. Cho
Morton Grove, IL

DUSTING SHAKER

When I need to dust my dough or surface with flour, I don't want to keep dipping my hand into the flour bag. So I keep a large shaker nearby filled with flour.

That way, whenever I need to flour my pasta machine or rolling pin, all I have to do is grab the shaker. It's less messy and I don't have to worry about the white powder ending up on my face and clothes.

A. Varma
St. Angelo, TX

Tips

TESTING THERMOMETERS

Check the accuracy of your thermometer by testing it in boiling water. Insert the thermometer stem (about 2 inches) into a pot of boiling water (don't touch the bottom of pan). It should read 212°—boiling point of water.

If you live at a high altitude, the boiling temperature will be about 2° lower for every 1000 feet you are above sea level.

CAPER EXTRACTION

For easy caper removal, use your basic vegetable peeler. Simply insert the peeler into the jar. The capers come out on the peeling blade while the brine drains out the slit.

SUGARED CRANBERRIES

To make the sugared cranberries that go with the Cranberry Napoleon on page 38, fill a cookie sheet with a bag of frozen cranberries. Sprinkle with 2 T. superfine granulated sugar and shake the pan to spread the sugar. Put in a 350° oven. After four minutes, remove pan and shake again. Bake for four more minutes or until all the sugar has melted.

SEND US YOUR TIPS

We'd like to hear from you. Just write down your cooking tip and mail it to Cuisine, Tips Editor, 2200 Grand Ave., Des Moines, IA 50312, or contact us through our E-mail address shown below. Please include your name, address, and daytime phone number in case we have questions. We'll pay you $25 if we publish your tip.
E-mail address: Cuisine@cuisinemag.com
Web address: http://www.augusthome.com

Photograph: Scott Little; Food Styling: Janet Pittman

ANTIPASTO

There's nothing worse to a writer than a blank page (believe me, I know), and there's nothing worse to an artist than a blank canvas. That's how it is when you

have a big white platter staring at you and a ton of stuff to put on it. You want it to look nice, but you have no clue how to start. No problem. I'm going to give you a paint-by-numbers approach to making the same gorgeous antipasto platter you see above.

I'll give you a few simple recipes, teach you about some Italian ingredients, then we'll put this thing together, step-by-step. Just follow along, and before you know it, you will have a thing of beauty.

What is antipasto?: Antipasto means "before the meal." In Italy, antipasto is not really the first course

like appetizers are here in America. It is an optional beginning to a meal, offered before the first course. The antipasto platter is enough to feed a small group at a cocktail party, too.

Ingredients: The key to the antipasto platter is high-quality ingredients. No matter what you plan to serve, even if it's just a plate of cured meats and some cheese, buy the best you can find.

I'm not going to give you a bunch of complex recipes here. The foods you put on your platter have to stand on their own merits, so you can't hide a poor product under a fancy sauce.

Keep it simple: Italians take great pride in the quality of their cured meats, cheeses, and fresh produce. Consequently, they don't want anything to take away from that quality. Recipes are relatively uncomplicated, and every ingredient serves a purpose. If it's not really necessary, it doesn't make the team.

The recipes I'm giving you for this platter are simple. You'll get a couple of basic marinades to help show off those good Mediterranean olives you found. The ricotta cheese filling for the Zucchini Rolls and Ricotta Cones is unadorned to let the flavor of your homemade ricotta show through.

Putting it together: Just follow my steps for assembling your platter, and you'll have a spectacular presentation. It's holiday time, after all, so don't work any more than necessary.

Olives: Olives are essential to antipasto. Don't get canned black or stuffed green olives, though. You want to get good unpitted imported olives. You can find brined or oil-packed olives in most supermarkets or at specialty stores. Marinate them for extra flavor.

SPICY MARINATED OLIVES
COMBINE AND MARINATE:
2 cups large green olives
1/3 cup extra virgin olive oil
1 large clove garlic, thinly sliced
1 t. fennel seed, toasted
1 t. crushed red pepper flakes
1/2 t. sweet paprika
1/2 t. dried oregano leaves

SWEET AND SOUR ONIONS
BLANCH AND PEEL:
10 oz. pearl onions (red & white)
SAUTE ONIONS IN 1 T. EXTRA VIRGIN OLIVE OIL WITH:
1 t. garlic, minced
ADD, THEN SIMMER:
1/4 cup white wine vinegar
1 T. sugar
6 whole cloves
1/2 t. cracked black pepper
1/4 t. salt
COOL; CHILL AT LEAST 24 HOURS.

Blanch onions in boiling water for 2 mins. Remove to bowl of ice water with slotted spoon. Trim roots and tips, then peel onions.

2 Saute onions and garlic in oil over medium-low heat for 3 mins. Add remaining ingredients. Simmer, partially covered, for 10 mins. Chill.

AROMATIC OLIVES
COMBINE AND MARINATE:
2 cups assorted olives
1/4 cup extra virgin olive oil
1 T. chopped fresh rosemary
1 t. garlic, minced
1/2 t. cracked black pepper

▲ *Toast whole fennel seeds in dry skillet over medium heat until they are lightly browned, shaking pan often.*

ROASTED PEPPERS WITH FRESH MOZZARELLA

Roast red bell peppers over a gas flame or under a broiler until blackened and blistered. Place in bag, seal, and let steam for 10 minutes.

2 Peel skin off steamed peppers (it's okay if a little black remains). Cut out stem and remove seeds. Cut peppers into 2–3" pieces.

3 Dip one side of mozzarella slices in olive oil, then sprinkle with chopped fresh basil. Do this just before serving or basil will brown.

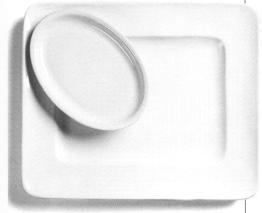

▲ *Put a small platter on a bigger platter to keep oily marinades separate from the rest of the ingredients. You don't want marinades to taint the other ingredients.*

▲ *Arrange two types of olives on opposite ends of small platter with onions in the middle. Make two batches of onions, one red and one white, and mix them up.*

▲ *Arrange pieces of roasted red pepper and mozzarella slices in an arc around end of the small platter. Slightly overlap them. Four or five pieces of each is enough.*

▲ *Arrange three or four Zucchini Rolls on each side of small platter to complete the arc started by the red peppers and cheese. Leave room in front for Ricotta Cones.*

▲ *Fill space in front of Zucchini Rolls with three or four Ricotta Cones. Put the points toward the rolls. You can prop up cones when you add more to the platter.*

▲ *Make a second arc on the platter with your meat selection. Group small slices together on one end. Overlap big slices, folding large pieces over, to complete arc.*

ZUCCHINI ROLLS

(MAKES 6–8 ROLLS)
THINLY SLICE, BRUSH BOTH SIDES WITH OLIVE OIL AND PEPPER; BAKE:
1   small zucchini
COMBINE AND PIPE INTO ROLLS:
2   cups ricotta cheese, see page 25
1/4   cup Parmesan cheese, grated
     Dash ground nutmeg
     Salt and pepper to taste

1 Use a vegetable peeler to slice zucchini really thin. Brush both sides with oil; sprinkle with pepper.

2 Roast zucchini on baking sheet at 375° for 8 mins. Wrap cooled slices around finger to make rolls.

3 Combine filling ingredients; place in pastry bag. Fill rolls on a flat surface. Pipe filling in straight up.

ITALIAN MEATS

An assortment of *salumi*, or Italian cold cuts, is probably the most common antipasto there is. In Italy, regional meats are featured on platters, showcasing the skills of the local sausage artisans.

When you go shopping, get the best cured meats you can find, but don't knock yourself out looking for a fancy selection. Get what you like. In fact, if you want to feature Uncle Bob's venison sausage, do it!

If you have an Italian specialty store or a big supermarket in your town, look for the following meats. They are what we used in this article, but are just meant as a guide. Ask to taste samples in the store, and again, buy what you like.

Prosciutto is uncooked, air-dried, salt-cured ham from Italy. It's sliced paper thin with a rim of fat around the edge. A good one should have a rosy color, and taste sweet and not too salty.

Mortadella, from Bologna, looks like American bologna with little circles of white fat and whole peppercorns throughout. The similarity stops there, though. Mortadella is made from delicately seasoned, high-quality pork.

Soppressata is a flavorful, meaty sausage from southern Italy. It is quite firm, but slices easily into small bright-red rounds.

RICOTTA CONES

1 Cut a slit halfway through 3" salami slices. Stack 8 slices and cut them all at once to make it easy.

2 Twist tips of cut salami slices to form cones. The salami will stick to itself to hold the cone closed.

3 Pipe ricotta filling into cones in a spiral fashion. They'll look like little ice cream cones.

PICKLED PRODUCTS

Good quality pickled, brined, or oil-packed foods are perfect for your antipasto platters. They are very easy to find and a no-brainer to use (just open the jar). These simple products add a tangy dimension to the platter.

I like pickled pepperoncini (Tuscan peppers). Their slightly sweet, moderately hot flavor offers a nice balance to the rich meats.

Artichoke hearts are available packed in an olive oil marinade that is either herb-laced or spicy. Drain them well, pick out the nicest ones, then fan them out on the edge of the platter for an attractive presentation.

There are a wide variety of other pickled vegetables available, too. Look for mushrooms, cornichons (gherkin pickles), and cherry peppers, to name a few.

ITALIAN BREAD

Good bread is essential to any part of a meal in Italy. You want one with a firm texture and chewy crust. It has to stand up to dipping in a fruity olive oil or sopping up marinades. It will also be toasted to be made into bruschetta or crostini. If you have an Italian market, buy your bread from them.

Bruschetta is a traditional garlic bread made by toasting slices of Italian bread, then rubbing them with a cut piece of garlic. The rubbed sides are topped with a drizzle of olive oil, salt, and freshly ground black pepper.

Crostini, a term often used interchangeably with bruschetta, actually means "little toasts." It refers to toasted bread that is finished with any number of savory toppings, like Gorgonzola Butter.

GORGONZOLA BUTTER

(MAKES ³/₄ CUP)

MIX TOGETHER UNTIL CREAMY:

- ²/₃ cup (3 oz.) crumbled Gorgonzola cheese
- ¹/₂ cup unsalted butter, softened

SPREAD ON:

Toasted Italian bread slices

Flavored butters are often used on crostini. Substitute shrimp, smoked salmon, or fresh herbs for Gorgonzola.

Blend in a food processor for a smooth spread, or mix with a fork to keep some chunks of cheese.

CHEESES

There are 450 different cheeses made in Italy, and it is served with almost every meal. Use four cheeses for your antipasto platter: ricotta, Parmigiano-Reggiano, Gorgonzola, and fresh mozzarella.

Ricotta is a perfect cheese for fillings. See page 24 for more on ricotta and making your own.

Parmigiano-Reggiano is the crown jewel of Italian cheeses. It's expensive stuff, but worth it for the antipasto platter. Use the tip of a knife, *see photo at right*, to break it into bite-size nuggets. That way its granular texture and complex flavors can be fully enjoyed. Look for the real thing in large supermarkets and specialty stores.

Truly *fresh mozzarella* is a ball of stringy, soft cheese kept in water or brine. Most grocery stores only

Stick the tip of a knife into a piece of Parmesan, then twist to make rough-looking chunks.

carry the firmer and saltier blocks of mozzarella (pizza cheese). It's alright to use this if you can't find the fresh stuff which only has a shelf life of a few weeks. Look for both types in the deli sections of supermarkets or specialty stores.

Gorgonzola is a mild, creamy, and slightly spicy blue cheese with greenish veins. It is from the Lombardy region in Italy.

▲ *Purchased pickled items fill opposite corners, giving the platter color balance. Fan artichoke hearts and arrange pepperoncini so stems can be easily grasped.*

▲ *Fill corner opposite the small platter with pieces of bruschetta and buttered toast. Serve extra Gorgonzola Butter on the side with more bread, if desired.*

▲ *Fill in obvious holes on the platter with chunks of Parmigiano-Reggiano cheese or another favorite cheese. Finally, garnish the platter with fresh rosemary. Enjoy!*

Photograph: Scott Little, Food Styling: Janet Pittman

RAVIOLI & TORTELLINI

During the holidays, we eagerly overindulge ourselves on too much turkey, dressing, and cranberries. But many of us share another tradition after the holiday

feast. It's a concept the Italians came up with. No, I'm not talking about what the Romans did after hours of gorging—I'm talking pasta. With family still hanging around and full of tryptophan, serving pasta the next day is a welcome relief.

We've made pasta before. The flat kind like fettuccine, linguine, and pappardelle. Now, you're going to learn how to fill pasta by making ravioli and tortellini.

Probably, ravioli and tortellini are the most well-known of the stuffed pastas. Ravioli consists of two layers of pasta folded over a vegetable or meat stuffing. Tortellini, on the other hand, is a little more difficult to describe. Maybe telling you how it came to be, will help you visualize it.

Long ago, there was an innkeeper in a small Italian town. One night, a beautiful woman, some think it was Venus, checked into his inn.

The innkeeper was totally taken back by her beauty and could hardly contain himself. Later that night, his boorish ways got the the better of him and he crept up to her room where he tried spying on her through the keyhole. All he was able to see, at that level, was her navel.

It was much too early for the invention of the camera, so the innkeeper ran down to his kitchen to recreate her image out of pasta. He worked diligently until he had perfectly fashioned the only part of her body that he saw—her navel. This was the beginning of tortellini.

Now, you can choose to believe this story if you want. But the fact of the matter is no matter how some pastas came to be, it's still a welcome change of pace after holiday feasting.

And let's face it—everybody loves pasta. As long as the whole family is hanging out, create a little entertainment by having them make their next dinner—fresh stuffed pasta. It's simple and they'll have fun helping.

BASIC PASTA

(MAKES 96 TORTELLINI OR 48 RAVIOLI)
WORK TIME: 30 MINUTES
COOK TIME: 5 MINUTES
BEAT TOGETHER:
5   eggs
2   t. extra virgin olive oil
COMBINE IN FOOD PROCESSOR WITH:
3   cups all-purpose flour

Our last pasta recipe called for 1 cup semolina to 2 cups of all-purpose flour. Now, I'm going to change the recipe to straight all-purpose. Why?

You may remember that semolina has a high gluten content which means that it's a harder flour than all-purpose. A semolina-based pasta is strong and tough enough to hold up to boiling, sauteing, and even baking that you might do with flat pastas.

However, for stuffed pastas, you want the dough's texture to be much softer and pliable so you can easily bend, shape, and seal it. This is best achieved with an all-purpose dough.

You'll also see that we're making the dough in a food processor rather than by hand. Last time, we mixed the dough by first forming a well in flour and mixing the eggs gradually right in the well.

This is fun and showy, but the truth is, the dough can be made quickly (about a minute) in your food processor. Achieving the proper moisture content is the key to stuffed pasta so you can get a tight seal around the edges. The dough consistency can be adjusted easily in a processor.

If you don't have a processor, don't fret. Refer back to Issue 1, page 8 for making it by hand.

1 Eggs make pasta soft so sauces are absorbed easily. Beat eggs (with oil) in a bowl rather than in processor. You can see shells easily.

2 Put flour in processor and turn it on. Gradually add egg/oil mixture. Keep dough on the sticky side. You'll add flour during kneading.

3 Shape the dough into a ball and divide it into quarters. Wrap each with plastic wrap so the dough won't dry out. Let rest 10 minutes.

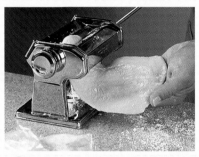

4 For kneading, set pasta machine to widest opening. Dust rollers with flour and crank dough through. At first, the dough will be ugly!

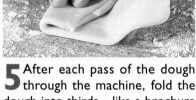

5 After each pass of the dough through the machine, fold the dough into thirds—like a brochure might be folded.

6 After you've folded dough into thirds, insert open end of pasta into machine and repeat. This rotation helps maintain an even shape.

PASTA MACHINES

There are a lot of pasta machines hitting the market, but I still like my Atlas (Imperia makes a good one too). I don't recommend equipment that either costs too much or could gather dust. But for less than $40, either one of these well-built machines are worth it.

Kneading is a breeze with both pasta makers. They transform a tough ball of dough into soft, velvet-like pasta in just a few minutes. Additional cutting attachments run about $25. Find them in kitchen stores or your favorite cooking catalogue.

7 Repeat kneading process until dough becomes smooth and satiny looking. It'll take about 10 passes. **Rewrap in plastic**.

FILLINGS

Be sure to let fillings chill before making ravioli or tortellini. It's *always* a safe practice to cool any food used for stuffing to prevent bacteria forming.

A cool filling is also easy to work with since chilling tends to bind the individual ingredients. When the pasta is folded, there's less chance that the filling will squirt out. And finally, a warm filling tends to make fresh pasta "pasty" and "soggy"—much too difficult to fold.

MUSHROOM/CHEESE FILLING

(MAKES 3 CUPS)
WORK TIME: 10 MINUTES
COOK TIME: 15 MINUTES
SAUTE IN $\frac{1}{2}$ CUP MARSALA; REDUCE:
6   cups mushrooms, chopped
$1\frac{1}{2}$ cups yellow onion, chopped
2   T. garlic, chopped
BLEND TO PASTE, ADD:
1   cup bread crumbs
$\frac{1}{2}$ cup Parmesan cheese, shredded
$\frac{1}{4}$ cup chopped fresh parsley
$\frac{1}{8}$ t. cayenne pepper

Use any filling you want. I'm just showing you a couple of basic ones here. Because you use so little filling in each tortellini or ravioli, the flavor should be pretty intense.

In the spinach filling, I used some chicken breasts that I ground in the processor. But use any poultry. Here's a thought: use the leftover turkey from Thanksgiving—it's better than making tetrazzini or soup out of it.

SPINACH/CHICKEN FILLING

(MAKES 3 CUPS)
WORK TIME: 10 MINUTES
COOK TIME: 20 MINUTES
SAUTE IN 2 T. OLIVE OIL:
2   cups ground chicken breast
1   cup yellow onion, chopped
$\frac{1}{2}$ cup ham, chopped
$\frac{1}{4}$ t. ground nutmeg
DEGLAZE WITH AND REDUCE:
$\frac{1}{3}$ cup dry marsala or sherry
SAUTE IN 1 T. OLIVE OIL:
3   cups fresh spinach
1   T. garlic, chopped
PROCESS WITH CHICKEN, THEN ADD:
$\frac{1}{2}$ cup Parmesan cheese, shredded
1   T. chopped fresh parsley

MUSHROOM/CHEESE FILLING

1 Chop mushrooms, onions, and garlic. You can cut them into rough pieces because they're going to be blended in the processor.

2 Saute onions and mushrooms until all moisture is gone. Add garlic and cook 1 minute. Now, add marsala. Reduce until evaporated.

3 Blend mushroom mixture in processor. I like small bits of mushroom rather than a paste, but it's up to you—the flavor's the same.

4 Finally, add bread crumbs, Parmesan, parsley, and cayenne. Blend by pulsing the processor. Season to taste and then chill.

SPINACH/CHICKEN FILLING

1 Over high heat, saute chicken just until it turns firm and white. Then add the onion and ham. Cook until onion turns translucent.

2 Add a pinch of nutmeg and then deglaze the mixture with dry marsala. Reduce until all the marsala is evaporated.

3 Remove the chicken mixture from the pan. Add 1 T. olive oil and saute the spinach until it's just barely wilted. It'll only take a minute.

4 Add chicken mixture and spinach to processor and blend until smooth. Then add Parmesan and parsley. Process until blended. Chill.

MAKING RAVIOLI

Every Italian city has at least two or three styles of pasta that they're known for. This can be a problem when it comes to putting a name with a shape. Ravioli can be square, rectangular, round, half moons, or they can be called tortelloni and totelli.

We're making the most common ravioli which is two squares of pasta sealed face to face. The size varies, but is usually between 1¹/₂–2¹/₂ inches.

Keep it Moist: The key to any filled pasta is keeping it moist and preventing it from drying out. *Always* keep your dough wrapped in plastic wrap before shaping.

The more you work the pasta the longer it's exposed to air (which can quickly evaporate moisture in dough). If it dries out too much, shaping becomes difficult and the edges (the first area to dry out) can't form an adequate seal to contain the filling.

Storing: Ravioli easily sticks to itself and other surfaces. So when you roll out your pasta, make sure you have enough flour on the counter to prevent the finished ravioli from sticking. (Don't get any flour where the two sheets of pasta will join.)

And after making the ravioli, make sure you have a sheet pan that's covered with *plenty* of cornmeal or flour to prevent sticking. Don't worry, the extra cornmeal will come off in the boiling water when cooked.

Finally, between each batch, put the whole sheet pan (with ravioli) in the freezer. It'll freeze enough, between batches to prevent sticking.

1 Begin rolling out pasta—only work with one quarter of pasta at a time from start to finish. First run pasta through largest opening.

2 Keep rollers dusted. Make the pasta by sequentially setting rollers to next smallest setting each time. I take it to next to the last setting.

3 Cut dough in half and lay the two pieces side by side. Place 1 t. filling every 2 inches. Be sure to flour counter to keep pasta from sticking.

4 Put the other half of pasta on top of the fillings (sticky side down on top of fillings). Press around each mound of filling to seal tightly.

5 Cut the individual ravioli into squares at each seal. I use a pastry wheel but you can use a pastry crimper or even a knife.

6 Place finished ravioli on a tray covered with cornmeal. They're very sticky now. Put tray in the freezer and start rolling out next batch.

COOKING FRESH PASTA

Whether you're cooking home-made fresh pasta or dried pasta from the store, the same rules apply—only the time is different.

The most important factor for proper pasta cooking is *plenty* of *boiling* water. A good rule of thumb is 1 gallon to 1 pound of pasta. And don't add oil! Plenty of water and stirring prevents sticking. Oil can keep the sauces from adhering to the cooked pasta.

This is a personal preference. I don't like rinsing my pasta after cooking. Rinsing removes the starch which can help hold a sauce.

The main difference (besides taste) between fresh and dried pasta is the cooking time. Fresh pasta only takes 2–4 minutes while dried takes up to 15 minutes. Since the filling is already cooked, ravioli and tortellini need to cook just long enough to heat the filling.

▲ *Add fresh ravioli to plenty of boiling water and then stir to prevent sticking. These took about 4 minutes.*

MAKING TORTELLINI

Tortellini is a little more difficult to make than ravioli, but the techniques are very similar.

Like ravioli, tortellini takes on many names for different shapes. It all depends on the region in which the pasta originated.

We're going to make a basic tortellini that's made from a 2–2¹⁄₂ inch round piece of pasta. A small amount of filling is put in the center, and then it's folded in two to form a half-moon. The half-moon is wrapped around to connect the points to form a ring. Simple? Yes, but it takes practice to build up a little speed.

Rolling Pasta: Start by rolling out the pasta, but don't take the dial to the last setting, *see Step 1*. For now, just take it to the next thinnest setting because the pasta could tear if it's too thin when you start folding it. As you get more proficient, roll it thinner for a more delicate finished tortellini.

Cutting and Filling: After rolling out the pasta, use a cookie cutter (2–2¹⁄₂ inch) to cut out circles in one sheet of pasta, *see Step 2*. Make sure there isn't any flour on side facing up, so the tortellini can seal easily.

Now, put a half teaspoon of *chilled* filling right in the *center* of each pasta round, *see Step 3*. Any filling that gets too close to the edge could squeeze out the sides messing up your seal.

Folding: Fold the pasta rounds over the filling to form a half-moon, *see Step 4*. The dough should be moist enough to form a secure seal. If not, dip your fingertip in water and moisten the edge before sealing.

Now, use the tip of your index finger as a mold to wrap the half moon pasta around. Join the two points together, *see Step 5*. Finally, fold the rounded flap down the back of the tortellini. Look closely—if it looks like a belly button, you've made it right!

TORTELLONI

Tortellini, tortelloni, and capelleti come from the Emilia-Romagna region (in the northeastern part of Italy). All 3 pastas are made similarly, but they vary in size. Capelleti is the smallest and means "little hat." Tortellini is the next size up and tortelloni are the biggest. You can make tortelloni out of square pasta and fold it like tortellini. If you don't fold down the back, it's known as a bishop's hat.

ROLLING AND SHAPING TORTELLINI

1 Roll out the pasta dough using a pasta machine as you did on Steps 1 and 2 of the ravioli, page 13. Keep the rollers dusted with flour.

2 Cut the dough in half and lay the two pieces on a lightly floured surface. Cut circles out of dough with 2–2¹⁄₂" diameter cutter.

3 Place ¹⁄₂ teaspoon filling in middle of each dough circle. You don't want more than this or the filling will squeeze out when you fold the pasta.

4 Fold each circle over to form a half-moon shape. Press down on the edges to seal. If the filling starts to squeeze out, it won't seal.

5 Wrap the half-moons around the tip of your finger until the points overlap. Firmly press the points together to secure them.

6 Fold the top flap over, away from the joined points, to achieve the infamous belly button. Place tortellini on a cornmeal-dusted tray.

SPINACH SAUCE
(MAKES 2 CUPS)
WORK TIME: 20 MINUTES
COOK TIME: 15 MINUTES
SAUTE:
1/2 cup pancetta/bacon, diced
ADD:
8 cups fresh spinach
    (roughly 10 oz.)
1 cup yellow onion, chopped
1 T. garlic, minced
DEGLAZE WITH:
1/2 cup white wine
1/2 cup chicken broth
WHIP IN FOOD PROCESSOR:
3/4 cup ricotta cheese
ADD SPINACH MIXTURE AND:
1/4 cup Parmesan cheese,
    grated
1/4 t. ground nutmeg
1/8 t. cayenne pepper
    Salt to taste

*NUTRITIONAL INFORMATION PER
3/4 CUP: CALORIES 150; TOTAL FAT
10(G); CALORIES FROM FAT 50%;
SODIUM 450(MG)*

I think pesto has suffered from overexposure so I changed it around a little. By using spinach and adding whipped ricotta, this sauce ends up having a great sweet, smooth flavor.

MARINARA SAUCE
(MAKES 5 CUPS)
WORK TIME: 30 MINUTES
COOK TIME: 25 MINUTES
SAUTE IN 1/4 CUP OLIVE OIL:
1 cup yellow onion, diced
ADD AND SAUTE:
1 T. garlic, minced
ADD AND SIMMER:
6 cups Roma tomatoes,
    seeded and diced
1/4 cup fresh basil, chiffonade
    Salt and pepper to taste

*NUTRITIONAL INFORMATION PER 1/4
CUP: CALORIES 41; TOTAL FAT 3(G);
CALORIES FROM FAT 60%; SODIUM
63(MG)*

No matter if it's the dead of winter, this marinara sauce still tastes good. Use fresh Roma tomatoes and basil, and you won't go wrong.

Cook the sauce only about 20–30 minutes, or just until the tomatoes turn a little dark. Process through a food mill. Then add the fresh basil.

A great variation is to make a tomato-cream sauce to go over pasta. Reduce 1 cup of cream by half and add to 3 cups marinara. It'll turn a beautiful pink.

ROASTED RED PEPPER SAUCE *(MAKES 4 CUPS)*
WORK TIME: 10 MINUTES
COOK TIME: 20 MINUTES
SAUTE IN 3 T. OLIVE OIL:
1 cup yellow onion, chopped
1 T. garlic, minced
ADD AND REDUCE:
1 cup dry white wine
*COMBINE IN BLENDER UNTIL
SMOOTH WITH:*
4 red peppers, roasted,
    peeled, seeded, and
    chopped, *see page 7 for
    roasting peppers*
*RETURN TO SAUCEPAN. ADD AND
REDUCE WITH:*
1 cup chicken broth
REMOVE FROM HEAT; BLEND IN:
3/4 cup whipped ricotta
2 T. chopped fresh oregano
1/2 t. crushed red pepper flakes
    Salt to taste

*NUTRITIONAL INFORMATION PER
3/4 CUP: CALORIES 180; TOTAL FAT
11(G); CALORIES FROM FAT 55%;
SODIUM 450(MG)*

This is an ambiguous sauce. The intense flavor comes from roasting the red peppers. Adding blended ricotta makes this sauce smooth and mild. Be sure to add the ricotta after the sauce has cooled or it'll curdle.

GORGONZOLA MUSHROOM SAUCE
(MAKES 3 CUPS)
WORK TIME: 10 MINUTES
COOK TIME: 30 MINUTES
SAUTE:
1/2 cup pancetta or bacon, diced
DRAIN ALL BUT 2 T. DRIPPINGS. ADD:
6 cups mushrooms, chopped
1/3 cup shallots, minced
ADD AND REDUCE:
2 cups heavy cream
2 T. chopped fresh parsley
REMOVE FROM HEAT; ADD:
1/3 cup Gorgonzola cheese

*NUTRITIONAL INFORMATION PER 1/4 CUP:
CALORIES 191; TOTAL FAT 19(G);
CALORIES FROM FAT 87%; SODIUM
111(MG)*

All of the sauces above are pretty low in calories. You can make them even lower in calories by substituting cottage cheese for ricotta. But I had to throw this cream-based sauce in because it's so popular.

The key to this rich sauce is reducing the cream by almost half and then adding it to mushrooms that have been sauteed until all their liquid has disappeared.

If there is any consolation to the high amount of calories, it's that you only use about a half cup of sauce per serving. The cream and cheese together are strong enough so that a little goes a long way.

10 GIFT IDEAS FOR COOKS

This is the issue where we consider the holidays. What should we buy for our cooking friends, spouses, and others? Here are some ideas from the Cuisine staff.

It seems that every year around this time we all end up with gifts of three different types: those that are painfully practical (like socks), those that are simply fun (a heated massage chair), and those we'll "recycle" (like a fruit cake) that can be passed on next year.

Last year, the *Cuisine* staff gave ideas for some gifts for the cooking enthusiast. Once again, we discussed the kitchen tool we can't live without and ones we think are pretty neat.

We've tried to steer you in the direction of fun, yet practical, kitchen gadgets (the best of both worlds), for you or anyone on your holiday list. And you're bound to find at least one in your price range.

Some of these you may really need (like the triple timer). Others you know you really don't, but you think it just might be fun to have (like the oyster opener). Some you'll use often (like the sink colander) and others you may only take out every once in awhile (the portable cook stove).

All these prices could fluctuate a little. They may even be less!

▲ OYSTER OPENER

Leave the old days of gouging an oyster knife into your palm behind. For a quick, easy, and *safe* way to open your oysters, just place an unopened oyster in the groove and push down on the handle.

Adjustable to fit oysters of any size. The sturdy oyster shucker is made of stainless steel and solid oak. Call **Sur La Table** at **(800) 243-0852** (item #18316), $24.95.

◀ SINK COLANDER

You can rinse, drain, and wash fresh produce in this adjustable stainless steel colander that fits right over your sink. It's big enough to clean and hold a mess of greens and sturdy enough to drain pounds of pasta. I like this colander a lot.

Call **Crate & Barrel** at **(800) 323-5461** (item #1134), $29.95 or **Baker's Catalogue** at **(800) 827-6836** (item #7503), $34.95.

▲ PORTABLE COOK STOVE

We never seem to have enough burners in our kitchen. We have three portable ones, and we're always needing just one more.

This portable stove has a high heat output (7600 BTUs), and requires one can of butane (not included). The controls are easy-to-operate, and the ignition system automatically shuts off. It will come in handy during holiday preparations and on vacations.

Call **Chef's Catalog** at **(800) 338-3232** (item #7453), $69.99.

TRIPLE TIMER ▶

Here's a way to avoid kitchen disasters when you're trying to bake the pie, roast the turkey, and bake the stuffing, all at once. The West Bend® Triple Electronic Timer lets you keep a close watch on all three. Each timer has a distinctive alarm and counts down from 10 hours to one second. Plus the large display is easy to read. The triple timer comes with a one-year warranty.

Call **Sur La Table** at **(800) 243-0852** (item #0281), $39.95 or **Chef's Catalog** at **(800) 338-3232** (item #6005), $39.99.

▲ SCREEN-TOP DREDGERS

Dusting, whether it's cake tops or table tops, has always been tough with my converted salt shakers. Sometimes, my desserts would look like they have ant hills of cocoa or sugar.

But these stainless steel sugar dredgers, with tight-fitting mesh lids, will show you what dusting means. Their fine, mesh tops are ideal for powdered sugar and cocoa. Or fill one with flour (*see Page 5*). The one-cup dredger comes with a plastic lid to prevent spillage and drying out.

To order, call **Sur La Table** at **(800) 243-0852**. One-cup Sugar Dredger (item #4027), $8.95. Two-cup Sugar Dredger (item #4153), $10.95.

▲ FOOD MILL

This is one gadget that is always in use in our test kitchen. This stainless steel food mill from Italy separates as it purees, and it comes with three interchangeable discs.

The fine disc works well for smooth purees, the medium for applesauce, and the coarse for ricing potatoes. The food mill can mash and puree tomatoes, potatoes, apples, or berries. Holds up to two quarts.

Call **Chef's Catalog** at **(800) 338-3232** (item #6469), $34.99.

SPATULAS ▶

How many times have you laid your spatula a little too close to a stove burner and suddenly smelled smoldering plastic? And what about opening the dishwasher only to find a melted mess lying on the heating element?

These flame-proof Le Creuset spatulas are made of all-purpose silicone and resist heat up to 650°. No need to worry about melted plastic any more. And they come in a variety of colors, like flame or blue.

Call **Chef's Catalog** at **(800) 338-3232** (item #7966). A set of two costs $22.00. Call **Kitchen & Home** at **(800) 414-5544**. Select an extra large spatula (item #615850B), $12.00; a small spoon spatula (item #615852B), $8.00, or a large spoon spatula (item #615848B), $10.00.

JUMBO PASTRY TIPS ▶

I don't care what skill level you are in cooking, you can always use more pastry tips. And these Ateco jumbo stainless steel tips are for you. The large size equals easier handling (and fewer frustrations).

The tips are seamless, which helps prevent rusting and makes them easier to clean. The package comes with 12 assorted tips, a storage container, and cleaning brush.

Call **Sur La Table** at **(800) 243-0852** (item #18287), $21.95.

◀ SPIRAL SLICER

Quickly turn your favorite vegetables into ribbons and noodle-like strings with the Saladacco Japanese spiral cutter. You can also create tiny cubes, thin slices, or julienne strips. We tried it out on potatoes, cucumbers, zucchini, and beets. It worked great and had a blast making garnishes.

The blade adjusts to change the width of your garnishes. Clean up is easy since it's dishwasher safe.

Call **The Wooden Spoon** at **(800) 431-2207** (item #T6441), $36.00 or **Sur La Table** at **(800) 243-0852** (item #18458), $35.95.

◀ SET OF PASTRY BAGS

Work on several decorating projects at one time with this set of three plastic-coated canvas bags. The combination of plastic and canvas makes them durable and easy to wash. Each bag comes with its own coupler. Use them to make our Cranberry Napoleon (*see page 38*).

Call **Sur La Table** at **(800) 243-0852** (item #2211), $12.95.

TUSCAN BEAN SOUP

PREPARING THE BEANS

1 Spread the beans on a baking sheet and sort through them to remove any stones, dirt, or imperfect beans. Rinse and drain.

2 Place rinsed beans in a large soup pot and add enough cold water to completely cover the beans by 2".

3 Bring the beans to a boil over high heat. Cover with a tight-fitting lid, reduce the heat, and simmer 10 minutes.

4 Remove beans from heat and let sit in the water, covered, for 1 hour. Drain beans, discarding the soaking liquid. Set aside.

Now, you wouldn't think people nicknamed "bean eaters" would make great culinary contributions. But this Tuscan Bean Soup is proof that these guys know beans about beans.

Why are they so tuned in to this humble vegetable? Well, it's mostly due to geography—Tuscany, in central Italy, is rocky and mountainous, so cattle (or any other livestock) are tough to raise. Tuscans had to be pretty resourceful and found that beans provided a major source of protein.

But what Tuscans didn't know was that they were on the edge of food greatness. These days, beans are a high-fashion food—high protein, high fiber, and high flavor.

Italian cannellini beans are the traditional choice for this soup but can be hard to find. The more common Great Northern beans make a fine substitute and are readily available.

You might think it's strange to see diced green chiles here. I was surprised, too, but many of the bean soups from this region include some kind of chile in the recipe. These won't "hurt" you—they're just spicy enough to add another flavor kick.

TUSCAN BEAN SOUP
(MAKES 8 CUPS)
WORK TIME: 30 MINUTES
COOK TIME: 3 HOURS

COVER WITH COLD WATER:
- 1/2 lb. dried Great Northern beans, sorted and rinsed

SWEAT IN 2 T. OLIVE OIL:
- 1 cup yellow onion, diced
- 2 t. garlic, minced

ADD:
- 1/2 cup celery, diced
- 1/4 cup carrots, diced

ADD WITH BEANS:
- 8 cups chicken broth
- 1 can (4.5 oz.) diced green chiles
- 3 T. chopped fresh parsley
- 2 T. chopped fresh rosemary leaves
- 1/4 t. pepper

DIVIDE AMONG SERVING BOWLS:
- 6 oz. fresh spinach leaves, stemmed

GARNISH SERVINGS WITH:
- 1/2 cup red pepper, diced
- Shaved Parmesan curls
- Italian bread croutons
- Fresh rosemary sprigs

NUTRITIONAL INFORMATION PER 1 CUP (NO GARNISH): CALORIES 159; TOTAL FAT 6(G); CALORIES FROM FAT 31%; SODIUM 198(MG)

Soup's On!

There are two things that make me nervous in the kitchen—desserts and soups. So, I'm never afraid to call in an expert for help with either. It just so happens that our new test kitchen director, Kim, is just such an expert. Here are some of her pointers.

Beans: Instead of soaking the beans overnight, quick-soak them, *see Page 18*. Soaking only shortens cooking time—it won't get rid of "gas."

Be sure to cook the beans properly—not too firm or too mushy. Like pasta, they have to be *al dente*, or firm to the bite. Check continuously after cooking for two hours.

Garnish: Simple garnishes can turn this simple soup into an entree.

Float a couple of Parmesan cheese croutons in the center. So they don't wind up too soggy, toast them on *both* sides before broiling with cheese.

And instead of adding spinach right to the pot (it'll overcook), add leaves to the bowls and ladle soup on top keeping the spinach bright green.

Finally, top with diced red pepper for color, shaved Parmesan for flavor, and a fresh rosemary sprig for looks.

SHAVING PARMESAN

It's tough (and dangerous!) to use a knife on a hard block of Parmesan. But this "Y" peeler makes those thin strips you want for the croutons (and the turkey dishes on pages 32 and 34). "Peel" the Parmesan like a carrot, shaving the cheese off in long strips. For best results, shave in one direction.

PREPARING THE SOUP

5 In the same pot, saute onion and garlic in olive oil until soft, about five minutes. Add celery and carrots, and saute five more minutes.

6 Now add the chicken broth, chiles, herbs, pepper, and the drained beans. Stir to combine and bring the soup to a boil.

7 Cover the soup with a lid and reduce heat to a simmer. Cook, stirring occasionally, for two hours. Check beans for doneness.

8 To make the croutons, toast both sides of Italian bread slices. Top with shavings of Parmesan cheese and broil just until melted.

9 To serve, place some spinach leaves into each soup bowl and ladle hot soup over the spinach. It will wilt almost immediately.

10 Gently swirl the wilted spinach with a spoon—this is just to make sure the spinach is heated all the way through.

11 Garnish the soup by sprinkling some diced red pepper over the top. It not only adds great flavor to the soup, but also great color.

12 Finish the dish by floating two croutons in the soup. Sprinkle with more Parmesan curls, and top with a sprig of fresh rosemary.

PANZANELLA

Translated, Panzanella means "little swamp"... but don't let the name fool you! This classic Italian salad literally explodes with color and intense flavor. Even

during the dead of winter, this Italian bread salad, made with tomatoes and day-old bread, is a refreshing respite from many of the heavy dishes you expect this time of the year.

Panzanella [pahn-zah-NEHL-lah] was an invention of necessity. Italian cooks waste nothing. And this was one way to utilize stale bread and prolific vegetables from the garden. So even though I'm giving you an exact recipe, feel free to add your own ingredients—just remember, Panzanella starts with bread and tomatoes.

Bread: A good Italian bread will absorb all the strong, wonderful flavors you can throw at it and still hold its shape when tossed.

As simple as it may seem, bread-making requires patience, skill, and time. For this reason, many cooks in Italy prefer to buy bread from the baker. And that's just what I want you to do. Look for a bread with a very simple ingredient list (flour, yeast, salt, water) and no preservatives. Bread labeled "peasant" or "Tuscan" will point you in the right direction.

Rehydrating: There are many ways to prepare the bread for Panzanella. Some recipes call for soaking the stale bread in water and then squeezing the water out. But I want you to toast the bread, and *then* soak it—with olive oil, capers, anchovies, garlic, and vinegar. This is powerful!

Freshness: Italians are sticklers for quality ingredients and produce. We all should be. Find the freshest tomatoes possible. In the winter, smaller tomatoes usually have a fresher, more intense taste. Romas are a good choice.

If you're fortunate enough to have an Italian market nearby—go. The owners are proud of the products and will encourage you to sample cheeses and olives you're not familiar with.

Variations: There are many ingredient variations to Panzanella, and all of them are acceptable—things like balsamic vinegar, crushed red pepper, herbs, sun-dried tomatoes, or your favorite cheese.

And don't limit this Panzanella to just salad. It's also a great bed for main dishes—try it under the turkey entrees on page 30.

PANZANELLA SALAD

(MAKES 12 CUPS)

WORK TIME: 30 MINUTES
COOK TIME: 5 MINUTES

TOAST UNDER THE BROILER:

4 cups day-old Italian bread, cut into ¹/₂" cubes

TOAST IN 1 TSP. OLIVE OIL:

¹/₃ cup pine nuts

MIX WITH MORTAR AND PESTLE:

1 T. capers, drained
2 t. garlic, minced
1 t. anchovy fillets, diced

COMBINE WITH:

¹/₂ cup extra virgin olive oil
¹/₄ cup red wine vinegar
¹/₄ cup chicken broth

ADD BREAD AND PINE NUTS; TOSS WITH:

2 cups tomatoes, seeded and diced
1 cup cucumber, peeled, seeded and diced
1 cup red onion, halved and thinly sliced
¹/₂ cup mixed red and yellow peppers, diced
¹/₂ cup mozzarella cheese, cubed
¹/₄ cup kalamata olives, pitted
¹/₄ cup fresh basil, chiffonade
Freshly ground black pepper

NUTRITIONAL INFORMATION PER 1 CUP:
CALORIES 166; TOTAL FAT 13(G); CALORIES FROM FAT 69%; SODIUM 159(MG)

WHAT'S A CAPER?

Capers are not usually one of my favorite things, but they're wonderful in this salad!

Capers are the flower buds of a bush native to the Mediterranean and parts of Asia. The buds are picked, sun-dried, and then pickled in a vinegar brine. They range in size from the petite nonpareil variety from southern France (considered the finest), to those from Italy, which can be as big as your little fingernail.

Capers are generally packed in brine but can also be found dry-packed in salt. If you use the salted kind, rinse them before adding to a recipe.

The pungent flavor of capers is best in sauces and vinegar-based salad dressings.

1 Cut day-old bread into ¹/₂" thick slices, then cut into ¹/₂" cubes. *Carefully* toast the cubes under the broiler, turning often.

2 To bring out their flavor, toast the pine nuts in 1 tsp. olive oil over medium-high heat. Stir often and watch carefully—they'll burn!

3 Mash the capers, garlic, and anchovies with a mortar and pestle until you have a smooth paste. Transfer the paste to a mixing bowl.

4 Whisk olive oil, red wine vinegar, and broth into the paste until combined. Add the toasted bread cubes and toss thoroughly.

5 Cut the tomatoes across their middles, squeeze out the seeds, and dice. Dice the cucumber and peppers. Add to the mixing bowl.

6 Peel the onion and cut it across its middle, too. Now, thinly slice the onion half. Separate the pieces and add them to the bowl.

7 Add the pine nuts, cheese, and pitted olives (use a cherry or olive pitter). Add the basil, and season with freshly ground pepper.

8 The last thing to do is to give it all a toss. My hands are the best tool I can use. Toss from the "bottom up" to mix all the ingredients.

BALSAMIC VINEGAR

What's the difference between a fine bottle of
champagne and an aged bottle of balsamic vinegar?
The vinegar will probably cost more. It's not that tart,

acidic stuff that tightens up those glands under your jaw like you've just bitten into a lemon. It's more like a liquid velvet that rolls down your throat. Deep purple-brown in color, an aged balsamic vinegar is a perfect match of sweet and sour.

This vinegar is like an Olympic athlete who has trained his whole life with one purpose in mind: to be the best in the world.

Cooking Grape Must: Balsamic vinegar is made from Trebbiano grapes grown in the Northern Italian provinces of Modena and Reggio. Harvested as late as possible (they're the sweetest), the grapes are crushed into "must" (grape juice), which is filtered from the "marc" (the pulp, skins, and seeds). Before the must turns into alcohol (wine vinegar), it's simmered and reduced by a third. Then the must is cooled, filtered, and stored in wooden casks.

Blending in Wooden Barrels: True traditional balsamics come in two grades: those at least 12 years old and others that are 25 years or older. Both are aged in a series of wooden barrels housed in airy attics. The different types of wood and fluctuations in the attic climate add character.

First Barrel: The first and largest barrel holds 16 gallons and is made of oak. As the vinegar ages in this barrel, the sugar starts to turn acidic. This gives vinegar its sour taste.

Second Barrel: The second barrel holds 13 gallons and is typically made of chestnut. In this barrel, the vinegar develops its scent, taste, and color.

Third Barrel: The $10^{1}/_{2}$-gallon third barrel is made of cherry. The rich flavor continues to slowly develop.

Final Barrels: The vinegar's flavor, texture, and color continue to mature in the final two barrels. The eight-gallon barrel is typically made of ash, and the final five-gallon barrel is crafted from either mulberry or juniper.

Topping Up: Finished balsamic vinegars are drawn from the smallest and oldest barrels. But the barrels are not drained completely. The part that is removed for judging (then marketed) and the part that has evaporated has to be replaced. The replacement vinegar comes from the next largest oldest barrel up the line. This once-a-year process is called "topping up."

Every barrel in the series goes through this process. Topping up is similar to the "solera" system used to make sherry. It's during blending that balsamic vinegar becomes a combination of all the ages and flavors of each type of wood used in the barrels.

But it's the vinegar eventually drawn off the smallest barrel that faces the toughest challenge.

Judging the Vinegar: True balsamic vinegar is judged by one of two consortiums in Italy. They are either from Modena or Reggio.

The judges in these consortiums are not told the owner or age of the vinegar. In fact, in Italy, it is illegal to put the age of balsamic vinegar on the label. If a bottle says it contains "15-year-old" vinegar, that may mean that any amount, even a teaspoon, could have started out in the largest barrel 15 years ago and eventually made it to the smallest. If you see an age on the label, it's not a "true" balsamic—it's not from the balsamic regions and it didn't go through the rigorous scrutiny of the consortium.

Want-to-be balsamics go through 90 tests to examine aroma, texture, color, and taste. If it passes, it's labeled balsamic vinegar. If not, the rejected vinegar is sent back to the owner.

Once passed, the consortium gives out a registration number, seal, and code indicating where it's from—API MO (Modena) or API RE (Reggio).

Traditionally, balsamics were placed in a distinctive bottle—a glass globe sitting on a rectangular stand. Some still maintain this tradition.

What to Look For: There are three basic types of balsamic you can buy. The first and best is an artisan-made, tested balsamic from Modena or Reggio. Second are commercially produced balsamics from these two regions. Finally are imitations made outside these regions, including balsamics made with additives such as wine vinegar or sweeteners.

The best way to find a great balsamic is to taste it. Trust me, when you get a hold of a good one, you'll know it. But since it's practically impossible to taste them, you'll have to rely on your other senses.

Sight: This is your next best sense. Look for a dark brown or black color that's similar to molasses. If the bottle has a screw top rather than a cork, it's probably a good indication of some inexpensive vinegar.

Finally, a true balsamic should be thick—like a good maple syrup. The best way to test for this consistency is to tip the bottle. If the neck remains coated, you've got a good one. The one thing I've noticed after testing 20 different vinegars is that all the good ones had clear bottles—obviously to show off their quality. In general, be suspicious of colored bottles.

Common Sense: Be sure to use common sense when buying and using balsamic vinegar. You probably aren't going to spend more than $6 for a commercially produced balsamic. Authentic balsamics can cost between $25–$200. Most of the ones I like (and could afford) range between $25–$50. But don't think of your $5 bottle as inferior or substandard—just think of it as a different vinegar.

Uses: Consider what you're using the vinegar for. If it's for sauces, soups, or marinades (anything you mix *into*), use a commercial balsamic.

This is true balsamic vinegar. Check out the bottle shape and registration number. Balsamics can cost hundreds of dollars!

However, there are times when only a true balsamic will do. Brush *sparingly* on poultry, meats, or seafood just at the end of grilling. Or drizzle some over fresh fruit such as strawberries, raspberries, or orange sections.

And finally, a really good bottle of balsamic can just be sipped as an after dinner drink. And you thought this was just vinegar! **AH**

(Page 22, from left to right)
***Carandini Extravecchio**, 8.5 oz., $149.95.*
***Carandini Primavera**, 8.5 oz., $17.95.*
***Carandini Europa**, 8.5 oz., $31.63.*
***Carandini Noé**, 8.5 oz., $83.95.*
***Grosoli Del Duca**, 8 oz., $28.50.*
***Campagnia Del Montale (25 yr.)**, 3.4 oz., $165.00.*
(Page 23, from left to right)
***Elsa**, 8.5 oz., $26.95.*
***Giusti**, 8.5 oz., $47.50.*
***Campagnia Del Montale (12 yr.)**, 8.5 oz., $32.50.*
***Antica Italia**, 17 oz., $5.96.*
***Raccanto**, 17 oz., $3.19.*
***Vecchia dispensa**, 8.5 oz., $18.00.*

MAKING RICOTTA CHEESE

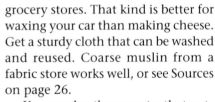

Photograph: Scott Little

Ricotta cheese was not a staple in my mother's kitchen. In fact, we had never heard of it back then. Lasagna was made with cottage cheese. Sound familiar? The

first time I ate lasagna at a *real* Italian trattoria, it had ricotta cheese. It was a whole different experience.

But trying to duplicate that lasagna at home (using grocery store ricotta), came up short. The ricotta was grainy and dry. I finally found some whole milk ricotta at an Italian market that made my lasagna (and ravioli) almost as good as what I had at the trattoria.

But most of us don't have an Italian grocer down the street—good ricotta isn't always available to us. So why not try making your own? It will be creamier and smoother than what you find in most grocery stores.

I'm going to show you how to make homemade ricotta, so you can taste the difference yourself. We'll also make mascarpone because it, too, is a great cheese used in Italian cooking.

Ricotta: Ricotta means "recooked" and is actually made from whey, a by-product of cheesemaking. Generally, all cheeses are made when the whey (liquid) is separated from the curd (solids). Most cheeses are made from solid curds—except ricotta. It is traditionally made using the whey.

Mascarpone: Mascarpone [mahs-kar-POH-neh] gets its name from the Italian verb *mascherare*—to "dress up" or "camouflage." This makes sense, since mascarpone is basically dressed up cream (crème fraîche) that has been drained.

THE BASICS

Before you start making cheese, there are some basics you'll need to know. These quick points are only relevant to soft cheeses. There is a lot more to cheesemaking than this.

Cleanliness: All of your utensils need to be absolutely clean—wash them in very hot, soapy water and rinse well. Impurities in your cheese make it spoil faster.

Sterilizing utensils isn't necessary; however, you'll want to go through the process of boiling your cheese-cloth in water for five minutes. This gets rid of any soap residue that may still be in the cloth from washing it.

Utensils: For making ricotta, you probably already have most of the items in your kitchen. They are: 6-quart stockpot, skimmer, slotted spoon, colander, cheesecloth, and an accurate thermometer.

Your *pot, skimmer, colander, and spoon* should be stainless steel, glass, or enamel-coated. Since milk becomes acidic during cheesemaking, the acid could cause metallic compounds to leach from more porous equipment. These compounds can affect flavor and, possibly, your health. Wooden spoons are just too hard to clean well, so I don't mess with them.

The *cheesecloth* you use should be a fine-mesh cloth, not the loosely woven stuff you find in hardware or

grocery stores. That kind is better for waxing your car than making cheese. Get a sturdy cloth that can be washed and reused. Coarse muslin from a fabric store works well, or see Sources on page 26.

You need a *thermometer* that gets up to 220°. A long-stemmed one that clips to the pot is handy, *see Sources*. I used my trusty instant-read, though, and it worked fine.

Milk: Since I'm guessing you don't have any whey at home, we're going to make ricotta with whole milk.

I tested different kinds of milk, from half & half (too rich) to skim (rubbery). The best results came from whole cow's milk.

I didn't try unpasteurized milk (it's supposed to make the best cheeses), because it's not available unless you have a dairy farm next door. So, just use pasteurized whole milk from the grocery store.

Curds: Curds are formed when the protein part of the milk solids (casein) curdles and releases liquid. Most of the milk's fat stays in the curd. As I said, traditional ricotta is made from whey, but we're using curds.

Whey: Whey is the yellowish liquid left after curds form. It's mostly water that contains soluble proteins, sugars, and minerals, but little fat. Don't throw this away. It really adds flavor and body to soups and breads.

WHOLE MILK RICOTTA

(MAKES 1+ POUNDS)
WORK/DRAIN TIME: 5 MINS./2 HRS.
COOK TIME: 30 MINUTES
COMBINE IN POT:
1   gallon whole milk
1   t. citric acid
1   t. kosher (flake) salt
HEAT SLOWLY TO 185°. SET ASIDE, THEN DRAIN.

Citric Acid: You need an acid to make milk curdle. For ricotta, you'll use citric acid. Citric acid is a white powder extracted from the juice of citrus and other acidic fruits. You can't find the pure stuff in the grocery store (it's an ingredient in Fruit Fresh®, but that won't work in cheese). You'll have to order some from one of the sources on the next page. Don't worry. It's cheap and a little goes a long way.

Making the Cheese: First, stir the citric acid and salt into cold milk. Now, gradually heat the milk over medium-high heat until it reaches 185°. You'll need to stir it occasionally to keep the milk from scalding, but be gentle. A few delicate curds will form right away, and you don't want to damage them. Also, try not to scrape the bottom of the pot. You don't want to release any scorched particles into the forming curds which could give an off-taste to the cheese.

 Most of the curds form after the milk has reached 185°. Letting the pot sit undisturbed (off heat) for 10 minutes gives more curds a chance to form and float to the top. This curd layer (about 2") is what you'll drain to make the ricotta cheese. Also, skim down into the whey for stray curds.

Draining the Cheese: Finding a place to drain the cheese bag is a trick. I looped mine over a broom handle and hung it between two chairs. Just make sure you put a bowl under it to catch the dripping whey (you'll want to save the whey.)

It should only take two hours to drain ricotta, but if it seems too wet, the cloth may be clogged. Remove the cheese from the cloth, scrape the cloth, then return the cheese to finish draining. Of course, how much you drain is up to you. I like mine a little moist for making lasagna.

1 Combine fresh milk, citric acid, and salt in a large stainless steel stockpot. Make sure the pot and utensils are absolutely clean.

2 Heat the milk over medium-high heat to 185°. Stir it gently every so often, so it doesn't scald. Check the temperature after stirring.

3 Sterilize cheesecloth by boiling it for 5 minutes in water. Line a colander with the cheesecloth. Place the colander in a sink.

4 When milk reaches 185°, take it off the heat and let stand for 10 minutes. Gently skim curds out of pot and place them in lined colander.

5 Gather two corners of cheesecloth in each hand. Gently rock cheesecloth like a see-saw to drain out most of the whey.

6 There are 4 corners to the cheesecloth. Gather 2 corners on each side, tie together firmly. This will form a bag that can hang.

7 Hang the cheesecloth bag by its loops and let it drain over a bowl. You can hang it from a broom handle between two chairs, on a hook, over the sink faucet—whatever works for you.

8 Let the cheese drain for about 2 hours. The longer it drains, the drier it will be. Turn ricotta out of cheesecloth and use in recipes.

CRÈME FRAÎCHE MASCARPONE

(MAKES 1 POUND)
WORK TIME: 5 MINUTES
STAND/DRAIN TIME: 24 HRS./12 HRS.
COMBINE:
2 cups heavy cream
2 T. buttermilk
2 T. fresh lemon juice, strained
ALLOW TO THICKEN FOR 24 HOURS,
THEN DRAIN.

Mascarpone is an extremely thick cream that is on the verge of becoming butter. Many Italian restaurants use mascarpone in fillings for ravioli and tortellini because it's so rich.

This mascarpone uses crème fraîche that you make a day ahead—then drain it to make mascarpone.

Most store-bought mascarpones are slightly sweet, but ours has a bit of a tang from the lemon juice and buttermilk used to make the crème fraîche. If you want less tartness, omit the lemon juice.

Fresh mascarpone is very perishable, so use it right away. Try it in the Cranberry Napoleons on page 38, or the Ricotta Torta on page 42. You can also make different mascarpone fillings for the tortellini and ravioli.

MAKING THE CRÈME FRAÎCHE MASCARPONE

1 Start this 2 days before you want mascarpone. Combine cream, buttermilk, and juice. Let stand 24 hours at room temperature.

2 The crème fraîche is ready when cream thickens to about the consistency of soft whipped cream. It gets tangier the longer it sits.

3 Line a sieve or colander with white paper towels. Put crème fraîche in sieve. Cover with plastic wrap. Drain in refrigerator overnight.

4 Mascarpone is ready when it's like soft cream cheese. It's best to use right away since it doesn't have a long shelf life (about 3 days).

LEMON CHEESE

(MAKES 1 1/2–2 POUNDS)
WORK TIME: 15 MINUTES
COOK TIME: 20 MINUTES
DRAIN TIME: 2 HOURS
HEAT TO 100°:
1 gallon whole milk
REMOVE FROM HEAT AND ADD:
1 cup fresh lemon juice, strained
DRAIN CURDS. BLEND CHEESE WITH
SALT; STIR IN CRACKED PEPPERCORNS.

Let's say you want to make cheese, but don't want to mail-order any products. Here's a simple recipe to try.

If you don't have any cheesecloth, use muslin, or even a colander lined with plain white paper towels.

Follow the same procedure for ricotta when you make lemon cheese. But there are a few differences that you have to follow carefully.

Point 1: Only heat the milk to 100°.
Point 2: Don't add the lemon juice until after the milk has heated.

Once you have heated the milk to 100°, take the pot off the heat and stir in 2/3 cup lemon juice. If there doesn't seem to be any curds forming after a minute of stirring, then add the remaining 1/3 cup. Let curds form for 15 minutes before draining.

Lemon juice produces a softer curd than citric acid, so this cheese will be different than ricotta. Because it's soft and creamy, this cheese makes a great spread or dip. **AH**

▲ *Lemon juice produces a stringy curd. Use a skimmer to ladle the curd into a cheesecloth-lined colander.*

▲ *Blend drained curds in a food processor until creamy. Stir in salt to taste and crushed peppercorns. Serve as a spread.*

SOURCES
Lehman's (330) 857-5757;
e-mail: www.lehmans.com

New England Cheesemaking
Supply Co. (413) 628-3808;
e-mail: www.cheesemaking.com

WHAT'S HAPPENING IN FOOD?

◄ PROVENÇAL-INSPIRED CUISINE ►

San Franciscans have long appreciated enticing dishes from Restaurant LuLu's Provençal-inspired menu. The combination of Mediterranean flavors and the freshness of California produce have proven irresistible to diners from around the country. Now, Chefs Jody Denton and Marc Valiani have captured the LuLu essence in a line of products for use at home. Stock your pantry with distinctive vinegars (like Fig Balsamic, or Wild Fennel and Thyme), or other condiments such as their Romesco Sauce—a flavorful Spanish paste made of red peppers, almonds, and garlic. To order, call **(888) 693-5800**.

▼ WINE BISCUITS

Here's a cracker that goes with just about anything, including our Lemon Cheese, *see facing page.* American Vintage Wine Biscuits' unique blend of wine and black pepper pairs well with cheeses and dips, or just on their own. Give them a try with ice cream. Call **(718) 361-1003** to order.

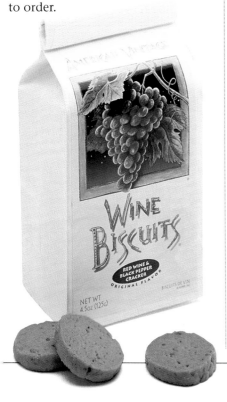

◄ STRETCH-TITE WRAP

I love this stuff. This plastic wrap can stick to almost anything. Although it clings to metal and wood, it grips glass like a neurotic clenches a stress ball. As a test, I stretched a sheet of **stretch-tite**®over a glass bowl. Then I placed two smaller bowls filled with leftovers on top of the plastic-sealed bowl—it didn't cave in! Not even after sitting all night. The wrap is thinner than others, but it doesn't matter. Call **Polyvinyl Films, Inc.** for more information or to order: **(800) 343-6134**.

SUZANNE'S MUFFINS ►

Looking for a wonderful (and tasty) gift to send to those who are far away or need a little cheering up? Suzanne's Muffins are it. I've already sent two boxes to my daughter at college. These muffins come in 16 different flavors, both traditional (Blueberry) and sinful (Chocolate Cream Cheese). They are sent FedEx®the day they're baked. And for those of you who need consistency in your life, join their Muffin of the Month Club. To order, call **(800) 742-2403**.

PLACE SETTING

By fifteen, I had been forced to take etiquette classes so I'd be polished and proper. The training finally paid off when I attended a debutante ball. Unfortunately, at dinner, I consumed the lemon water in my finger bowl.

At least I used my consommé spoon—the rest of the bumblers at the table used their dessert spoons!

I haven't forgotten that night. So the few formal dinners I throw each year aren't squeaky formal. To me, a formal dinner is the way a menu is put together, not the amount of silver on my table, or ways I can intimidate guests. After all, we're talking about one of life's celebrations—eating.

Of Course: Menus for a formal dinner are different from the day-to-day stuff because of courses. A *course* is part of a meal served at one time. A TV dinner is a one-course dinner, while a more formal meal is staged into several courses of food. I might have a first course (appetizer), soup course, salad course, meat course, and then a dessert course.

Each course, being a distinct piece of the whole dinner, has its own equipment, and at times, even its own drink. Silver and crystal have to show up on the table at the beginning—they serve as guides for the whole dinner. But following the one-time use rule, they don't hang around from course to course.

The classic framework of courses was a belt-busting total of 13 different ones, starting with an hors d'oeuvre and finishing with dessert. I don't think it would be proper to eat that much, anymore, at one sitting. Imagine 13 sets of equipment per place. This is a streamlined version of the dining experience.

Not Hoity, Proper: Before you think I'm ready to tuck a napkin into my collar, I'll tell you that etiquette hasn't gone out of style—it's just a little more relaxed now. Table setting still has rules, but they're simple ones.

The first rule: The menu drives the setting of the table. How many courses will the dinner have? Once you've decided on the menu, you've outlined the set of the table.

The second rule: Nothing extra goes on the table. Nothing to trick or overwhelm your guests.

The third rule: Everything has a proper position, according to how and when it will be used.

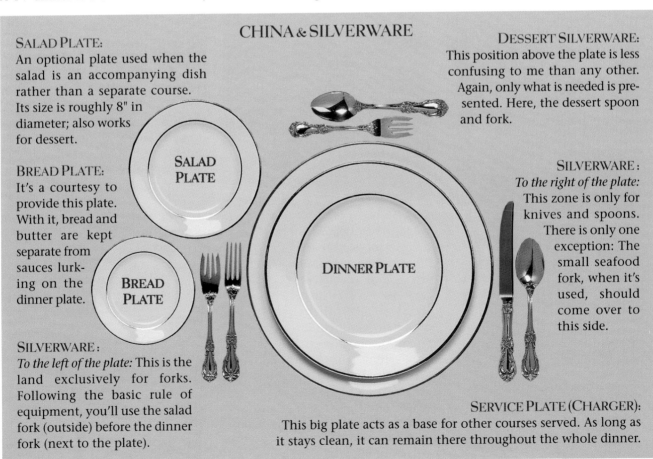

CHINA & SILVERWARE

SALAD PLATE:
An optional plate used when the salad is an accompanying dish rather than a separate course. Its size is roughly 8" in diameter; also works for dessert.

BREAD PLATE:
It's a courtesy to provide this plate. With it, bread and butter are kept separate from sauces lurking on the dinner plate.

SILVERWARE:
To the left of the plate: This is the land exclusively for forks. Following the basic rule of equipment, you'll use the salad fork (outside) before the dinner fork (next to the plate).

DESSERT SILVERWARE:
This position above the plate is less confusing to me than any other. Again, only what is needed is presented. Here, the dessert spoon and fork.

SILVERWARE:
To the right of the plate: This zone is only for knives and spoons. There is only one exception: The small seafood fork, when it's used, should come over to this side.

SERVICE PLATE (CHARGER):
This big plate acts as a base for other courses served. As long as it stays clean, it can remain there throughout the whole dinner.

SETTING PLACES

It's time to set an "informal" formal table. You first have to consider the menu. There will be a soup, salad, meat, and dessert. Different wines will be served with three of the courses. And bread will tag along with the salad course. Following rule #1, you'll need china and silver for four courses, plus crystal for wines and water.

China: Go to your closet and pull out the china you'll need for each place: a salad plate, a dinner plate, a bread plate, a dessert plate, and a rimmed soup bowl.

But it's best to start with a service plate. It's the base plate for all courses served during a meal. No guest sits at an empty place before or between courses, so its major purpose is to occupy space. It's also a big honking plate, perfect for designating places.

Silverware: Next comes the silver, and you have to consider rules #2 and #3, too. For each place, you'll need a tablespoon, salad fork, dinner fork, dessert fork and/or spoon (depending on the dessert), and a dinner knife. Since you're using bread plates, you'll need butter spreaders all around, too.

With silver, forks are on the left, spoons and knives on the right, with blades facing the plate. Silver is *always* used from the outside of the plate in. This means that the fork farthest from the plate is the first one to be used.

Crystal: With crystal, positions are according to content. The water goblet (iced beverage) is straight up from

CRYSTAL

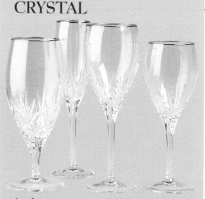

A place setting of crystal can be four or more glasses, all on stems. Before you rush to buy an armload, remember rules #1 and #2: Use only what your menu needs, never anything extra. If you're not going to offer white wine, don't worry yourself or your guests by putting a white wine glass at each setting.

Like this set of four glasses, iced beverage is the one with the shortest stem and biggest bowl—use this one for water. The tallest, larger-stemmed glass is the goblet for red wine. The one like it, only smaller, is the white wine glass. And, of course, there is the champagne flute.

LINEN

For most formal and semi-formal table settings, white is best: *the white-is-always-right rule.*

Natural fabrics are better than anything synthetic because they can be bleached and starched. And they last forever.

Dinner napkins are the biggest size and hors d'oeuvres napkins are the smallest. Lunch napkins are in-between. But don't substitute small when you should have large. A dinner napkin should be about 20" square, or large enough to cover a lap.

The napkin is placed either on the service plate, or to the left of the forks. Don't fold them into wine goblets—this top-heavy setup begs for an accident.

A word about paper napkins: they're just right...for outdoor barbecues only.

the knife tip, with red wine to its right, and white to the right of that. If you're serving champagne with dessert, it sits slightly behind the other glasses.

Linens: All this nice china and silver, stored since your wedding, sits on a tablecloth—white and creased straight down the center. A crooked center on a tablecloth is like having a crooked part in your hair (it bothers people). Place the napkins on the service plate rather than to the left of the forks. If a guest goofs and grabs the wrong one, it throws everyone into a quandary. There no disputing ownership when it's on the service plate.

A PLACE IS SET

So here is what your final table setting will look like with everything in the right place. When dinner guests take a seat, this is what they'll see:

A service plate with a napkin folded into its center. The adjacent bread plate with a butter spreader positioned on the rim (blade facing in).

All the silver to be used is in place: A spoon for soup. A salad fork for salad. Dinner knife and fork for the meat course. And a spoon and fork for dessert. A teaspoon appears on the rim of a coffee cup saucer when it is served after dessert.

The water goblet will be filled before the guests are seated. Wines will be poured in the proper glasses with their courses. Now, everything is in its place and ready—*just don't drink the finger bowl.* **AH**

Photograph: Scott Little, Food Styling: Janet Pittman

3 TURKEY DISHES

Norman Rockwell's Thanksgiving portrait is an injustice to turkey. It's a great image and tradition— a functional, spit-shined family gathered around a

perfectly roasted bird. But even though this image works for us, a good-tasting turkey deserves a little more than ending up overcooked and dried out from hours of roasting.

As conservative as I am, I must buck tradition. There's no good reason why turkey should be pigeon-holed into one traditional preparation only to be enjoyed on holidays. This American treasure deserves more.

Now, I'm not being sacrilegious. I love this annual overindulgence—the turkey dinner that feeds twice as many people as there are crammed around the dinner table. And all those hot turkey sandwiches that follow are reason enough for me to light the oven and roast another 26-pounder!

But we're going to do things differently—Italian-style. Here's what I'm thinking. Obviously, turkey isn't very common in Italian cuisine since it's native to America. But veal is big. So what about taking a couple of classic Italian dishes, like Parmigiana and Saltimbocca, and use turkey instead?

The Veal Deal: If veal's so traditional, why not use it? *Strike one*, not everyone's crazy about eating veal. *Strike two*, it's pricey. *Strike three*, veal can be tough to find.

Turkey makes a great designated hitter. It's widely acceptable, readily available, and fairly inexpensive. Its mild flavor is similar to veal, but not quite as delicate—it won't get lost in the flavorful sauces we'll be making.

Turkey Tenderloin: For these recipes, we're going to use a cut of turkey you might not know about— the tenderloin. You know "chicken tenders," right? It's the same thing here, only bigger—about six ounces.

A turkey tenderloin is the whole inside muscle lying directly underneath the breast. It's shaped like a beef tenderloin—thick and wide at one end, tapering down to the other.

And if your family likes white meat as much as mine, you'll love this— turkey tenderloins are *all* white meat. Finally—enough for everyone.

Preparation: None of these recipes calls for long preparation or cooking time. The turkey cooks in about 15 minutes, at most. And the sauces can be made the day before. Which is a good thing—there are football games to watch.

And, finally, look at how we're going to present this. It looks almost too dressy for turkey, doesn't it?

30 NOV/DEC 1998 CUISINE

TRIMMING AND POUNDING

Turkey tenderloins need just a little basic preparation before cooking.

Trimming: You need to trim out the thick, white tendon that runs through the tenderloin. Like silver-skin on a beef tenderloin, it can turn into a rubber band after it cooks. Plus, it shrinks and causes the meat to curl.

Look to the right and see how I'm trimming out the tendon. For the Parmigiana and Saltimbocca dishes, cut the tenderloin in half lengthwise, along the white tendon. Now, you can easily "fillet" the tendon from the meat. You'll have perfect pieces to portion into cutlets and medallions.

For the roast turkey on page 34, you'll use a "v" cut and won't slice all the way through the tenderloin.

Pounding: Usually, you'll pound tougher cuts of meat to tenderize them. But here, for the Parmigiana and Saltimbocca, *lightly* pounding the pieces of tenderloin is more for shaping than anything. Plus, it helps them cook quickly and evenly.

FOR THE PARMIGIANA AND SALTIMBOCCA

1 *For Parmigiana and Saltimbocca, first slice through the tenderloin, trimming along one side of tendon.*

2 *Then trim the tendon from the other side like you'd fillet a fish. Now cut each side in half, or into 4 medallions.*

3 *Gently pound pieces between plastic with flat side of a mallet to ¼" thick. Medallions are for Saltimbocca.*

FOR THE ROAST TURKEY

1 *For the roast turkey, create a pocket by making a "v" cut around the tendon to trim it out. Don't cut through the meat.*

PREPARING THE SAUCE FOR SALTIMBOCCA AND ROAST TURKEY

MARSALA SAUCE

(MAKES 3 CUPS)
WORK TIME: 15 MINUTES
COOK TIME: 20 MINUTES

IN A SAUCEPAN, HEAT:
¼ cup olive oil

ADD AND SAUTE:
1 cup shallots, minced
¼ cup garlic, minced

DEGLAZE AND REDUCE:
1 cup dry marsala
½ cup balsamic vinegar

ADD AND SIMMER:
2½ cups chicken broth

STRAIN; COMBINE AND WHISK IN:
2 T. cornstarch
2 T. chicken broth

FINISH WITH (OPTIONAL):
2 T. unsalted butter, cold

SEASON WITH:
2 T. dry marsala
1 T. fresh sage, chiffonade
½ t. salt
¼ t. freshly ground pepper

1 Heat oil in medium saucepan over high heat. Add shallots and saute until soft, about 2 minutes. Add garlic and saute another minute.

2 Deglaze with marsala and balsamic vinegar. Reduce until almost dry, about 3 minutes. Add chicken broth and simmer 5 more minutes.

3 Strain sauce through fine mesh sieve. Return to pan and bring to boil. In small bowl, whisk cornstarch and 2 T. broth until smooth.

4 Thicken sauce by whisking cornstarch mixture into boiling sauce. Simmer 3 minutes. Finish sauce with butter, marsala, sage, salt, pepper.

TURKEY PARMIGIANA WITH MARINARA SAUCE

(MAKES 6 SERVINGS)
WORK TIME: 50 MINUTES
COOK TIME: 20 MINUTES

REMOVE TENDON AND POUND OUT:
1½ lbs. turkey tenderloins

FOR HERB CRUST, COMBINE:
¾ cup unseasoned bread crumbs
½ cup chopped fresh parsley
¼ cup chopped fresh rosemary
¼ cup Parmesan cheese, grated
¼ t. crushed red pepper flakes
½ t. salt
   Zest from 1 lemon

FOR EGG MIXTURE, WHISK TOGETHER:
2 eggs
2 T. milk

DREDGE TURKEY CUTLETS IN:
¾ cup all-purpose flour
   Egg mixture
   Herb crust mixture

FRY CUTLETS IN:
¼ cup olive oil

TRANSFER TO SHEET PAN. TOP WITH:
6 oz. mozzarella cheese, sliced

SAUTE IN 2 T. OLIVE OIL UNTIL WILTED:
10 cups spinach, stemmed; or
   Swiss chard, cut into strips
   Salt and pepper to taste

GARNISH WITH:
3 cups Marinara Sauce, *see page 15*
   Parmesan cheese curls
   Italian parsley sprigs

NUTRITIONAL INFORMATION PER SERVING:
CALORIES 599; TOTAL FAT 31(G); CALORIES FROM FAT 46%; SODIUM 1,135(MG)

At first, there seems to be a lot of action going on all at once. Don't worry! Here are some tricks so you're not tied to the stove all evening.

First, make the Marinara Sauce in advance—the day before. Like most of us, it gets better with a little age.

Then, saute the turkey cutlets a couple hours before dinner and refrigerate. Heating the sauce, sauteing the spinach, and finishing the turkey in the oven will take about 10 minutes.

All these dishes are dressed up with "restaurant-style" presentations. Fun to do and impressive—but it still tastes good if you pass things "family-style."

And if you're not a fan of sauteed spinach, use the Panzanella on page 20 as a base for the turkey. It's a refreshing, light-tasting alternative.

PREPARING THE PARMIGIANA

1 Preheat oven to 400°. Trim and pound tenderloins as on page 31. Combine herb crust ingredients, and whisk together egg mixture.

2 Heat oil in large skillet over high heat. Dredge turkey cutlets first in flour; then dip in egg mixture, and coat in herb crust mixture.

3 Fry cutlets in ¼ cup oil until golden brown, about 3 minutes. Turn and fry other side until golden (2 minutes). Transfer to sheet pan.

4 Top each cutlet with a slice of mozzarella and finish cooking in oven, about 10 minutes. Meanwhile, warm Marinara Sauce in a saucepan.

5 While cutlets finish, heat oil in large saute pan over high heat. Saute spinach in batches, just until wilted. Season with salt and pepper.

6 To serve, spoon about ½ cup Marinara on each plate. Blot spinach dry with paper towels and mound some in center of each plate.

7 The turkey is ready when the mozzarella is melted and lightly browned. Arrange two cutlets against the mounded spinach.

8 Finally, garnish the plates with Parmesan cheese curls, *see page 19*. Leggy sprigs of Italian parsley make a great garnish.

TURKEY SALTIMBOCCA WITH MARSALA SAUCE

(SERVES 6)

WORK TIME: 50 MINUTES

COOK TIME: 30 MINUTES

PREPARE AND KEEP WARM:

Marsala Sauce, *see page 31*

REMOVE TENDON AND POUND OUT:

1½ lbs. turkey tenderloins, sliced
crosswise into medallions

DIP TURKEY IN:

Egg mixture, *see page 32*

DREDGE IN:

¾ cup all-purpose flour

SAUTE TURKEY IN:

¼ cup olive oil

ADD TURKEY TO WARM SAUCE WITH:

¼ lb. prosciutto, thinly sliced

IN ANOTHER PAN, HEAT THROUGH:

3 cans (15-oz. each) Great Northern
white beans, drained and rinsed

¾ cup chicken broth

3 T. Parmesan cheese, grated

2 T. fresh sage, chiffonade

¼ t. freshly ground black pepper

SERVE WITH:

Sauteed Swiss chard, *see page 32,*
Step 6

GARNISH WITH:

Fresh sage sprigs

NUTRITIONAL INFORMATION PER SERVING:
CALORIES 820; TOTAL FAT 33(G); CALORIES
FROM FAT 35%; SODIUM 727(MG)

Saltimbocca [sahl-teem-BOH-kah] is Italian for "jump in the mouth." There's no straight answer about where the name came from. But just taste this and see—it's flavor-packed.

Here, you're trimming the tenderloins into smaller medallions, like we did on page 31. Now when you pound them out, they'll be thinner than the cutlets—and saute faster.

Since this dish happens so fast, make the Marsala Sauce ahead of time, *see page 31*. Add butter, herbs, and Marsala when you reheat it.

For a good spinach substitute, try using a green called Swiss chard. There are two common types— red- and white- stemmed. You can use either, just as long as the leaves are bright and fresh. They taste like sweet turnip greens.

PREPARING THE SALTIMBOCCA

1 Pound medallions to ¼" thick, as on page 31. Heat oil in saute pan over high heat. Dip turkey in egg mixture, then dredge in flour.

2 Saute each side of turkey until golden brown (about 2 minutes each). Transfer to platter. Saute other pieces and set aside.

3 Now, prepare Marsala Sauce on page 31. Or, if you've made it ahead, rewarm in saucepan over low heat. Finish with butter, if desired.

4 In another saucepan, combine the rinsed beans, broth, cheese, sage, and pepper. Warm gently— don't overcook. They'll turn mushy.

5 Transfer Marsala Sauce to a large skillet; add sage and seasonings. Over medium heat, warm the turkey and slices of prosciutto in the sauce.

6 Saute strips of Swiss chard just like you did with the spinach on page 32. This red-stemmed chard adds color to the plate.

7 Divide white beans among serving plates. Blot the chard dry with paper towels, then arrange a mound in the middle of the beans.

8 Fan four slices of turkey and two or three prosciutto slices around the chard. Garnish each plate with a sprig of fresh sage.

HERB-CRUSTED ROAST TURKEY

1 Preheat oven to 450°. Trim tendon from tenderloin using a "v" cut, like on page 31. Fill in the cut with a layer of Parmesan, then 2 slices of prosciutto.

2 To truss tenderloins, insert wooden skewers through the cut. With scissors or poultry shears, trim off the ends, leaving about 1" on both sides.

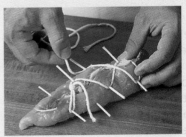

3 Tie one end of an 18" string to the first skewer, leaving a "tail" to tie off. "Lace" string around skewers, like a boot. Tie the end to the tail and trim off.

4 Dredge tenderloins like the cutlets on page 32. Saute in oil over high heat until golden. Refrigerate, or transfer to roaster lined with a rack.

HERB-CRUSTED ROAST TURKEY *(MAKES 6 SERVINGS)*

WORK TIME: 60 MINUTES
COOK TIME: 40 MINUTES

REMOVE TENDON FROM:
1¹/₂ lbs. turkey tenderloins, *see pg. 31*

STUFF WITH; SECURE THEN TIE:
¹/₄ lb. prosciutto, thinly sliced
¹/₄ lb. Parmesan, shaved into strips

DREDGE TURKEY IN:
³/₄ cup all-purpose flour
  Egg mixture, *see page 32*
  Herb crust, *see page 32*

BROWN TURKEY IN:
¹/₄ cup olive oil

FOR CRANBERRY SAUCE, SAUTE IN
¹/₄ *CUP OLIVE OIL UNTIL SOFT:*
1 cup shallots, minced
¹/₄ cup garlic, minced

DEGLAZE AND REDUCE:
1 cup dry white wine
¹/₄ cup balsamic vinegar

ADD AND SIMMER:
2¹/₂ cups chicken broth
¹/₄ cup sugar

STRAIN; COMBINE AND WHISK IN:
2 T. cornstarch
2 T. chicken broth

JUST BEFORE SERVING, ADD:
2 cups whole fresh cranberries
1 T. chopped fresh thyme
  Salt and pepper to taste

Let's say you *don't* have all the relatives at your place for the holidays this year. But your resident traditionalists still want to see turkey on their plates. How can you do it without going all out with a big bird?

Well, these stuffed tenderloins are your answer. Let me tell you, they're the way to go—they roast in a fraction of the time it takes for a whole turkey (about 20 minutes!). And, just like we've been doing all along, you can get ahead of this game, too.

First, put this Cranberry Sauce together in advance. It's a lot like the Marsala Sauce on page 31. The main difference is that you'll be adding whole fresh cranberries. This serves up an unusual tart flavor and a needed red color accent to the brown dish.

But be careful: don't let the berries cook too long—they'll make the sauce pink and too tart. Add and simmer them just before serving.

Second, you can tie and saute these tenderloins in advance. Keep them refrigerated until you're ready to roast.

I really suggest you tie the tenderloins like I'm doing in Steps 2 and 3. It helps them cook evenly, hold their shape, and secure the filling inside. Don't worry, it's an easy process.

SAUTEED VEGETABLES

FOR THE BRUSSELS SPROUTS —
SAUTE IN 3 T. OLIVE OIL:
2   lbs. Brussels sprouts, trimmed
    and halved
ADD AND SAUTE:
1   T. garlic, minced
DEGLAZE WITH AND SIMMER:
3/4   cup dry white wine
SEASON WITH:
1/4   t. salt
1/4   t. freshly ground black pepper
SERVE TURKEY WITH OVEN-ROASTED POTATOES AND SAUTEED SWISS CHARD, SEE SPINACH, PAGE 32.

Simply prepared vegetables make the best accompaniment to this turkey.

Brussels Sprouts: There were a few turned-up noses when I brought Brussels sprouts to the test kitchen—people just whined about them.

But let me tell you something—we ate these babies right out of the saute pan. We had converts that day.

For the best-tasting and freshest Brussels sprouts, see if you can buy them right on the stalk—many times, you'll find them this way in the store. If you can't, buy sprouts the same as you would cabbage—with tight heads and no yellowing leaves.

Potatoes: I want you to do a restaurant-type presentation, so you need to include roasted potatoes.

Peel and quarter russet or Yukon gold potatoes (use 1–2 potatoes per person). Toss the potatoes in olive oil to coat and season with salt and pepper. Roast on a sheet pan at 450° for 25–30 minutes, until they're golden brown and tender. Stir once or twice during roasting to prevent sticking.

Presentation: Everything should now be cooked—all that's left is the presentation. This is the way pro chefs would plate this dish.

First, place about a cup of cooked Swiss chard in the center of the plate. Now, lean the potatoes and Brussels sprouts on either side of the chard.

Next, pour some sauce at the base of the chard. You can see all of this plainly in Step 10.

Finally, cut each turkey tenderloin into eight slices. This will serve two. Fan the slices between the vegetables so they lean up against the chard. *AH*

5 Preheat oven to 450°. Roast browned tenderloins to an internal temperature of 145°, about 20 mins. Remove and rest 5–10 mins.

6 You'll make the Cranberry Sauce like the Marsala Sauce on page 31. Just substitute white wine for the Marsala and add sugar.

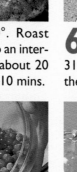

7 Thicken this sauce with the cornstarch mixture, like you did before. Just before serving, add cranberries, thyme, salt, and pepper.

8 Saute prepared Brussels sprouts in oil over high heat—about 3 minutes (a little browning is okay). Add garlic and saute another minute.

9 Deglaze with wine. Simmer 2 minutes. Season and reduce heat. Keep the sprouts warm, but don't cover—they'll turn "army green."

10 This is where it all happens—saute the chard, then plate all the vegetables while the turkey rests. Then add some Cranberry Sauce.

11 Work quickly and remove skewers and string from tenderloins. Slice turkey on the bias using a sharp carving knife.

12 Fan slices of tenderloin over the Cranberry Sauce, leaning on the chard. Garnish with a sprig of thyme. Serve immediately.

Q *I bought an old cast iron skillet at a flea market last week and it is pretty rusty. What's the best way to get rid of the rust and how do I season it?*

A After hundreds of years, cast iron remains an inexpensive and popular alternative to other types of skillets.

One downside to cast iron is that it requires regular care. Because it's not a nonstick pan you need to create a sheen on the skillet's surface (called seasoning) so your food won't stick. Seasoning also helps prevent rust from developing.

And if you find an old cast iron lying around, just scrub it with a 00 or 000 steel wool pad and vegetable or olive oil. Then just reseason your skillet and it's ready to use.

To season, spread a layer of vegetable or olive oil (just not a salted fat like butter) all over the inside of your skillet. Put the skillet in the oven at 350° and bake for one hour.

Q *When a recipe calls for lemon juice, can I use bottled lemon juice instead of fresh?*

A Of course, I'll always encourage you to use anything fresh over prepackaged. But bottled lemon juice is always an option if you don't keep fresh lemons handy.

However, there are occasions when bottled lemon juice is not only recommended, *it's imperative* if the recipe calls for it.

When canning, especially tomatoes, the acidity level needs to remain constant. This helps prevent bacteria from developing. The canning environment is perfect for bacteria growth—moisture and warm temperatures are abundant. Bottled lemon juice offers this benefit. Its acidity level is consistent, while it varies in fresh lemon juice.

ReaLemon® says their juice goes through a "pasteurization process" that kills bacteria—another reason to use bottled juice in canning.

Otherwise, fresh is best.

Q *I purchased a fennel bulb the other day and I noticed it was also labeled anise. Are they the same thing?*

A Wow! Mass confusion when it comes to fennel and anise. Most likely, when you go to the produce section in your grocery store, and you see a bulbous plant with flat stalks (like celery) and dill-like leaves, you've got fennel, or more correctly, "Florence fennel."

Anise is usually sold as an herb, not a vegetable. And although both vegetables look very similar, the anise *herb* looks nothing like the fennel vegetable. The herb has leaves that are shaped like flat parsley and are topped by creamy-white flowers that are said to resemble Queen Anne's lace.

Sometimes fennel is incorrectly called "sweet anise," which is more a reference to its taste. Although both have a licorice flavor, fennel has a much sweeter and delicate taste which becomes lighter as it cooks.

▲ *This is fennel! Don't get confused if you see it by other names in the grocery store.*

Q&A

We'll find answers to your cooking questions, and help find solutions to the unique problems that occur in the kitchen. Any questions? Send your cooking questions to *Cuisine, Q & A Editor,* 2200 Grand Avenue, Des Moines, IA 50312, or contact us through our E-mail address: *Cuisine@cuisinemag.com*

Q *I went to the store to purchase arborio rice to make risotto. My store didn't have it, but they did have sushi rice. Will that work?*

A Grown in Italy, arborio [ar-BOH-ree-oh] is the traditional rice used in risotto. It's a short-grain rice—as wide as it is long. Arborio is perfect for risotto because it has a firm center and soft outer shell, which other short grains don't. This helps arborio hold its creamy yet firm texture through the slow cooking process.

Rice contains two types of starch: one makes it sticky and one keeps it firm. It's the ratio of the starches that determines if it clings together or falls apart. That's why arborio works well in risotto: it has a good balance of both types.

The U.S.A. Rice Federation says sushi rice, a short grain, wouldn't work well in risotto because it gets too sticky. Also, if you use sushi rice, you won't get the slight crunch that risotto is famous for.

Other short grains won't work either because the starch ratio (it has too much of the clingy kind) causes it to become sticky, which is ideal when you're using chopsticks but not for risotto.

Don't use a long grain. It can become mushy and won't withstand risotto's lengthy preparation.

Medium-grain is the next best thing to arborio for risotto. The starch in medium-grain rice is fairly balanced so it doesn't get too sticky and won't break apart.

So substitute a medium grain if you can't find arborio.

Q *You've used a meat called "chorizo" in a recipe before. I'm not familiar with it. Do I have to go to a speciality food store to find it?*

A Yes, we used chorizo in our Spanish Paella recipe in Issue 4. Chorizo [chor-EE-zoh] is a highly seasoned pork sausage that's flavored with chili powder, garlic, and other spices.

Chorizo is used in both Spanish and Mexican dishes. But there is a difference between Spanish and Mexican chorizo. Spanish chorizo is a smoked pork while the Mexican chorizo is fresh pork.

Some chorizo is sold raw so don't be tempted to slice a piece and eat it.

Chorizo is readily available in Mexican markets and most large grocery stores.

GLOSSARY

Dredge: To lightly coat food (usually with flour, cornmeal, or bread crumbs) that's to be fried. Dredging aids in browning.

Marsala: [mahr-SAH-lah] A rich wine from Sicily to which brandy has been added to increase the alcohol. The sweet version is used in the Italian custard, *zabaglione*; the dry to stimulate the appetite.

Mascarpone: [mahs-kar-POH-neh] A rich, silky Italian cream cheese made with 60% to 75% milk fat. The mild, buttery flavor works well in desserts (such as the coffee-flavored *tiramisu*), or as a filling for ravioli.

Pancetta: [pan-CHEH-tuh] Italian bacon that's rolled like a jelly roll. It's unsmoked, cured with salt and spices. Look for a roll with more pink (meat) than white (fat).

Prosciutto: [proh-SHOO-toh] This "ham" is Italy's gift to the food world. The cities of Parma and San Daniele (where it's mainly produced) argue over whose is better. Its production is a secret. It's first seasoned and salt-cured (but not smoked). Then it's air-dried, pressed, and sold thinly sliced. The best hams are aged 18 to 24 months.

Springform pan: A round pan with tall, straight sides that "unbuckle" from a removable bottom. Is most often used with tortes and cheesecakes. Allows you to easily unmold a cake and still retain its shape.

Swiss chard: A member of the beet family with crinkly green leaves and celery-like stalks (either red or white colored). Leaves and stalk can be eaten raw, or prepared like spinach.

ABBREVIATIONS

t. = teaspoon

T., Tbsp. = tablespoon

oz. = ounce

lb. = pound

Pinch = $1/16$ of a teaspoon

Dash = scant $1/8$ of a teaspoon

STATEMENT OF OWNERSHIP, MANAGEMENT AND CIRCULATION (Required by 39 U.S.C. 3685)

1) Publication title: Cuisine. 2) Publication no.: 1089-6546. 3) Filing date: September 14, 1998. 4) Issue frequency: bimonthly. 5) Number of issues published annually: six. 6) Annual subscription price: $21.94. 7) Complete mailing address of known office of publication: 2200 Grand Avenue, Des Moines, (Polk county), Iowa 50312-5306. 8) Complete mailing address of headquarters or general business office of the publisher: 2200 Grand Avenue, Des Moines, Iowa 50312-5306. 9) Full names and complete mailing addresses of publisher, editor, and managing editor: Publisher: Donald B. Peschke, 2200 Grand Avenue, Des Moines, Iowa 50312; Editor: John F. Meyer, 2200 Grand Avenue, Des Moines, Iowa 50312. 10) Owner: August Home Publishing Company, 2200 Grand Avenue, Des Moines, Iowa 50312; Donald B. Peschke, 2200 Grand Avenue, Des Moines, Iowa 50312. 11) Known bondholders, mortgagees, and other security holders owning or holding 1 percent or more of total amount of bonds, mortgages or other securities: none. 12) Does not apply. 13) Publication title: Cuisine. 14) Issue date for circulation data below: May/June 98. 15) Extent and nature of circulation:

		Average no. copies each issue during preceding 12 months	Actual no. copies of single issue published nearest to filing date
A.	Total number copies (net press run)	138,297	128,938
B.	Paid and/or requested circulation		
	1. Sales through dealers and carriers, street vendors and counter sales (not mailed)	11,074	9,977
	2. Paid or requested mail subscriptions	91,574	89,159
C.	Total paid and/or requested circulation	102,648	99,136
D.	Free distribution by mail	5,797	341
E.	Free distribution outside the mail	0	0
F.	Total free distribution	5,797	341
G.	Total distribution	108,445	99,477
H.	Copies not distributed		
	1. Office use, leftovers, spoiled	6,093	9,528
	2. Returns from news agents	23,759	19,933
I.	Total	138,297	128,938
	Percent paid or requested circulation	94.65%	99.66%

16. This statement of ownership will be printed in the Nov/Dec '98 issue of this publication.
17. I certify that the statements made by me above are correct and complete. (signed) John F. Meyer, Editor

CRANBERRY NAPOLEON

CRANBERRY NAPOLEONS
(MAKES 4 NAPOLEONS)
WORK TIME: 40 MINUTES
COOK TIME: 1 HOUR

FOR COOKIES —
CREAM TOGETHER:
$^1/_2$ cup unsalted butter
$^1/_2$ cup sugar
BLEND IN:
1   egg
1   t. vanilla extract
$^1/_2$ t. salt
MIX IN:
$1^1/_4$ cups all-purpose flour
SPREAD OUT AND BAKE.

FOR CABERNET SAUCE —
SIMMER, STRAIN, REDUCE:
12   oz. fresh cranberries
1   cup Cabernet wine
1   cup orange juice
$^3/_4$ cup sugar

FOR FILLING —
BLEND TOGETHER:
2   cups mascarpone
$1^3/_4$ cups heavy cream
$^1/_2$ cup powdered sugar

BUILD AND GARNISH WITH:
Cabernet Sauce
Sugared cranberries, *pg. 5*
Fresh mint sprigs

MAKING CRANBERRY NAPOLEONS

1 Preheat oven to 350°. Cream butter and sugar until light. Blend in vanilla, salt, and egg. Stir in flour.

2 Drop batter by tablespoons onto ungreased sheet pans. With a small knife, spread in 3" rounds.

3 Bake 10–13 mins., until golden. Transfer while hot to a cooling rack. Store airtight until ready to serve.

4 For the sauce, simmer all ingredients just until berries pop. Strain; reduce until thick (15 mins.). Cool.

5 Blend filling ingredients just to soft peaks— **don't overmix!** Transfer to piping bag with star tip.

6 Prepare sugared cranberries, *see Page 5*. To assemble, anchor a cookie on plate with a little filling.

7 Just before serving, pipe 5 rosettes on cookie. Add some berries; top with cookie. You'll make 3 tiers.

8 Spoon sauce around the base of napoleon. Garnish with berries and mint. Serve immediately.

CALZONES

The coolest thing about calzones is that I found out I can make great ones at home. I thought they were only an "eat out" treat—but you can turn out perfect

calzones in your own kitchen without *any* special equipment. You might have thought that calzones were only reserved for Friday nights down at Big Tony's Pizzeria and Lanes.

Why make calzones at home when you can get them at Tony's? Simple. Everything is better! The fillings are top-quality (and abundant), the crust is crispier, and you're eating it piping hot, right out of the oven. Tony can get sidetracked by league shoe rentals.

What is Calzone? Okay. Let's get serious. A classic calzone [kahl-ZOH-neh] is really just a pizza folded in half. It literally means "trouser or pant leg." Apparently the half-moon shape of calzone is reminiscent of billowing pants worn by Italian men.

A good calzone should end up with an outstanding crust that surrounds flavorful ingredients. And when cut in half, the calzone oozes out plenty of melted, gooey cheese.

Fillings: I'm giving you the recipes for four sure-fire fillings (the cheese is the same for all of them). There's even one using leftover holiday turkey! Use your imagination to come up with your own combinations. Anything goes, but these will get you started.

Crust: The crust isn't just a vehicle for the great stuff inside. A good crust is critical to an outstanding calzone—it can make or break it.

Rather than proofing yeast right before making the dough, I begin a day ahead and make a simple starter (*don't panic, it takes all of five minutes*). A starter dramatically improves the crust's flavor and texture. The final dough can be made 15–24 hours later.

Serving: To serve calzones, be sure to have some marinara sauce on the side for dipping! You can find my recipe for Marinara on page 15. It's a perfect match with a great calzone.

Follow this carefully. Make the starter first and let it sit. Then, the next day, make another mixture of yeast and oil to add to the starter. This is all mixed with the final flour and salt.

CALZONE DOUGH

(MAKES 4 CALZONES)
KNEAD TIME: 8–10 MINUTES
REST AND RISE TIME: $1^1/_2$ –$2^1/_2$ HOURS
FOR THE STARTER—
WHISK TOGETHER:
$^1/_3$ cup + 1 T. all-purpose flour
$^1/_4$ t. kosher salt
DISSOLVE, STIR IN DRY INGREDIENTS.
COVER, LET SIT 24 HOURS:
$^1/_4$ t. active dry yeast
3   T. cold water
FOR THE DOUGH—
DISSOLVE:
$^1/_2$ cup + 2 T. warm water (85–95°)
1   t. active dry yeast
ADD TO YEAST:
1   T. olive oil
POUR OVER SPONGE. COMBINE WITH:
$1^2/_3$ cups all-purpose flour
1   t. kosher salt

Use a sponge (a yeast starter) for this dough. It makes all the difference in the flavor and texture of the final crust. A sponge is a simple mixture of flour, water, and yeast (sometimes salt). This stiff mixture "ferments" at room temperature 15–24 hours before being mixed with the rest of the ingredients to form a final dough.

Again, don't worry. Making the sponge is a five-minute task. This isn't a drawn-out process.

1 In a large mixing bowl, whisk together flour and salt. In a small bowl, dissolve yeast in water. Pour liquid over flour and stir with a fork.

2 Stir until all flour is incorporated. Mixture will be a stiff, heavy blob. Cover tightly with plastic wrap and let sit at room temperature.

3 After fermenting for 15–24 hours, the starter has grown and is ready for the final dough. It's bubbly and smells very yeasty.

MAKING CALZONE DOUGH

4 Whisk the yeast in warm water (85–95°). After foam appears (about 5 minutes), whisk in oil. In separate bowl, combine flour and salt.

5 To loosen the sponge, pour the liquid yeast mixture around the edge. Stir it lightly. The sponge will begin to pull away from the bowl.

6 Add dry ingredients to the sponge mixture and stir until all the flour is moistened. The dough will be sticky and full of lumps.

7 It's time to knead. Turn dough out onto floured work surface. Lift and fold half of dough towards you. Flour hands and surface as needed.

8 Press down and away from you with heel of hand. Keep hands floured. Give dough quarter-turn; repeat steps 7 & 8. Knead 8–10 mins.

9 Form 1 large ball. Dust with flour. Cover with plastic. Let rest 20 minutes. Cut into quarters. Tuck into 4 balls. Cover and let rise 2 hours.

CALZONES
(FOR 1 CALZONE)

FILL EACH DOUGH WITH:

10 rounds Italian sausage, browned
1/4 cup red pepper, diced, sauteed
1 t. rosemary, chopped

MIX TOGETHER AND TOP WITH:

1/4 cup mozzarella cheese, grated
1/4 cup provolone cheese, grated
2 T. Parmesan cheese, grated

BRUSH CALZONE WITH EGG WASH:

1 egg
2 T. milk

FILLING OPTIONS—
HAM & SPINACH

2 slices prosciutto or ham
1/2 cup fresh spinach, sauteed
1/3 cup roasted red pepper, diced

TURKEY & ONION:

1/3 cup cooked turkey or chicken, cubed
1/3 cup sauteed onions, sliced
1 T. sundried tomatoes, sliced

EGGPLANT & TOMATO:

3 slices eggplant (egg washed, floured, and fried)
1/3 cup tomatoes, seeded and diced

Making the crust is crucial, but how you fold it is just as important.

Shaping and Folding: When you rotate the circle of dough as in step 11, it stretches as it hangs briefly in the air. If the circle isn't enlarging easily, you can slow down your rotation.

Now, lay the dough on parchment to finish shaping. Sometimes, there will be thin spots where the filling can poke through. Find these areas and repair them by pinching the dough together. And be sure to keep the rough underside of the dough facing up. This way, the smooth part of the crust is on the finished outside.

Here's the secret to folding a calzone. Look at step 14. Take the whole rounded backside and grip it with the entire length of both your hands. Now, pull the dough over the filling in one smooth motion. This minimizes tearing in thin spots.

Finally, keep the filling away from the edges. This, as well as the crimping in step 15, helps form a tight seal. **AH**

10 After dough has risen 1–2 hours, flour surface. Flip 1 ball over (keep others covered). Press dough with fingertips to form circle.

11 With both hands at top of dough, grasp the edge and rotate. This stretches dough and enlarges circle to 7–8" in diameter.

12 Lay down the dough circle and check for any uneven spots. With your fingers, gently lift and stretch out any thick spots.

13 Put dough on parchment-lined baking sheet. Place fillings on half of circle leaving 3/4" clean border at edge of dough. Top with cheese.

14 Lift edge of unfilled side and pull slightly towards you. This stretches dough so you can cover filling to meet edge on other side.

15 Press edges to create seal. Crimping ensures a tight bond between the two edges. Press each indentation twice to really seal it.

16 Calzones look better with an egg wash. Lightly brush each one with egg mixture. Careful: Too much liquid in crimps makes it soggy.

17 Bake 10–12 minutes in 500° oven until calzones are golden. If a little cheese oozes out, eat it! This is better than the calzone itself!

RICOTTA TORTA

Photograph: Scott Little; Food Styling: Janet Pittman

RICOTTA TORTA *(MAKES A 9" TORTA)*
WORK TIME: 1 HOUR
BAKE TIME: $1^1/_4$–$1^1/_2$ HOURS
FOR PASTRY DOUGH, COMBINE:
$2^1/_2$ cups all-purpose flour
$^1/_2$ cup sugar
$^1/_2$ t. salt
     Zest from one lemon, minced
BLEND IN:
1   cup cold unsalted butter, cubed
MIX IN; THEN CHILL, ROLL, AND BAKE:
2   eggs
FOR FILLING, PULSE IN PROCESSOR:
$4^1/_2$ cups part-skim ricotta cheese
$^1/_2$ cup mascarpone cheese
STIR IN:
$^1/_2$ cup sugar
$^1/_4$ cup all-purpose flour
$^1/_4$ cup fresh lemon juice, strained
$1^1/_2$ t. vanilla extract
3   egg yolks
2   whole eggs
BRUSH OVER LATTICE TOP:
1   egg, beaten

Ricotta Torta isn't like the "tux and tails" Cranberry Napoleon on page 38. It's more rustic—like jeans and a sweater. But it's just as good.

We'll start with a buttery, cookie-like pastry crust. Prebaking keeps it crisp—a nice contrast to the filling.

Now, this torta isn't dense like a New York cheesecake. The ricotta lightens things up—in flavor *and* calories (serving 12, there's 500 calories a slice). You can actually eat a piece of this after a big meal and not feel *too* stuffed. Plus, it's not too sweet.

A lattice is the traditional top crust on an Italian torta. If you've never tried weaving one before, this is a great place to start. The more mistakes you make, the better it'll look. Straight lines and even spacing are *not* the objective here—the idea is rustic and casual.

If this torta is a little underdressed for your holiday party, you can deck it out with some white chocolate sauce and sugared cranberries—check out the dynamite back cover.

MAKING THE PASTRY DOUGH

1 Mixing the pastry dough by hand lets you really *feel* what's going on. Toss together flour, sugar, salt, and lemon zest on a work surface.

2 Add cold butter cubes to flour. Press butter between fingers, blending it into flour. You just want to soften, not mix it in completely.

3 Make a well in middle of flour mixture; add eggs. Here's the messy part—gradually blend eggs into the flour using your fingertips.

4 Knead pastry dough just until it's smooth (like putty). Then flatten into a disk, wrap in plastic, and chill at least $^1/_2$ hour before rolling.

5 Preheat oven to 375°. On a lightly floured surface, trim off ⅓ of chilled dough; wrap and chill again. You'll use it for the lattice top crust.

6 Roll remaining dough into a 14" circle, about ⅛" thick. Rotate dough often; keep table and dough lightly floured to prevent sticking.

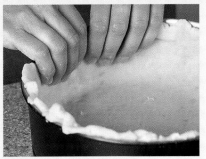

7 Transfer dough to a 9" x 2½" springform pan. Press gently into pan without stretching. Fit dough tightly in the corners and up the sides.

8 Line dough with foil and fill with 3 cups dried beans. Prebake crust in lower half of oven 15 minutes, or until surface of crust is dry.

9 For ricotta filling, pulse cheeses together in food processor until light, smooth, and blended—just 10 or 11 quick pulses will do the job.

10 Transfer cheeses to a mixing bowl. Stir in sugar, flour, lemon juice, vanilla, egg yolks, and whole eggs. Cover and chill until ready to fill.

11 Remove foil and cool crust completely before filling with cheese mixture. Fill and trim excess dough with pastry wheel.

12 For lattice strips, roll reserved dough ⅛" thick and cut into ½" wide strips. Place four strips across top of torta, about 1" apart.

13 Fold back every other strip halfway. Then lay a strip across middle, *on top of* the unfolded strips, and *right next to* the folded ones.

14 Now, *unfold* the folded strips over the middle strip. Then *fold* the straight ones back, like Step 13. Add a strip across and repeat.

15 Weave until torta is covered. Then trim the strips slightly longer than width of torta. "Glue" them to the crust with egg wash.

16 Brush egg wash over strips. Bake at 375° for 1¼–1½ hrs. Center will be soft. Cool; remove pan sides. Serve at room temp. or chilled.

GRAND FINALE

DRESSING UP THE RICOTTA TORTA

For the White Chocolate Sauce: Finely chop 8 oz. white chocolate and place it in a mixing bowl. Meanwhile, bring 1/2 cup heavy cream to a simmer in a small pan. Pour the cream over the chocolate and whisk until smooth.

Painting the Plate: Transfer the sauce to a squeeze bottle. Now, "paint" the plate—this is easiest if you keep the tip right on the plate, like you're writing with a pencil. Make a long heart shape and fill it in.

Placing the Cranberries: Place some of the sugared cranberries from page 5 in the pool of white chocolate sauce. Arrange them so they look like a grape cluster. Finally, garnish the berries with a sprig of mint—gorgeous!

Cuisine VOLUME 2 INDEX